The Lost World of Classical Legal Thought

The Lost World of Classical Legal Thought

Law and Ideology in America,

1886–1937

William M. Wiecek

OXFORD
UNIVERSITY PRESS

OXFORD

UNIVERSITY PRESS

Oxford   New York
Athens   Auckland   Bangkok   Bogotá   Buenos Aires   Calcutta
Cape Town   Chennai   Dar es Salaam   Delhi   Florence   Hong Kong   Istanbul
Karachi   Kuala Lumpur   Madrid   Melbourne   Mexico City   Mumbai
Nairobi   Paris   São Paulo   Singapore   Taipei   Tokyo   Toronto   Warsaw

and associated companies in
Berlin   Ibadan

First published in 1998 by Oxford University Press, Inc.
198 Madison Avenue, New York, New York 10016

First issued as an Oxford University Press paperback, 2001

Oxford is a registered trademark of Oxford University Press

Library of Congress Cataloging-in-Publication Data
Wiecek, William M., 1938–
The lost world of classical legal thought : law and ideology in America,
1886–1937 / William M. Wiecek.
p.   cm.
Includes index.
ISBN 0–19–511854-5   0-19-514713-8 (ppk)
1. Law—United States—Philosophy—History.   2. Juriprudence—
United States—History   I. Title.
KF380.W54   1998
349.73'01—dc21   97-28858

1 3 5 7 9 8 6 4 2
Printed in the United States of America
on acid-free paper

To Judy, again
with all my love
L'Chaim

Preface

A comment about the origins of this study may help the reader place it in a larger interpretive framework. This book is the first installment of a work-in-progress on the history of the United States Supreme Court from 1941 to 1953. It is what historians call a prolegomenon, or an introduction, to that parent study.

In late 1994, the Permanent Committee for the Oliver Wendell Holmes Devise and Stanley N. Katz, the general editor of the *History of the Supreme Court of the United States* series, offered me the magnificent opportunity of preparing the Holmes Devise volume covering the years 1941–1953. I projected two introductory chapters for the Holmes Devise book, one situating the Court in the context of American society on the eve of Pearl Harbor, and the other summarizing the state of constitutional doctrinal development at that time. I hoped thereby to re-create for the reader the world as it might have appeared to a Justice of the United States Supreme Court at the start of October Term 1941.

Approaching the book that way, it became apparent to me that one of the Stone Court's most important responsibilities was its search for a jurisprudential paradigm that would replace the recently abandoned ideology that I refer to in this book as "legal classicism." One of the defining characteristics of the Roosevelt Court was the fact that a hitherto dominant way of thinking about law and the role of courts in American society had been discarded in 1937–1938. By 1941, nothing had emerged to take its place. There seemed to be a modern scholarly consensus about the origins, content, vogue, and weaknesses of the abandoned ideology. So I thought it would be a simple matter to summarize that consensus, note the challenges to it posed by recent revisionist writings, and present that doctrinal-historical sketch as the entrée to the story of the Roosevelt and Truman Courts.

But then that introductory doctrinal chapter took on a life of its own. I found myself in the position of an author of fiction who sits at the word processor observing his characters as they come to life. They tell their own story, and the author merely records it as their amanuensis. So it was with my introduction to legal classicism. As soon as I began writing, interpretive questions presented themselves in ways that I could not ignore. Many questions remained unanswered or even unasked about this body of thought. Conventional and revisionist accounts alike assume important issues that seemed to me to require further exploration. Little has been written about the roots and origins of orthodox thought, or about how that body of lawyers' thinking related to the larger intellectual and social background against which it appeared. Most important, neither critic nor admirer seemed to have fully appreciated how comprehensive and powerful orthodoxy was as an explanation of what law is, and as a justification for the role of courts in expounding it.

So what was to have been a brief introductory summary evolved into a long chapter, then cloned itself into two chapters, then continued a dismaying process of mitotic division, until a fortuitous opportunity intervened. The speaker who had been invited to deliver the annual lecture of the American Society for Legal History at its 1995 meeting was unable to fulfill his engagement. The chair of the program committee, Professor Don Nieman, asked me if I would substitute at the last minute. I took the opportunity to integrate my thinking up to that point, and to present a synopsis of what I was writing.[1] Comments from members of the society enabled me to see, at last, the real scope and significance of the book that I had inadvertently written. You now hold that book in your hands.

Though writing is a solitary experience, many persons helped bring this book into print. Stanley N. Katz has for thirty years been a friend and mentor. His counsel did much to shape this book and the one that is to follow. Friends and colleagues, Richard D. Friedman foremost among them, have read parts of the manuscript or all of it, and offered insights and comment. Historian friends who have patiently listened to my ideas and offered advice or criticism include Harold M. Hyman and Sandra Van Burkleo. Syracuse University and the community of its College of Law have been unstintingly supportive. I thank particularly Vice Chancellor for Academic Affairs Gershon Vincow, Deans Daan Braveman and Sarah Ramsey, and my colleagues on the law and history faculties, especially Chris Day, Brian Bromberger, and David Bennett. Louise Lantzy and members of the Law Library staff, in particular Wendy Scott, Elmer Masters, Mike Poitras, and Ted Holynski, have provided essential support. Karen Bruner assisted with research in exemplary ways. Morton Horwitz and Duncan Kennedy of the Harvard Law School have been generous in their encouragement. The hospitality of John P. and Martha Chandler in New Hampshire, and of Marvin Gettleman and Ellen Schrecker in the Catskills, provided an emotional environment that later buoyed this work in a difficult time. Linda Zimack's interest and support during that period was crucial. The flaws of this book remain my sole responsibility, but whatever virtues it may have are owing in some measure to the help of friends.

Note

1. That presentation was derived from a précis of this book that will appear as "The Lost World of Classical Legal Thought: Prolegomenon to the Modern Constitution," in Sandra Van Burkleo, ed., *Time to Reclaim: American Constitutional History at the Millennium* (forthcoming).

Contents

The Lost World of Classical Legal Thought

The Challenge of
Classical Legal Thought

During the half-century between 1886 and 1937, a distinctive outlook dominated the thinking of American lawyers and judges. It was an ideology as defined by the historian Eric Foner: a "system of beliefs, values, fears, prejudices, reflexes, and commitments — in sum, the social consciousness — of a social group."[1] Scholars have designated this ideology by various phrases: "legal orthodoxy," "classical legal thought," "legal formalism," "the orthodox ideology." I call it "legal classicism" because I seek a label that is as neutral as possible yet that retains some descriptive and suggestive content. "Formalism" is excessively narrow and potentially misleading, while "orthodoxy" carries pejorative connotations for some readers.

Classicism was both an ideology and a structure of thought created by an intellectual community,[2] the elite American bar and bench. Robert Gordon refers to this elite as a "community of intellectual discourse," which is a useful way of thinking about the men who shaped — and were shaped by — classicism.[3] This coterie included half the Justices of the United States Supreme Court in those years, and most of the Chief Justices.

As a phenomenon of legal consciousness or *mentalité*, classicism comprised a coherent set of beliefs, values, and assumptions about law and the role of courts in construing law. It was not a jurisprudential school and was something both more and less than a jurisprudential theory. Classicism rested on a deeper underlying ideological structure, which consisted of beliefs shared by most middle-class contemporaries about liberty, power, human nature, rights, and republican government. It identified the values that define Americans as a people and their government as a republic.

The classical outlook provided an explanation of the nature and sources of law; it justified judicial review and the place of courts in American democracy; it offered a plausible account of the way that judges and lawyers think; most important, it legitimated the Supreme Court's power to construe the Constitution. Though classical thought was profoundly and irremediably flawed, we lost something valuable in our

3

constitutional discourse when we discarded it in 1937, and we have not yet found a replacement.

In this prologue, I summarily sketch the substance of classical legal thought, by way of identifying and defining the subject of the book in a generalized description. Ensuing chapters elaborate those generalizations, trace their historical evolution, and explore the causes of classicism's demise.

Classical Legal Thought Briefly Described

Most recent writers on American law take the existence of classicism as a given, either as formalist method or as laissez-faire policy preference. But some scholars have begun to investigate it more systematically.[4] The account of classicism in this study begins with their conclusions and extends their inquiry. Going backward in time, it seeks classicism's origins in the public law of the early republic; moving "horizontally" in the era of classicism's dominance, it identifies classicism's linkages to contemporary thought about society and the economy; carrying the story forward in time, it traces classicism's overthrow.

Legal classicism constituted a coherent body of thought that provided answers to some of the most enduring questions of jurisprudence: What are the sources of law? How does law promote the goals of society — and which goals? What legitimates the authority of legal institutions? Why is legal obligation binding? What is law's relationship to politics? Classicism offered a justification of law and judicial power that was persuasive, even compelling, in its time. So powerful was its explanatory and legitimating power that it continues to echo today in our legal discourse, a half-century after it was consigned to a dishonored burial. To paraphrase Maitland on the forms of action: classicism may be dead, but it rules us from the grave. Like the tolling of the drowned bells in Debussy's "Sunken Cathedral," legal classicism's muffled, ghostly peal rings throughout modern law.

Classical legal thought may be presented in terms of (1) patterns of reasoning, (2) social values, and (3) sources of law.

Patterns of Reasoning

Legal classicism was, first, a way of thinking about law and, behind that, a way of thinking, period. It was abstract, formal, conceptualistic, categorical, and (sometimes) deductive. One reason for classicism's bad repute in our time is that this way of thinking overstayed its welcome. It lingered on in law long after it had been abandoned in other fields. It was discredited among other intellectuals, dysfunctional in light of law's goals, and ever more distanced from social and economic reality. In the end, classical legal thought hung on only as empty dogma, and its critics could condemn it as nothing more than a rationalization for illicit power.

The innovations in legal education instituted by Dean Christopher C. Langdell at the Harvard Law School after 1870 inculcated the claim that the Langdellian law school teaches students "to think like a lawyer." Preposterous though that idea is, it does contain an element of truth. Classical jurists did organize their thought in ways that were distinctive and that we may ascribe to them as characteristic. Their processes of reasoning furnished the methodological foundation of classicism.

Classical thought aimed at a high level of abstraction and generality. Parties appeared in opinions and treatises as "A" and "B," "purchaser" and "seller," "the contracting parties," "a reasonable man." When such bloodless impersonality was not possible, judges seldom took more notice of the parties than to refer to them in status terms as "appellant's intestate," or "one Jones, a brakeman." Abstraction promoted neutrality, purportedly diverting the judge from being swayed by personal sympathy or aversion. This self-reassuring posture of impartiality enabled judges to ratify their assumptions and biases, or — what amounts to the same thing — to assume that those views were universally valid. Generalization served the same end by enabling law's universality. The justice at which classicism aimed was not a fair, equitable result in the particular case, but rather a uniform, undeviating, impartial application of supposedly neutral rules in all cases. Law must apply in the same way to all similarly situated. The more general and unqualified the statement of the rule, the more likely that it would approach such universal scope.

Professional Americans a century ago enjoyed a luxury no longer within our reach today: they were confident that they could attain objective truth. Such premodern confidence in objectivity, grounded in beliefs about the moral and the material universe — both being governed by universal laws — enabled them to believe that concepts like property or race had objective validity. They thought that such legal categories were innate in nature, not socially constructed. Absolute standards and truth were attainable by complying with unquestioned norms. The moral and legal order could be identified with certitude and should be imposed because it was objectively just. For the pious, this moral/legal order was divinely ordained; for others, whatever its origins, it was as patent and as binding as the law of gravity. Fortified by such epistemological confidence, classical jurists derived notions of fact, causation, and proof that were certain and objectively verifiable. It would have struck them as perverse and socialistic, for example, if someone had suggested that property relationships were legally and socially constructed (and thus subject to legislative control), rather than being the objective, determinate relationship between a man and a thing that he owned.

Generalization, abstraction, and certitude were components of a larger classical enterprise, the creation of a legal science. The very notion of law being a "science" challenges us moderns. So fatuous does the idea seem, in the light of modern understandings both of science and of law, that no one has yet been able to compose a satisfactory account of what legal science meant to the classical jurists in the United States. To grasp their aspiration to legal science, the modern reader must leap by imagination back into a world before Rutherford and Einstein and Planck and Heisenberg, before Freud, before Marx and Durkheim and Weber, sometimes, it almost seems, before Galileo and Copernicus. Legal science encouraged lawyers to think that they were expounding principles of universal validity, applicable to all legal categories they fit, beyond human power to manipulate or modify. The right principles would solve the problem of precedential anomalies, which were often caused by the pesky impulse to achieve justice in a particular case. In the "Formal Style" discerned by Karl Llewellyn, "'principle' is a generalization producing order which can and should be used to prune away those 'anomalous' cases or rules which do not fit." The "rules of law are to decide the cases; policy is for the legislature, not for the courts."[5]

A ready technique for assigning things to their appropriate categories was to construct simple dichotomies: "direct" versus "indirect," "fact" versus "law," "manufacturing" versus "commerce." Categories usually identified the appropriate principles to be applied. Legal relations turned on whether, for an example drawn from the law of agency, someone acting on behalf of another was an agent, a servant, or an independent contractor. Such patterns of thought were reductionist, hurrying classicism on in its flight from fact-specificity toward abstraction, resolving reality's complexity into simplified binary patterns.

Classical lawyers reveled in systematization. Though its underlying patterns varied over time, classicism sought to identify a hierarchy of principles, doctrines, and norms. This structure generated results, which accreted into precedents. In going from precedents to principles and back down again, classical lawyers functioned both inductively and deductively. Generally the deductive method was better suited to appellate adjudication, while the inductive mode of reasoning was more at home in the academy, especially in two lasting Langdellian innovations, the casebook and the Socratic method.

Some scholars have called this way of thinking systematically "formalism," or "formalistic."[6] That designation usually connotes a mode of thought and sometimes of literary expression as well, but it has jurisprudential implications that render it potentially misleading. We encounter a substantive difficulty in dismissing classical thought simply as formalistic. "Formalism" might properly imply rule-boundedness, the idea that judges are constrained by extant norms and achieve justice by applying those norms.[7] Taken in this sense, the label is not adequate for an understanding of classicism. It evokes the dilemma forcefully expressed by the German savant Rudolf von Jhering, who wrote of the philosopher's confrontation with formalist reasoning in law: "[W]ho can see in formalism nothing but a superficial way of seeing things, a purely external impulse of looking at things, a positive disruption of the relation between form and substance. . . . This overemphasis of the dry, bare form, this angst-ridden, pedantic worship of a symbol that is totally worthless and meaningless in itself, the poverty and meanness of spirit that animates and dominates formalism." Yet, Jhering went on, formalism, "because it is grounded in the innermost essence of law, repeats itself in the law of all peoples, and always will."[8]

Like Jhering, we are repelled by formalism's exaltation of form over substance, rule over justice, yet bound by the need ever to return to the command of rules and their disciplined application. Charles Fried has identified this characteristic of formalism as its "constitutive rationality," necessary to law anywhere.[9] In any event, the classical enterprise cannot be written off simply because it was formalist either in logic or in application of rules.[10] Its ultimate failure was determined by other characteristics.

Given classicism's premises about how lawyers ought to think, the role of the courts followed logically. Drawing on pre–Civil War suppositions, legal classicism held that judges did not "make" law; they "found" it. This is sometimes called a declaratory theory of judging, from the commonplace or legal maxim that stated that the judicial function was "ius dicere et non ius dare": to declare the law and not to make it. The judge supposedly had no more discretion to invent a legal rule on instrumentalist grounds or policy preferences than a chemist had to dictate the outcome of an experiment. In both cases, scientists discovered results; they were not supposed to control or manipulate them.

This view of the judge's role led lawyers of the classical period to ascribe to him an almost automaton-like quality, a superhuman achievement of impartiality that assumed James I's claim to be *lex loquens*. William Blackstone provided the canonical justification for this view: "[T]he judgment, though pronounced or awarded by the judges, is not their determination or sentence, but the determination and sentence of *the law*. It is the conclusion that naturally and regularly follows from the premises of law and fact. . . . Which judgment or conclusion depends not therefore on the arbitrary caprice of the judge, but on settled and invariable principles of justice."[11]

Social Values

The foregoing patterns guided lawyers in *how* they thought about law and society. Equally important was the substance of their beliefs, or *what* they thought about society, about the economy, about law, about courts, about themselves.

Traditional liberal accounts of classicism ascribe ideologies of laissez-faire and social Darwinism to the legal elite. The most influential imputation of this idea was Justice Oliver Wendell Holmes's *Lochner* dissent: "This case is decided upon an economic theory which a large part of the country does not entertain. . . . The 14th Amendment does not enact Mr. Herbert Spencer's Social Statics."[12] Holmes's assertion was not wrong, but some qualifications are in order.

Lawrence Friedman overstated the case when he claimed that "neither the United States Supreme Court nor the state supreme courts as a whole ever judged social legislation on the basis of any consistent pattern of ideas which can properly bear the name of an economic theory. . . . No consistent ideological pattern emerges from the case law."[13] Ideology there was, in abundance, but not consistency. Classical jurists proclaimed a set of beliefs; they did not maintain them with the ideological rigidity of a Richard Epstein, but they were guided by those beliefs in their thinking and their judging.

Laissez-faire — which Max Lerner called "the philosophical anarchism of the rich and successful"[14] — did find a more enthusiastic reception in the United States than it did in England, the home of Herbert Spencer, its foremost exponent. But few American lawyers had ever actually read Spencer or his American disciple, William Graham Sumner. They were no better acquainted with the writings of the French physiocrats, Adam Smith, Jeremy Bentham (whose contempt for the common law would have closed their minds to his thought in any event), John Stuart Mill, or the leading exponents of the Manchester school, Richard Cobden and John Bright. For that matter, even their acquaintance with John Locke was, at best, third-hand. By the time laissez-faire thought reached these shores, experience had long overtaken theory in England: repeal of the Corn Laws was a distant memory.[15] The social order over which Gladstone and Disraeli presided was no more consecrated to laissez-faire dogma than was contemporary Wilhelmine Germany.

Laissez-faire called for limited governmental intervention in the economy — constrained, but by no means weakened. Yet American legal conservatives were almost unanimously supporters of tariffs and the gold standard. The English visitor James Bryce noted in 1888 that "one half of the capitalists are occupied in preaching laissez faire as regards railroads, the other half in resisting it . . . in tariff matters."[16] But the men who enacted the Payne-Aldrich and Hawley-Smoot tariffs would have proclaimed themselves believers in laissez-faire and disciples of Spencer (if they had known who he was).

Laissez-faire also implied dedication to a free market economy, yet here too consistency and doctrinal purity evaporated in the heat of self-interest. The night-watchman state was a figment of classical-liberal rhetoric. An unregulated market society might be a suitable means of allowing the price of labor to sink to levels set by penury, but it certainly would not do when private enterprise called for subsidies or protection from competition.

Classical lawyers have been portrayed as social Darwinians. That, too, is true, but only with qualifications. Belief in a free market, however much it may be compromised by self-interest, is not the same thing as a vulgarized social Darwinian outlook. Jurists of the classical era believed in competition, for labor at least, and they thought that the struggle for survival should provide an effective incentive to workers. So a theoretical social Darwinism was a natural complement to their let-alone outlook. Yet here again consistency gave way to opportunistic pursuit of the main chance, especially among large economic competitors. Struggle, competition, and survival were scarcely desirable among corporate giants, or among suitors for scarce or unique natural resources. Indeed, one of the most powerful impetuses for national economic regulation came from industrialists trying to escape from competition among themselves.

Thus, to label legal classicism the judicial expression of free market economics or survival-of-the-fittest social outlook is only an approximation to reality. Those dogmas or social philosophies were weapons in an ideological armory: available but not constantly in use. The Justices of the Supreme Court drew on them opportunistically, some more frequently than others. Rufus Peckham and David J. Brewer endorsed laissez-faire dogma confidently, but most of their brethren refrained from avowing such ideological commitments. The labels of laissez-faire and social Darwinism are catchalls rather than precise analytical tools.

Our search for more comprehensive and accurate ways of describing the classical outlook would be better directed toward morally based values. Like most other Americans in the late nineteenth century, classical lawyers were captives of an individualist outlook. In nineteenth-century law, as in other areas of Victorian culture, the individual was the exclusive focus of concern in legal, moral, and political reasoning. Lawyers of the time did not think of society as a congeries of groups, which is the assumption of interest-group pluralism that dominates twentieth-century political analysis. Instead, they placed great store on the autonomy of the individual will. Applauding Henry Maine's celebrated observation that "the movement of the progressive societies has hitherto been a movement from Status to Contract,"[17] they regarded the centrality of individual will as the supreme achievement of modern legal systems. It represented progress beyond feudal societies where individuals were constrained by status, rank, or class, locked permanently into the station in which they had been born. Progress toward nineteenth-century liberalism carried society away from tyranny, superstition, and constraint, to a legal order characterized by freedom, rationality, and individual mobility. All modern law seemed to be a realization of that progress: slavery, the most total of status constraints, had been abolished; first married women, then their spinster sisters, had been emancipated into full legal capacity; political status based on religion or property ownership had given way to universal suffrage (to classical judges, a mixed blessing, though).

Both private and public law exalted the primacy of individual will. The law of contracts contrived doctrines of offer and acceptance to give it effect. The public law doctrine of liberty of contract endued contractual capacity with constitutional status. In property law, common law courts sloughed off restraints on alienation to encourage the free transferability of both realty and personalty. Commercial law promoted negotiability to create a commercial society composed of innumerable individual economic actors. In all these ways, the law celebrated its progressive tendencies, freeing human creative capabilities to enhance both personal growth and the common welfare.

Certain consequences followed from the centrality of individual will. One was its correlate, individual responsibility. Classical law proclaimed hostility toward state paternalism. "The paternal theory of government is to me odious," trumpeted Justice David J. Brewer in 1892.[18] Classical judges stressed the necessity for all people to be responsible for their own destiny, and condemned intervention by the state meant to protect individuals from misfortune and their own folly or inadequacy.

Because the law exalted will, it had to regard all individuals as juristic equals. This had pervasive consequences. In contractual relationships, the law could not take account of disparities in bargaining power, for to do so would be to invite the sort of state intervention that the antipaternalist ethos condemned. Collectivities were suspect, at least those formed by working people, because they threatened to interpose an external entity like a union into binary economic relationships that presumed one person freely contracting with another. (It should go without saying that classical law often overlooked legal arrangements inconsistent with this presumed individualism. Thus, for example, classical lawyers saw nothing regrettable about the elaborate structure that conservative white regimes erected in the post-Reconstruction South to constrain and repress black labor. Nor were classical lawyers much troubled by pooling, trusts, or manufacturers' associations unless they ran afoul of specific antitrust restraints.)

The primacy of individual will had an important grounding in political theory. A free state must not be coercive. In theory, and as much as possible in practice, the state must rest on the consent of the governed. Consent was presumed from continuing presence in the jurisdiction, and had been ever since the Laws and Liberties of Massachusetts had made the point explicit in 1648. That is not to say that the state could not act coercively, of course. On the contrary: classical lawyers became rapturous about the coercive might of the state when it was deployed to crush labor unions or other impediments to the pure theoretical one-to-one contractual employment relationship.

The basic condition for the exercise of individual will was liberty, which classical lawyers understood in the sense that Isaiah Berlin has described as "negative liberty."[19] Liberty in this sense required restraints on the state's power to assure that the individual would not be oppressed by its authority. Positive liberty, providing an active role to a person as a member of society exercising civic responsibility together with others, was alien to the classical mind. The sort of active involvement in civic affairs that classical republicanism demanded was scarcely appropriate for the working classes and other lower orders, whose proper role was limited to contributing labor to society's productive capacities. The Jeffersonian yeoman farmer was a figure from a landscape long gone. The bucolic idyll had no place in the industrial United States of the late nineteenth century, except in Currier and Ives nostalgia. Governance, as Alexander Hamilton had insisted, was the prerogative of those fitted for it by education, wealth, command, and status. But all men equally enjoyed negative liberty, the freedom from unwarranted state coercion. (There was no appropriate direct role for women in governance, any more than there would be for children or lunatics. Theirs was the domestic sphere.)

Classical lawyers had only a partial conception of equality, and that was limited to the narrow scope of jural equality: all persons were presumed equals in bargaining relationships. The state could not properly endow any individual with formal advantages not based on services rendered or other indicia of merit, nor could it impose disabilities unrelated to the public welfare. Beyond that, however, state-enforced equality would conflict with the ideal of liberty. Equality of opportunity, if not pressed too vigorously on behalf of the poor, was a harmless social ideal, possibly even a useful one if it propagated a Horatio Alger myth of vertical social mobility. But equality of results or equality of condition was abhorrent, for several reasons. It could be achieved only by redistribution of extant wealth. It would derange the presumptively neutral and just results of industry and would be bad policy to boot, rewarding the indolent or the unfit at the expense of the productive members of society. Inequality of status or fortune was inevitable in all free societies, and attempts to rectify such inequality could only infringe individual liberty in one way or another.

Classical legal thought cherished an understanding of rights derived from the tradition of natural or higher law. In the nineteenth century, lawyers thought of rights primarily in terms of contract and property. Rights were anterior to the state, recognized and protected by the Constitution but not created by it.[20] In this Lockean sense, the state existed to protect rights; that was indeed the whole point of the social compact, embodied in the federal and state constitutions. State interference with rights, as by, for example, intruding into bilateral individual contractual arrangements, would pervert the social contract and its implementation in law.

This understanding weakened around 1900 with the rise of the positive state. Rights are now seen as claims that are created by law on the state or against other individuals and entities. To understand classical thought, it is necessary for moderns to go behind that twentieth-century understanding of rights.

The liberty ideal also alerted American elites to the possibility that public law (constitutional, administrative, and criminal law) had a threateningly redistributive potential. Anticipating that, the Framers had carefully hedged public law about with constraints that protected property rights and contractual results: the contracts, due process, and just compensation clauses, for example. Most bodies of private law were nonredistributive; contract law, above all, assumed that negotiations resulted in wholly voluntary economic arrangements by bargaining equals based on their estimates of their own self-interest. Under a regime of freedom of contract, the state redistributed nothing; at most, it enforced the consequences of the parties' willed transactions.

Constitutional and administrative law, on the other hand, threatened to rearrange the status quo of power and material wealth, the most threatening form of state coercion. Taxation posed an obvious danger, but regulation of commercial enterprise was no less serious a threat, especially because it might often be more plausible and politically justifiable. For all these reasons, the distinction between public and private law had to be strictly policed. Private law had to evolve toward ever more effective realization of individuals' wills, while public law had to inhibit state authority. (In recent times, this older emphasis has been revived in "public choice" theory. Fearing redistribution, or what they term "wealth transfers," public choice theorists call for an activist judiciary to police legislative policies to root out the influences of interest group "rent-seeking.")[21]

The classical lawyers' fear of redistribution lent a distinctly antidemocratic cast to their thought. Continuing to work within a structure of assumptions and beliefs established a century earlier during the American Revolution, they worried that numerical majorities in a state might combine politically to despoil the virtuous and wellborn of their accumulated wealth, the fitting reward of industry. They shared James Madison's anxieties about majority power, without his offsetting confidence that structural limitations on majority rule could constrain the masses. The steady progress of democracy since Madison's day was scarcely encouraging. Democratic majorities in state and municipal government had indulged themselves in such appalling adventures as debt repudiation and modification of corporate charters. Democracy threatened to become the handmaiden of plunder. Woe betide the state when the hordes of new immigrants, improvidently enfranchised by the Democratic Party prostituting itself for their votes as it had earlier done for the Irish vote, augmented the forces of radical farmers, silverite monetary inflationists, labor unions, and agrarian radicals rallying to the Farmers Alliances!

Classical jurists placed the highest value on certainty, stability, and predictability, both in society and in law. They feared the disruption of either. "Anarchy" was for them a code word expressing their inmost anxieties, a fear of loss of control and of descent into a Hobbesian war of all against all. The social turmoil that marked the last quarter of the nineteenth century frightened them. Labor unrest and the turbulence of the cities seemed to realize their fears, with the promise of worse to come. Legal elites turned to law to do what they could to suppress disorder. This response has led unsympathetic observers to write them off as conservative, if not reactionary. They were that, to be sure, but our understanding of their outlook is incomplete if we conclude our inquiry at that point.

The Nature and Sources of Law

Classical lawyers understood law in ways significantly different from the way that we do a century later. We risk misunderstanding their thought, and parodying their achievements, if we fail to take those differences into account.[22]

Given classicists' yearning for order and stability, it was ironic that one of the traditional foundations of those values in the legal order was no longer accessible. Natural law, "the Laws of Nature and Nature's God" to which Jefferson appealed in the Declaration of Independence, had long been retired as a plausible basis for the legal order. Living in what had become for American elites a secular age, classical lawyers (themselves seldom pious or traditional Christians)[23] faced the challenge of identifying a credible secular alternative, but one of equally compelling authority.

Nevertheless, they believed that law was derived from universal principles of justice and moral order. These were as prevalent, unchanging, and authoritative as the law of gravity, to which classical lawyers sometimes compared them. Because these principles were rooted in absolute justice, their faithful application would produce just and correct results. For those who took comfort in such things, the principles that underlay law were harmonious with the commands of the Decalogue and with Christian morality generally.

Viewed as a system, the body of law was comprehensive and complete unto itself. At the tier of principle, the system was closed: no one expected to discover new transcendent principles of justice. New norms might evolve to accommodate social or economic change, and the application of norms certainly would evolve. But doctrinally integrated principles were fixed. Judges had an obligation to maintain the internal coherence and consistency of the system. They did this by incorporating valid decisions into the structure and sloughing off flawed precedent.

In the next tier of law's hierarchy came doctrine, a lawyers' systematization of the rules that principles generated. Doctrine may be essential to coherent development of the law, as Charles Fried has argued,[24] but it remains something imposed on the otherwise spontaneous evolution of the common law. In a common law system, doctrine is academic in origin, identified when lawyer-scholars stepped outside the day-to-day concerns of practice to reflect and write about law's development. Two innovations, debuting a half-century apart, made it possible for lawyers to expound doctrine: the legal treatise, which appeared in the 1820s, and the modern law school, begun in the innovations of Langdell at Harvard and Theodore W. Dwight at Columbia in the 1870s. Together, they provided first the medium, then the environment, in which academic lawyers could systematize legal rules into coherent doctrinal structures.

Doctrinal exposition in treatises provided the interface between supralegal principles and the actual rules of law generated by common law adjudication. These rules were the product of a mode of litigation having certain specific characteristics.[25] Classical litigation was bipolar, between two private parties; retrospective, attempting to restore a status quo disturbed by a tortious act or a contractual dispute; confined in its impact, limited in its immediate consequences to the actual parties, and, at law, resolved by the payment (or not) of money damages; and fertile, generating a legal rule in a regime of stare decisis capable of resolving the next dispute presenting similar facts.

The forms of classical adjudication contributed to attaining classicism's highest goal, the rule of law. Judgment was to depend on impartial administration of fixed rules, not on uncontrolled judicial discretion, empathy, or whim. Only such neutral impartiality could guarantee that the application of law would be predictable, and its substantive rules not dictated by those who stood to benefit from them.

Central to the classical constitutional vision was the imputed differentiation, if not antagonism, between state and society. Society, defined by the primacy of the individual and the role of institutions like family and church, was prior to the state (that is, government), in both time and precedence. According to orthodox Lockean theory, the state existed to protect society and its constituent institutions, but it had the sinister tendency of itself threatening them. Control of state power, therefore, became one of the most pressing needs of free societies.

In the nineteenth century, the rule of law was the principal means of assuring society's dominance over the state. The idea of a rule of law was not new in industrial America; John Adams was responsible for one of its ancestral formulations in the Massachusetts Constitution of 1780, whose Declaration of Rights mandated the separation of powers, "to the end it may be a government of laws and not of men."[26] Nor was it unique to the United States; it was the American cousin of the contemporary German ideal of the *Rechtsstaat*. But the concept took on new connotations in the heated social atmosphere of the late nineteenth century. In Adams's time, the rule of law assumed the neutral state, governmental power impartial among conflicting interests, lending its force to none except by the operation of majoritarian republican politics, constrained by constitutional norms established by the sovereign people themselves through ratification of the Constitution. But in the industrial America of a century later, the rule-of-law ideal had come to be, for many, a fiction justifying use of the state's power to sustain the privilege and position of wealthy elites.

This threat to the rule of law had a dangerously destabilizing potential, threatening the legitimacy of the law itself. Across the ideological continuum, both contemporary and modern, the rule of law is considered essential to law's place in a democratic society. Even in a Marxian view, where law is seen as a form of ideology that legitimates class power through its hegemonic operation, the rule of law operates to require inclusion of equitable principles valued by nonhegemonic groups like workers.[27] From more centrist perspectives, the modern Court has reaffirmed the necessity and the supremacy of the rule of law in solemn language suited only to the gravest occasions.[28] Such near universal[29] allegiance to the rule of law, at least as aspirational ideal, confirms its centrality in the American legal regime.

Lawyers considered American legal culture in the classical era to be autonomous. They regarded their system as self-contained and characterized by a quality that today is known in cardiac physiology as "automaticity": capable of generating its own animating impulses, keeping itself going along by an endogenous capability of activating itself.[30] This automaticity assured law's independence from political controversy and legislative struggle. To extend the cardiac metaphor, if disturbance or trauma affected other organs (legislative or executive, church or private association) the heart of law, the common law system, would continue to beat, pumping life-sustaining order throughout the body politic.

Law's autonomy led classical jurists to regard social science data with Olympian indifference (until the Supreme Court permitted itself to be influenced by the Brandeis Brief in 1908). What did it matter that legal doctrine or norm might or might not be compatible with a reality disclosed by the emergent social sciences like economics or sociology? The imperial sway of a general principle like *pacta sunt servanda* was not to be deflected by discordant social conditions (such as the relative bargaining power of the parties) any more than it was to be diverted by a party's unilateral preference.

Classical lawyers disdained resort to the emergent social sciences because their legal system was sufficient in itself, endogenously generating whatever impetus to its own development might be required. In this attitude, they followed in a tradition established by Edward Coke in the seventeenth century, reaffirmed by John Austin in the nineteenth, and most recently restated in an extreme form amounting to intellectual autarky by Alan Watson,[31] that insists on law's autonomy from the rest of society.[32]

In a similar sense, law was amoral (though expressing the thought that way might have troubled classical lawyers). Its legitimacy rested not on an individual judge's own ethical compass, nor on the customary or popular moral values of contemporary society, nor even on the Christian moral order. Classical lawyers boasted of law's independence from popular morality. Nathan Dane, acclaimed as "the American Blackstone," explained that "the law of the land and morality are the same [only in] some special cases." The become divorced "when policy, or arbitrary rules must also be regarded. Virtue alone is the object of morality, but law has also often, for its object, the peace of society, and what is practicable."[33] Joseph H. Beale, one of the last classicist academics, wrote in 1916 that "law as the lawyer knows it is absolutely distinct from any rule of conduct based on a moral ground however strong."[34]

Some classical lawyers, such as James C. Carter, believed the common law method was "historicist" in the continental sense, emanating out of the customs and experience of the people. This assured law's authenticity and confirmed the legitimacy of its results. Their common law bias imbued judges with a suspicion of legislative intrusion into the economy or into social relationships. Since the natural evolution of common law kept it harmonious with society, legislative intervention could only disturb that harmony. Thus classical lawyers often repeated the old precept that statutes in derogation of the common law are to be strictly construed. The public law counterpart was vigilant judicial oversight of legislation to insure its conformity with constitutional limitations.

The Structure of This Book

Legal classicism held sway for half a century because its roots reached down into the origins of the American constitutional order and intertwined with some of our most fundamental normative republican commitments. Its legitimating function traced back to the republic's beginnings, and was derived from republican "foundational principles" concerning the nature of government and the social order.[35] Thus lawyers could invoke it as "normative history"[36] to sanction policy positions that were implicit in legal doctrines. Chapter 1 surveys the first century of legal growth in America, outlining the foundations of classical thought.

Classical ideology rose to ascendancy in the generation after the Civil War. It grew out of the social and economic conditions of the time, and constituted the elite bar's response to them. The second chapter explores American society in the Gilded Age and the anxieties it induced among American lawyers and judges, and summarizes the ideological content of classical thought.

Once formulated into a coherent whole, the classical outlook quickly dominated the work of the United States Supreme Court in constitutional law. Although its reign was not exclusive — rival lines of precedent contemporaneously developed that undermined its authority — legal classicism constituted *a* dominant way of expounding the law of the constitution, but not the only way. Chapter 3 evaluates classical constitutional law in the era of classicism's reign, 1886 through 1937.

American law has developed through continual discourse over centuries of time, which has led constitutional theorists to see it as the product of a community of discourse.[37] One way of interpreting our constitutional history is to consider the Court engaged in a dialogue with the American people over the direction of republican values. This discourse has not always been harmonious. The impact of classical adjudication on American society, government, and the economy provoked hostile political and intellectual reactions. Legal classicism tried to control the attitudes of laypeople toward law and courts, but it never commanded universal respect. On the contrary, the history of American public law has been marked by recurrent political efforts to overthrow classical beliefs.

In the political arena, different interest groups threatened by the consequences of classical adjudication sought to curtail the power of courts or to overturn specific decisions. Some judges and scholars not in the thrall of classical ideology produced a critique of the ways that its assumptions determined results in both private and public law. Meanwhile, by the First World War (if not earlier), the intellectual vitality of legal classicism had drained away. It ceased to be intellectually fecund just as its legitimating authority was beginning to wane. Chapter 4 explores this political and intellectual decline.

One of the greatest challenges confronting the student of classicism is to explain why an explanatory paradigm of such power, scope, and legitimating authority collapsed so suddenly and completely in 1937–1938. Chapter 5 and the epilogue offer some explanations.

Classicism succumbed in a surprisingly brief period and was defunct as a legitimating ideology by 1938. When it disintegrated, a new paradigm, announced offhandedly by Justice Harlan Fiske Stone in a footnote in *United States v. Carolene Products* (1938), partially supplied its place. It anticipated the next half-century of constitutional development, announcing a shift in the Court's concern from economic to noneconomic issues. After Stone became Chief Justice in 1941, the Court began implementing the new legal order.

But the *Carolene Products* paradigm, prescient though it proved to be, did not supply a comprehensive legitimating authority for the system that it had displaced. As an innovation, it did not enjoy the aura of legitimacy that had validated classicism. In the half-century since Stone announced the new paradigm, the legal system has not yet produced a comprehensive structure of thought comparable to classicism, and therefore much of the Court's work today remains vulnerable to challenges to its legitimacy.

Finally, a historiographic appendix surveys the ways that historians have presented legal classicism. Lawyers and others who are not historians sometimes do not appreciate the extent to which our understanding of the past is nothing more than a digest of what historians have written about it. Lay readers sometimes attribute greater authority to our interpretations than is warranted. The writing of history is as contingent, as culturally bound, and as ideological as the writing of judicial opinions. A survey of how historical interpretations of classicism have evolved might prove useful or interesting to some readers, and it appears in the appendix.

Notes

1. Eric Foner, *Free Soil, Free Labor, Free Men: The Ideology of the Republican Party before the Civil War* (1970), 4.

2. I borrow the phrase from G. Edward White, "Transforming History in the Modern Era," 91 *Mich. L. Rev.* 1315, 1323–1324 (1993) (reviewing Morton J. Horwitz, *The Transformation of American Law, 1870–1960: The Crisis of Legal Orthodoxy* [1992]; I will hereafter refer to this book as Horwitz, *Transformation II*).

3. Robert W. Gordon, "Legal Thought and Legal Practice in the Age of American Enterprise, 1870–1920," in Gerald L. Geison, ed., *Professions and Professional Ideologies in America* (1983), 72.

4. Duncan Kennedy, "Toward an Historical Understanding of Legal Consciousness: The Case of Classical Legal Thought in America, 1850–1940," *Research in Law and Sociology* 3 (1980), 3; Morton J. Horwitz, *The Transformation of American Law, 1780–1860* (1977), 253–68 (hereafter: Horwitz, *Transformation I*); Horwitz, *Transformation II*, 3–63; Elizabeth Mensch, "The History of Mainstream Legal Thought," in David Kairys, ed., *The Politics of Law: A Progressive Critique*, 2nd ed. (1990), 13–37; Gordon, "Legal Thought and Legal Practice in the Age of American Enterprise," 70–110; Thomas C. Grey, "Langdell's Orthodoxy," 45 *U. Pitt. L. Rev.* 1 (1983); Stephen A. Siegel, "Lochner Era Jurisprudence and the American Constitutional Tradition," 70 *N.C. L. Rev.* 1 (1991); Neil Duxbury, *Patterns of American Jurisprudence* (1995), 9–64; Donald J. Gjerdingen, "The Future of Our Past: The Legal Mind and the Legacy of Classical Legal Thought," 68 *Ind. L.J.* 743 (1993); Howard Gillman, *The Constitution Besieged: The Rise and Demise of Lochner Era Police Powers Jurisprudence* (1993).

5. Karl Llewellyn, *The Common Law Tradition: Deciding Appeals*, (1960), 38.

6. E.g.: William E. Nelson, "The Impact of the Antislavery Movement upon Styles of Judicial Reasoning in Nineteenth Century America," 87 *Harv. L. Rev.* 513 (1974); William M. Wiecek, *Liberty under Law: The Supreme Court in American Life* (1988), ch. 5, "The Formalist Era, 1873–1937."

7. Frederick Schauer, "Formalism," 97 *Yale L.J.* 509 (1988).

8. Rudolf von Jhering, *Der Geist des Römischen Rechts*, vol. 2, part 2, 478–79 (1858). I thank my colleague Peter Herzog for guiding my translation of this passage. Duncan Kennedy quotes a different translation in "Legal Formality," 2 *J. Legal Studies* 351 (1973).

9. Charles Fried, "Constitutional Doctrine", 107 *Harv. L. Rev.* 1140, 1145 (1994).

10. Edward A. Purcell Jr. denies that legal thought in the 1870–1930 period can usefully be described as formalist. He maintains that judges' decisions were informed by substantive value choices and thus were instrumentalist: *Litigation and Inequality: Federal Diversity Jurisdiction in Industrial America, 1870–1958* (1992), 253–254.

11. William Blackstone, *Commentaries on the Laws of England* (1765–68), vol. 3, 396.

12. Lochner v. New York, 198 U.S. 45, 75 (1905) (Holmes, J., dissenting). A minor economy of wordage: since I do not refer to Holmes *père* anywhere in this study, I omit the Jr. in the name of Holmes *fils*.

13. Lawrence M. Friedman, "Freedom of Contract and Occupational Licensing 1890–1910: A Legal and Social Study," 53 *Cal. L. Rev.* 487, 525–26 (1965).

14. Max Lerner, "The Triumph of Laissez-Faire," in Arthur M. Schlesinger Jr. and Morton White, eds., *Paths of American Thought* (1963), 148.

15. Arthur J. Taylor, *Laissez-Faire and State Intervention in Nineteenth-Century Britain* (1972).

16. James Bryce, *The American Commonwealth*, 2nd ed. rev. (1891), vol. 2, 292.

17. Henry Maine, *Ancient Law* (1861; rpt. 1917), 100.

18. Budd v. New York, 143 U.S. 517, 551 (1892) (Brewer, J., dissenting).

19. Isaiah Berlin, *Four Essays on Liberty* (1970), ch. 2, "Two Concepts of Liberty."

20. Cf. a modern echo of this belief: "[W]e deal with a right of privacy older than the Bill of Rights . . . .": Douglas, J., for the majority in Griswold v. Connecticut, 381 U.S. 479, 485 (1965).

21. Jonathan R. Macey, "Public Choice: The Theory of the Firm and the Theory of Market Exchange," 74 *Cornell L. Rev.* 43 (1988); Macey, "Transaction Costs and the Normative Elements of the Public Choice Model: An Application to Constitutional Theory," 74 *Va. L. Rev.* 471 (1988).

22. Although the subhead to this section is almost identical to the title of John Chipman Gray's classic, *The Nature and Sources of the Law* (1909), the following paragraphs do not reflect the theses or contents of that magisterial book.

23. For a pious exception, see Stephen A. Siegel, "Joel Bishop's Orthodoxy," 13 *Law and Hist. Rev.* 215 (1995). Thomas M. Cooley was another.

24. Charles Fried, "Constitutional Doctrine," 107 *Harv. L. Rev.* 1140 (1994).

25. Abram Chayes, "The Role of the Judge in Public Law Litigation," 89 *Harv. L. Rev.* 1281 (1976); Louis L. Jaffe, "The Citizen as Litigant in Public Actions: The Non-Hohfeldian or Ideological Plaintiff," 116 *U. Pa. L. Rev.* 1033 (1968); Owen M. Fiss, "The Social and Political Foundations of Adjudication," 6 *Law & Hum. Behavior* 121 (1982); Fiss, "Foreword: The Forms of Justice," 93 *Harv. L. Rev.* 1 (1979).

26. William F. Swindler, *Sources and Documents of United States Constitutions* (1973–1979), vol. 5, 96.

27. E. P. Thompson, *Whigs and Hunters: The Origin of the Black Act* (1975), 258–269.

28. Planned Parenthood of Southeastern Pennsylvania v. Casey, 112 S. Ct. 2791 (1992) (joint opinion of O'Connor, Kennedy, Souter, JJ.; dissenting opinion of Rehnquist, C.J.).

29. Morton Horwitz is, or was, an exception: "The Rule of Law: An Unqualified Human Good?," 86 *Yale L.J.* 561 (1977).

30. The human heart generates its own electrical impulses in the sinoatrial and atrioventricular nodes, which cause depolarization and repolarization of cardiac muscle fibers, producing contractions and relaxations of the atria and the ventricles.

31. Alan Watson, *Slave Law in the Americas* (1989), 64, 76, 130–133.

32. Charles Fried makes a more moderate claim for law's autonomy in "Jurisprudential Responses to Legal Realism," 73 *Cornell L.J.* 331 (1988); see also Richard Posner, "The Decline of Law as an Autonomous Discipline," 100 *Harv. L. Rev.* 761 (1987) (noting shrinkage of law's autonomy since 1960).

33. Nathan Dane, *A General Abridgement and Digest of American Law* (1823–29), vol. 1, 100.

34. Joseph H. Beale, *A Treatise on the Conflict of Laws*, 1st ed. (1916), vol. 1, 153.

35. On foundational principles in constitutional adjudication, see Kennedy, J., concurring in United States v. Lopez, 115 S. Ct. 1624, 1634 (1995).

36. Paul W. Kahn, *Legitimacy and History: Self-Government in American Constitutional Theory* (1993), 180.

37. Robert Cover, "Foreword: Nomos and Narrative," 97 *Harv. L. Rev.* 4 (1983); Bruce Ackerman, "The Storrs Lectures: Discovering the Constitution," 93 *Yale L.J.* 1013 (1984); Frank Michelman, "Foreword: Traces of Self-Government," 100 *Harvard L. Rev.* 4 (1986); Kahn, *Legitimacy and History*, 171–189; Gillman, *The Constitution Besieged*, 200 (who refers to a "legal" ideology as understood by "interpretive communities in particular historical contexts"). These authorities differ among themselves, however, about just who constituted the discursive community: the American people, the Court itself, the Court plus the professional elite, Congress, etc.

Chapter One

The Foundations of Classical Legal Thought, 1760–1860

Classical legal thought did not appear suddenly and without precedent in 1890, nor was it an innovation. It grew instead out of the previous century of constitutional growth, evolving in an organic development of antebellum legal culture. Its origins go back to the creation of the American republics. Classicism arose from the original eighteenth-century constitutional foundations and derived its legitimating power from them.

In the ideology of the American revolution,. in the early state constitutions, in the national constitution of 1787, and in early precedents of the state and federal courts, Americans created a constitutional system that privileged certain substantive values, particularly those relating to contracts, property, and security for personal liberty. The Framers of the state and federal constitutions assigned the courts' place in the constitutional order and legitimated the use of judicial power.

The American Revolution

From the American Revolution, classical legal thought derived some defining elements of American constitutionalism:

the sense of a higher law controlling ordinary legislation
a fear of governmental power as a threat to individual liberty
the dominance of legal culture in American public life
commitment to a stable legal order .
the tendency to convert political and ideological divisions into legal argument
the centrality of the common law in the American legal order
a dedication to limited government and regularized procedure

a fear of popular democratic power
commitment to Lockean values of life, liberty, property, and security
a strong central government
judicial review

To a modern lawyer, three characteristics of the American Revolution[1] stand out: it was ideological, it was legalistic, and it was radical.

Revolutionary Ideology

As Americans became aware of their grievances and disagreements with the mother country after 1760, they articulated their views incessantly in newspaper essays, pamphlets, broadsides, letters, and state papers. Within a decade, this accumulation of constitutional argument identified the principles by which Americans thought they had been governed, and by which the meant to be governed in the future.[2]

Americans extolled the British constitution as a source of their liberties. In this, they thought themselves true disciples of Sir Edward Coke and William Blackstone. They cherished the "mixed constitution," a coincident balance of principles of government and estates of society. The Crown embodied executive authority, Lords the deliberative principle, and Commons the liberties of the people. The equipoise achieved by this balance of functions and estates was essential to preserve popular government.

Whig Americans[3] viewed power as the defining characteristic of government, and liberty as the defining characteristic of the people. These root principles, power and liberty, each had characteristic, innate degenerative tendencies. Power unchecked would degenerate into tyranny, liberty into licentiousness and anarchy. The principles were therefore mutually related in a constitutional zero-sum game: the growth of governmental power threatened popular liberty, and vice versa. A wise and just constitutional order sought to strike a balance of the two so that government was sufficiently energetic for its responsibilities while preserving the people's liberties. Those liberties were derived from "the natural absolute personal rights of individuals" and the "original, inherent, indefeasible, natural rights" of the people collectively.[4] They were God-given, "founded on the immutable maxims of reason and justice."[5]

Throughout the colonial period, Americans held to a belief in higher or fundamental law. Eighteenth-century Americans concurred with William Blackstone that natural law, which was "dictated by God himself, . . . is binding over all the globe, in all countries, and at all times: no human laws are of any validity, if contrary to this."[6] Thomas Jefferson confidently called on "the Laws of Nature and of Nature's God" to justify the Declaration of Independence. James Wilson, Justice of the Supreme Court, identified the law of nature as the divinely instituted foundation of all law, immutable, universal, knowable by humans through intuition and conscience.[7]

The ideological stresses of the Revolution disclosed that this tradition actually confounded two different branches of fundamental-law thought.[8] One, expressed in the preceding quotations, appealed to sources of higher law outside the mundane legal order, such as divine law. The other, more relevant to the later classical tradition, operated wholly within the earthly legal order, holding that a legislature might not infringe legally created rights, such as those recognized by common law (e.g., property rights) or by traditional institutional procedures (e.g., protection against searches under general warrants). These legal rights were the product of social evolution and were identified by judicial precedent. The source of their authority lay in the English constitutional tradition, of which Chief Justice Sir Edward Coke was the supreme exponent. This tradition emphasized the supremacy of law over arbitrary power, the role of custom and reason in law's evolution, and judicial authority of the sort Coke claimed in *Dr. Bonham's Case* (1610).

Because the constitution was superior to positive law, it was a limitation on legislative authority. The Georgia minister John Zubly insisted in 1769 that the constitution "is permanent and ever the same." Parliament "can no more make laws which are against the constitution or the unalterable privileges of British subjects than it can alter the constitution itself. . . . The power of parliament, and of every branch of it, has its bounds assigned by the constitution."[9] This understanding of higher law readily transferred to the new republican environment.

Americans originally found sources of higher law indiscriminately in the British constitution, the common law, the divine ordinances found in the Bible, natural law as defined by Scholastic philosophers, or universal norms of behavior somehow implanted in the human spirit. In the crucible of revolution and republican constitution-making, however, Whig leaders definitively identified the source of fundamental law in the American republics as the constitutive act of the people in their sovereign capacity, expressed in written constitutions — first of the states, then of the national government. Higher law thereby became subsumed in the supremacy of written constitutions.

Revolutionary Legalism

The American Revolution was intensely legalistic, due partly to the fact that half its political leaders were lawyers. The Revolution began with attorneys' arguments in two cases and culminated in a lawyer's brief.

The public debates of the Revolution were framed in constitutional terms. To an extent without parallel in the upheavals of the modern era, the American Revolution was a struggle over constitutional principles,[10] and over the legitimacy of government. In some senses, this may have been a conservative achievement. Americans reluctantly resisted British power to preserve what they considered their ancient liberties against modern innovation. Americans devised new state and national constitutions, not as an afterthought or ceremonial formality, but as the core creation of their revolutionary experience. The heritage of the Revolution was a structure of legal institutions, not a body of revolutionary dogma. But in a longer view, functioning institutions of popular government, with the potential for ever increasing democratization, were the Revolution's truly radical achievement.

Elsewhere revolutions have been made by desperate crowds storming the Bastille, by workers' soviets, or by people's armies on the Long March; in America, the Revolution began in lawyers' arguments about the constitutionality of a court's process. In 1761, James Otis Jr. attacked the use of writs of assistance, a kind of general search warrant, issued by the Court of Exchequer in the enforcement of the

Navigation Acts, condemning them as "against the fundamental principles of law" and therefore "illegal": "An act against the Constitution is void [Otis declaimed]; an act against natural equity is void; and if an act of Parliament should be made, in the very words of this petition it would be void. The executive Courts must pass such acts into disuse."[11] Two years later, a Virginia attorney, Patrick Henry, developed the theme of popular consent in his arguments in the litigation known variously as the "Two-Penny Act Case" or "The Parsons' Cause" (1763). Henry argued that by disallowing a statute made for the general welfare, the king had violated the compact between himself and his people and forfeited "all rights to his subjects' obedience."[12]

Throughout the course of the Revolution, attorneys advanced elaborate legal arguments extending the ideological positions of the American cause. All the major state papers issuing from town meetings, provincial legislatures, and national congresses, as well as many of the tracts arguing the Whig viewpoint, were lawyers' arguments. Among them were the Declarations of the Stamp Act Congress (1765), the Massachusetts Circular Letter of 1768, the 1773 debate between Governor Thomas Hutchinson and the Massachusetts House of Representatives, and the Declaration and Resolves of the First Continental Congress (1774).[13] John Adams and Josiah Quincy, both members of the Massachusetts bar, insisted on scrupulous legality in the prosecution of the officer and soldiers responsible for the Boston Massacre (1770), and got acquittals or release by plea of benefit of clergy. Two of the most influential tracts of the Revolution, James Wilson's *Considerations on the Authority of Parliament* and Thomas Jefferson's *A Summary View of the Rights of British-America* (both 1774), were extended constitutional arguments.

This prominent role of law and lawyers in the Revolution reflected a legal culture in which, as Alexis de Tocqueville noted later, all political questions sooner or later become transformed into legal issues, and in which lawyers play a central role in national life. In the thought of influential lawyers, including Otis, Alexander Hamilton, and John Adams, revolutionary legalism took on a conservative coloration, protecting the rights of property and the obligations of contract from legislative meddling.

Higher or fundamental law provided one component of revolutionary legalism. Otis, Jefferson, and other lawyers assumed that higher law underlay and determined all human laws. God's law provides "the laws of our nature . . . founded on the immutable maxims of reason and justice," John Dickinson wrote in 1766.[14] Higher law was a vital component of all revolutionary thought.[15]

A revolution begun by lawyers fittingly found its leading spokesman in another lawyer and its justification in a piece of transcendent propaganda that took the form of a legal pleading, Jefferson's Declaration of Independence. Though its immortal two opening paragraphs are the only part remembered or even read by moderns, the bulk of the document consisted of twenty-seven items in an extended bill of complaint or indictment, twenty of which involved legal or constitutional issues, not matters of mere policy.

Revolutionary Radicalism

The American Revolution was the most radical governmental upheaval in modern history.[16] Its fundamental premise was that the people are capable of ruling themselves, and it realized that ideal in actual working governments.[17] The people displaced the Crown as the source of sovereignty, authority, and legitimacy of govern-ment. From their experience rather than as a matter of theoretical speculation, Americans adopted John Locke's insistence on the consent of the people as the basis of legitimacy.[18] Alexander Hamilton wrote in 1775 that "no laws have any validity or binding force without the consent and approbation of the people."[19]

The revolutionary generation secured the sovereignty of the people in several ways. In the Declaration of Independence, Jefferson asserted that governments "deriv[e] their just power from the consent of the governed," so that when a govern-ment loses its legitimacy "it is the Right of the People to alter or to abolish it, and to institute new Government." This was not merely a rhetorical call to arms; it became a working principle of government. The Virginia Declaration of Rights (1776) and the New Hampshire Constitution of 1784 affirmed the right of revolution, a notion that in any other system would have to be dismissed as oxymoronic: "[W]henever the ends of government are perverted, and public liberty manifestly endangered, and all other means of redress are ineffectual, the people may, and of right ought, to re-form the old, or establish a new government. The doctrine of non-resistance against arbitrary power, and oppression, is absurd, slavish, and destructive of the good and happiness of mankind."[20]

The legitimacy of a government itself became a contested question in the Rev-olution. At the national level, sovereignty, and with it, legitimacy, were transferred from the Crown to the Continental Congress in the years 1774 through 1776.[21] At the state level, legitimacy came to inhere in the popular legislatures as the inheri-tance of the colonial charters, compacts, covenants, and common law.[22]

The first of the republican constitutions, Virginia's of 1776, proclaimed that "all power is vested in, and consequently derived from, the people; that magistrates are their trustees and servants, and at all times amenable to them."[23] Pennsylvania's con-stitution of 1776 attempted to assure popular control of government by procedural devices, such as requiring that the doors of the unicameral assembly be open at all times, and that all bills and votes be printed for the public.[24]

While Pennsylvania's first constitution was egregiously democratic, the entire revolutionary experience was one of increasing democratization. The Revolution was driven from below, by "the people out of doors," as much as from above by a law-yerly elite, because as Carl Becker noted long ago, it was a contest over "who should rule at home" as well as over "home rule" (the contest with England).[25] These con-current struggles were not harmonious with each other. "Who should rule at home" involved more than power struggles among differing factions of local governing elites. In all the colonies, new popular groups, often representing frontier or artisan inter-ests, contested the dominance of established coteries of political power. They rudely challenged the provincial political culture that for a century and a half had been based on the common people's deference to social and political elites.[26]

A reaction to democratizing tendencies set in soon after Independence, though. Erstwhile revolutionaries invoked social compact theory to check wealth-redistributive exercises of legislative power, channeling the revolutionary impulse into constitu-tional forms.[27] The radical revolutionary tradition thus evoked a countertradition that emphasized restraints on popular, democratic power. From John Adams's "Thoughts on Government" (1776) through George Washington's farewell address (1796), con-servative revolutionaries appealed for stability and legality. The farewell address (ghostwritten first by James Madison and then Alexander Hamilton) summed up two decades of resistance to revolutionary democratic tendencies that might upset the status quo of wealth and power:

> The basis of our political systems is the right of the people to make and alter their constitutions of government. But the constitution which at any time exists till changed by an explicit and authentic act of the whole people is sacredly obligatory upon all. The very idea of the power and the right of the people to establish government presupposes the duty of every individual to obey the established government.[28]

Together, the radical and conservative traditions have coexisted as a polarity of American constitutionalism. Subsequent constitutional development has oscillated between them.

Hamilton and Washington could not have issued their appeal for obedience in 1796 unless they anticipated that the people would heed it. Their confidence rested on the abiding popular respect for order and legitimacy that characterized the revolutionary experience. At the moment of Independence, Whig Americans did not believe that the legal order had been suspended or discarded by the break with the mother country. They abhorred the thought that the legal order was dissolved by revolution. Law as a principle of order and stability balanced the centrifugal tendencies of democratic government.

Republican State Constitutions

Revolutionary Republican Theory

The state constitutions adopted between 1776 and 1790 converted republican ideology and aspiration into actual working state charters.[29] Written constitutions occupy a central place in republican theory as the documentary specification of republican government. The first state constitutions comprised another part of legal classicism's foundations.

Nowhere was the regime of law suspended or legitimate authority put in abeyance at the culmination of the Revolution. Legitimacy simply transferred from royal to popular bodies, paralleling and realizing the theoretical changeover from sovereignty in the Crown to popular sovereignty. Americans lived up to their well-deserved reputation for being a consistently law-respecting people, preserving (self-)government under law even at the climax of their revolutionary struggle. (They were to reconfirm this commitment to legality repeatedly in mining camps, westward trails, and frontier settlements.)[30] To restate the Turner frontier hypothesis in legalist terms: it was on the advancing frontier that legalism constantly renewed itself and replicated the legal order.

The new republican legislatures enacted statutes or adopted constitutional provisions declaring that the common law, including appropriate British statutory law, was received as the basis of the state's legal order.[31] Thus at the beginning, the American republics installed their ancestral private law system as an essential element of their constitutions. Classicism built on these common-law foundations.

The earliest state constitutions, adopted between 1776 and 1779, instantiated the revolutionary legal order. All of them[32] affirmed republicanism, popular sovereignty, liberty, property, the commonwealth idea, representation, and separation of powers.[33] These charters attest to the high value revolutionary Americans put on the written constitution as a specification and limitation of governmental powers. The constitutions typically consisted of two components, a "Frame of Government" and a "Declaration of Rights." The Frame of Government provided the structure and mechanics of government, providing for such things as powerful but bicameral legislative assemblies,[34] a weak governor, and state courts. Checks and balances and separation of powers secured limited government, in order to protect the liberty of the people.

The declarations of rights were compendia of revolutionary constitutional theory. Virginia's, being the first,[35] was the prototype of most other state bills of rights. It emphasized popular sovereignty and the people's right of revolution; separation of powers among the three branches of government; expansive, but not necessarily universal (and implicitly white) male suffrage; protection for individual rights, beginning with freedom (but not for enslaved people),[36] life, and property.[37] Individual liberty was secured by "the law of the land," Magna Charta's ancestor of due process. The declaration enumerated the rights of those accused of crimes (slaves again excepted) and civil jury trial. It also specified collective rights: free exercise of religion, freedom of the press, and prohibition of standing armies. It concluded with a ringing reminder of the need for popular virtue ("justice, moderation, temperance, frugality"), and mutual charity.[38]

Conservative Republican Theory

Throughout the decade after Independence, republican ideology was corrected by experience.[39] From all points of the ideological compass, Americans weighed in with critiques of the hastily drafted constitutions of 1776–1777. Throughout the war and after, Whigs in the states pursued policies of economic opportunism, unconstrained by the lofty principles of the revolutionary constitutional order. They confiscated enemy and Loyalist property without a thought of compensation or regular judicial procedure. After the war, republican legislatures repudiated British debts, and persisted in that policy even though the Treaty of Paris and Jay's Treaty of 1794 stipulated that those debts were to be honored. In reaction to the postwar depression that set in after 1783, the legislatures enacted various forms of debtor relief, including inflationary paper money schemes and debt moratoria. Urban artisans continued to demand legislative wage and price controls, as they had throughout the Revolution.[40] The debtor-creditor struggle was reflected in alarming incidents of instability, amounting to insurrections, challenging the new governments, the worst being Shays's Rebellion in the winter of 1786–1787. Even after creation of a supposedly powerful national government, popular, economically driven resistance continued to threaten national authority, in the Whiskey Rebellion of 1794 and Fries's Rebellion in 1799.

Nationalists like James Madison were distressed by this legislative behavior of the states. Madison catalogued the states' failings in an essay, "Vices of the Political System of the U. States," that he drew up in 1787, which reflected his experience in

the Confederation Congress. High on his list of complaints was the variety, mutabil-
ity, and instability of state legislation.[41] He and Alexander Hamilton, writing as "Publius" in the *Federalist* papers, railed at the "enormities" and "iniquitous measures" of
the debtor-relief laws of Rhode Island.[42] North Carolina attorney general James Iredell (later Justice of the United States Supreme Court) exaggerated for rhetorical effect when he condemned his state's laws as "the vilest collection of trash ever formed
by a legislative body," but he expressed a widely held sentiment.[43]

John Adams, representing the more conservative pole of Whig political thought,
demanded that the executives' powers be enhanced. He also advocated a strong
upper house in the state legislatures that would be more removed from the people
and organized on a different representative basis than the lower house so as to give
added structural protection to the interests of property owners.[44] Article XXX of the
Declaration of Rights of the Massachusetts Constitution of 1780, Adams's handiwork,
mandated the separation of powers, "to the end that it may be a government of laws
and not of men," a touchstone of revolutionary republican ideology and an expression of the rule-of-law ideal.[45] From the other end of the ideological spectrum,
Thomas Jefferson criticized the "very capital defects" of Virginia's constitution of
1776, including disfranchisement, malapportionment, an overpowerful legislature,
and an enfeebled separation of powers.[46]

Distilled from these discrepant views, an emerging consensus held that law was
necessarily something more than merely statutes and codes. Law had to create a
regime of order, stability, and justice. Americans rejected a strong version of legislative positivism in favor of preserving a correspondence between statutory law and
some form of higher law.

Whig Americans learned a great deal through reflection and experience from
1776, when they drafted their first republican constitution, Virginia's, until 1790,
when adoption of Pennsylvania's conservative constitution (replacing the radically
democratic 1776 original) brought the constitutional era to a close. The evolution of
George Mason's views exemplified this trend away from popular control of government and toward protections for economic interests. He had been the author of the
Virginia Declaration of Rights in 1776, but by 1783, he wrote in disillusionment of
"frequent Interference with private Property & Contracts, retrospective Laws destructive of all public Faith, as well as Confidence between Man & Man, and flagrant Violations of the Constitution must disgust the best & wisest Part of the Community, occasion a general Depravity of Manners, bring the Legislature into Contempt, and
finally produce Anarchy & public Convulsion."[47] In response to such anxieties, Americans wrote extensive securities for property into their state and federal charters. Almost all of these appeared in the 1780 Massachusetts Constitution.

The first article of the Virginia and Massachusetts declarations of rights identified the inherent right of "acquiring, possessing, and protecting property."[48] Whigs
condemned preferential inequality: they required that "no man, nor corporation, or
association of men, have any other title to obtain advantages, or particular and exclusive privileges, distinct from those of the community, than what arises from the consideration of services rendered to the public"; but this was linked to a condemnation
of hereditable officeholding, not to the antimonopoly sentiment that appeared later,
in the Jacksonian era.

The constitutions protected property explicitly in due process or law-of-the-land clauses, and prohibited uncompensated takings: "[N]o part of the property of any individual can with justice, be taken from him, or applied to public uses, without his own consent or that of the representative body of the people. . . . And whenever the public exigencies require that the property of any individual should be appropriated to public use, he shall receive a reasonable compensation therefor." The judicial system existed to protect property, among other interests: "[E]very subject of the commonwealth ought to find a certain remedy, by having recourse to the laws, for all injuries or wrongs which he may receive in his person, property, or character." And "it is essential to the preservation of the rights of every individual, his life, liberty, property, and character, that there be an impartial interpretation of the laws, and administration of justice," this last being the rationale for good-behavior judicial tenure. In addition to these, the federal Constitution prohibited the states from impairing the obligation of contracts.[49]

In *Federalist* Number 37, James Madison expressed the dilemma of revolutionary republican constitution-making: "combining the requisite stability and energy in government with the inviolable attention due to liberty and to the republican form."[50] By this time, Madison had come to fear the power of legislative majorities. As he wrote to Thomas Jefferson, "[W]herever the real power in a Government lies, there is the danger of oppression. In our Governments the real power lies in the majority of the Community, and the invasion of private rights is chiefly to be apprehended, not from acts of Government contrary to the sense of its constituents, but from acts in which the Government is the mere instrument of the major number of the Constituents."[51]

The Framers believed that they had successfully met this challenge. They not only preserved their almost otherworldly ideals but actually organized their new governments around them. They guided their states through a revolution at once radical, yet conservative and legalistic. In doing so, they crystallized the revolutionary experience and its ideals in successful state governments that protected liberty and property.

The Federal Constitution and the Judiciary

As they created republican state governments, the revolutionary generation also brought forth a national government. They sought a balance between the autonomy of the states and vigorous national authority. The First Congress supplied two deficiencies in the Constitution of 1787, sending a bill of rights out to the states for ratification and enacting the first Judiciary Act (1789), which created a national court system. State and federal judges began exploring the potential of judicial power, broaching the delicate problem of judicial review and asserting the binding force of higher law principles as limits on legislative power. They laid the foundations on which their successors, the judges of the nineteenth century, erected the edifice of classical legal theory.

Nationalists like James Madison despaired of reforming states' laws that threatened the security of property and contract. But they came to realize that state-by-state revision would not be necessary if they could establish a strong national government with authority over the substance of state legislation. This new national government would derive its authority from a national constitution that contained substantive protections for the citizens' rights. The Virginia Plan, authored by Madison, would have achieved this through such structural devices as a congressional veto over state legislation and a council of revision to superintend Congress's work.[52] But such ultra-nationalist provisions ran afoul of a lingering attachment to state authority, and they were discarded, to Madison's chagrin.

In rejecting judicial participation in the aborted Council of Revision, the delegates to the Philadelphia convention made it plain that they did not expect federal courts to pass on the wisdom, policy, or desirability of legislation, but only on its conformity with the Constitution. Elbridge Gerry averred that "it was quite foreign from the nature of ye. office to make them judges of the policy of public measures," and John Dickinson added that "the Judges must interpret the Laws they ought not to be legislators."[53] The Framers did succeed, however, in creating a powerful national government having direct authority over individuals in the states.[54]

The drafting of the federal Constitution and, two years later, the Bill of Rights, provided occasions for resolving the critical issue of protecting property interests in a republican constitutional regime.[55] The Framers of the federal Constitution, as well as several state constitutions, including Massachusetts (1780) and Pennsylvania (1790), determined to protect individual liberty (including property claims) against governmental power, restraining democratic control of state legislatures. Property became the focus of a larger problem, protecting minority rights against majority power while nevertheless preserving majoritarian self-government. By drafting special constitutional securities for economic liberties, such as the contracts, due process, and just compensation clauses, the Framers exalted the liberty/property interest over majoritarian democracy.

This primacy both stunted democratic control of state legislatures, and enhanced the political power of wealthier Americans.[56] It affirmed economic inequality as legitimate and natural in the American political system. Constitutional inhibitions protected not only property but inequality from legislative reformation. The constitutional order prohibited redistribution and, potentially, all other legislative controls over property, implicitly inviting the judiciary to assert itself as the protector of an almost supraconstitutional privileged position for property.

Jennifer Nedelsky has demonstrated the linkages that the Framers created between judicial authority and constitutional protections for the unequal distribution of property. The constitutional order of 1787–89 provided insufficient "protection for certain basic rules and rights — property and contract in particular. Property was thus one of the crucial issues around which judicial review and the law-politics distinction was built. The courts could make a strong claim that property belonged in a distinctly legal realm, which had the sanction of the long and honorable tradition of common law." Judicial power to protect property claims "could be seen to rest on a neutral legal tradition." "Once the crucial boundaries [protecting property and contract] were defined as a matter of law, then judiciary's claim to draw them was virtually unassailable."[57]

One of the signal achievements of the Philadelphia Convention was the creation of a national judiciary. Federal courts enabled the new national government to enforce its laws through its own courts and thereby to extend its coercive reach to individuals. The Convention left three major questions unanswered about the national judiciary: would that judiciary consist of more than just the Supreme Court?[58] (The Convention left that to the determination of Congress.) Would the federal courts have the power of judicial review? And would federal courts have jurisdiction over appeals from the decisions of state courts?

Federalist *Number 78 and Judicial Review*

Hamilton, Madison, and John Jay published the authoritative commentary on the Constitution in the *Federalist* papers in 1787–1788. The problem of judicial review presented a difficult challenge to Publius. In the politicoideological environment of the 1780s, legislative supremacy characterized the constitutional regime of the states, deriving its appeal from the doctrine of popular sovereignty. In such a climate, anyone proposing judicial review undertook a daunting task. Hamilton met that challenge superlatively in *Federalist* Number 78, where he claimed the full power of judicial review for the federal courts.

Hamilton began with what seemed to be a disarming concession: the judiciary is the "least dangerous" branch of government, and must depend on the executive for enforcement of its decrees.[59] Since judges control neither purse nor sword, they "may truly be said to have neither Force nor Will, but merely judgment." Confounding review's opponents, Hamilton then turned their sword against them by grounding judicial review on popular sovereignty. As the people, he explained, were superior to their representatives in the legislature, so the charter they ratified, the Constitution, was superior to the legislative product, statutes. Just as the legislature could not claim superiority to the people, so statutes must defer to the Constitution. To preserve this superiority, "the courts were designed to be an intermediate body between the people and the legislature, in order, among other things, to keep the latter within the limits assigned to their authority."

Hamilton established the legitimacy of judicial review in an elegantly simple way: "[T]he interpretation of the laws is the proper and peculiar province of the courts. A constitution is in fact, and must be, regarded by the judges as a fundamental law." Hamilton's syllogism seemed to dispel all objections:

Major premise: Judges interpret the law.

Minor premise: The Constitution is a law.

Conclusion: Therefore judges interpret [and apply] the Constitution.

The subsequent century of struggle over judicial review would disclose that it was not as simple as all that, but the conceptual brilliance of Hamilton's logic provided John Marshall, Joseph Story, and other precursors of the classical tradition with ample justification for their exercise of sweeping judicial power.

Several state courts had approximated judicial review before 1787, but in only one case, *Bayard v. Singleton* (North Carolina, 1787) did a court unequivocally hold a legislative act to be unconstitutional and therefore unenforceable.[60] Alexander

Hamilton, appearing as counsel in the 1784 New York Mayor's Court case of *Rutgers v. Waddington*, made a precocious argument in favor of the power of judicial review.[61] After 1787, state supreme courts in Georgia, New Jersey, Virginia, Ohio, Maryland, Tennessee, Pennsylvania, and South Carolina exercised review power, approving one aspect or another of Hamilton's argument in *Federalist* Number 78. By 1820, nineteen states knew some form of judicial review.[62]

Both state and federal courts drew on the doctrines of higher law to monitor state legislation. In a 1795 grand jury charge, Justice William Paterson of the Supreme Court, sitting as a circuit judge, instructed the jury that "the constitution is the work or will of the people themselves, in their original, sovereign, and unlimited capacity." From this it followed that "every act of the legislature, repugnant to the constitution, is absolutely void." Thus an act of the Pennsylvania legislature divesting one person of real property and vesting it in another was "contrary to the letter and spirit of the constitution."[63]

Calder v. Bull

The epitome of judicial review and higher law appeared in the 1798 case of *Calder v. Bull*.[64] Justice Samuel Chase's seriatim opinion articulated what the twentieth-century constitutional authority, Edward S. Corwin, termed "the basic doctrine of American constitutional law."[65] The Connecticut legislature voided a probate decree[66] and ordered a new hearing, which would have had the effect of invalidating title to real or personal property. The Supreme Court's reaction to this statute[67] epitomized the enduring division in American legal thought between advocates of broad judicial power to hold statutes void and judges who take a more self-restrained approach.

Operating within the legalist natural law tradition, Chase asserted that state legislatures cannot be omnipotent. "Certain vital principles in our free republican governments" render state statutes unconstitutional, such as making an act criminal that was not so when it was committed (that is, an ex post facto law), a law impairing contracts, "or a law that takes property from A. and gives it to B." "The genius, the nature and the spirit of our state governments, amount to a prohibition of such acts of legislation," even if they do not come under the ban of a specific constitutional provision. Chase's position expressed the doctrine of higher law in its purest and most potent form. Under it, a court could hold a statute unconstitutional whenever it thought that the statute violated nontextual "republican principles," even if no textual constitutional provision was violated.[68]

Justice James Iredell emphatically disagreed, speaking for those then and later skeptical about free-ranging judicial power. No court can declare a statute void "merely because it is, in their judgment, contrary to the principles of natural justice. The ideas of natural justice are regulated by no fixed standard: the ablest and the purest men have differed upon the subject." Only a statute violating a clear textual provision can be declared unconstitutional. And even then, Iredell admonished, "as the authority to declare it void is of a delicate and awful nature, the court will never resort to that authority, but in a clear and urgent case."[69]

The Marshall Court, 1800–1830

Chief Justice John Marshall and his associates built on the deep-laid foundations of revolutionary ideology and constitution-making. Marshall definitively but ambiguously established judicial review on the Supreme Court. At first he continued, and then abandoned, the higher law tradition of late-eighteenth-century adjudication, leaving Joseph Story its sole exponent on the Court. Marshall and Story confirmed federal judicial supremacy over state legislation and the judgments of state supreme courts, suppressing inconsistent doctrines of state sovereignty. Marshall exalted the contracts clause as a constraint on state legislative power. On this broad base, later jurists erected the superstructure of legal classicism.

Marbury v. Madison

Marbury v. Madison (1803)[70] provided another essential component for the foundation of classical doctrine. Without judicial review, legal classicism could not have developed beyond the speculative musings of treatise writers and the after-dinner rhetoric of elite lawyers. Judicial review was the prerequisite for turning theory into operational doctrine. In *Marbury*, Marshall asserted ideas that constituted the earliest components of classic legal thought.[71]

He began grandly by reaffirming John Adams's formulation of the rule of law: "[T]he government of the United States has been emphatically termed a government of laws, and not of men."[72] From this it followed that every person may demand "the protection of the laws" for redress of injury, and that government is bound "to afford that protection."

Marshall virtually plagiarized *Federalist* Number 78, adapting Hamilton's thought and embedding it in American constitutional law. *Marbury*'s core idea was that the written Constitution was "a superior, paramount law" established by the people in their sovereign capacity. The people's sovereign "authority" is "supreme"; "the powers of the legislature are defined and limited" by the Constitution itself, and therefore subordinate to it. The Hamilton/Marshall identification of the Constitution as a *law*, enforceable by courts like any other law, is the fulcrum of American constitutionalism.

From there, Marshall easily (and simplistically) went on to assert that since courts routinely apply law, when they confront a conflict between two laws, Constitution and statute, they simply apply the law of superior authority. "This is of the very essence of judicial duty." The seductive power of this reductionist idea persisted into the twentieth century. In *United States v. Butler* (1936),[73] Justice Owen Roberts wrote that

> when an act of Congress is appropriately challenged in the courts as not conforming to the constitutional mandate, the judicial branch of the government has only one duty; to lay the article of the Constitution which is invoked beside the statute which is challenged and to decide whether the latter squares with the former. All the court does, or can do, is to announce its considered judgment upon the question. The only power it has, if such it may be called, is the power of judgment. This court neither approves nor condemns any legislative policy.

There was a latent ambiguity in Marshall's easy identification of the Constitution with law, and in his conclusion that "it is emphatically the province and duty of the judicial department to say what the law is." In exercising this power, did judges act in their ordinary judicial role, adjudicating a legal dispute that happened to involve a constitutional question? Or did Marshall's words about "the province and duty" endow the Court with some authority as *the* expositor of the Constitution, superior to the authority of legislators?[74] The Supreme Court in modern times, acting in moments of constitutional stress, has chosen the latter alternative, identifying itself the "ultimate interpreter of the Constitution" and its interpretations as "the supreme law of the land."[75]

Marbury is also the often overlooked source of the political-question doctrine, not fully developed until the 1849 case of *Luther v. Borden*.[76] After drawing a distinction that remains viable in the late twentieth century between ministerial responsibilities of the executive branch (which may be enjoined) and discretionary "political acts" (which may not), Marshall stated in dictum that "questions, in their nature political, or which are, by the constitution and laws, submitted to the executive, can never be made in this court."

This embryonic political question doctrine assumed a distinction between law and politics. Building on the differences Hamilton noted in *Federalist* Number 78 among "Force" (executive branch), "Will" (legislature), and "judgment" (judiciary), Marshall's *Marbury* opinion assigned the political realm to the legislature, which exercised "Will," that is, raw power realized through majoritarian voting. Legislators appropriately made choices about public policy. Law, on the other hand, was the domain of courts, because it was founded on reason.

The concept may be expressed diagrammatically:

Table 1.1 John Marshall's Conception of the Law-Politics Distinction

Branch of Government	Mode of Action	Result
Courts	Reason (Hamilton: "Judgment")	Law
Legislature	Will (Power)	Politics

This distinction between politics as the business of the legislature and law as the business of the courts has become a leitmotif of American legal experience. To lawyers, it is essential to the realization of the rule of law. Policy is determined by legislative majorities in the political process. Law is the domain of judges, above politics and beyond its reach, except in the ways explicitly provided in the Constitution, such as the manner of appointing judges.

McCulloch v. Maryland

In his opinion in *McCulloch v. Maryland* (1819),[77] Marshall provided the definitive treatise on how to interpret the Constitution.[78] Again he trod in a path originally blazed by Alexander Hamilton. In the 1791 cabinet debate over the constitutionality of the bill chartering the first Bank of the United States, Hamilton defended his concept of "implied powers" by ends-means reasoning: "If the end be clearly comprehended within any of the specified powers, and if the measure have an obvious relation to that end, and is not forbidden by any particular provision of the Constitution, it may safely be deemed to come within the compass of the national authority."[79] Referring to the necessary-and-proper clause,[80] he contended "that it was the intent of the [Philadelphia] Convention to give a liberal latitude to the exercise of the specified powers."

In *McCulloch*, Marshall adapted Hamilton's conclusions and once again elevated them to the status of constitutional dogma. He employed a rhetorical strategy that gave his utterances exceptional force.[81] He began with a broad statement of seemingly incontrovertible principles: "[T]he government of the Union . . . is, emphatically, and truly, a government of the people"; "Though limited in its powers, [it] is supreme within its sphere of action." He then used those principles as an interpretive key to unlock the meaning of constitutional text (here, the necessary-and-proper clause and its companions in Article I, Section 8). From this operation, he was able to derive a secondary, nontextual, and more specific principle, which inherited constitutional stature from its parentage. In *McCulloch*, the process yielded this sweeping formulation, an improvement on Hamilton: "[L]et the end be legitimate . . . and all means which are appropriate, which are plainly adapted to that end, which are not prohibited, but consist with the letter and spirit of the constitution, are constitutional."

Most importantly, both for the contemporary controversy over the Court's power and for legal classicism later, Marshall claimed for his Court exclusive and ultimate interpretive authority. "If it"—Marshall was referring to the great issues of federalism and national power—"is to be so decided, by this tribunal alone can the decision be made. On the Supreme Court of the United States has the constitution of our country devolved this important duty."

Marshall also expanded the power of the Court through what has come to be known as the "pretext clause." "Should Congress, under the pretext of executing its powers, pass laws for the accomplishment of objects not entrusted to the government; it would become the painful duty of this tribunal . . . to say that such an act was not the law of the land."

Marshall further anticipated the classical view of the judicial function in a newspaper skirmish with states'-power Virginians over his *McCulloch* opinion. A coterie known as the Richmond Junto, which included Judge Spencer Roane of the Virginia Supreme Court of Appeals, Thomas Ritchie, publisher of the Richmond *Inquirer*, John Taylor of Caroline, John Randolph, and William Brockenbrough, a group that enjoyed the warm support of the aged Jefferson, attacked the decision and Marshall's reasoning. Marshall responded by drafting anonymous rebuttal essays in which he elaborated the major points of his opinion.[82] He insisted that a judge interprets constitutional language only by a "fair construction which gives to language the sense in which it is used, and interprets an instrument according to its true intention." He defended judicial power on the grounds that judges were independent and impartial, "selected from the great body of the people." The judge is "as exempt from any political interest that might influence his opinion, as imperfect human institutions can make him."

McCulloch was one of a triad of cases the Supreme Court decided in 1819 that marked the emergence of the Supreme Court as the ultimate arbiter of constitutional questions in the United States, both among the branches of the federal government, and over the states in the Union. (The other two, discussed below, were *Dartmouth College v. Woodward* and *Sturges v. Crowninshield.*) Warren Dutton, a Boston attorney, approvingly noted that in these decisions the Supreme Court has "protect[ed] the rights of the citizens of a state against the injustice of their own legislatures" and has kept "within their constitutional bounds the legislative and executive powers of the union."[83] He predicted that the Court would prove to be "the strongest barrier against the tide of popular commotions, or the usurping spirit of popular assemblies." He concluded with a grand peroration that foretold the emergence of legal classicism:

> By subjecting legislative bodies to rule, and holding them under the restraints of those fundamental principles and enactments, which we call the constitution, we have given a new dignity and higher duty to LAW, and realized the noble idea of a moral supremacy, clothed with power, to hold not only subjects of the government to a just performance of their various individual duties, but also the government itself, in all its departments, in its proper place and sphere.

Higher Law and Constitutional Text

The Marshall Court definitively established the principle that the United States Constitution imposes substantive limits on state legislative power. It returned to the higher-law precedent of *Calder v. Bull* in 1810 in the politically charged case of *Fletcher v. Peck*, the Yazoo land litigation.[84] In striking down a Georgia statute divesting individuals of title to lands because their ancestors-in-title had obtained the land patents by bribing state legislators, Marshall held that "the state of Georgia was restrained, either by general principles which are common to our free institutions, or by the particular provisions of the constitution of the United States" from attempting the divestiture.[85] This utterance was doubly significant. The "general principles [of] our free institutions" reaffirmed Justice Chase's nebulous *Calder* higher law doctrines. The "particular provisions of the constitution" was probably the contracts clause,[86] and *Fletcher* represented a breath-taking expansion of that provision's scope, beyond anything the Framers had anticipated for it. Marshall applied it to executed, as well as executory, contracts, and to contracts in which the state was a party. Neither of these were in the contemplation of the Philadelphia Convention.[87]

The Court lived with *Fletcher*'s ambivalence a bit longer. In the 1815 case of *Terrett v. Taylor*,[88] Story relied on "the principles of natural justice, upon the fundamental laws of every free government, upon the spirit and the letter of the constitution of the United States, and upon the decisions of most respectable judicial tribunals" to void a Virginia statute that purported to sell glebe lands to which it had previously confirmed title in the Episcopal Church.

Property and Insolvency

Marshall's ambivalence — relying both on higher law and on specific textual provisions — could not be sustained much longer, though. Chase's eighteenth-century *Calder* conception of property was becoming inadequate to the needs of industrializing America's evolving economic relationships. The nation, and with it its Supreme Court, was passing from an era when property was mostly tangible, to a new age that saw the rise in importance of intangible forms of property, such as corporate charters, franchises, and monopoly rights. The source of these new forms of property was state grants. Property was coming to be defined not in static terms, which emphasized its immediate market value, but rather in dynamic terms looking to a potential rise in value due to speculation, or to anticipated income streams derived from it. G. Edward White captured this well: America was changing, from being "a society whose primary economic indicator was speculation in and control of undeveloped land (*Fletcher v. Peck*) . . . to a society in which the corporate franchise was the primary unit of economic activity (the *Charles River Bridge* case)."[89]

The transformation of property was actually more complicated than that. The nation was passing from an eighteenth-century stage of social and economic development centered on landed wealth in local communities, to a national economy dominated first by commercial, and then by financial, activity. Economically conservative *rentier* interests in the early nineteenth century were facing competition from dynamic forms of mercantile capitalism. Even in the most economically conservative region of the nation, the principal form of wealth was not landholding but slaveholding. Slaveowners, in Gavin Wright's phrase, were "laborlords," not "landlords," their wealth measured not in acres but in anticipated income streams from enslaved (and capitalized) labor.[90]

The republican conception of real property as the basis of individual autonomy and civic participation was receding into irrelevance. The beginnings of the Industrial Revolution, the concomitant rise of a landless urban proletariat, and the expansion of slave-based agriculture into the West destroyed the Jeffersonian yeoman idyll, which had never been a realistic image to begin with. The "commonwealth idea," which called for the state to assume a partnership role with private enterprise in stimulating economic development,[91] and Henry Clay's "American System," which sought federal financial support for infrastructure development to stimulate the economy, coexisted uneasily with ever more antique republican property conceptions. But the eighteenth-century republican conception of vested rights in property lingered on as a powerful, mischievous legal paradigm.

The corporate/mercantile economy, increasingly interstate in its reach, introduced complications into older conceptions of property and the social order.[92] The paper instruments of this increasingly national economy, and specifically the endorsement and negotiation of promissory notes, created special problems.[93] The new private business corporation added another overlay of complexity on the already perplexing picture of property. Could the state modify the franchise of a corporation that it had originally granted, and if it could, could it do so in ways detrimental to the control or profit expectations of incorporators and shareholders? Was the business corporation itself, or its charter, or its shares, a form of property? Could a corporation hold property, and was its title any different from that of an individual?

These questions came before the Court in *Dartmouth College v. Woodward* in 1819,[94] the second of great triad of cases that year. There Marshall thwarted an attempt by the New Hampshire legislature to revoke the college's charter and convert it into a state university. This is conventionally and correctly seen as a precedent that protected corporate charters from arbitrary state repeal or modification.[95] As such, it marked another expansion of the contracts clause. Marshall admitted that "it is more than possible, that the preservation of rights of this description was not particularly in the view of the framers of the constitution, when the [contracts] clause . . . was introduced into" the Constitution. Nothing deterred, he held that "the term 'contract' must be understood . . . to restrain the legislature in future from violating the right to property." This was Marshall at his most expansive. He read into the contracts clause a protection for property in the eighteenth-century "vested rights" sense. This reading implied constitutional protection for traditional forms of property. Under the new doctrine, when traditional property rights "vested," the legislature could not interfere with them unless it paid just compensation. Why then did Marshall not simply rely on the Fifth Amendment, instead of contorting the contracts clause by forcefeeding property precepts into it?

There are two explanations. First, it was not clear in 1819 that the Fifth Amendment was a restraint on the states, and in *Barron v. Baltimore* (1833) the Court was to hold that it was not.[96] Moreover, the contracts clause offered Marshall an opportunity to employ a favorite technique: identifying a general principle, loading it up with doctrinal implications, and then importing the whole conglomeration into a specific clause of the Constitution, so that the clause as construed would now incorporate the whole cluster of doctrine that Marshal had packed around the original principle.

Marshall's *Dartmouth College* opinion resolved the lingering ambivalence of *Fletcher* and *Terrett*. Higher law disappeared from his reasoning altogether, replaced by explicit reliance on the contracts clause. Justice Joseph Story alone forlornly continued to invoke "the fundamental maxims of a free government" and "the great and fundamental principles of a republican government" after the demise of pure higher law.[97] As if intellectually sleepwalking, he continued to maintain in his *Commentaries on the Constitution of the United States* (1st edition 1833) that "since the American revolution no state government can be presumed to possess the transcendental sovereignty, to take away vested rights of property; to take away the property of A and transfer it to B by a mere legislative act. . . . The fundamental maxims of a free government seem to require that the rights of personal liberty and private property, should be held sacred."[98] For the moment, the tides had of constitutional thought had ebbed, leaving this doctrine beached. But fifty years later, the tide would flood back in and float it once more.

With *Fletcher*, the intervening case of *New Jersey v. Wilson* (1812),[99] and *Dartmouth College*, the Marshall Court launched the contracts clause on its remarkable career as the nineteenth century's chief textual inhibition on state regulatory power. Contract became the fundamental paradigm of law in the nineteenth century: a voluntaristic economic relationship created by free individuals pursuing individual gain. The implications of centering law's development on the contract paradigm would unfold as the nation's economy expanded and its society changed in unpredictable and destabilizing ways.

Though the extension of the contracts clause to cover property relationships was remarkable, it did not force the Court to confront the tensions and contradictions posed by the new forms of intangible, commercial, corporate, and financial property. The insolvency cases did that. Bankruptcy and insolvency in the early nineteenth century involved people who were embarked on profit-making "ventures": they speculated in land, endorsed negotiable commercial paper, borrowed venture capital, assumed the risks of an almost totally unregulated currency that fluctuated wildly, and were ruined every decade or so by economic depressions (1819, 1833, 1837, 1857, 1873, 1882, 1893). Whipsawed by conflicting economic interests, Congress was unable to enact permanent bankruptcy legislation until 1898, so the states had the insolvency field to themselves.[100]

One of the few unqualified generalizations that can confidently be made about the intentions of the Framers is that they despised state legislation that inflated the currency or stayed debt collection. They were determined to use national power to crush state debtor-relief legislation. In the Philadelphia Convention debates immediately preceding Rufus King's proposal to insert the contracts clause into the draft Constitution, Madison noted: "Mr. [Roger] Sherman thought this a favorable crisis for crushing paper money."[101] It was in that mindset that they incorporated the contracts clause in the Constitution. So invocation of the clause to void debtor-friendly state laws at least had the virtue of being congruent with the Framers' intent.

But that did not resolve the underlying clash between differing forms of property interests. The old *Calder* higher-law formula of taking the property of A and giving it to B proved useless and irrelevant in mediating the rival jurisprudential claims of static and venture capital. This tension forced itself into the Court's consciousness in the third case of the 1819 triad, *Sturges v. Crowninshield*.[102] There, in a compromise opinion drafted by Marshall, the Court struck down a New York insolvency statute's retrospective application as an impairment of contract. To the extent that there had been a Framers' intent on this matter, this result was compatible with it. In the contracts clause debates, when George Mason pleaded for some latitude for state regulatory power, James Wilson replied: "The answer to these objections is that *retrospective* interferences only are to be prohibited."[103] But the *Sturges* result failed to provide doctrinal stability or clarity; it raised, rather than answered, questions about the protection of property in a regime of contract.

The Antebellum Era, 1830–1860

In the 1820s, the development of classicism's foundation shifted out of the Supreme Court and into different intellectual venues. Treatise writers and state supreme courts played important roles in articulating innovative legal principles. The bar rose to greater heights of influence, while the bench, chiefly the state judiciaries, basked in the glow of what has been called the "Golden Age of American Law."[104] Lawyers and judges refined foundational assumptions, just when their critics began to achieve important reforms, including codification and the elective judiciary, that impinged on judicial power.

Tawney

The Taney Court

At first it seemed that the Supreme Court would continue along the trajectory set by John Marshall. The debut opinion of his successor Roger B. Taney in the *Charles River Bridge Case* of 1837[105] drew the Court into the most significant economic policy debate of the era: how best to promote economic development in the capital-scarce young nation. The state court predecessor of Marshall's last great constitutional decision, *Gibbons v. Ogden* (1824),[106] had involved just that issue. In *Livingston v. Van Ingen* (1812),[107] New York's Chancellor John Lansing condemned monopoly grants as an outdated relic of mercantilist theory and endorsed the competitive economic model of Adam Smith. His colleague on the Court of Errors, Chief Justice James Kent, defended state-conferred monopolies as necessary to encourage investment.

This conflict between the policies of competition and monopoly was involved in the *Charles River Bridge Case*, where Daniel Webster argued for an implicit grant of exclusive powers and privileges in a corporate franchise.[108] Taney finessed this issue neatly and avoided having to make a choice between the antagonist policies, thereby preserving both the potential for democratic control of economic policy and security for investors' legitimate expectations. He did so by affirming a point that Story had originally made in his *Dartmouth College* concurrence: a state could reserve the power to alter a corporate charter at the time it granted that charter.[109] But where the state had not made such a reservation, Taney held, the Court would not read into the charter an implied monopoly. Taney concluded his opinion with an eloquent paean to the blessings of technological innovation. The antebellum Court's sensitivity to law's influence on technological development displayed its preference for dynamic rather than static investment ventures.[110] This was potentially disruptive of property relationships, however, and demonstrated that John Marshall's line between law and politics, between adjudication and policy making, was not fixed, obvious, or impermeable.

Aside from its forward-looking sensitivity to issues implicating economic growth, technological development, and the allocation of political power,[111] though, the Taney Court contributed little to the progress of legal classicism. That responsibility was taken up by treatise writers and state court judges.

The Science of the Law (Phase 1)

The period known in politics as "the Era of Good Feelings" was a boom time for lawyers. The influence of the legal profession grew; lawyers founded several law schools; and they wrote treatises that directed the course of legal development. Above all, they undertook systematic exposition of the science of the law.

In 1817, David Hoffman proposed to create a law school at the new University of Maryland by publishing *A Course of Legal Study*,[112] an outline of his proposed law curriculum. Joseph Story, not yet the Dane Professor at the Harvard Law School but merely a Justice of the Supreme Court, enthusiastically hailed Hoffman's proposal as the debut of "legal science" in the United States.[113] Hoffman, Story, and other early commentators nurtured the science of the law, a "regular system" characterized by "a scientific arrangement and harmony of principles." "Scientific research" gives law "a systematic character" enabling its votaries to "arrive at its principles by regular analysis [and] teach its elements and distinctions by a nice synthesis."

The "science of the law" recurred as a refrain for the rest of the nineteenth century, and lingered on in attenuated form to the middle of the twentieth.[114] The legal scientists were unsure among themselves whether their science was inductive or deductive; perhaps both. Harvard Law School professor Simon Greenleaf thought that "by the process of induction, [the legal scientist's] mind ascends to the higher regions of the science."[115] On the other hand, a later legal scientist, Theodore Dwight of the Columbia Law School, claimed that "no science known among men is more strictly deductive than the science of a true Jurisprudence."[116] An evaluation of the legal curriculum at one of the nation's leading law schools, Transylvania, summed up the objective bent of early legal science: "When we say that a branch of human knowledge is a science, we mean in general that it is founded on principles inherent in the subject to which it relates. We mean also that those principles serve as a basis whereon we may classify the subjects of that particular branch of knowledge. We mean, further, that such branch of knowledge may be taught by commencing with generals and descending to particulars."[117]

The scientists of the law claimed Francis Bacon as their patron and Blackstone as the first legal scientist.[118] As a science, law must be taught in a university setting, where students could obtain a "more thorough and deep-laid juridical education . . . and a more methodical and extensive range of studies."[119] Anomalies might appear from time to time: "those comparatively rare and unimportant cases which happen occasionally in the system . . . in violation of its general harmony." To resolve these, "only . . . the positive decision of a tribunal" was competent.[120]

By midcentury, the legal scientists were confident that they had established the authority of law:

> Like other sciences, [law] is supposed to be pervaded by general rules, shaping its structure, solving its intricacies, explaining its apparent contradictions. Like other sciences, it is supposed to have first or fundamental principles, never modified, and the immovable basis on which the whole structure reposes; and also a series of dependent principles and rules, modified and subordinated by reason and circumstances, extending outward in unbroken connection to the remotest applications of law.[121]

Legal science identified law's basic character: it rested on a relatively few "fundamental principles"; its precepts were universal in their applicability; it was apolitical, neutral as between parties or interest groups; it was predictable, uniform, and systematic. It should not be diverted by the biases of an individual judge. Its principles could be applied to resolve actual disputes through the application of pure logic. "Sound theories will take the place of false ones, and the rules of genuine logic will direct their application to particular cases," according to Peter Du Ponceau, the foremost American authority on international law at the time.[122] Because law was founded not on will but on reason, legal science was an inappropriate subject for legislative action.

"The science of the law is, of all others, the most sublime and comprehensive," exulted an early scientist: "[A]ll creation [is] governed by laws, universal, eternal, immutable, and fixed. In whatever relation we view them, they are important to man, to society, and to nations; they comprise in them the sublime precepts of revealed truths; they point out those rules, which are to regulate him in society, and lay down those fundamental principles, which govern the affairs of states, countries, and nations."[123]

The science of the law was objective. Leopold von Ranke identified the ideal of historical research: to describe the past *wie es eigentlich gewesen [ist]* ("as it really was"). The science of the law aspired to a similar objectivity. Chancellor James Kent, another early legal scientist, described his method in his *Commentaries on American Law* (1826–1830): he refused "to indulge in general theory on law subjects, or to think it of much value. The first duty of a law book is to state the law *as it is*, truly and accurately."[124]

Not coincidentally, legal science appeared just at the time that a new vehicle was emerging to propagate its tenets: the legal treatise. To scoffers who might deride their pretensions to scientific stature, Story, Kent, and their contemporaries could point to the impressive body of treatise literature that expounded their scientific ideals.[125] Generally, the treatises followed a similar pattern of approach, though not of format. The core of the early treatise was a systematic exposition of legal principles, followed by deductive identification of specific legal rules. This approached demonstrated that law was coherent, integrated, and grounded on axioms of universal (or at least nationwide) validity.

Beginning with Zephaniah Swift's *System of the Laws of the State of Connecticut* (1795) and continuing with St. George Tucker's *Blackstone* (1803),[126] American commentators composed a large body of commentary on American law that compared favorably with anything English. Kent's *Commentaries on American Law* (1826–1830) achieved such authoritative stature that its author was sometimes referred to as "the American Blackstone." Nathan Dane compiled his *General Abridgement and Digest of American Law* in nine volumes, published in 1823. "Dane's *Abridgement*," as it was called, was the first systematic treatise covering the entire field of American law. Its author used the proceeds to endow the Dane chair at the Harvard Law School, and insisted that Story be its first occupant. Establishment of the Dane chair marked the effective creation of the law school in Cambridge, which had been struggling to survive since its inception in 1817.[127]

Story himself brought out a monumental string of treatises, beginning at the time of his academic appointment: *Bailments* (1832), *Conflict of Laws* (1834), *Equity* (1836), *Equity Pleadings* (1838), *Agency* (1839), *Partnership* (1841), *Bills of Exchange* (1843), and *Promissory Notes* (1845). The capstone of this prodigious output was his *Commentaries on the Constitution of the United States* (1833).[128] In all his treatises, Story drew on the precepts of legal science that he had done so much to create, conforming American law to his vision of the national economy and republicanism — an outlook that was rapidly becoming antique.[129]

Many of the early treatises, as well as lesser-known popularizing works or school texts, expounded constitutional law. These included, to name only the most influential, William Rawle's *A View of the Constitution of the United States of America* (1825), Thomas Cooper's *Two Essays . . . on the Constitution of the United States*

(1826), Nathaniel Chipman's *Principles of Government . . . Including the Constitution of the United States* (1833), Peter S. Du Ponceau's *A Brief View of the Constitution of the United States* (1834), Henry Baldwin's *A General View of the Origin and Nature of the Constitution* (1837),[130] William A. Duer's *A Course of Lectures on the Constitutional Jurisprudence of the United States* (1843), and Henry St. George Tucker's *Lectures on Constitutional Law* (1843). It was no coincidence that all these men except Rawle had academic positions; several of the commentaries were in fact written-out versions of their law lectures. As a group, the authors of the antebellum constitutional commentaries may have had as great an influence on legal development as their jurist contemporaries.

The Antebellum Bar

The French magistrate Alexis de Tocqueville witnessed the emergence of the classical tradition, and his observations provide us an incomparable contemporary view of the process. His reflections on judicial review explained the sources of the courts' authority and the limitations on their powers. He traced the jurisdiction of the federal courts with an accuracy remarkable for a civil-law magistrate from a unitary state. He demonstrated the special force that laws have in open, democratic systems. His sociological observations on why both rich and poor found it in their differing interests to obey laws were acute, particularly his perception that "it is the opulent classes who frequently look upon the law with suspicion."[131]

Tocqueville realized that lawyers would be "the most powerful existing security against the excesses of democracy." Their "habits of order, a taste for formalities, and a kind of instinctive regard for the regular connection of ideas" make lawyers "hostile to the revolutionary spirit and the unreflecting passions of the multitude." They see themselves as "masters of a science," "a privileged body in the scale of intellect." This station imbues them with "a certain contempt for the judgment of the multitude." The American bench and bar constituted a natural aristocracy in a nation that had formally prohibited titles of nobility.[132] Yet though their "tastes [incline them] towards the aristocracy and the prince," their interests force lawyers to serve the needs of the people. "Lawyers belong to the people by birth and interest, and to the aristocracy by habit and taste; they may be looked upon as the connecting link between the two great classes of society." Democracy would probably be impossible without this mediating function of lawyers.

"The courts of justice are the visible organs by which the legal profession is enabled to control the democracy." The American lawyer, infused with "the instincts of the privileged classes," inhibits democratic legislation and helps channel popular demands in directions that do not threaten redistributions of wealth or power. Lawyers instinctively oppose innovation and support the existing order. "Their general spirit will be eminently conservative and anti-democratic." Lawyers value "public order beyond every other consideration." "If they prize freedom much, they generally value legality still more."

Tocqueville's oft-quoted observation, "[S]carcely any political question arises in the United States that is not resolved, sooner or later, into a judicial question," was only half his explanation for the pervading influence of law in a democratic society.

The jury supplied the other half. Because juries, both grand and petit, function throughout American society, "the language of the law [becomes] a vulgar tongue," while "the spirit of the law . . . descends to the lowest classes."

Tocqueville the civilian found the common law dauntingly obscure. The American lawyer "resembles the hierophants of Egypt, for like them he is the sole interpreter of an occult science." Lawyers might think of themselves as scientists of the law, but by a stroke of good luck (for them), their methods were comprehensible to the people and legitimate in the popular estimation.

Tocqueville did not mention Rufus Choate, and so far as is known never met or heard him,[133] but the Massachusetts attorney-statesman personified the American lawyer whom the Frenchman described. Choate's career validated Tocqueville's generalizations. More importantly, Choate's beliefs and attitudes expressed the embryonic concepts of classical legal thought. He was, at the least, a precursor of classicism.

Choate was a paragon of the Massachusetts and American bars, second only to Daniel Webster in popular as well as professional esteem as a lawyer and orator. A lifelong Whig,[134] he served in the United States House of Representatives from 1831 to 1834 and in the Senate from 1841 to 1845. In 1850, he provided this accurate self-portrait: "I am a conservative of the strictest type, and maintain conservatism in all its forms."[135] With an ideology formed by Edmund Burke, Choate professed the political beliefs of northern Whiggery.[136]

Whigs at first sought to temper the effects of industrialization by paternalistic attempts at imposing social harmony from above. When this failed, and the effects of industrialization began to divert American society irreversibly away from the old republican ideal, Whigs lapsed into gloomy pessimism, demanding that social control be left to impersonal market forces, reinforced by the military power of the state when the market economy proved inadequate to maintenance of civil peace. Whigs preached the identity of interests between capital and labor, rejected claims of class stratification in American society, and held out the hope of vertical social mobility to the increasingly impoverished working classes. Materialist and individualistic, Whigs extolled commerce and factory production as the bases of economic development.

A persistent strain of dark doubt ran through Whig thought in the 1840s, however. They were as aware as other Americans that the republican era had been left behind irretrievably, and in their inmost thoughts Whigs realized that they offered nothing to replace its ideals. Even if the market economy could allocate scarce resources optimally by an invisible hand, there was no social equivalent to replace the republican virtue and its socioeconomic preconditions that the revolutionary generation had identified as essential to the maintenance of republics. Anticipating the failure of such automatic mechanisms, Whigs turned to law as the ultimate guarantee of social cohesion and protection for the rights of property.[137]

In 1845, as he was retiring from the Senate, Choate accepted an invitation from the Harvard Law School to address its graduating class. Coincidentally, Joseph Story, Dane Professor of Law there, died three months later. Symbolically, as Story's death closed out the old republican era, Choate's address opened the new epoch of legal conservatism. With "The Position and Functions of the American Bar, as an Element of Conservatism in the State," Choate inaugurated the new age.[138] German idealist philosophy, which Choate had imbibed through the prose essays of the English romantic poet Samuel Taylor Coleridge, exerted a powerful yet unseen influence on the classical tradition.

Choate exhorted the young lawyers listening to him to pursue legal careers as "an element of conservation" in the state. It was their professional duty to inculcate "the sacred sentiments of obedience and reverence and justice, of the supremacy of the calm and grand reason of the law over the fitful will of the individual and the crowd." He identified the distemper of the modern age, derived from an "unreasoning liberty": the popular belief that law is "no more nor less than just the will — the actual and present will — of the actual majority of the nation." Far from it. "Law is not the transient and arbitrary creation of the major will, nor of any will. It is not the offspring of will at all. It is the absolute justice of the State, enlightened by the perfect reason of the State." This idealist view of law "raise[s] the law itself, in the professional and general idea, almost up to the nature of an independent, superior reason, in one sense out of the people, in one sense above them." In any event, law is not the product of "the actual will of the existing generation."

In such a conception, "the judge does not make" the law; he merely finds it, discerns it in the spirit of the age, the product of ages of development, "one mighty and continuous stream of experience and reason, accumulated, ancestral . . . our own hereditary laws." The current generation's right "to make all the law" is only theoretical, certainly not to be taken literally. "Property and good name and life . . . the great body of the *ius privatum* . . . our civil and social order, our public and private justice, our constitutions of government" must be maintained by a learned, conservative bar and judiciary against democratic majorities. The age of reform was over; the only reform left to be accomplished "is the reformation of our individual selves, the betterment of our personal natures," but not the reform of social institutions. "No, no!" he exclaimed. "Government, substantially as it is; jurisprudence, substantially as it is; the general arrangements of liberty, substantially as they are; the Constitution and the Union, exactly as they are."

Choate linked public order to the protection of property. Itemizing the old republican structural arrangements of written constitutions, representative government, checks and balances, bicameral legislatures, fundamental law, and judicial review, he hailed "our jurisprudence of liberty, which guards our person from violence and our goods from plunder . . . which makes every dwelling large enough to shelter a human life its owner's castle which winds and rain may enter but which the government cannot." In this idealized postrevolutionary world, beyond the need of any further reform, Justice anthropomorphized "has come down from her golden and purple cloud to walk in brightness by the weary ploughman's side, and whisper in his ear as he casts the seed with tears, that the harvest which frost and mildew and canker-worm shall spare, the government shall spare also." (Exactly half a century later, Choate's distant relative Joseph Choate would translate his ancestor's fulsome imagery to an argument against the constitutionality of the federal income tax.)

Rufus Choate fairly spoke the mind of the antebellum bar, perhaps more conservative than that of his contemporaries, but prefiguring its reaction to the crises that would burst forth in a generation.

State-Court Activism

As Choate spoke, state court judges in a sustained burst of judicial creativity were transforming the common law. Through the eighteenth century in England and America, the common law had slowly developed as a body of principle and doctrine. In the nineteenth century, judges harnessed it to serve the social and economic needs of the young nation, as they understood those needs. Adopting an instrumentalist view of the judicial role, judges were coming to believe that "the direction of [legal] change was a matter of choice from among competing policies rather than deduction from shared first principles."[139] (Not that belief in principles was disappearing: on the contrary, it lingered for the remainder of the century. But the allure of policy choice enticed antebellum judges, and they succumbed to the temptation of taking a hand in its formulation.) In the process, the common law became an instrument of economic policy.[140] Lawrence Friedman has contended that "in modern times, law is an instrument; the people in power use it to push or pull toward some definite goal. The idea of law as a rational tool underlies all modern systems."[141]

Tapping Reeve and James Gould, Connecticut judges and proprietors of the Litchfield Law School, instructed their students that "theoretical[ly] courts make no law[,] but in point of fact they are legislators."[142] Zephaniah Swift, another Connecticut jurist, wrote that the rules of evidence are not necessarily "founded on abstract principles of justice. They are positive regulations founded on policy."[143] New York judges determined that they should not adopt rules for the interpretation of insurance contracts "that would tend to embarrass commerce or injure the assured; . . . we are at liberty to adopt such a construction as shall most subserve the solid interests of this growing country."[144]

This frankly instrumentalist attitude betokened a new role for state judges: they actively participated in policy formation, and their role became increasingly accepted as legitimate. Judges did not abandon principles, precedents, or traditional modes of adjudication; rather, they poured the new wine of instrumentalist policy formulation into the old bottles of traditional judicial role and legal doctrine, justifying policy innovations by adapting or inventing principles. Their instrumentalist outlook was not indifferent or neutral toward varying economic interests in American society, however. It was selective, favoring some economic groups at the expense of others.

The law of property is a good place to glimpse this process of transformation in the early-nineteenth-century American legal order. Earlier judges had conceived of property primarily as a body of law governing interests in land.[145] They invoked the common law maxim *sic utere tuo ut alienum non laedas* ("use your own [property] in such a way that you do not burden [that of] another") to protect landowners from the consequences of innovative land use by others. In the nineteenth century, property law mutated to emphasize dynamic, profit-oriented uses of real property (including fixtures), personalty, and intangible forms of property. American property law stressed efficiency, balanced one owner's interest against another's based on considerations of social policy, and encouraged development of natural resources. That approach responded to early America's fundamental economic equation: abundant land and resources, scarce capital, labor, and managerial skills.

Justice Story's opinion in *Van Ness v. Pacard* (1829) nicely illustrated this instrumentalist reorientation of property law. Story rejected the English doctrine that a tenant could not remove agricultural fixtures such as a barn that he had erected. Such a rule was incompatible in America, he wrote, because "the country was a wilderness, and the universal policy was to procure its cultivation and improvement."[146] In the leading case of *Cary v. Daniels* (1844), Chief Justice Lemuel Shaw of the Supreme Judicial Court of Massachusetts modified the "prior appropriation" doctrine of watercourse law to take into account the "usages and wants of the community" and "the progress of improvement in hydraulic works"— that is, to support economic policy and technological change.[147] In a similar pro-development spirit, the New York courts rejected the doctrine of ancient lights, to encourage urban construction.[148] Decisions like these reflected economic and technological competition among turnpikes, bridges, ferries, canals, and railroads.

Looking back on this course of development after the Civil War, the New York Supreme Court in *Losee v. Buchanan* (1873) summarized the radical reorientation of doctrine that had taken place: "The general rules that I may have the exclusive and undisturbed use and possession of my real estate, and that I must so use my real estate as not to injure my neighbor, are much modified by the exigencies of the social state. We must have factories, machinery, dams, canals and railroads. They are demanded by the manifold wants of mankind, and lay at the basis of all our civilization." Property rights in modern urban society "are not absolute but relative . . . and they must be so arranged [as] to promote the general welfare."[149]

Courts cheerfully sacrificed the rights of individuals to social policy by liberal application of the concept of *damnum absque injuria* (injury without liability). The Maine Supreme Judicial Court explained why an injury to property does not always give a right to recover: "[T]he general good is to be consulted and promoted, though in many respects operating unfavorably to the interests of individuals."[150]

Chief Justice Taney provided one of the most forceful articulations of judges' role in public policy-making in the eloquent peroration of his *Charles River Bridge* opinion. He asked, rhetorically, what the consequences would be of the doctrine Webster demanded, which would imply monopoly grants in corporate charters. "To what results would it lead us?" He answered his own question:

> [If] such charters carry with them these implied contracts, . . . you will soon find the old turnpike corporations awaking from their sleep, and calling upon this court to put down the improvements which have taken their place. The millions of property which have been invested in rail-roads and canals upon lines of travel which had been before occupied by turnpike corporations, will be put in jeopardy; we shall be thrown back to the improvements of the last century; and be obliged to stand still, until the claims of the old turnpike corporations shall be satisfied, and they shall consent to permit these states to avail themselves of the lights of modern science, and to partake of the benefit of those improvements, which are now adding to the wealth and prosperity, and the convenience and comfort of every other part of the civilized world.[151]

Such exquisite sensitivity to the combined impact of technological change and policy implications characterized antebellum legal developments in state courts as well. As Stanley Kutler has demonstrated, antebellum judges did not flinch from the "creative destruction" of existing property rights, to say nothing of expectations, when they believed that by so doing they might contribute to promoting the public welfare.[152] Material progress was not to be held captive to disappointed landowners.

Yet despite — or perhaps, because of — the extent to which instrumentalist judging disrupted legal relationships and rights, judges after the Civil War felt compelled to assert law's timeless, objective, policy-neutral nature. The tension this generated, between what judges did and what they claimed they were doing, made them vulnerable to charges of dissimulation, if not hypocrisy.

State judges, led by Chief Justice Shaw, virtually created a whole new domain of law, torts, to structure the increasing volume of litigation occasioned by accidents occurring because of the Industrial Revolution. New doctrines shifted the risks and costs of industrial accidents from employer/producers to employees or consumers, thereby permitting corporations to accumulate capital for reinvestment, rather than paying it out to injured employees or consumers.[153]

The centerpiece of the new law of torts was *Brown v. Kendall* (1850),[154] in which Shaw established fault as an essential criterion of unintentional torts. Plaintiff must prove "either that the [defendant's] intention was unlawful, or that the defendant was in fault; for if the injury was unavoidable, and the conduct of the defendant was free from blame, he will not be liable." The standard of "ordinary care" determined fault: "that kind and degree of care, which prudent and cautious men would use, such as is required by the exigency of the case, and such as is necessary to guard against probable danger." In that same case, Shaw also invented the concept of contributory negligence (here, a complete bar to recovery). Finally, he adopted the doctrines of efficient and proximate cause.

Earlier cases in South Carolina, New York, and Pennsylvania had pioneered the concept of negligence or "carelessness."[155] This innovative criterion came to dominate the emergent field of torts, submerging the law's earlier tendency toward absolute liability. The House of Lords revived the old concept in *Rylands v. Fletcher* (1868),[156] but American jurists balked. Strict liability imposed the costs of industrial activity without regard to fault, and thus to American judges it was both irrational and redistributive. They attempted to rid American law of the rule, which they considered archaic, anomalous, and alien. The highest courts of New York and New Hampshire repudiated the doctrine in two leading 1873 cases, *Losee v. Buchanan* and *Brown v. Collins*.[157] A judicial finding of contributory negligence took the case away from the jury. Jurors tended to sympathize with plaintiffs and against corporations or other deep-pockets defendants. Judge Seward Barcolo of the New York Supreme Court candidly explained that "in certain controversies between the weak and strong — between a humble individual and a gigantic corporation, the sympathies of the human mind naturally, honestly and generously run to the assistance and support of the feeble and apparently oppressed." In such cases, the jury's compassion "is wholly inconsistent with the principles of law and the ends of justice."[158]

Railroads were the darlings of nineteenth-century judges. Shaw's opinion in *Farwell v. Boston and Worcester Railroad* (1842)[159] sheltered them from liability by impeding employees' suits against employers for work-related injuries. Shaw there created the doctrines of assumption of risk and the fellow-servant rule for American law:[160] the employee "takes upon himself the natural and ordinary risks and perils" of the workplace. Both doctrines raised the threshold for employee litigation. The fellow-servant rule quickly acquired a spurious patina of antiquity and pseudoconstitutional status. In that guise, it impeded enactment of workers' compensation statutes into the twentieth century.

Risk-shifting captured the imagination of nineteenth-century judges, especially as the insurance industry expanded. In *Ryan v. New York Central Railroad* (1866),[161] the New York Court of Appeals exonerated a railroad for damage to the plaintiff's building 150 feet from the railroad right-of-way that had been caused by a fire set by sparks from defendant's engine. "In a commercial country," the Court explained, "each man, to some extent, runs the hazard of his neighbor's conduct, and each by insurance against such hazards, is enabled to obtain a reasonable security against loss."

By the Civil War, American courts had thus reversed the old *sic utere* principle. Where it had previously been meant to inhibit the potential aggressor, it now tied the hands of the potential victim and liberated the aggressor. The Massachusetts Supreme Judicial Court held in a 1865 case that "the right of the party to the free and unfettered control of his own land above, upon and beneath the surface cannot be interfered with or restrained by any consideration of injury to others."[162]

Judges also permitted some potential defendants to contract out of tortious liability. At common law, railroads were held to absolute liability for damage to baggage.[163] That was obviously undesirable from a corporation's point of view, and some risk-shifting was in order. Joseph Story obliged in the fourth edition of his *Commentaries on the Law of Bailments* (1846), proffering the opinion that common carriers could contract out of liability for ordinary negligence (but not for gross negligence).[164] The Supreme Court affirmed this doctrine the next year.[165]

Comparable trends occurred in the antebellum law of contracts.[166] Nineteenth-century jurists promoted commercial and industrial growth, with the inevitable effect of rewarding some players and disappointing others. Contract law was instrumentalist, promoting specific economic policy choices, careless of the costs these choices imposed on their victims. Contract law exalted the individual acting in an economic capacity, upheld the role of parties' wills, and abhorred attempts at righting bargaining inequalities.

Eighteenth-century English and American decisions had reflected conceptions of fairness in bargaining. Judges refused to enforce contracts when they believed consideration inadequate. South Carolina Chancellor Henry W. Desaussure thought it "a reproach to the justice of the country, if contracts of very great inequality obtained by . . . the skillful management of intelligent men, from weakness, or inexperience, or necessity could not be examined into, and set aside."[167] To John Adams, "it is a natural, immutable Law that the Buyer ought not to take Advantage of the sellers Necessity, to purchase at too low a Price."[168] Equity readily intervened to set aside unconscionable contracts, courts frequently implied warranties of soundness or merchantability, and judges applied community standards of fairness.

Such a regime of law was unsuited to an expanding commercial economy where commodities were traded across great distances. The subjectivity and unpredictability of earlier fairness standards impeded commercial growth and frustrated expectations or disappointed merchants' needs for regularity. Older doctrines stood in the way of speculation, first in state debt obligations arising out of the War for

American Independence, then later in commodities, and finally in the early counterpart of futures contracts (a form of hedging). Where the value of currency fluctuated and the economy ran through regular boom-bust cycles, with attendant insolvencies, precommercial contract doctrines were a drag on economic development.

The will theory, predicated on the meeting of minds of freely bargaining parties who were presumed to stand on an equal footing toward each other, replaced older equitable considerations like fairness and adequacy of consideration. "Every contact is founded on the mutual agreement of the parties," proclaimed William W. Story, Joseph Story's son and author of what was in its time (1844) the definitive treatise on contracts.[169] In the leading case of *Seymour v. Delancey* (1824), the New York Court of Errors rejected a plea of inadequacy of consideration, noting "how much property is held by [executory] contract; that purchases are constantly made upon speculation; that the value of real estate is fluctuating."[170] Joseph Story dismissed the doctrine of adequacy of consideration: "[T]he Common Law knows no such principle."[171]

Courts discarded theories that value was objective, and instead located value in the bargained-for agreement of the parties. "Price depends solely upon the agreement of the parties, being created by it alone," wrote Gulian Verplanck in one of the earliest American contracts treatises.[172] His implicit conflation of price and value itself spoke volumes. Implied warranties, implied promises, implied contracts themselves, withered where express contracts supplied terms. The New York Supreme Court adopted the doctrine of *caveat emptor* in *Seixas v. Woods* (1804),[173] exalting the autonomy and individual responsibility of the parties. The United States Supreme Court's decision in *Laidlaw v. Organ* (1817)[174] provided the foundation for modern commodities trading. The Supreme Court upheld expectation damages in commodities contracts in *Shepherd v. Hampton* (1818),[175] a rule essential to cotton speculation.

American jurists and commentators realized that the new configuration of contracts doctrines would reinforce inequality of bargaining power. "All know what a wide difference exists among men in these points," explained Verplanck, "and whatever advantage may result from that inequality, is silently conceded in the very fact of making a bargain." "It is a superiority on one side — an inferiority on the other, perhaps very great," he conceded, "but they are allowed."[176] More conservative jurists like Chancellor James Kent condemned the very concept of equality in the economic sphere:

> A state of equality as to property is impossible to be maintained, for it is against the laws of our own nature; and if it could be reduced to practice, it would place the human race in a state of tasteless enjoyment and stupid inactivity. . . . Liberty depends essentially upon the structure of government, the administration of justice, and the intelligence of the people and has very little concern with equality of property.[177]

In the closely related field of commercial law, American courts rejected privity requirements and upheld the negotiability of promissory notes against remote endorsers. But this came only after a long struggle, not only against judges wedded to earlier doctrines,[178] but against state legislators, especially in the western states, who smelled a rat (eastern creditors, as usual) and enacted legislation preserving the original endorser's defenses against remote assignees. In his path-breaking treatise on *Promissory Notes*, published in the year of his death, 1845, Joseph Story inveighed against such hindrances to negotiability.[179]

Story's opinion in the landmark case of *Swift v. Tyson* (1842)[180] made it possible for the Supreme Court to topple these state-created barriers to negotiability. In *Swift*, the Court held that a state statute impeding negotiability was "a violation of the general commercial law."[181] This cleared the way for development not only of a uniform commercial law throughout the United States, but of a flourishing traffic in commercial paper of all kinds as an essential supplement to the money supply and a basis of credit throughout the nation.

Swift was an ancestor of classical adjudication in a more significant way: it enabled an extraordinary expansion of federal judicial power, inviting federal judges to create federal common law doctrines at will in numerous fields besides commercial law. By the early twentieth century, Progressives and other reformers came to view the *Swift*-bloated federal jurisdiction in diversity cases as a roadblock to state regulatory power, and were determined to dismantle it.

Concurrent with these modernizing doctrinal trends in antebellum state courts was a flourishing but backward-looking higher law jurisprudence. Carrying on in the spirit of *Calder v. Bull*, antebellum courts in nearly half the states of the Union struck down state statutes on the grounds of their inconsistency with

> a fundamental principle of right and justice, inherent in the nature and spirit of the social compact, . . . the character and genius of our government, . . . that rises above and sets bounds to the power of legislation, which the legislature cannot pass without exceeding its rightful authority. It is that principle which protects the life, liberty, and property of the citizen from violation, in the unjust exercise of legislative power.[182]

Judges elsewhere drew on doctrines of the social compact, common law, vested rights, republican government, natural law, limited government, just compensation, retained rights, obligation of contracts, principles of right and justice, personal liberty, and any other concept that might occur to them as inherent limitations on legislative power.[183]

Although state judges at first assumed that the due process or cognate law-of-the-land provisions of the state constitutions were to be construed in a procedural sense only,[184] higher law principles and the due process clauses attracted each other and tended to merge toward mid-century. Provoked first by married women's property acts and then by various state prohibition laws, state judges interpreted the due process clauses to be substantive limitations on state legislative power.[185] In an early North Carolina case,[186] the court held that persons "shall not be so deprived of their liberties or properties, unless by a trial by jury in a court of justice, according to the known and established rules of decision derived from the common law and such acts of the legislature as are consistent with the Constitution." From this, courts read into the due process clauses generalized prohibitions on discriminatory or retrospective legislation, as well as requirements that laws be general and equal in their application.[187]

This trend culminated in *Wynehamer v. New York* (1856),[188] the earliest case in which the doctrine of substantive due process explicitly emerged. This decision may be regarded as the first adjudication in the classical tradition. In it, Judge George F. Comstock held that a state prohibition statute destroying property rights in extant stocks of liquor violated the state constitution's due process clause. He gave voice to many of the basic propositions of legal classicism as they would be expressed forty years later. If the public policy rationale behind prohibition "can be allowed to subvert the fundamental idea of property, then there is no private right entirely safe, because there is no limitation upon the fundamental discretion of the legislature." The legislature could not discriminate among kinds of chattels, because "all property is alike in the character of inviolability."

"In a [republican] government like ours," Judge Comstock cautioned, "theories of public good or public necessity may be so plausible, or even so truthful, as to command popular majorities. But whether truthful or plausible merely, and by whatever numbers they are assented to, there are some absolute private rights beyond their reach, and among these the constitution places the right of property." He considered, but dismissed, *Calder v. Bull* theories of natural rights unattached to some specific constitutional clause as mischievous, "by giving to private opinion and speculation a license to oppose themselves to the just and legitimate powers of government." Rather, the state's due process and just compensation clauses provided ample protection for fundamental rights like property: "[W]here rights are acquired by the citizen under the existing law, there is no power in any branch of the government to take them away."

The New York court's interpretation of the due process clauses was echoed the next year in Chief Justice Taney's dictum in the *Dred Scott Case* (1857), where he averred that "an act of Congress which deprives a citizen of the United States of his liberty or property [Taney was referring to enslaved people who, in contemplation of law, were chattels] merely because he came himself or brought his property [slaves] into a particular territory of the United States and who had committed no offense against the laws could hardly be dignified with the name of due process of law."[189]

Dred Scott closed a circle. Marshall had dropped higher law from Supreme Court adjudication in 1819, but it lived on in the state courts, gradually becoming mingled, then fused, with the due process clause. Thus strengthened, it was available to Taney when he was casting about for a doctrine, any doctrine, that would inhibit Congress's power to interfere with the southern states' control over enslaved people. Higher law, now tricked out in the costume of the due process clause, reentered Supreme Court discourse.

Legal Reform

The antebellum "transformation of American law," as Morton Horwitz calls it, was assailed by a powerful contemporary critique of common law and the institutions that made it. In this, antebellum reformers anticipated a pattern that reappeared in the late nineteenth century, when legal classicism was confronted by its own political and intellectual challenges.

Reformers attacked the common law itself. The English philosopher Jeremy Bentham denounced the common law as a "dunghill" and lawyers as "casuists."[190]

He condemned the common law process as inherently ex post facto, retroactive and unknown till the judge pronounced the rule. Bentham said that judges make common law "as a man makes laws for his dog. When your dog does anything you want to break him of, you wait till he does it, and then you beat him for it."[191] But Bentham was not popular in America, and few cited him. The American critique of common law was largely homegrown.

William Sampson, the talented Irish-American lawyer and reformer,[192] the anonymous "P. W. Grayson" (whose identity remains unknown),[193] and the Massachusetts lawyer and Democratic Party reformer Robert Rantoul scorned the common law as incompatible with popular sovereignty and democracy, violative of the very idea of a rule of law, which presupposed an existing and known norm to guide conduct. They saw only one solution: "[T]he whole body of the law must be codified."[194]

Americans had been codifying their law, in a sense, since the seventeenth century, whenever they revised the accumulated statutes on a subject, weeding out anomalies and obsolete provisions, rationalizing the organization of session laws. But this was not what codification's proponents demanded in the Jacksonian era. Instead, they called for a thorough rewriting of the common law, so that all law would emanate from legislative rather than judicial authority. The law's substantive content should embody policy choices made by elected legislators, and its procedures would be rescued from the tangled obscurities of the writ system, the forms of action, and common law pleading.[195] Such attacks on common law adjudication and preferences for codification alarmed conservatives, who considered respect for law as essential to protection of private rights. Legal reform only hardened their suspicion of democracy and legislative majorities.

Some legal conservatives did concede the need for a carefully limited codification, and even proposed it to head off more radical law revision. Joseph Story in 1821 proposed a cautious codification of selected bodies of law to bring law closer to "scientific accuracy," provided the legislature did not do more than "reduce the past to order and certainty" by rationalizing and reorganizing common law though what would be little more than a digest.[196] Story, Kent, and other conservatives were troubled by the mounting volumes of American reports, which they regarded as a mixed blessing. On the one hand, appellate cases were the fount of the authentic American jurisprudence that they had been calling for; on the other hand, the sheer mass of the state reports made them indigestible and useless to the ordinary practitioner.

Story accordingly served as chair of an advisory committee on codification for the Massachusetts General Court[197] in 1837 and recommended three codes: the "general principles" of property, contracts, and personal rights; substantive criminal law; and evidence.[198] But more thoroughgoing codifiers dismissed such limited codification as half-hearted. David Dudley Field, the leading exponent of codification at mid-century, persuaded the New York Constitutional Convention of 1846 to mandate appointment of a commission to recommend codification. As head of this commission, Field proposed three comprehensive codes: civil, criminal, and procedural. Only the last enjoyed any success, but its triumph was total.[199]

By World War I, the Field procedural codes had been adopted in nearly all American jurisdictions. They introduced what lawyers called "code pleading" to replace common law pleading. But conservatism, ameliorative partial reform, and the appearance of ancillary legal research aids like digests and treatises combined to block adoption of the substantive codes. Classical lawyers instinctively resisted wholesale codification, and tolerated less sweeping legislative revisals, like code pleading, only reluctantly. Joel Bishop, an influential treatise writer of the later nineteenth century, expressed their attitude:

> Our common law is a particular system of reason. It is one of the great departments of our government structure; and the study, practice, and administration of it produce that training of the reason necessary to the carrying on of the government in other departments. Statutes are not reason, they are mere command. And if we convert our common law of reason into statutes, we in effect abolish reason in things legal and governmental. . . . Such is the end of total codification.[200]

The antebellum period witnessed many substantive legal reform efforts. The constitutions of the new states admitted in the 1830s and 1840s, plus constitutional conventions in the older states, introduced revisions throughout the body of law comparable in scope and impact to the legal reforms that Thomas Jefferson had promoted for Virginia after Independence. Married women's property acts enhanced the legal status of married women. The antimonopoly sentiment of Jacksonian politics led the states to adopt general incorporation acts for nonbanking corporations, somewhat democratizing access to this form of amassing investment capital.

The political process itself was reformed. The New York Constitutional Convention of 1821 led the way in reducing or abolishing franchise qualifications, looking toward white and male but otherwise universal suffrage. States reduced the malapportionment of their legislatures, sometimes only after violent struggles, as in Rhode Island's Dorr Rebellion of 1842. By the Civil War, religious and property qualifications to vote had been discarded almost everywhere. This loss of structural protection for wealth only heightened the sense of urgency that gripped conservatives about the need to secure protection for property.

Despite the sweep of these legislative reforms, judges' creation of two new doctrines ironically did more to threaten the economic status quo than all reform movements combined. In the antebellum period, state court judges legitimated eminent domain and the police power. Legal classicism was born of lawyers' efforts to constrain these potent legal concepts. They sought to articulate constitutional limits on the power of legislatures to act in ways that threatened property rights and contractual relationships.

For centuries the common law had recognized the state's power to appropriate privately held property. But because Revolutionary-Era Americans concurred with John Locke's concept of property ownership as an element of civil liberty, they hedged the states' takings power with inhibitions in state constitutions and in the Fifth Amendment. John Adams went to great lengths in the Bill of Rights of the Massachusetts Constitution of 1780 to protect the right of "acquiring, possessing, and protecting property" (art. I). Article X stated that every individual has a "right to be protected" in that possession and use, and then provided that protection: "[B]ut no part of the property of any individual can, with justice, be taken from him, or applied to public uses, without his own consent, or that of the representative body of the people. . . . And whenever the public exigencies require that the property of any individual should be appropriated to public uses, he shall receive a reasonable compensation therefore." Thus from the beginning, the constitutional order imposed requirements of just compensation and public use on the taking of property. Seven other articles in the Massachusetts Bill of Rights provided additional explicit protections for property rights, and at least two others did so indirectly.[201] The First Congress accomplished the same end with greater economy of language: "[N]or shall private property be taken for public use without just compensation."[202]

These just compensation provisions received surprisingly little attention in the nation's first half-century, though local governments continued to take lands for roads and the states' milldam acts authorized riparian owners to flood upstream lands for hydropower. These milldam acts provided a precedent for the taking that was involved in the first American case to explicitly recognize the concept of eminent domain, *Beekman v. Saratoga and Schenectady Railroad* (1831).[203] New York's Chancellor Reuben Walworth there upheld the constitutionality of a state statute authorizing a railroad to condemn lands for its right of way. He defined eminent domain as "the highest and most exact idea of property, [which] remains in the government." All property privately owned is nevertheless held of the people in their sovereign capacity, and can be resumed by their representative, the government, in the "public interest."

In neighboring Massachusetts, the General Court extended the eminent domain power to manufacturing corporations, permitting them to flood lands for low-head hydropower, and Chief Justice Shaw upheld it as constituting the "public uses" required by Article X.[204] The Supreme Court upheld the use of a state's eminent domain powers to condemn a corporate charter in 1848,[205] so a broad and flexible power of eminent domain was well established under the state and federal constitutions.

Three years later Chief Justice Shaw established the police power doctrine, just as state judges were voicing concern over property divestitures under the married women's property acts and prohibition. Shaw confronted this issue when the state prohibited wharves in Boston harbor beyond the "commissioners' line," even though the riparian owner's fee in the tidal mud flats extended to the low-water line. In *Commonwealth v. Alger* (1851),[206] Shaw distinguished the police power from eminent domain, the principal difference between them being that the exercise of eminent domain requires compensation, while the exercise of police power does not. He defined the police power as "the power vested in the legislature, by the constitution, to make . . . all . . . reasonable laws . . . not repugnant to the constitution as they shall judge to be for the good and welfare of the commonwealth" and its people. "All real estate derived from the government is subject to some restraint for the general good," he explained. Defined thus broadly, police power was coterminous with government's sovereign power. *Alger* seemed to recognize no significant limitations on it.

Legal reform and innovation undermined some foundations of the early American constitutional order, especially as these were meant to secure property and the legitimacy of wealth distribution. Alarming in itself, this trend intensified conservatives' insecurity about the stability of the constitutional regime, providing an impetus for creating classical legal doctrine.

On the eve of the Civil War, Americans had created a constitutional order that prized individual liberty as its most cherished goal; that accorded property and contract the highest levels of legal security; that subordinated ordinary legislation to the higher law of the Constitution, as construed by a uniquely powerful, activist judicial corps; and that revered law both as an instrument of social policy and as the guarantor of all other values.

The Civil War reinforced these values. The Constitution emerged from its holocaust reborn, the phoenix arising out of its ashes. The victorious Union vindicated the supremacy of the Constitution, only to have the legal order threatened anew by social and industrial change. The legal elites' response to that later challenge produced the world of classical legal thought.

Notes

1. In this study, the phrase "the American Revolution" refers to the events that occurred between 1760 and 1776, culminating in the Declaration of Independence. The phrase is not used in the popular sense that identifies (and confuses) it with the War for American Independence, 1775–1783, or for that matter with any event after 1776. By 1776, the Revolution was completed; all that was left was the military defense of its permanence and success. The establishment of the American republics, beginning in May 1776, began the next era.

2. Bernard Bailyn, *The Ideological Origins of the American Revolution* (1967); Donald S. Lutz, *The Origins of American Constitutionalism* (1988). John P. Reid has produced a stunning corpus of work on the Revolution, emphasizing its lawyerly and ideological nature, reinstating constitutional arguments at the core of American revolutionary experience. His most sustained argument is the four-volume series (in reality a thousand-page book published in four book-length fascicles): *Constitutional History of the American Revolution: The Authority of Rights* (1986); *Constitutional History of the American Revolution: The Authority to Tax* (1987); *Constitutional History of the American Revolution: The Authority to Legislate* (1991); *Constitutional History of the American Revolution: The Authority of Law* (1993). In addition to these, he has published five studies of more discrete topics: *In a Defiant Stance: The Conditions of Law in Massachusetts Bay, the Irish Comparison, and the Coming of the American Revolution* (1977); *In a Rebellious Spirit: The Argument of Facts, the Liberty Riot, and the Coming of the American Revolution* (1979); *In Defiance of the Law: The Standing-Army Controversy, the Two Constitutions, and the Coming of the American Revolution* (1981); *The Concept of Liberty in the Age of the American Revolution* (1988); *The Concept of Representation in the Age of the American Revolution* (1989). See also his documentary edition, *The Briefs of the American Revolution: Constitutional Arguments between Thomas Hutchinson, Governor of Massachusetts Bay, and James Bowdoin for the Council and John Adams for the House of Representatives* (1981).

3. I use the term "Whig" at this point to refer to that portion of the American populace (both of European and of African descent), estimated by John Adams to be a third of the whole, which in 1776 supported independence and the establishment of republican governments.

4. [James Otis], *A Vindication of the British Colonies against the Aspersions of the Halifax Gentleman* (1765), 8; declaration of Boston Town Meeting, 28 Oct., 2 Nov. 1772, *Votes and Proceedings of the Freeholders and Other Inhabitants of the Town of Boston*, 8.

5. [John Dickinson], *An Address to the Committee of Correspondence in Barbados* (1766), 4.

6. William Blackstone, *Commentaries on the Laws of England* (1765), vol. 1, 41.

7. James Wilson, "The Law of Nature," in Robert G. McCloskey, ed., *The Works of James Wilson* (1967), vol. 1, 126–147.

8. Thomas C. Grey, "Origins of the Unwritten Constitution: Fundamental Law in American Revolutionary Thought," 30 *Stan. L. Rev.* 843 (1978); Charles F. Mullett, *Fundamental Law and the American Revolution* (1933).

9. [John J. Zubly,] *An Humble Enquiry into the Nature of the Dependency of the American Colonies upon the Parliament of Great-Britain, and the Right of Parliament to Lay Taxes on the Said Colonies* (1769), 5. Zubly was a Swiss-American Whig and Presbyterian minister in Savannah, forgotten today perhaps because he ended his days a Loyalist.

10. Charles M. Andrews, "The American Revolution: An Interpretation," *American Historical Review* 31 (1926), 219–232; Edmund S. Morgan, *The Birth of the Republic, 1763–1789*, rev'd ed. (1977); Peter C. Hoffer, *Law and People in Colonial America* (1992), 96–123.

11. The first and last quotations are from John Adams's recollection of Otis's argument (Adams was present in the Superior Court as an attorney-spectator): Charles Francis Adams, ed., *The Works of John Adams* (1850), vol. 2, 521–522. The claim of illegality is from George R. Minot's reconstruction of Otis's speech from Adams's notes in a version approved by Adams himself: Minot, *Continuation of the History of the Province of Massachusetts Bay, from the Year 1748* (1803), vol. 2, 98.

12. Quoted in Lawrence H. Gipson, *The Coming of the Revolution, 1763–1775* (1954), 53.

13. Reprinted in Jack P. Greene, ed., *Colonies to Nation, 1763–1789: A Documentary History of the American Revolution* (1975), 63–64, 134–135, 182–187, 243–246 respectively.

14. [Dickinson], *Address to the Committee of Correspondence in Barbados*, 4.

15. Edward S. Corwin, *The "Higher Law" Background of American Constitutional Law* (1929; rpt. 1955); J. W. Gough, *Fundamental Law in English Constitutional History* (1971), 192–193; Grey, "Origins of the Unwritten Constitution."

16. Gordon S. Wood, *The Radicalism of the American Revolution* (1992). Different perspectives on revolutionary radicalism are considered in the essays in Alfred F. Young, ed., *The American Revolution: Explorations in the History of American Radicalism* (1976).

17. On the origins and early development of popular sovereignty, see Edmund S. Morgan, *Inventing the People: The Rise of Popular Sovereignty in England and America* (1988).

18. John Locke, *Two Treatises of Government*, Peter Laslett, ed. (1690; rpt. 1967), *Second Treatise*, § 212.

19. [Alexander Hamilton,] *The Farmer Refuted*, in Harold C. Syrett and Jacob E. Cooke, eds., *The Papers of Alexander Hamilton* (1961–1987), vol. 1, 105.

20. Virginia Declaration of Rights (1776), art. 3, and New Hampshire Bill of Rights, art. X, in William F. Swindler, comp., *Sources and Documents of United States Constitutions* (1973–1979), vol. 10, 49, and vol. 6, 345, respectively.

21. Jerrilyn G. Marsden, *King and Congress: The Transfer of Political Legitimacy, 1774–1776* (1987).

22. Lutz, *Origins of American Constitutionalism*, 96–100.

23. Art. 2, in Swindler, comp., *Sources and Documents of United States Constitutions*, vol. 10, 49.

24. Sections 13–15, in Swindler, comp., *Sources and Documents of United States Constitutions*, vol. 8, 280–281.

25. Carl Becker, *The History of Political Parties in the Province of New York, 1760–1776* (1909; rpt. 1968), 22.

26. See generally Merrill Jensen, *The Founding of a Nation: A History of the American Revolution, 1763–1776* (1968); Jensen, *The American Revolution within America* (1974). On traditional politics of deference, see Charles S. Sydnor, *Gentlemen Freeholders: Political Practices in Washington's Virginia* (1952).

27. Thad Tate, "The Social Contract in America, 1774–1787: The Role of Contract Theory in the American Revolution," *William and Mary Quarterly* 22 (1965), 375.

28. "First Draft of Farewell Address," in John C. Fitzpatrick, ed., *The Writings of George Washington from the Original Manuscript Sources, 1745–1799* (1931–44), vol. 35, 51–61; Hamilton to Washington, 10 May 1796, in Syrett and Cooke, eds., *Papers of Hamilton*, vol. 20, 169–183; Victor H. Paltsits, ed., *Washington's Farewell Address . . .* (1935).

29. On the development and use of political theory in the first republican period, 1776–1790, see Donald S. Lutz, *Popular Consent and Popular Control: Whig Political Theory in the Early State Constitutions* (1980).

30. John P. Reid, *Law for the Elephant: Property and Social Behavior on the Overland Trail* (1980); James Willard Hurst, *Law and the Conditions of Freedom in the Nineteenth-Century United States* (1956), ch. 1.

31. See, e.g.: Ordinances of the Virginia Convention, ch. 5, art. VI (May 1776), in William W. Hening, comp., *The Statutes at Large of Virginia* (1821), vol. 9, 127 (receiving common law of England and parliamentary statutes enacted prior to 1607 [date of the first permanent English settlement in Virginia]); New York Constitution, art. XXXV (1777), art. XXXV, in Swindler, comp., *Sources and Documents of United States Constitutions*, vol. 12, 177–178 (receiving English common law and British statutory law enacted prior to 19 April 1775 [date of battles of Lexington and Concord]). See generally Elizabeth G. Brown, *British Statutes in American Law, 1776–1836* (1964).

32. All eleven, that is. Connecticut and Rhode Island did not adopt republican constitutional charters until 1818 and 1843 respectively; for the interim, they merely updated their seventeenth-century royal charters, an entirely reasonable course since they were charter colonies, not royal colonies.

33. See generally Willi Paul Adams, *The First American Constitutions: Republican Ideology and the Making of the State Constitutions in the Revolutionary Era* (1980); Lutz, *Popular Consent and Popular Control.*

34. Except in Georgia and Pennsylvania, which at first were unicameral.

35. It was adopted 12 June 1776, two weeks before the Continental Congress approved the Declaration of Independence.

36. See A. E. Dick Howard, *Commentaries on the Constitution of Virginia* (1974), vol. 1, 61; *accord* Hudgins v. Wright, 1 Hen. & M. (1 Va.) 134 (1806)(opinion of Tucker, J.).

37. Arts. 2, 3, 5, 6.

38. Arts. 8–10, 11, 16, 12, 13, 15–16.

39. See generally Gordon S. Wood's modern classic, *The Creation of the American Republic, 1776–1787* (1969) and Edward S. Corwin's early one, "The Progress of Constitutional Theory between the Declaration of Independence and the Meeting of the Philadelphia Convention," *American Historical Review* 30 (1925), 511.

40. Gary B. Nash, *The Urban Crucible: Social Change, Political Consciousness, and the Origins of the American Revolution* (1979); "Artisans and Politics in Eighteenth Century Philadelphia," in Nash, *Race, Class, and Politics: Essays on American Colonial and Revolutionary Society* (1986), 243.

41. [Madison], "Vices of the Political System of the U. States," in Robert Rutland, ed., *The Papers of James Madison* (1962–1991), vol. 9, 345–358.

42. *The Federalist*, Jacob E. Cooke, ed. (1788; rpt. 1961), Nos. 7 (Hamilton), 44 (Madison), 63 (Madison?), 51 (Madison?).

43. James Iredell to Hannah Iredell, 18 May 1780, in Griffith J. McRee, ed., *Life and Correspondence of James Iredell* (1857–1858), vol. 1, 446.

44. John Adams, *A Defence of the Constitutions of the United States* in Adams, ed., *Works of John Adams*, vol 6, 288–290, 414, 585. On the upper houses, see Jackson Turner Main, *The Upper House in Revolutionary America, 1763–1788* (1967).

45. Swindler, comp., *Sources and Documents of United States Constitutions*, vol. 5, 96.

On the 1780 Massachusetts Constitution, see Ronald M. Peters Jr., *The Massachusetts Constitution of 1780: A Social Compact* (1978) (a study of political theory), and Oscar and Mary Handlin, *The Popular Sources of Political Authority; Documents on the Massachusetts Constitution of 1780* (1966) (documentary collection).

46. Thomas Jefferson, *Notes on the State of Virginia*, 1st Am. ed. (1788), 125.

47. Robert A. Rutland, ed., *The Papers of George Mason, 1725–1792* (1970), vol. 2, 768.

48. All quotations are from the Massachusetts 1780 Constitution, arts. I, VI, X, VII, XI, XXIX, in Swindler, comp., *Sources and Documents of United States Constitutions*, vol. 5, 93–96.

49. U.S. Const. art. 1, § 10.

50. Cooke, ed., *Federalist* No. 37, 233.

51. Madison to Jefferson, 17 Oct. 1788, in Rutland, ed., *Papers of Madison*, vol. 21, 298.

52. Max Farrand, ed., *The Records of the Federal Convention*, rev'd ed. (1937), vol. 1, 21.

53. Farrand, ed., *Records of the Federal Convention*, vol. 1, 97–98, 108 (4 June, notes of Madison and Rufus King).

54. The latest evaluation of the Convention's achievements is Jack N. Rakove, *Original Meanings: Politics and Ideas in the Making of the Constitution* (1996).

55. Jennifer Nedelsky, *Private Property and the Limits of American Constitutionalism: The Madisonian Framework and Its Legacy* (1990).

56. See the corpus of the work of Merrill Jensen, especially *The Articles of Confederation: An Interpretation of the Social-Constitutional History of the American Revolution, 1774–1781* (1940); *The New Nation: A History of the United States during the Confederation, 1781–1789* (1950); *The American Revolution within America* (1974); *The Founding of a Nation: A History of the American Revolution, 1763–1776* (1968). See also Elisha P. Douglass, *Rebels and Democrats: The Struggle for Equal Political Rights and Majority Rule during the American Revolution* (1955).

57. Nedelsky, *Private Property and the Limits of American Constitutionalism*, 8.

58. To achieve another small economy of wordage, in this study the unmodified phrase "the Supreme Court" will always refer to the United States Supreme Court. All references to state supreme courts will specify the state, e.g., "New Hampshire Supreme Court."

59. All quotations are from Cooke, ed., *Federalist* No. 78, 522–523, 525.

60. 1 N.C. (Martin) 42 (1787). Other early cases involving possible exercise of the power of judicial review are collected at James Bradley Thayer, *Cases on Constitutional Law* (1895), vol. 1, 63–80.

61. Julius Goebel Jr., ed., *The Law Practice of Alexander Hamilton: Documents and Commentary* (1964–1981), vol. 1, 282–419. See also Hamilton to Jefferson, 19 April 1792, in Syrett and Cooke, eds., *Papers of Hamilton*, vol. 11, 316–317.

62. See William E. Nelson, "Changing Conceptions of Judicial Review: The Evolution of Constitutional Theory in the States, 1790–1860," 120 *U. Pa. L. Rev.* 1166 (1972).

63. Vanhorne's Lessee v. Dorrance, 2 Dall. (2 U.S.) 304, 308, 310 (1795) (grand jury charge per Paterson, C.J.).

64. 3 Dall. (3 U.S.) 386 (1798).

65. Edward S. Corwin, "The Basic Doctrine of American Constitutional Law," 12 *Mich. L. Rev.* 247 (1914).

66. That is, a judicial decision that had the effect of vesting real or personal property in some devisee, legatee, or heir.

67. The Court declined to hold the statute void as an ex post facto law, on the grounds that the Constitution's ex post facto clause (art. I, § 10) applied only to criminal statutes. See Julius Goebel Jr., *Antecedents and Beginnings to 1801* (vol. 1 of the Holmes Devise *History of the Supreme Court of the United States*) (1971), 782–784.

68. 3 Dall. (3 U.S.) 386, 388 (1798).

69. 3 Dall. at 399.

70. 1 Cranch (5 U.S.) 137 (1803).

71. On Marbury, see generally George L. Haskins and Herbert A. Johnson, *Foundations of Power: John Marshall, 1801–15* (vol. 2 of the *Holmes Devise History of the Supreme Court of the United States*) (1981), 182–204; William W. Van Alstyne, "A Critical Guide to Marbury v. Madison," 1969 *Duke L.J.* 1; and on later interpretations of the case, Robert L. Clinton, *Marbury v. Madison and Judicial Review* (1989).

72. The quotations that follow are from 1 Cranch 163, 164–166, 170, 177–178.

73. 297 U.S. 1, 62–63 (1936).

74. See the discussion in Gerald Gunther, *Constitutional Law*, 12th ed. (1991), 14, 21–28.

75. "The supreme Law of the Land": United States Constitution, art. VI; Baker v. Carr, 369 U.S. 186, 211 (1962) (per Brennan, J.; dictum); Cooper v. Aaron, 358 U.S. 1, 18 (1958) (per each of the Justices; dictum); see also United States v. Nixon, 418 U.S. 683 (1974). Cf. Daniel A. Farber, "The Supreme Court and the Rule of Law: Cooper v. Aaron Revisited," 1983 *U. Ill. L. Rev.* 387 with Gerald Gunther, "Judicial Hegemony and Legislative Autonomy: The Nixon Case and the Impeachment Process," 22 *UCLA L. Rev.* 30 (1974). On the Court's overassertion of its authority when it is goaded by fears of social conflict, see Robert Burt, *The Constitution in Conflict* (1992).

76. 7 How. (48 U.S.) 1 (1849).

77. 4 Wheat. (17 U.S.) 316, 405, 421, 400, 423 (1819). The discussion in text focuses only on those portions of that monumental opinion directly relevant to the emergence of legal classicism and passes by without comment other issues, such as the nature of the Union.

78. On McCulloch, see generally G. Edward White, *The Marshall Court and Cultural Change, 1815–35* (vols. 3–4 of the *Holmes Devise History of the Supreme Court of the United States*) (1988), 237–240, 246–249, 933–935, and esp. 541–567.

79. [Hamilton,] "Opinion on the Constitutionality of an Act to Establish a Bank," in Syrett and Cooke, eds., *Papers of Hamilton*, vol. 8, 107.

80. U.S. Const. art. I, § 8, cl. 18.

81. G. Edward White, *The American Judicial Tradition: Profiles of Leading American Judges* (1976), 25, 27–30.

82. These essays, and those of Spencer Roane, writing as "Hampden," have been collected and edited by Gerald Gunther, *John Marshall's Defense of McCulloch v. Maryland* (1969). Quotations that follow are from pp. 92, 211–212.

83. [Warren Dutton,] "Constitutional Law," *North American Review* 10 (1820), 83, 113. The attribution to Dutton is made in White, *Marshall Court and Cultural Change*, 938.

84. On the case itself, see C. Peter Magrath, *Yazoo: Law and Politics in the New Republic; The Case of Fletcher v. Peck* (1966).

85. 6 Cranch (10 U.S.) 87, 139 (1810).

86. U.S. Const. art I, § 10.

87. Farrand, ed., *Records of the Federal Convention*, vol. 3, 439 (Rufus King offered a motion to add what became the contracts clause, limited to "private contracts"). But cf. Madison in *Federalist* No. 44, p. 301: state laws modifying obligation of contracts "are contrary to the first principles of the social compact, and . . . are prohibited by the spirit and scope of these fundamental charters [state constitutions]."

88. 9 Cranch (13 U.S.) 43, 52 (1815).

89. White, *Marshall Court and Cultural Change*, 597. The latter half of the formulation is an exaggeration for 1825: while the corporation was rising in importance, most economic activity was carried on in the forms of sole proprietorships, various kinds of partner-

ships, or specialized adaptations like the business trust. Nevertheless, White's formulation is striking and, in a long view, essentially correct.

90. Gavin Wright, *Old South, New South: Revolutions in the Southern Economy since the Civil War* (1986), 18, 49.

91. Louis Hartz, *Economic Policy and Democratic Thought: Pennsylvania, 1776–1860* (1948; rpt. 1968); Oscar Handlin and Mary Handlin, *Commonwealth: A Study of the Role of Government in the American Economy: Massachusetts, 1774–1861*, rev'd ed. (1969); Harry N. Scheiber, *Ohio Canal Era; A Case Study of Government and the Economy, 1820–1861* (1968).

92. Tony A. Freyer, *Producers versus Capitalists: Constitutional Conflict in Antebellum America* (1994).

93. See generally Horwitz, *Transformation I*, 211–252.

94. 4 Wheat. (17 U.S.) 518, 644, 628 (1819).

95. Francis N. Stites, *Private Interest and Public Gain: The Dartmouth College Case, 1819* (1972), 99–100.

96. 7 Pet. (32 U.S.) 243 (1833).

97. Wilkinson v. Leland, 2 Pet. (27 U.S.) 627, 634, 657 (1829).

98. Joseph Story, *Commentaries on the Constitution of the United States* (1833), vol. 3, 268.

99. 7 Cranch (11 U.S.) 164 (1812) (holding that the contracts clause inhibited a state from revoking a tax exemption).

100. Peter Coleman, *Debtors and Creditors in America: Insolvency, Imprisonment for Debt, and Bankruptcy, 1607–1900* (1974), 16–30.

101. Farrand, ed., *Records of the Federal Convention*, vol. 2, 439.

102. 4 Wheat. (17 U.S.) 122 (1819).

103. Farrand, ed., *Records of the Federal Convention*, vol. 2, 440 (emphasis in original). It should be noted that Marshall could not have known this: Madison's *Notes of Debates* were not published until 1840, four and five years after his and Marshall's deaths respectively.

104. Charles M. Haar, ed., *The Golden Age of American Law* (1965).

105. 11 Pet. (36 U.S.) 420 (1837).

106. 9 Wheat. (22 U.S.) 1 (1824).

107. 9 Johns. 507 (1812). The New York Court for the Trial of Impeachments and the Correction of Errors, the state's highest court at that time, was a peculiar hybrid, comprised of the Justices of the Supreme Court, the chancellor, and members of the state senate.

108. On the Bridge Case, see Stanley I. Kutler, *Privilege and Creative Destruction: The Charles River Bridge Case* (1971), and Carl B. Swisher, *The Taney Period, 1836–64* (vol. 5 of the *Holmes Devise History of the Supreme Court of the United States*)(1974), 71–98.

109. "[T]he rights legally vested in a corporation, cannot be controlled or destroyed by any subsequent statute, unless a power for that purpose be reserved to the legislature in the act of incorporation. These principles are so consonant with justice, sound policy, and legal reasoning, that it is difficult to resist the impression of their perfect correctness." Dartmouth College v. Woodward, 4 Wheat. at 708 (Story, J., concurring).

110. J. Willard Hurst, *Law and the Conditions of Freedom in the Nineteenth-Century United States* (1956), 27–28.

111. See Luther v. Borden, 7 How. (48 U.S.) 1 (1849); Propeller Genesee Chief v. Fitzhugh, 12 How. (53 U.S.) 443 (1851); Pennsylvania v. Wheeling and Belmont Bridge Co., 13 How. (54 U.S.) 518 (1852).

112. David Hoffman, *A Course of Legal Study: Respectfully Addressed to the Students of Law in the United States* (1817).

113. Joseph Story, "Course of Legal Study," *North American Review* (1817) (review essay), reprinted in William W. Story, ed., *The Miscellaneous Writings of Joseph Story*, (1852), 66–92.

114. See generally Perry Miller, *The Life of the Mind in America from the Revolution to the Civil War* (1965), ch. 3, "The Science of the Law."

115. Greenleaf quoted in Miller, *Life of the Mind*, 159.

116. Theodore Dwight, *The Inaugural Addresses of Theodore W. Dwight and of George P. Marsh in Columbia College, New York* (1859), 39–40.

117. Quoted in A. W. B. Simpson, "The Rise and Fall of the Legal Treatise: Legal Principles and the Forms of Legal Literature," 48 *U. Chic. L. Rev.* 632, 672 (1981).

118. On Bacon and Blackstone as patron saints, see Josiah Quincy, *An Address Delivered at the Dedication of Dane Law College in Harvard University* (1832). On the diffuse influence of Blackstone, especially on legal science and legal education, see Dennis R. Nolan, "Sir William Blackstone and the New American Republic: A Study of Intellectual Impact," 51 *N.Y.U. L. Rev.* 731 (1976).

119. Story, "Course of Legal Study"; Story, "The Progress of Jurisprudence," (1821) in Story, ed., *Miscellaneous Writings of Story*, 232.

120. John Pickering, *A Lecture on the Alleged Uncertainty of the Law: Delivered before the Boston Society for the Diffusion of Useful Knowledge*, March 5, 1830 (1834), 26, 15.

121. "Nature and Method of Legal Studies," 3 *U.S. Monthly Law Mag.* 381–382 (1851).

122. Peter S. Du Ponceau, *A Dissertation on the Nature and Extent of the Jurisdiction of the Courts of the United States* (1824), 128–129.

123. D. T. Blake, *A Discourse Introductory to a Course of Law Lectures* (1810), 10.

124. James Kent, *Commentaries on American Law* (1826–1830), vol. 3, 88 (emphasis in original).

125. See Roscoe Pound, *The Formative Era of American Law* (1938), ch. 4, "Doctrinal Writing."

126. St. George Tucker, ed., *Blackstone's Commentaries: With Notes of Reference to the Constitution and Laws of the Federal Government of the United States and of the Commonwealth of Virginia* (1803).

127. Arthur E. Sutherland, *The Law at Harvard: A History of Ideas and Men, 1817–1967* (1967), 92–98.

128. Story even boiled his constitutional *Commentaries* down into two school versions, *The Constitutional Class Book: Being a Brief Exposition of the Constitution of the United States* (1834) and *A Familiar Exposition of the Constitution of the United States* (1840), to indoctrinate younger students.

129. Kent Newmyer, *Supreme Court Justice Joseph Story: Statesman of the Old Republic* (1985).

130. Baldwin was a Justice of the Supreme Court at the time of publication.

131. Alexis de Tocqueville, *Democracy in America*, trans. Henry Reeve (1835, 1840; rpt. 1945), vol. 1, 102–107, 143–147, 256–258, 283–290.

132. U.S. Const. art. I, §§ 9, 10.

133. George W. Pierson's thorough study, *Tocqueville and Beaumont in America* (1938), contains no mention of Choate, though Pierson notes Tocqueville's and Gustave de Beaumont's extensive contacts with other New England lawyers.

134. In contrast to the usage earlier in this chapter, I now use the term "Whig" to refer to members of the political party of that name that emerged by 1832 in opposition to the Jacksonian Democrats and that was immolated in the fiery furnace of the Kansas-Nebraska controversy in 1854.

135. Quoted in Jean V. Matthews, *Rufus Choate: The Law and Civic Virtue* (1980), 163.

136. For an excellent synopsis of Whig conservative thought, see Matthews, *Choate*, 70–92 and the sources cited in her fns. 44–47 there, to which might be added William M.

Wiecek, "'A Peculiar Conservatism' and the Dorr Rebellion: Constitutional Clash in Jacksonian America," 22 *Am. J. Legal Hist.* 237–253 (1978).

137. Matthews, *Choate*, 174–182, 191.

138. Choate, "The Position and Functions of the American Bar, as an Element of Conservatism in the State: An Address Delivered before the Law School in Cambridge, July 3, 1845," in Samuel G. Brown, ed., *The Works of Rufus Choate with a Memoir of His Life* (1862), 414, 417, 430, 436.

139. William E. Nelson, *Americanization of the Common Law: The Impact of Legal Change on Massachusetts Society, 1760–1830* (1975), 172; see generally chs. 8–9.

140. The following pages summarize the theses of Horwitz, *Transformation I*. For a defense of Horwitz's ideas against his critics (some of whom are noted below), see Wythe Holt, "Morton Horwitz and the Transformation of American Legal History," 23 *Wm. & Mary L. Rev.* 663 (1982).

141. Lawrence M. Friedman, *A History of American Law*, 2nd ed. (1985), 29.

142. Quoted from student ms. notes in Horwitz, *Transformation I*, 23; *see also* James Sullivan, *The History of Land Titles in Massachusetts* (1801), 345.

143. Zephaniah Swift, *A Digest of the Law of Evidence, in Civil and Criminal Cases* (1810), xi.

144. Vandenheuvel v. United Insurance Co., 2 Cai. Cas. 217, 286, 289 (N.Y. Sup. Ct. 1805).

145. As in Blackstone's *Commentaries* (1765–1768), vol. 2, "Of the Rights of Things."

146. 2 Pet. (27 U.S.) 137, 145 (1829).

147. 8 Met. (49 Mass.) 466, 476–477 (1844).

148. Parker v. Foot, 19 Wend. 309 (N.Y. Sup. Ct. 1838).

149. 51 N.Y. 476, 484–485 (1873) (denying liability, absent proof of negligence, for property damage caused by explosion of boiler).

150. Spring v. Russell, 7 Greenl. 273, 289–290 (Me. 1831).

151. 11 Pet. at 477.

152. Kutler, *Privilege and Creative Destruction*.

153. The next few paragraphs follow what have by now become the standard interpretations of the beginnings of tort law in Lawrence M. Friedman, *A History of American Law*, 2nd ed. (1985), 299–302, 467–478; Leonard W. Levy, *The Law of the Commonwealth and Chief Justice Shaw* (1957; rpt. 1987), 166–182; G. Edward White, *Tort Law in America: An Intellectual History* (1980), 3–19; and Horwitz, *Transformation I*, 85–101. Elements of this interpretation have been criticized: Richard A. Posner, "A Theory of Negligence," 2 *J. Legal Stud.* 29 (1972); Gary T. Schwartz, "Tort Law and the Economy in Nineteenth-century America: A Reinterpretation," 90 *Yale L.J.* 1717 (1981). Prof. Schwartz notes, however, that his criticisms do not apply to tortious liability in the employment context, the major area of innovation.

154. 6 Cush. (60 Mass.) 292, 296–297 (1850).

155. Clark v. Foot, 8 Johns. 421 (N.Y. Sup. Ct. 1811); Lehigh Bridge v. Lehigh Coal & Navigation Co., 4 Rawle 8 (Pa. 1833); Snee v. Trice, 2 Bay 345 (S.C. 1802) (this last possibly anomalous, in that the persons responsible for setting the fire were enslaved and the issue was apportionment of loss as between an innocent third party and the master, on a theory of respondeat superior in the context of enslavement).

156. L.R. 3 H.L. 330 (1868).

157. 51 N.Y. 476 (1873); 53 N.H. 442 (1873).

158. Haring v. New-York and Erie R.R., 13 Barb. S.C. 2, 15–16 (N.Y. Sup. Ct. 1852).

159. 4 Met. (45 Mass.) 49, 57 (1842).

160. The doctrine had been anticipated in England in Priestly v. Fowler, 3 Mees. & W. 1, 150 Eng. Rep. 1030 (1837)

161. 35 N.Y. 210, 217 (1866).

162. Gannon v. Hargadon, 10 Allen (92 Mass.) 106, 109 (1865).

163. Redfield on railways: Isaac F. Redfield, *The Law of Railways: Embracing Corporations, Eminent Domain . . .* , 4th ed. (1869), vol. 2, 36–46.

164. Joseph Story, *Commentaries on the Law of Bailments*, 4th ed. (1843), § 549.

165. New Jersey Steam Navigation Co. v. Merchants Bank, 6 How. (47 U.S.) 344 (1847).

166. Horwitz, *Transformation I*, 160–252. A. W. B. Simpson attacked this treatment in "The Horwitz Thesis and the History of Contracts," 46 *U. Chic. L. Rev.* 533 (1979). See also Nelson, *Americanization of the Common Law*, 54–63.

167. Reporter's comment in Clitherall v. Ogilvie, 1 Des. 250, 259n. (S.C. Eq. 1792).

168. Lyman H. Butterfield, ed., *Diary and Autobiography of John Adams* (1961), vol. 1, 112.

169. William W. Story, *A Treatise on the Law of Contracts Not under Seal* (1844), 4.

170. 3 Cow. 445 (1824).

171. Story, *Commentaries on Equity Jurisprudence* (1836), vol. 1, 249–250.

172. Gulian C. Verplanck, *An Essay on the Doctrine of Contracts: Being an Inquiry How Contracts Are Affected in Law and Morals, by Concealment, Error, or Inadequate Price* (1825), 115.

173. 2 Cai. 48 (N.Y. Sup. Ct. 1804).

174. 2 Wheat. (15 U.S.) 178 (1817) (executory contract for sale of tobacco; purchaser need not communicate information that would enhance the sale price).

175. 3 Wheat. (16 U.S.) 200 (1818).

176. Verplanck, *Essay on Contracts*, 120.

177. Kent, *Commentaries on American Law*, II, 328, 330.

178. Including, perhaps surprisingly, John Marshall: Mandeville v. Riddle, 1 Cranch (5 U.S.) 290 (1803).

179. Joseph Story, *Commentaries on the Law of Promissory Notes* (1845), 10.

180. 16 Pet. (41 U.S.) 1 (1842). Of the voluminous commentary on Swift, Tony Freyer's *Harmony & Dissonance: The Swift & Erie Cases in American Federalism* (1981), 1–75, provides the most useful historical account, elaborating on the same author's *Forums of Order: The Federal Courts and Business in American History* (1979), 53–99.

181. Watson v. Tarpley, 18 How. (59 U.S.) 517, 521 (1855) per Daniel, J! (Daniel's state-power predilections made him an unlikely spokesman for this nationalizing commercial doctrine.)

182. Regents of the University of Maryland v. Williams, 9 Gill & J. 365, 408–409 (Md., 1838).

183. Ham v. McClaws, 1 Bay 93 (So. Car., 1789); Turpin v. Locket, 6 Call. 113 (Va., 1804); Trustees of the University of North Carolina v. Foy, 1 Murphey 310 (N.C., 1804); Dash v. Van Kleeck, 7 Johns. 477 (N.Y., 1811); Gardner v. Village of Newburgh, 2 Johns. Ch. 162 (N.Y. 1816); Bedford v. Shilling, 4 Serg. & R. 400 (Pa., 1818); Merrill v. Sherburne, 1 N.H. 199 (1819); Rice v. Parkman, 16 Tyng (16 Mass.) 326 (1820); Goshen v. Stonington, 4 Conn. 209 (1822); Hoke v. Henderson, 4 Dev. 1 (N.C., 1833); In re Dorsey, 7 Porter 293 (Ala., 1838); Taylor v. Porter, 4 Hill 140 (N.Y. Sup. Ct. 1843); Rice v. Foster, 4 Harr. 479 (Del. Ct. Errors & Apps., 1847); Holmes v. Holmes, 4 Barb. 295 (N.Y. 1848); Sohier v. The Massachusetts General Hospital, 3 Cush. (57 Mass.) 483 (1849); White v. White, 5 Barb. 474 (N.Y. Sup. Ct. 1849); Benson v. The Mayor, 10 Barb. 223 (N.Y. Sup. Ct. 1850); Welch v. Wadsworth, 30 Conn. 149 (1861).

184. E.g., Taylor v. Porter, 4 Hill 140 (N.Y. 1843); see Rodney L. Mott, *Due Process of Law: A Historical and Analytical Treatise of the Principles and Methods Followed by the Courts in the Application of the Concept of the "Law of the Land"* (1926), 106–124, 208–255.

185. See Edward S. Corwin, "Due Process of Law before the Civil War," 24 *Harv. L. Rev.* 366, 460 (1911).

186. University v. Foy, 5 N.C. 57, 63 (1804).

187. Holden v. James, 11 Tyng (11 Mass.) 396, 405 (1814).

188. 13 N.Y. 378, 385, 387, 393–393 (1856).

189. Dred Scott v. Sandford, 19 How. (60 U.S.) 393, 450 (1857).

190. *The Works of Jeremy Bentham*, comp. John Bowring (1962), vol. 4, 494; vol. 3, 209.

191. *Works of Bentham*, vol. 5, 235.

192. William Sampson, *An Anniversary Discourse . . . 1823: Showing the Origin, Progress, Antiquities, Curiosities, and the Nature of the Common Law* (1824), excerpted in Perry Miller, ed., *The Legal Mind in America from Independence to the Civil War* (1962), 119–134.

193. "P. W. Grayson," *Vice Unmasked, an Essay: Being a Consideration of the Influence of Law upon the Moral Essence of Man* (1830), excerpted in Miller, *Legal Mind in America*, 191–200.

194. Robert Rantoul, *Oration at Scituate . . . 1836*, excerpted in Miller, *Legal Mind in America*, 222–227; quotation at 225.

195. See generally Charles M. Cook, *The American Codification Movement: A Study of Antebellum Legal Reform* (1981).

196. Story, "The Progress of Jurisprudence" in Story, ed., *Miscellaneous Writings of Story*, 237–238.

197. Not a court, at least since the seventeenth century, but the proper name of the Massachusetts legislature.

198. Story, "A Report of the Commissioners . . . 1837" in Story, ed., *Miscellaneous Writings of Story*, 699–734.

199. On Field and his influence, see Daun Van Ee, *David Dudley Field and the Reconstruction of the Law* (1986). For his writings promoting codification, see *Speeches, Arguments, and Miscellaneous Papers of David Dudley Field* (1884–1890), vol. 1.

200. Joel P. Bishop, *Common Law and Codification; or, The Common Law as a System of Reasoning* (1888), 3.

201. Massachusetts Constitution of 1780, Bill of Rights, arts. I, II, and X (property cannot be taken for religious uses, except as provided), XI ("recourse to laws" to protect property), XII (property protected by "the law of the land"), XIII (criminal juries), XIX (search and seizure), XV (civil juries), XXIX (good-behavior tenure for the judiciary); XXVII (soldiers may not be quartered in homes), XXIII (taxation); in Swindler, comp., *Sources and Documents of United States Constitutions*, vol. 5, 93–97.

202. U.S. Const. amend. V.

203. 3 Paige 44, 72 (N.Y. Ch. 1831).

204. Hazen v. Essex Co., 12 Cush. (66 Mass.) 475 (1853). See Levy, *Law of the Commonwealth and Chief Justice Shaw*, 118–139.

205. West River Bridge v. Dix, 6 How. (47 U.S.) 507 (1848).

206. 7 Cush. (61 Mass.) 53, 85, 95 (1851). See Levy, *Law of the Commonwealth and Chief Justice Shaw*, 229–265.

Chapter Two

The Emergence of
Legal Classicism,
1860–1890

*I*n the generation after the Civil War, classical legal thought emerged and attained its greatest authority. By the turn of the twentieth century, classicism had become the authentic expression of American law. Classicism provided an explanation of what law was, what its sources and sanctions were, why it could command the obedience of all, how it animated society and directed the economic order. Classical thought identified the legal ideals that directed the course of American national destiny. Classical legal thought integrated society, economy, and law as it sanctioned the status quo of the American social order. Classicism subordinated state to society and governmental power to individual liberty. It selectively constrained state authority, yet blessed the application of state power for certain purposes, justifying the subordination of some groups of Americans and their domination by others.

Classical legal thought was nothing less than a unified field theory of law and society. In the secular republic of the United States, it provided the sanction for the extant distribution of power and privilege that elsewhere was supplied by church, hierarchy, and creed.

Classical thought providentially triumphed at the moment when it was most needed. Traditional structures of governmental authority and community, together with their religioethical underpinnings, were ceding place to new and troubling replacements. Cities towered over the small town, while labor unions struggled to achieve legitimacy as centers of power in the state. Corporations outgrew the regulatory and disciplinary powers of the states that had created them. Corruption was endemic at all levels of government. Religious belief was shaken by the Higher Criticism. Middle-class angst drove legal development as the century drew to a close.

The Social Climate of the Late Nineteenth Century

Reconstruction and Gilded Age America

The first century of American independence had laid the foundations of legal classicism. The Civil War and the struggle over Reconstruction from 1861 to 1877 remade the constitutional order.

The constitutional regime of 1776–1876 had governed an agrarian society. The postwar constitutional order had to adapt to an industrializing society that was undergoing profound social and economic transformation. Some of the major impacts of this transformation were[1]

- Nonagricultural production now took place principally in factories rather than small workshops, and was organized on an ever larger industrial scale, shipping products into national and international markets.
- The organization of industrial labor changed, and the status of the worker along with it, from journeyman to factory hand. Workers organized themselves in unions, which were coordinated in national, crafts, and industrial federations. Employers ferociously resisted all forms of labor organization. When earlier legal weapons against unions like the conspiracy doctrine grew enfeebled, employers deployed new ones, principally the labor injunction, or resorted to private and public armed force to suppress unions by violence.
- The profit-oriented private corporation emerged as the principal legal and economic vehicle for amassing capital, organizing production and distribution, and defining the powers and claims of investors, managers, employees, and others affected by the legal activities of the firm. Scholars refer to this as "corporate capitalism," as opposed to the earlier stage of "proprietary capitalism," where the basic economic unit was the sole proprietorship, partnership, or family.
- Investment banking firms reorganized public and private credit sources, coming to dominate American finance. This is often referred to as "finance capitalism," and was thoroughly documented by the investigations of the Pujo Committee in 1913.[2] (In response to this private control of the nation's finance and credit, the Wilson administration and Congress created a central banking system in 1914, the Federal Reserve, to assert public control over capital formation.)
- Local organization of society and the economy gave way to national controls. Nationwide organizations such as the American Bar Association presided over the professionalization and bureaucratization of previously local activities, in parallel with the nationalization of industry, manufacturing, and transport. The pervasive symbol of this trend toward nationalization was congressional creation of standardized time by imposing four national time zones for the continental United States in 1883, responding to demands from the private sector (the railroads) for standardization, uniformity, and national control.

- As a result of the constitutional settlements that followed the Civil War, the federal government emerged dominant within the federal system. Antebellum state power constitutionalism receded, though it by no means disappeared. States' power constitutional doctrine remained powerful in establishing the political regime of white supremacy in the southern and border states.
- Both private economic activity and governmental regulatory authority became increasingly bureaucratized.
- Administered markets, whether controlled by nongovernmental cartels or state/federal agency regulation, replaced unmediated competition.
- Transportation and communications were transformed. The railroad, telegraph, steamship, telephone, internal combustion engine automobile, and radio reduced distance and isolation.
- American society assumed a middle-class, increasingly urban identity. Bourgeois values triumphed, while most Americans claimed or at least aspired to middle-class status. Americans denied as steadfastly as ever that their nation was riven along class lines.
- Women and black Americans became increasingly assertive in demanding civic participation (the vote) and protection for their basic civic rights, including legal capacity. The women's struggle was successful, at least nominally, by World War I, while the African American effort was rolled back by apartheid.
- Farm and rural populations inexorably shrank, while city populations swelled because of internal migration and the immigration of Europeans and Asians.
- The nation elbowed its way into competition for imperial status. After its appetite for landed expansion was sated by acquisition of Alaska (1867), America avidly pursued naval-commercial expansion in the Caribbean and Pacific.

The United States was not unique in this modernization. Martin Sklar offers this comparative summary, with particular reference to Germany but including other industrializing European states and, to a less extent, Japan:

> Land, goods, property rights in general and, of critical importance, labor-power, became freely salable or mobile, and subject to diminishing restraint from religion, custom, or other prescriptive norms. Market and contractual relations displaced kinship, communal, and older status relations as the paramount mode of social organization. A market-directed division of labor generated both specialization of function and complex patterns of integration in the sphere of production and exchange, as well as in the sphere of politics and government.[3]

Capitalism in this view was not merely an economic system, but the integrative organization of an entire society, shaping its values, laws, social organization, even its family structure and religious bodies.

These jarring dislocations of the antebellum order created a cultural lag. Hurtling social and economic change — the triad of industrialization, urbanization, and immigration in the late nineteenth century — outran the ability of Americans to formulate ideological structures that would help them understand such change, much less control it. This disconnect between social reality and outmoded patterns of thought is sometimes described as a misfit between "society" (economic and social change) and "state" (governance capacity).

In the domain of legal thought, cultural lag took the form of jurists and lawyers attempting to adapt legal concepts and structures of thought (ideologies) that had governed an earlier age to the drastically changed circumstances of the new environment. Had social change come at a more leisurely pace, that adaptation might have gone more smoothly and produced a legal culture better suited to the economy that it controlled. But the bar of a century ago did not enjoy the luxury of leisurely change. Instead, the phenomenon that in our times would be called "future shock"[4] struck American lawyers unprepared, and they scrambled intellectually to catch up.

Bruce Ackerman has described the period of Reconstruction as a "constitutional moment," a "self-conscious act of constitutional creation that rivaled the Founding Federalists' in . . . scope and depth."[5] In 1787–1791, the Framers created the first of three successive "constitutional regimes, the matrix of institutional relationships and fundamental values that are usually taken as the constitutional baseline in normal political life." These constitutional regimes were the periods from the founding to Reconstruction, Reconstruction to the New Deal, and the New Deal to the present. At the beginning of each, the American people in their sovereign capacity constituted or reconstituted the fundamental values of their constitutional order. Those values were embodied first in the Constitution of 1787 and the Bill of Rights; next in the Thirteenth through Fifteenth Amendments; and last in the constitutional settlement that evolved out of the constitutional crisis of 1937, signaled first in the *Carolene Products* footnote (1938).[6]

Ackerman contends that the constitutional status quo is regularly subjected to critique by the legal profession and the people. Over time, that "critique finally gains the considered support of a mobilized majority of the American people" as the result of a "deep and sustained popular commitment required for a legitimate transformation in fundamental values." This induces a constitutional moment, a time when the president and Congress "speak in the authentic higher lawmaking accents of We the People of the United States." When this occurs, the constitution is transformed through an "intergenerational . . . interpretive synthesis," and the new principles thus inducted into the constitution take on the pervasive generality and authority of the old.

Reconstruction was such a moment, the first in our history since the founding. In the Thirteenth through Fifteenth Amendments, Congress revised the constitutional order in generalized language that embodied three new principles — universal freedom, equal protection of the laws, and congressional enforcement authority — and extended three older ones — citizenship, privileges and immunities, and due process.

Lawyers perforce had to adapt old materials, suitable for the stage of proprietary capitalism, to new uses in this transformed environment and new constitutional order. Sometimes the adaptation proceeded slowly and with a maximum of confusion, as was the case with the legal understanding of the nature of the corporation. At other times, older notions appeared ill adapted to modern needs, the law of industrial relations being an example. Infrequently, this process of adaptation and bricolage[7] might produce a functional innovation, such as federalized habeas corpus.[8] Usually, though, lawyers found themselves in the awkward position of trying to define a world they feared and understood only imperfectly with concepts that were outmoded and ill suited to the task.

Reconstruction also marked a shift from an earlier era, dating back to the first European settlements of North America, marked by pervasive local regulation of the society and economy, to a time when an individualistic liberal ethos struggled to displace regulation. Before 1870, Americans resorted to law to promote public safety, stimulate economic development, police public spaces, control morals, protect public health, and in general promote collective welfare. They did not waste a moment's concern about overriding individual interests in doing so.[9]

Liberalism's contemporary and modern triumphs, both propagandistic and historiographic, have almost obliterated the memory of this "well-regulated society," as William Novak calls it, and replaced it with an edenic state of minimal governmental regulation. Constructing myths of statelessness (weak government), individualism, cultural transformation, and exceptionalism, the liberal countertradition would have it that America has always been the home of the free market, laissez-faire, and minimal governance.

In reality, antebellum Americans took seriously the maxim *salus populi suprema lex esto* (let the welfare of the people be the supreme law), and used governmental regulation pervasively to promote the people's welfare. Powerful local self-government was the norm, not only in the long settled East, but all along the frontiers as well. Law was central in this thoroughly regulated social order, identifying the loftiest ideals of the people as well as prescribing the minutiae of their social intercourse. The doctrine of the police power provided the all-pervasive reality of government presence in antebellum America.

Seen in this light, the rise of the classical legal order was revolutionary, seeking to overthrow a regime of governance sanctioned by two and a half centuries of experience. Part of the explanation for its ultimate failure in 1937 lay in the fact that classical ideology attempted a wrenching displacement of a venerable tradition.

Industrialization and the American Economy

At the end of the Civil War, the Supreme Court had to adapt existing legal forms to the radically changed conditions of the postwar world.[10] Like other Americans, judges and lawyers were awed by the achievements and prospects of industrial organization, even as industry itself was undergoing violent dislocations. The small antebellum productive unit of a master plus a few journeymen and apprentices, organized as a sole proprietorship, gave way to the factory and its integrated assembly line, organized under corporate forms. Large internal corporate bureaucracies developed to control information flows, to provide staff services (legal, accounting, personnel), and to structure decision-making.[11] This private bureaucratization created industrial structures of command and control. Divided decision-making authority was unthinkable to management, which denied workers and their unions a share in decisional responsibilities. Hierarchical authority in the boardrooms and suites was replicated by petty command structures on the shop floor, where workers were subordinated to foremen and foremen to managers.

The factory system rationalized production by improving the efficiency of manufacturing and assembly processes, but in doing so, it regimented labor. The ever more tightly organized factory system required subordination and submission of the worker. Antebellum slavocrat predictions[12] of "wage slavery" in the free-labor North under a regime of laissez-faire seemed to be coming true, an irony that echoed Republicans' fears that they had won the war only to lose the peace. From the workers' point of view, a war that had been fought to vindicate Free Labor seemed only to have transferred fetters from the slave to the factory worker. Uriah Stephens, a founder of the Knights of Labor, demanded "emancipation . . . from the thraldom and loss of wage slavery."[13] Another spokesman for the Knights claimed "that the present industrial system of our country is but chattel slavery, in fact, if not in name, and . . . the laws that sanction and uphold this system must be changed by the power of organized labor."[14] Meanwhile, the New South devised novel forms of truly unfree labor for black Americans, including the convict lease system, prison labor, the chain gang, crop lien laws, and criminal surety statutes.[15] The Thirteenth Amendment's prohibition of involuntary servitude proved to be a dead letter when Euro-Americans tired of responsibility for the freedpeople's fate.

Industrial workers no longer owned their tools or controlled their time. They were now disciplined by artificial time and mechanical artifacts — clocks, bells, whistles — not by the rhythms of the days and the seasons. Factory work was repetitive and the worksite dangerous. Real per capita income rose steadily through the nineteenth century,[16] but with that secular rise, paradoxically, grew obvious poverty.

Antebellum energy sources for production were all derived from solar energy: falling water, wood, the sweat of animals and humans. The energy sources of the Industrial Revolution were fossil fuels: coal at first, later oil.[17] Accompanying this switch in energetic sources was a change in the machines that exploited them, from wood- and coal-burning external combustion steam engines to internal combustion engines fueled by petroleum. In this process, external combustion became restricted to stationary sources such as factories and power plants, except for the steamship and steam locomotive.

Urbanization and massive migration were essential parts of the Industrial Revolution. Cities grew inexorably, becoming milieux of poverty and violence that seemed to betray their historic role as centers of civilization. Anxious old-stock Americans recalled Thomas Jefferson's aversion to cities and their impact on the political system: "[T]he mobs of great cities add just so much to the support of pure government, as sores do to the strength of the human body. It is the manners and spirit of a people which preserve a republic in vigour. A degeneracy in these is a canker which soon eats to the heart of its laws and constitution."[18] Henry George published *Progress and Poverty* in 1879, exploring the paradox that industrial progress, which held out so much hope for the betterment of humanity's lot, seemed to be accompanied by unprecedented misery in the industrial slums. His readers need only have looked at the cities around them for proof of the paradox.

The cities filled with native-born migrants from the American countryside, and with the "new immigrants," as they were called. These were predominantly from

Eastern or Southern Europe and Asia. They included few Protestants, and there were no native English speakers among them. The newcomers were Roman Catholics, Jews, Orthodox, Confucian; Slavs, Magyars, Greeks, Sicilians, Mexicans, Chinese. Many of them were dark-skinned, uncouth in dress and culture. They spoke a babel of alien tongues bearing no relation to the Romance and Germanic languages of Western Europe. The new immigrants fed industrializing America's insatiable hunger for cheap labor, but that did not soothe the anxieties of Protestant, English-speaking Americans over this barbarian invasion.

Recoiling with terror from the labor violence of 1877 and 1886, bourgeois Americans clamored for repression of the striking workers. Even the religious press sounded a bloodthirsty note: "If the club of the policeman, knocking out the brains of the rioter, will answer, then well and good; but if it does not, . . . then bullets and bayonets, canister and grape . . . constitute the one remedy. . . . Napoleon was right when he said that the way to deal with a mob was to exterminate it." That from 1877; and in 1886: "When anarchy gathers its deluded disciples into a mob, as at Chicago, a Gatling gun or two . . . offers, on the whole, the most merciful as well as effectual remedy."[19]

The image of cities as theaters of class warfare preoccupied the middle-class imagination. Josiah Strong's 1886 best-seller *Our Country* expressed the fear of the northern elites that they were about to be overwhelmed by the new immigration (especially Catholics), city dwellers, racially inferior groups, and socialists. Ignatius Donnelly's dystopic novel *Caesar's Column* (1892)[20] predicted a twentieth-century New York City convulsed by class warfare between capitalist masters and oppressed workers. Jacob Riis sympathetically but anxiously portrayed *How the Other Half Lives* in 1890. Technological advances in flash photography and printing presses enabled newspapers to provide vivid portraits of Riis's subjects in their urban slums.

Republican Economic Policy

The Republican Party honored its Federalist-Whig antecedents by updating the fiscal policies that Alexander Hamilton had anticipated in his "Report on the Public Credit" (1790), report on the national bank (1791), and "Report on Manufactures" (1791), as well as the economic program of Henry Clay's American System. Both public and private finance were transformed by the war and its aftermath. Fiscal and monetary policies restructured the nation's credit and its money supply. Congress financed the war in three ways. It levied a variety of taxes, including excise, manufacturers', inheritance, and sales taxes, capped by an income tax (a flat-rate 3% tax on incomes over $800). It issued $450 million in paper money ("greenbacks"). Most important of all, it borrowed: almost $3 billion by 1865. The now-forgotten Section 4 of the Fourteenth Amendment confirmed the national war debt and repudiated the Confederate debt, a measure crucial to securing the economic components of Reconstruction. Thanks to the National Bank Act of 1865, the nation for the first time enjoyed a reliable national currency. A prohibitive 10 percent tax on state banknotes retired that circulating medium. These measures facilitated national commerce.

After the war, Republicans pursued a deflationary monetary policy, demonetizing silver and resisting Democrats' demands for payment of the national debt in greenbacks. This hard-money policy had the effect of reducing prices for agricultural produce and the value of farmland. Both farm foreclosures and tenancy rose in the Midwest and the South. Hard money also depressed factory workers' wages. At the same time, the Republicans refunded the national debt, thereby concentrating capital in the hands of wealthy investors, as Hamilton's funding program had done earlier.

These monetary and fiscal measures redistributed wealth upward and regionally, out of poorer and debtor classes, especially in the South and West, and into the coffers of eastern creditors and financiers. The resulting maldistribution of wealth at the turn of the twentieth century achieved extremes of inequality not attained again until the 1980s. Drawing on a contemporary estimate, Nell Painter writes that "the wealthiest 1 percent of families in 1890 owned 51 percent of the real and personal property; the 44 percent of families at the bottom owned only 1.2 percent of all the property. Together, the wealthy and well-to-do (12 percent of families) owned 86 percent of the wealth. The poorer and middle classes, who represented 88 percent of families, owned 14 percent of the wealth."[21]

The investor-beneficiaries of the Republicans' neo-Hamiltonian program plowed the sums they amassed into the railroads, factories, mines, and infrastructure of industrializing America, as well as into the conspicuous consumption that provided the cultural definition of the era. The national debt was serviced by revenues from the tariff (all other taxes having expired by 1872), draining the South and West for the benefit of the East, a point not lost on outraged southern and western Democrats who saw themselves once again victimized by national economic policy. Stock and bond markets flourished.

The federal government buoyed public credit by "economic Reconstruction," a continuation of such wartime policies as the Homestead Acts, land grants to subsidize railroad building, and the 1862 Morrill Land Grant College Act. Republicans thus found nearly cost-free ways to finance public works and infrastructure. The Contract Labor Act of 1864 authorized importation of thousands of Chinese men whose labor contribution was vital to the European "conquest" of the West.

Republican policy subordinated the southern regional economy, already devastated by war, to national economic policies, including the tariff and nationally imposed preferences for northern industry, such as the Pittsburgh basing-point system for steel pricing. In the southern states, "Redeemer" regimes overthrew Unionist governments through terror, racist violence, and voter intimidation by the Ku Klux Klan and similar night-riding organizations. Once back in power, Bourbon Democrats reinstated the South's tragic, perennial policy of exploiting its land and its peoples, both white and black, for the benefit of distant investors. As a result, southern taxes and public services, including education, lagged the rest of the nation, while the imposition of Jim Crow reinforced economic policies that assured stunted economic development for the region.

A dark cloud moved in over the national economy in 1873 and hovered there for two decades in what is sometimes called "the Great Depression of the nineteenth century." During the long-wave depression that ran from the investment banking crash of 1873 through the climactic year of 1896, prices steadily declined, and economic downturns recurred with dismaying regularity each decade. Capitalism's boom-bust cycle seemed sharper and more destructive. Banks failed at each decennial recession, and by the end of the decade almost a third of American railroad mileage was owned by lines in judicial receivership. The entire economy seemed manic.

Throughout this unusually long trough in the nineteenth-century business cycle, investment bankers like the house of J. P. Morgan extended their control of utilities, railroads, and manufacturing industries by placing their representatives on boards of directors as part of financing arrangements. Investment bankers perfected interlocking control devices like trusts and pools to cartelize much of American industry. Financiers and investors experimented with innovative legal devices adapted from the law of trusts to integrate and control multiple firms.

The corporation emerged in this era as the dominant form of large-scale capital investment, for better[22] or worse.[23] The legal device of the corporation permitted investors to amass capital, to centralize control of manufacturing enterprises, and to pursue efficiency by controlling production activities within the firm, rather than by contracting for those productive resources in the market.[24] While this benefited investors and created a new managerial class of corporate officers,[25] it separated ownership (by shareholders) from control (by corporate board and officers),[26] and encouraged monopolistic or anticompetitive corporate strategies and rent-seeking by corporate management. Justice Louis D. Brandeis later called these effects "the evils attendant upon the free and unrestricted use of the corporate mechanism."[27]

Labor and the Age of Anxiety

The final third of the nineteenth century seemed to many who lived through it to be an unending Age of Anxiety,[28] a nightmare era, anything but *la belle époque* of modern nostalgia.

Employers, whether small firms or large integrated corporate enterprises, reacted to the depression of 1873–1896 predictably. In times of contraction, they slashed wages, laid off employees, and shuttered plants. They tried to keep prices up by eliminating competition among themselves through different kinds of anticompetitive behavior, including cartelization. They also organized themselves in trade and employers' associations. Working people responded with their own efforts at organization.[29] Experiencing the loss of individual opportunity, they turned to collective action. But labor unions toiled in a demimonde of legitimacy.[30]

Early American workers' associations carried forward English guild traditions, including self-governance and regulation of members. Antebellum workers had a highly developed sense of their place in the Republic. Personal independence, pride of craft, a sense of community as solidarity with others of the "producer" classes, democratic self-government, and civic equality among all people (with racial and ethnic exceptions) defined the outlook of what we now call "labor republicanism."[31] Political activism, coupled with a growing sense of class differentiation among masters, journeymen, and apprentices, as well as artisans' hostility to monopoly and privilege, guided labor's antebellum civic involvements. Labor began to see the law as antagonistic to its interests. "The social, civil, and intellectual condition of the laboring classes of these United States," declared the a writer in the *National Trades*

Union in 1834, was threatened by "the erroneous customs, usages, and laws of society," which produced "the most unequal and unjustifiable distribution of the wealth of society in the hands of a few individuals."[32]

For much of the nineteenth century, the judicially defined conspiracy doctrine served as a major impediment to labor organization.[33] Judges deployed it in an effort to crush the formation of labor unions throughout what labor historians call the first moment of unionization, the 1830s,[34] when artisans began to develop the concept and vocabulary of class consciousness. Workers' attempts to organize labor associations and to unite in an effort to raise wages, restrict hours, or exclude unqualified workers ran up against old English common law traditions of hostility to conspiracies and to restraints on trade. The earliest American labor litigation, the Philadelphia and New York *Cordwainers' Cases* of 1806 and 1809 respectively, held journeymen's associations to be illegal attempts at coercing masters and nonmembers to the detriment of the public welfare and in restraint of trade.[35] These cases began a process that continued throughout the nineteenth century in which law privileged employers in their struggles with labor, but they did also begin the slow and painful emergence of authentically free labor from the chrysallis of their legal status under earlier labor law.[36]

In the 1835 decision of *People v. Fisher*,[37] New York's highest court criminalized the efforts of striking bootmakers to penalize scabbing. Chief Justice John Savage applied a statute prohibiting conspiracies to injure "trade or commerce" to declare workers' strike tactics illegal. Savage justified this reaffirmation of the *Cordwainers* doctrine by a discourse on the laws of economics (not the laws of New York, for there was little precedent supporting his position). "It is important to the best interests of society," he proclaimed, "that the price of labor be left to regulate itself, or rather be limited by the demand for it." Both private intrusions in the free market by labor unions and public involvement by governmental regulation were an "officious and improper interference" with economic freedom. He and judges who thought as he did assumed that the legal order hostile to unions was natural and just, not constructed and contingent.

Fisher and other cases involving organized labor before the Civil War constructed a paradigm of the employment relationship based on dominance and subordination. Judges went to lengths to protect the employers' property rights, conceived in ever broadening terms as including not only the workplace but the business itself. Thus judges eventually came to think that strikes deprived employers of property rights, disrupted existing contractual relationships, inhibited new ones, and increased the price of goods and services. In the legal construction of the workplace, employer-capitalists were masters, employees servants. In the North, labor was free, in the limited sense that courts would not impose criminal sanctions or decree specific performance to compel employees to labor.[38] But the legally sanctioned exploitation and inequality produced by labor law left that freedom illusory for most workers.

As real wages fell by a third during the Civil War, workers organized into city central unions, national trade unions (including the powerful railway brotherhoods), producers' cooperatives, and abortive national labor federations like the Knights of St. Crispin and the National Labor Union. These efforts evaporated with the onset of the 1873 depression. The early federations were replaced by the Knights of Labor,[39] a national industrial union that welcomed unskilled workers, women, and blacks (but not Chinese).[40] The nation was convulsed by widespread strikes, accompanied by scores of deaths, arson, and insurrection in some of the nation's major cities, first in 1877,[41] then again in 1886.[42] In the general railroad strike of 1877,[43] workers fought local militia to a standoff, forcing President Rutherford B. Hayes to send federal troops to Martinsburg, West Virginia, and Pittsburgh to reopen lines and impose order.

At the same time, radical European revolutionary parties, organizers, and ideas were making their way to American shores, led by the move of the First International's headquarters to New York in 1872. Marxian Socialists vied with Bakuninite anarchists in creating the Workingmen's Party (1877). The events of the Paris Commune of 1870–1871 convinced many Americans that communism, anarchism, socialism, syndicalism or related theories posed an actual threat to social order.[44] (Marx may as well have had them in mind when he wrote of the Commune: "[T]he old world writhed in convulsions of rage at the sight of the Red Flag, the symbol of the Republic of Labour, floating over the Hotel de Ville.")[45] Judges, including Stephen J. Field of the Supreme Court, followed the news of the siege of Paris in 1870, and the establishment of a communist government in the city, with fascinated horror. Their anxieties were not based on a complete delusion: workers in the St. Louis general strike of 1877 proclaimed a "genuine Commune" for governance of the city.[46]

A wave of anticommunist hysteria seemed to wash over the middle classes in the 1880s. "The spirit of communism is abroad," proclaimed Chief Justice Thomas Durfee of the Rhode Island Supreme Court in 1877.[47] Cleveland newspapers denounced striking Polish steelworkers as "Communistic scoundrels [who] have hoisted the red flag of Agrarianism, Nihilism and Socialism [and who] revel in robberies, bloodshed and arson."[48] Alien socialist radicals would lay "violent hands . . . on the throat of the social organism in attempts to stop the course of production," warned the economist Francis Amasa Walker, threatening "great cities . . . with darkness, riot, and pillage."[49] A communist state would mean that "tramping incendiaries [would] apply the torch to the edifice of American society, and cut the throats of all who resist."[50] Such rhetoric, and the social visions it embodied, inevitably seeped into the work of jurists. A New York judge sentencing striking workers convicted of extortion through boycotting noted that some of the defendants were aliens. "Socialistic crimes as [yours] are gross breaches of national hospitality. . . . [Y]ou and others of your union [have let down] a country that welcomed you and offered equal opportunity with its own native-born citizens. Common gratitude should have prevented you from outraging public opinion, and using here those methods of a socialistic character which you brought with you from abroad."[51]

In an 1888 commencement address at the University of Iowa, Justice Samuel F. Miller cautioned the graduates that "anarchists, nihilists, socialists or communists" seek "abolition of the right of property" and "redistribution of all the existing accumulations of wealth." He noted uneasily that in large American cities, "the palaces of the rich are surrounded by the hovels of the poor; the glaring lights of gas and electric lamps illuminating the wealthy in their hours of hilarity and festivity shine down upon the tenements of the lowly and the poverty stricken." In such circumstances, the poor would support communistic schemes of redistribution. European leftists "come here and form clubs and associations; they meet at night and in secluded places; they get together large quantities of deadly weapons; they drill and prepare themselves for organized warfare; they stimulate riots and invasions of the public peace; they glory in strikes."[52] In thirty years, and then thirty years again after that, Americans would be treated to identical lurid alarms in successive Red Scares.

The recurrent assassinations and attempts on princes, czars, emperors, kings, dukes et al.,[53] culminated in the killing of Archduke Franz Ferdinand and his wife at Sarajevo in 1914 and the conflagration that it triggered. This radical violence seemed to have its parallel in America as two Russian anarchists, Alexander Berkman and Emma Goldman, nearly succeeded in an attempt on Carnegie Steel's general manager, Henry Frick, in 1892. In response, several states enacted criminal-syndicalism statutes, making advocacy of revolutionary violence a felony. The middle classes were gripped by a fear of revolutionary labor radicalism comparable to the anxiety over terrorism and street crime a century later.

The eight-hour day was the focus of the general strike of 1886, precipitating what people of the time called "the Great Upheaval." Four hundred thousand workers went out on strike. Unions expanded the tactic of the boycott, scoring successes among sympathetic city populations. In the minds of America's middle classes, the Haymarket Massacre of 1886 and the ensuing judicial lynching of four anarchists fixed the image of the radical alien bomb-thrower on the labor movement.[54] In the same crisis year of 1886, trade unions formed the American Federation of Labor, which under the leadership of Samuel Gompers adopted the self-serving goals of business unionism and disavowed direct involvement in politics.

Both the trade unions and the industrial federations sought labor-protective legislation, in addition to the eight-hour day.[55] These included school attendance laws and restriction of child labor, wages-and-hours protection for women workers, factory inspection, curtailment of sweatshops, workers' compensation, mandatory arbitration of labor disputes, hours legislation for male workers, regulation of dangerous industries, and immigration restriction.

Employers did not greet labor's offensive passively. They too organized, eventually forming the National Association of Manufacturers. They fought unions and organizing drives with legal process and violence. Employers hired armed mercenaries leased by the Pinkerton Detective Agency; set up company unions; circulated blacklists of union organizers; fired union members and imposed the yellow-dog contract. A sympathetic bar denounced workers, their unions, and organized labor's tactics: "[S]trikes as now managed are notoriously lawless, reckless and dangerous conspiracies against the public peace and safety. They mean terror, incendiarism, violence, and bloodshed, and with these characteristics the law should deal, if patiently, yet decisively. . . . A mob of strikers is entitled to no more leniency than a mob of lynchers or common ruffians."[56]

In the courts, the conspiracy doctrine had weakened since 1842 when Chief Justice Shaw rejected the doctrine of *per se* criminality of labor organization in *Commonwealth v. Hunt*.[57] So lawyers representing employers perfected the labor injunction, which a sympathetic judge called a "Gatling gun on paper" when he issued it;[58] cultivated sympathetic state and federal attorneys and judges, procuring convictions for trespass, public nuisance, affray, and other common law offenses as stop-gaps until they could get legislation tailored to the new conditions; and propagandized tirelessly in the elite media, such as the *North American Review*, to promote their view of the labor struggle. Justice Holmes drew the connection between middle-class fears and legal development: "[W]hen twenty years ago [he was speaking in 1913] a vague terror went over the earth and the word socialism began to be heard, I thought and still think that fear was translated into doctrines that had no proper place in the Constitution or the common law."[59]

The Great Upheaval proved to be a run-up to the stunning labor violence of the 1890s. In 1892, seven men died in the Homestead Massacre at a Carnegie Steel plant near Pittsburgh.[60] In that clash, Andrew Carnegie and his lieutenant Henry C. Frick busted the union so completely that the steel industry was not unionized until the late 1930s. Judges sympathetic to management, such as Chief Justice Edward M. Paxson of the Pennsylvania Supreme Court, attempted to have the strike organizers indicted for treason against the state.[61] In that same year, martial law and federal troops broke a strike at the Coeur d'Alene silver mines in Idaho.

After a market panic intensified the depression in 1893, three million Americans lost their jobs. Coxey's "army" of the unemployed walked across the nation to demand that the federal government increase public spending to provide relief for jobless workers.[62] The newly formed United Mine Workers brought its men out in the bituminous coal fields that summer. A strike against the Pullman Palace Car company, reinforced by boycotts and sympathetic strikes, brought the Chicago hub of the American railway network to a standstill. United States attorney general Richard Olney and President Grover Cleveland responded by deploying federal marshals, the regular army, and labor injunctions to break the strike and the union.

This labor violence confirmed and intensified middle-class anxieties. Because many labor radicals, like the Haymarket defendants and Frick's would-be assassins, were of European birth, some Americans sought emotional refuge in nativism and xenophobia, fearing Europe's social turmoil was about to wash up on American shores. They scapegoated aliens and nonwhites for the social disintegration that they thought they saw all around them. The anti-Catholic American Protective Association, formed in 1887, demanded a cutoff of all immigration. Others, including many labor leaders, called on Congress to end Asian immigration, punctuating their demands with occasional vigilante violence like the San Francisco "Sandlot Riots" of 1877. Congress complied by restricting Chinese immigration in 1882, then excluding Chinese entirely in 1902.

Racism was the sibling of xenophobia. By 1890, northern whites washed their hands of any obligation to protect freedpeople in the South from terrorism. Lynchings peaked in the 1890s; in 1892 alone, whites killed 160 black people, sometimes after torture, sometimes with much of the white community as participants or onlookers. By 1950, whites had lynched some 4,000 blacks. Whites imposed a regime of Jim Crow on southern society, weakly imitated in the northern and western states, an all-pervasive practice of deliberate racial degradation. Segregation and legal oppression enforced by the legal system created a system of servitude that effectively replaced slavery as a system of race control and enforced labor. Comparable discrimination against Asians and Mexicans in the Chinatowns and barrios of the western states mirrored the social degradation and economic exploitation of blacks in the South.

By the early twentieth century, these racial and nativist policies were rationalized by elaborate theories of scientific racism. Building on the racial thought of Thomas Jefferson, Josiah Nott, and John H. Van Evrie among the Americans, and Arthur de Gobineau and Houston Chamberlain among the Europeans, American amateurs at the turn of the century developed the pseudosciences of eugenics and racial classification. Madison Grant and Henry P. Fairchild compiled influential proofs of Nordic superiority and the inferiority of all races they consigned below the Aryan in their racial hierarchies. Josiah Strong, Albert Beveridge, and even Theodore Roosevelt popularized ideas of nonwhite inferiority.

This witches' brew of threatening social change and destabilizing economic development had political repercussions. The Wormley Compromise of 1876 was a pivotal moment in national policy. It gave the Republicans control of the White House and direction of national economic policy, for as long as they could hold onto congressional majorities. In return, the Democrats got a free hand to implement a policy of reaction in the South.[63] Republicans reviewed their mixed heritage of Whig economic policy and moderate antislavery and concluded the two were incompatible. Framing the choice in that way, it was never a contest: with scarcely a shrug, Republicans abandoned the freedpeople of the South to their fate, freeing themselves to pursue a policy of economic development unencumbered by moral baggage.

The result has been called "the Great Barbecue": mindlessly high tariffs, the economic integration of the South into the national economy, federal support for industrialization and the national market, a free hand for finance capitalists to accumulate capital, congressional dominance of policy making throughout a generation of weak Republican presidents. The Democrats for their part rebuilt their national influence by reaffirming positions established since the times of Jefferson and Jackson: local white control of all matters affecting black Americans, hostility to the tariff, hospitality to European immigrants.

Reform Political Movements

Reformers were revolted by the politics of the Gilded Age, and they tried to restore what they imagined to be the purity of the early republic. Fastidious Mugwumps of the 1880s, derided as "goo-goos" (good government) by their opponents, espoused middle-class, moderate, and moralistic reforms to the structure of government, hoping to improve efficiency and eliminate spoils politics.[64] Their vision embraced more than civil service reform, however. They were among the earliest advocates of regulation and administrative expertise, and they helped create the regulatory apparatus of the modern administrative state.[65]

In that same decade, the Populists began to coalesce as a movement out of farmers' cooperative efforts in the Farmers Alliances and from the remains of the Greenback-Labor Party, which had declined since its peak in 1880. The Populists were that rarest of American political phenomena: an authentically radical movement that began at the grass roots and flourished on the basis of wide popular support.[66] The People's Party formed out of an uneasy coalition of three farmers' groups trying to create cooperative economic structures: southern whites, southern blacks, and middlewesterners.[67] They realized that they could achieve their broader goals only through political action, fusion among themselves across racial lines, and cooperation with urban industrial labor. To everyone's surprise, they achieved this cooperation in a mere two years, uniting the farm groups at the Ocala convention of 1890, then emerging as a national third party running candidates on the radical program of the St. Louis platform in 1892.

In this manifesto, the Populists proffered a lurid vision of *fin-de-siècle* America that even their conservative enemies could endorse:

> [W]e meet in the midst of a nation brought to the verge of moral, political, and material ruin. Corruption dominates the ballot-box, the Legislatures, the Congress, and touches even the ermine of the bench. The people are demoralized . . . business prostrated. . . . A vast conspiracy against mankind has been organized on two continents [the other being Europe], and it is rapidly taking possession of the world. If not met and overthrown at once it forebodes terrible social convulsions, the destruction of civilization, or the establishment of an absolute despotism.[68]

When the Depression of 1893 struck the next year, Populist rhetoric seemed if anything an understated description of reality.

But the People's Party offered a different diagnosis of the nation's ills than might be heard at contemporary bar association meetings:

> [L]abor [is] impoverished, and the land concentrating in the hands of capitalists. The urban workmen are denied the right to organize for self-protection, imported pauperized labor beats down their wages, a hireling standing army, unrecognized by our laws, is established to shoot them down. . . . The fruits of the toil of millions are boldly stolen to build up colossal fortunes for a few . . . and the possessors of these, in turn, despise the Republic and endanger liberty. . . . [Republicans and Democrats] propose to drown the outcries of a plundered people with the uproar of a sham battle over the tariff, so that capitalists, corporations, national banks, rings, trusts, watered stock, the demonetization of silver and the oppressions of the usurers may be lost sight of. They propose to sacrifice our homes, lives, and children on the altar of mammon.

And so on and on. Even in an era of bloody-shirt rhetoric, this was heady stuff. Populists and many other Americans received it as literal truth.

The Populist vision touched off a spasm of reaction from middle-class America. Terrified that labor's demands might have found an effective political voice, middle-class Americans, and a large segment of the working classes as well, united behind Republican candidate William McKinley in the climacteric 1896 election. The voters rejected both the Democratic-Populist fusion candidate William Jennings Bryan and whatever element of Populism was left in the campaign — but only in the short term.

Many of the specific planks demanded by the Populists later became law: a graduated income tax, postal savings, the secret ballot, immigration restriction, an eight-hour workday for some occupations, initiative and referendum (in some western states), direct election of United States senators. The Populist movement itself, traduced by its cowbird, free silver, turned rancid and vanished. Some of its leaders, like Tom Watson, turned on their black allies with a regressive racism; others, like Bryan, espoused religious fundamentalism. After Populism's defeat in 1896, capitalism reigned unchallenged.

Meanwhile, different congeries of reform movements developed in the states, grew into a loose national coalition, and extended their influence pervasively through American life. The term "Progressivism" suggests more unity and cohesion than ever characterized the congeries of reforms. Originating at the state level,[69] Progressivism never developed the cohesion that would enable it to function as a third party at the national level (though the Progressive Party candidate Robert M. La Follette did make a respectable showing in the 1924 presidential election). Instead, Progressivism influenced the thought of many political leaders and lawyers, preeminent among them Louis D. Brandeis. Like Protestantism, its lack of a monolithic organization or ideology enabled it to sprawl across the ideological spectrum, claiming as adherents both democratic reformers like Brandeis and conservatives like Elihu Root. Progressives depended on the new professions like economics and social work for information and analysis, and on sympathetic journalists for publicity.[70]

Legal Classicism: Foundations

Fear of disorder and social disintegration constituted the matrix of legal classicism in its triumphant phase from 1873 to 1905.[71] Anxiety drove lawyers to articulate a comprehensive vision of law — legal classicism — in a determined, even desperate, attempt to preserve social order, individual liberty, and republican government.

The Civil War was a trauma for the bench and bar. Like other northerners, lawyers in the Union states regarded secession and what the North officially termed "the War of the Rebellion" as a threat to law and order, to social stability and civilized society, and as an eruption of anarchy.[72] Their fears were not eased as they pondered the problems of Reconstruction, when the war's lawlessness seemed to extend indefinitely into the peace. Pogroms against freedpeople in Memphis and New Orleans in 1866 proved that the spirit of rebellion was alive and lethal. Night-riding and the incessant intimidation of Freedmen's Bureau officers, army personnel, Unionists, and Republicans throughout the South demonstrated that whites could be the objects of terror as well as blacks. Then, as the North was abandoning Reconstruction and the freedpeople in the political settlement of 1876, the nationwide railroad strike of the next year threatened to paralyze national commerce, transferring violence related to race to the arena of labor relations.

One symptom of diminished respect for law, in the eyes of the Justices of the Supreme Court, was the widespread inclination by states and municipalities to shrug off their debt obligations.[73] In a group of cases that constituted an early microcosm of classicism's response to perceived disorder, the Supreme Court rebuked those states and municipalities that tried to repudiate their debt obligations, and recalled them to their sense of public honor.[74] In the best known of these, *Gelpcke v. Dubuque* (1863)[75], the Supreme Court chastised a state supreme court for upholding the validity of repudiating legislation. Dubuque had issued bonds to invest in railroad stock, then sought to repudiate them on the grounds that the obligation exceeded the state's constitutional debt ceiling. When the Iowa Supreme Court sustained this position, Justice Noah Swayne consigned its holding to "unenviable solitude and notoriety," and intoned: "[W]e shall never immolate truth, justice, and the law, because a State tribunal has erected the altar and decreed the sacrifice."

In the same year as *Gelpcke*, John Norton Pomeroy brought out his influential *Introduction to Municipal Law* in an effort to inculcate the fundamental principles of Anglo-American liberty in the American people, reiterating the principles that protect life, liberty, and personal security.[76] John F. Dillon's treatise on state and local government[77] was instinct with a scrupulous regard for the binding obligation of railroad aid bonds, unless they were *ultra vires* under state constitututional law.

The municipal bond cases were the first clear instance of classicism's reaction to threats to the legal order. They also marked the earliest expansion of the federal courts' power to identify and enforce a general federal common law, a power originally claimed by Justice Story in *Swift v. Tyson* (1842).[78] Such an enlargement of federal judicial power was a precondition for realizing classicism's potential.

The municipal bond cases prefigured classicism's basic paradigm: the legal elite perceived signs of social disintegration and a threat to existing legal rights (bondholders' expectation of interest and repayment of the principal of their investments). Reactively, they did what they could to suppress policy initiatives of local and state governments. Moral obligation coincided, in judges' eyes, with sound public policy: governments had to honor debt obligations in order to keep investment resources open. The cases' result had a wealth-redistributing effect, as farmers and other taxpayers in the western states were forced to bear the financial burden of disappointed investment hopes, even though defaulting railroads failed to provide the infrastructures the taxpayers had underwritten.

Philosophical Assumptions

Jurists of the classical era were, like American lawyers of any period, notoriously indifferent to philosophical inquiry. Thus, attributing a philosophical outlook to them seems both pretentious and misleading, if it suggests that their reasoning and beliefs were grounded in disciplined abstract inquiry. Nevertheless, in their writings we can detect lawyers' assumptions about reality, truth, justice, and human destiny. That they did not self-consciously adopt or review these assumptions is irrelevant. Lawyers were all the more captive of their philosophical outlook for being unaware that they had one.

The term "classical," when used to describe the dominant mode of adjudication in the late nineteenth century, suggests characteristics of music, architecture, and art of the "classical" period a century earlier: balanced, harmonious, composed, bounded, rational, symmetrical, Appollonian in spirit. (The analogy extends to the Progressive and realist rejection of formalism as well, which resembled romanticism in its Dionysian spirit, impatient of forms and formulas.)

Children of their era, classicist lawyers believed not just in the possibility but in the reality of objective truth, based on universal laws and principles, which could be found by human reason. People could attain certainty in their pursuit of truth and justice. The American philosopher Richard Bernstein has recently described the urgent need for certainty that objectivism assuaged in its "quest for some fixed point, some stable rock upon which we can secure our lives against the vicissitudes that constantly threaten us. The specter that hovers in the background of this journey is not just radical epistemological skepticism but the dread of madness and chaos where nothing is fixed." The only alternative to chaos for the objectivist lawyers of the late nineteenth century was their belief in "some fixed, permanent constraints to which we can appeal and which are secure and stable."[79] Truth therefore had to be a reality independent of human volition: it existed outside human activity and thus could be a criterion of human approximations toward it.

The classical lawyers were, in an elementary way, philosophical idealists in the sense that Holmes ascribed to Christopher C. Langdell: "If Mr. Langdell could be suspected of ever having troubled himself about Hegel, we might call him a Hegelian in disguise, so entirely is he interested in the formal connection of things, or logic, as distinguished from the feelings which make the content of logic, and which have actually shaped the substance of the law." (It was this observation that provided the platform from which Holmes launched his best-known aphorism: "The life of the law has not been logic: it has been experience.")[80]

Lawyers' reasoning proceeded by an uncluttered, reductionist Aristotelian logic, preferring where possible to confine reality to binary alternatives and antinomies: fact *or* law, politics *or* law, tax *or* expropriation, manufacturing *or* commerce, federal *or* state. Not for them the complexities of Russell, Whitehead, Wittgenstein, or Quine. This lent a rigidity to their thought that served them poorly when their premises came under attack. But at the same time, they were blessedly free of epistemological angst or even of doubt.

Classical method emphasized deduction and logic, rejecting empirical scientific or social science research. Such an approach led judges to ignore inconvenient facts in a burlesque of the modern aphorism, "My mind's made up; don't confuse me with the facts." The best-known example is Justice Rufus Peckham's pontifical utterance dismissing proffered medical evidence in the *Lochner* case: "We do not believe in the soundness of the views which uphold this law."[81] In place of disciplined factual enquiry, judges would substitute their own uninformed musings about social reality, as Peckham did about the occupation of a baker.

Language, especially of text and precedent, took on a life of its own. In vain did Holmes exhort contemporary judges: "We must think things, not words."[82] In a method as heavily dependent on logic and as indifferent to social reality as classicism, words held sway, providing verbal formulas that were endlessly manipulable by judges. Once match text to principle, and results followed with certainty and predictability.

Lawyers were much taken with mathematical models, though they conceded that legal reasoning could not produce the precision or certainty of mathematical demonstration. Their geometry was simply Euclidean, but it provided them with a persuasive metaphor for legal reasoning, and one that reassured them of the validity of their thought.[83] The law's "decisions come like the answer to an algebraic problem, without partiality."[84] Their image of the physical world was Newtonian, a universe governed by underlying laws of ubiquitous validity, expressible mathematically, discoverable by reasoned investigation. Their innocent faith in the certitudes of science as they understood it is revealed in a comparison one of them made: "To characterize [John Marshall's] reasoning as sophistry is childish. A school boy might as well challenge a proposition of Euclid, or attempt to ridicule the *Principia* of Newton."[85] The balance and harmony of creation derived ultimately from a divine hand. Human laws therefore had to be complementary to divine laws. None of the lawyers noted in this study displayed any awareness that their Newtonian certainties were being subverted by Darwin, Freud, and Rutherford.

Economic and Social Outlook

Classical lawyers' economic predispositions were of a piece with their science. They were no more systematic in economic investigation than they were in philosophical inquiry, so we can only infer their beliefs from occasional comments in oral arguments and speeches. Elite lawyers' sophistication in economics had not progressed beyond platitudes derived from Adam Smith's *Wealth of Nations* (1776). The free market was their *summum bonum*, so government regulation was suspect. They believed that the market impersonally set the natural and just price for labor and capital. Lawyers assumed that if the market was not distorted by legislative meddling or private anticompetitive collusion, it would reward inputs according to their objective value. Only free competitive struggle for advantage could provide a reliable pricing mechanism. Combinations to raise prices, especially union activity by working people, deranged this precious mechanism. Monopolies and other anticompetitive tendencies also threatened the beneficent workings of the market. (This did not prevent the elite bar from representing monopolistic and oligopolistic enterprises as clients, however.)

The elite bar drew on indistinctly understood Rousseauist or Lockean images of a state of nature existing before government began to intervene in economic affairs. In this fantasy, the status quo was neutral, being based on the natural conditions of people and environment. State interference only disturbed that primordial condition of natural justice. Lawyers were incapable of imagining that the state has always intervened in the economic relations among human actors, usually in support of existing distributions of wealth and power. The status quo at any given time was itself a product of antecedent state action, and its preservation amounted only to further use of state force to protect what the state, not nature, had already formed.

When lawyers extolled equality, it was strictly equality of opportunity, which for them meant the opportunity to compete, with no artificial advantages. Equality of results was as reprehensible to them as it had earlier been to Chancellor Kent. Socialism was a melancholy example of humanity's episodic propensity to collective madness, and yet another confirmation of the need to constrain democratic majorities on a short leash. They would not have seen anything funny in Anatole France's contemporary send-up of their attitude, which hailed "the majestic equality of the laws, which forbid the rich as well as the poor to sleep under bridges, to beg in the streets, and to steal bread."[86]

In 1888, James Bryce commented on the grip that classical liberal economics had on the American mind: "so far as there can be said to be any theory on the subject in a land which gets on without theories, *laissez aller* is the orthodox and accepted doctrine in the sphere both of Federal and State legislation."[87] (He noted, however, that Americans disregarded this theory in practice, preferring extensive government intervention in the economy.) To whatever extent that a Spencerian outlook of laissez-faire can be said to have influenced American legal thought, it was being undercut by technology, the complexity of social organization, bureaucratization, modernism, the rise of the large corporation, and the collectivism of large enterprise. Its vulgarized blend of natural law, the Calvinist ethic, preference for a weak state, and fixation on competition in the natural world was rapidly proving ill suited to the needs of modern society.

The classical lawyers' social outlook corresponded with their economic views. In an industrializing society, where social values were predicated on a free market economic outlook and an ethos of individualism, lawyers thought of society as composed of autonomous individuals having a natural right to their bodies and to the fruits of their labor. This principle was grounded in antebellum moral teaching. Francis Wayland, the nation's premier moral philosopher (and a classical economist to boot) had taught in his magisterial *Elements of Political Economy* (1837) that a "man's possessions are his talents, faculties, skill, and the wealth and reputation which these have enabled him to acquire; in other words, his industry and his capital. In order that industry be applied to capital with the greatest energy, it is necessary that every man be at liberty to use them both as he will; that is, that both of them be free."[88] This outlook was reinforced by the terrible human costs of the Civil War.

Wayland's moral principle, which was also a commonplace in classical economics, brought with it a corollary in political economy, expressed by the classical economist Arthur L. Perry: "[T]he legislature should give to capital and labor equal rights — no more . . . leav[ing] both to take care of themselves, subject only to the general laws relating to person and property." If the legislature were to prescribe maximum hours or minimum wages, it would be "an economic abomination." The "just and comprehensive rule" governing all labor relations was "[W]hen men exchange services with each other, each party is bound to look out for his own interest . . . and to make the best terms for himself which he can make."[89] Individuals must be able to contract with each other freely to exchange their services or goods. Such an outlook would necessarily be unfriendly toward any form of coercion imposed on these contracting relationships, except the supposedly "natural" one represented by the status quo. Law, as the old common law maxim had it, took the parties as it found them. "In a free government like ours," boasted a delegate to the 1853 Massachusetts constitutional convention, "employment is simply a contract between parties having equal rights. . . . In the eye of the law, they are both freemen."[90]

Social life no less than biological was driven by competition for the resources that enabled survival. The superior would vanquish the inferior; the losers would succumb and vanish. In the social world, this was no more cause for regret or moral censure than predation by carnivores in the oceans and forests. It was an inescapable part of the natural order of things, and it determined indifferently the fate of individuals and groups, especially racial and ethnic groups. Herbert Spencer, prophet of the era, cheerfully observed that "the poverty of the incapable, the distresses that come upon the improvident, the starvation of the idle, and the shouldering aside of the weak by the strong, which leave so many in shadows and in miseries, are the decrees of a large, far-seeing benevolence." "Under the natural order of things," he benignly went on, "society is constantly excreting its unhealthy, imbecile, slow, vacillating, faithless members," consigning "to early graves the children of diseased parents, [singling] out the low-spirited, the intemperate, and the debilitated."[91] Spencer and his disciple Sumner taught that poverty performed the socially useful function of culling the unfit, much as predators did in natural environments.[92]

But the outlook of Gilded Age lawyers was not nearly so upbeat as this realization of social and industrial freedom might suggest. Classical legal thought in the years between the Great Upheaval of 1886 and the turn of the century was infected with a morose pessimism that derived from anxieties about the approaching demise of Western Civilization.[93] Few of the men whose thoughts are represented here are known to have read Herbert Spencer[94] or William Graham Sumner,[95] but they moved to the measure of their thought.[96] They might have gladly embraced as their motto William Graham Sumner's aphorism: "Let it be understood that we cannot go outside of this alternative: liberty, inequality, survival of the fittest; not-liberty, equality, survival of the unfittest."[97]

In common with the social elites in America and England, lawyers lapsed into a gloomy fear that the growing proletariat, maddened by diverging extremes of wealth and poverty, would lash out in an expropriating frenzy to seize the accumulations of the rich.[98] In 1878, the historian Francis Parkman, unnerved by the general railroad strike of the year before, depicted an American society in which the middle classes were threatened on both sides by an "ignorant proletariat and a half-taught plutocracy." The proletariat posed the greater threat: "dangerous classes," "greedy and irresponsible crowds" constituted a "barbarism . . . ready to overwhelm us," if not by outright violence, then by democratic politics. "The dangerous classes are most numerous and strong, and the effects of flinging the suffrage to the mob are most disastrous."[99] In that same year, *The Public*, a New York financial paper, bewailed "Granger railroad laws, scaling of debts, Bland silver bills, convertible bond schemes, and war against banks and bondholders [which] are all merely phases of Communism in America."[100]

John F. Dillon, sometime president of the American Bar Association, echoed Parkman in a dire Malthusian prophecy, warning lawyers of "an overcrowded population pressing with augmenting force on the means of subsistence, with the hopeless separation of the rich and the poor into distinct, hostile, and incommunicable classes, without common interests and common sympathies, and with the growth of a proletariat armed with the ballot in one hand and a gun in the other."[101]

It may be, as Antonio Gramsci suggested, that the comfortable elites are incapable of understanding the lives of the poor: "[F]or a social elite the features of subordinate groups always display something innately barbaric and pathological."[102] At a minimum, elites bemoaned what they feared was their loss of dominance and mastery of the lower orders, made all the more threatening by the apparent organization of workers into unions and their growing influence in municipal and state government. Lawyers were not exempt from these class anxieties. Law was an antidote to manhood suffrage. Lawyers extolled the legal order as "the conservative power which has . . . held the safeguards of life and property secure amid this surging sea of popular suffrage."[103] Echoing Tocqueville, Chief Judge Thomas Durfee of the Rhode Island Supreme Court maintained that lawyers were "lovers of order, foes to innovation, followers of precedents, and so the natural counterpoise to popular excesses."[104]

Justice Stephen J. Field, commemorating the Supreme Court's centennial in 1890, explicitly linked his apocalyptic social vision with his judicial philosophy in a dire prediction:

> As population and wealth increases [*sic*]— as the inequalities in the conditions of men become more and more marked and disturbing — as the enormous aggregation of wealth possessed by some corporations excites uneasiness lest their power should become dominating in the legislatures of the country, and thus encroach upon the rights or crush out the business of individuals of small means — as population in some quarters presses upon the means of subsistence, and angry menaces against order find vent in loud denunciations — it becomes more and more the imperative duty of the [Supreme] court to enforce with a firm hand every guarantee of the Constitution.[105]

Later, scientific racism and its applied science offspring, eugenics, fused the struggles of class and race. At the Second International Congress of Eugenics (1921) held at the American Museum of Natural History and orchestrated by the two principal American scientific racists of the time, Madison Grant and Henry Fairfield Osborn, the French eugenicist G. V. de LaPouge warned that "a great movement has begun among the inferior races and classes, and this movement which has the air of being turned against the whites and against the rich, is turned against the superior intellectual element and against civilization itself. . . . The war of classes is indeed the war of races."[106]

Only the reality of this vision and the fear that it provoked can account for the superheated quality of lawyers' rhetoric during the last two decades of the nineteenth century. To cite a few of the most influential examples: Christopher Tiedeman's *Treatise on the Limitations of Police Power* (1886)[107] announced that "Socialism, Communism, and Anarchism are rampant throughout the civilized world. The State is called on to protect the weak against the shrewdness of the stronger, to determine what wages a workman shall receive for his labor, and how many hours daily he shall labor."

Justice David J. Brewer warned the New York State Bar Association that unions and democratic government threatened the rights of property and especially wealth. While democracy and unions were an ineradicable part of American life, they were cousins to "the black flag of anarchism, flaunting destruction to property, and, therefore relapse of society to barbarism" and "the red flag of socialism, inviting a redistribution of property . . . in order to secure the vaunted equality."[108] Brewer thought it inevitable that "the wealth of a community will be in the hands of a few," who are constantly in danger of being stripped of "the magnificence and luxuriousness" they enjoy by "the multitudes — the majority, with whom is the power." He foresaw the most likely course of this spoliation in "the improper use of labor organizations to destroy the freedom of the laborer" and in legislative regulation of fees of property subjected to public uses. Unions were trying to limit the number of apprentices, restrict the hours of labor, compel equal wages for all employees, and blockade employers' premises. If unions got away with such schemes, "the next step will be a direct effort on the part of the many to seize the property of the few."

Gilded Age lawyers, echoing the laissez-faire economist David A. Wells, equated taxation with confiscation, decrying "organized communism and destruction of property under the guise of taxation."[109] An eminent member of the Supreme Court bar, Joseph H. Choate, denounced the federal Income Tax Act of 1894 as "communistic in its purposes and tendencies, and . . . defended here upon principles as communistic, socialistic — what shall I call them — populistic as ever have been addressed to any political assembly in the world."[110] (He was criticizing arguments in favor of the statute's validity made by two quintessential conservatives who had preceded him, Richard Olney and James C. Carter.) Justice Stephen J. Field resonated with Choate's arguments: in his concurrence, he declaimed from the bench: "[W]here is the course of usurpation to end? The present assault upon capital is but the beginning. It will be but the stepping-stone to others, larger and more sweeping, till our political contests will become a war of the poor against the rich; a war constantly growing in intensity and bitterness."[111]

In his most important public address, "The Path of the Law" (1897), Holmes, then Chief Justice of the Supreme Judicial Court of Massachusetts, spoke candidly about these anxieties and their impact on the work of judges: "When socialism first began to be talked about, the comfortable classes of the community were a good deal frightened. I suspect that this fear has influenced judicial action both here and in England, yet it is certain that it is not a conscious factor in the decisions to which I refer."[112] Conscious, no; but a factor? Certainly.

In their more relaxed moments, the bar could entertain a more soothing vision of the future, derived from the progressive emphasis of the English constitutional historians William Stubbs, Edward A. Freeman, and Henry Maine, whose interpretations stressed an inevitable progress out of legal status relationships and unfreedom into individualism and liberty.[113] They also drew on the pre–Civil War intellectual antecedents of Republican Party policies toward labor. Abolitionists had attacked slavery on the grounds, among others, that every person has a right to his or her own labor and to the rewards for that labor. This evolved from being a negative critique of the political economy of the slave states into the positive Free Labor ideology of the Republican Party, which extolled the superiority of northern free labor as the realization of the American ideal of liberty.[114]

The theory of possessive individualism, as C. B. MacPherson has termed it,[115] posited that all persons had a property right in their bodies and in their labor: "[T]he individual was seen neither as a moral whole, nor as part of a larger social whole but as an owner of himself. . . . The human essence is freedom from dependence on the wills of others, and freedom is a function of possession [while] society consists of relations of exchange between proprietors." Given such assumptions, "political society becomes a calculated device for the protection of this property."

The Free Labor idea was not the invention of political philosophers or lawyers: antebellum workers themselves proclaimed it in their losing effort to preserve their independence. "Our labor is our property," proclaimed New York sailmakers in 1836, "and we have the inherent right to dispose of it in such parcels as any other species of property."[116] The National Trades Union in the previous year declared that "as the mechanic is not possessed of any other property than his labor, he has an undoubted right to dispose of it" as he pleases.[117]

Such working-class republicanism became transformed into something else altogether when judges insisted that workers could alienate their "property" rights in their own labor through contractual arrangements. Where all adults have a contractual capacity to bargain for the terms on which they will sell their labor, labor became a commodity to be traded on the open market, a defining characteristic of capitalism. Thus was the liberating vision of antislavery transformed, none too subtly, into an ideology that threw the individual worker onto an unregulated labor market dominated by powerful employers, who were in a position to dictate terms. It represented, in Boaventura de Sousa Santos's apt phrase, "the collapse of emancipation into regulation."[118]

Contractual liberty was the moral counterpart to the worker's right to keep what he or she earned; indeed, it was the precondition to that right. Thus the moral crusade against enslavement was linked to a defense of a free market economy. A regime of contract characterized the passage of society from feudal status relationships to individual freedom, mobility, and opportunity. The problem that arose, however, was that contract law itself, while enabling freedom, reinforced existing inequality.[119]

These background elements of their culture provided the classical lawyers with a coherent and persuasive social vision. Drawing on their republican (as well as Republican) heritage, classicist lawyers affirmed the centrality of the individual as the object of political and legal philosophy. The individual's liberty and property were threatened both by the power of the state and by different social groups. Protecting that liberty against redistributionist threats became the imperative duty of statecraft. Violent assaults on the security of property, such as robbery or burglary, could be dealt with by adequate military and police force and needed no special moral condemnation in a civilized society. It was in this period that states built militia armories in tactically strategic locations in American cities; created paramilitary state police forces; organized, equipped, and armed uniformed urban police forces. Lawless theft therefore was of little concern to classic jurists. The more troubling threat came from nonviolent expropriation of property.[120]

In addition to securing the individual's property, lawyers were concerned to protect everyone's right to contract, as an essential aspect of individual freedom. Contractual capacity became the defining characteristic of individuality, the means by which an individual organized personal economic affairs and pursued his or her own conception of self-interest. In this pursuit, all people had to be assured of an equality of opportunity, defined as freedom to own what property they could accumulate, and to contract for their labor or their property. Public affairs were founded on the theory of consent, private affairs on the basis of individual will.

Lawyers of the late nineteenth century could have boasted of a recent actual realization of this centrality of property and contract, but curiously they did not. The Civil Rights Act of 1866[121] marked the North's first explicit effort to define the legal meaning of freedom and its distinction from enslavement. In this statute, property and contractual capacity figured conspicuously as essential attributes of human freedom. Yet the classical jurists never claimed this achievement, one of the most magnificent in American historical experience and a clear experiential vindication of their political theories. They contented themselves with merely rhetorical, theoretical, and abstract disquisitions about liberty instead of pointing with pride at what they had actually achieved to establish the human freedom about which they rhapsodized endlessly. Why they chose to ignore their own noble accomplishment must be the subject of another book. Briefly, it was because of the pervasive racism that infected white American society in the Gilded Age and beyond. European Americans entertained growing doubts about whether African Americans could handle civil capacity or were worthy of it. In this attitude, the legal elite was not singular.

The Lawyers' Intellectual Milieu

Two developments occurred in American law after Story's time that destabilized the intellectual world of lawyers. First, the outpouring of reported cases that had troubled Story in the 1830s now reached flood levels. Lawyers were being overwhelmed by common law developments that they could not absorb. West Publishing Company's National Reporters, begun in 1879, which printed the appellate decisions of all the state supreme courts, plus its project for publishing all federal decisions in the *Supreme Court Reporter*, the *Federal Reporter*, the *Federal Supplement*, and (retrospectively) *Federal Cases*, realized Story's nightmare of an unmanageable mass of appellate opinions that no lawyer could read or systematize. Even legal treatises, helpful as they were, could not hope to keep up, no matter how diligent the writer. American lawyers and judges of the late nineteenth century found themselves in the predicament described by Gibbon that led to the compilation of the *Corpus Juris* in the sixth century:

> When Justinian ascended the throne, the reformation of the Roman jurisprudence was an arduous but indispensable task. In the space of ten centuries, the infinite variety of laws and legal opinions had filled many thousand volumes, which no fortune could purchase and no capacity could digest. Books could not easily be found, and the judges, poor in the midst of riches, were reduced to the exercise of their illiterate discretion.[122]

To make a bad situation worse, most American jurisdictions were abolishing common law pleading and the forms of action at common law in favor of code pleading, building on the success of New York's Field procedural code of 1848. The forms of action had lent common law development an innate if unthinking system. A lawyer who mastered the intricacies of *Chitty on Pleading* had acquired the program code of the common law in its procedural aspects. Deprived of that intellectual scaffolding for their litigation, lawyers now had to rethink the premises of substantive law every time they filed a complaint.

Lawyers desperately sought some way to systematize the law.[123] In this quest, they encountered a rival, and a most unlikely one at that: West itself. Into the crisis that it had contributed so much to bringing on, West stepped in with two ingenious solutions: the digests, comprised of the *Century* and *Decennial Digests*, and the key number system for organizing them.[124] Practicing lawyers now had, literally at hand, some devices for accessing and organizing common law decisions. But West's solutions did little to harmonize inconsistencies; indeed, to the extent that they enabled more thorough legal research, West's devices only amplified incompatibilities and contributed to the proliferation of inconsistent precedents. Something more was needed to organize unwieldy common law growth in the forty-plus American jurisdictions of 1900.

That something was the systematization afforded by legal science. It promised to do what West's gimmicks could not: it would cull out from the mounds of decisional rubbish the correct, valid, "right" opinions, based on the fundamental principles that underlay the common law.

Lawyers were rescued from the avalanche of reports by the revitalized legal science pioneered at the Harvard Law School. This legal science was expounded in a second generation of influential treatises that showcased classical legal thought. In the law schools, lawyer-scholars were indoctrinating the foundations of the American legal system. Their dogma was legal science, their vehicle the casebook, their tactic the Socratic method.

THE SCIENCE OF THE LAW (PHASE 2)

The legal science of the late nineteenth century differed from its predecessor of Story's time. As originally expounded by Blackstone,[125] early legal science presumed the existence of universal principles, resting on theological or moral foundations. From these principles, judges deduced and applied norms of human conduct. In contrast, modern legal science was inductive in its approach, viewing cases as sources of law, from which judges derived principles inductively. The legal scientist's responsibility was to arrange those principles into a system. The "scientific jurist," wrote Christopher G. Tiedeman (a prominent treatise writer and legal academic) does not resort to cases to determine what the law *is*, "but to discover, as the scientific investigator hopes by his experiment with the forces of nature, the fundamental principles underlying the concrete manifestations of their influence [i.e., cases]."[126]

Late-nineteenth-century American legal science was homegrown, but it resembled the more fully developed legal science of the Continent, which derived from Roman law.[127] Contemporary legal science in Germany differed in roots and erudition from its unsophisticated cousin in North America, due in large measure to the advantage continental law enjoyed of being able to draw on its Roman law antecedents and almost two millennia of its "scientific" development. German scholars, led by Karl Friedrich von Savigny, developed a systematized, historical science of the law (*Rechtswissenschaft*) that provided a model for American aspirations.[128] Some of Savigny's disciples, including Georg Friedrich Puchta and Bernhard Windscheid, produced an abstract, systematized body of law, the *Pandektenrecht*, the "law of the Pandects," based on Justinian's *Digest* (533 A.D.).[129] To the pandectists, as they were called, the sources of law, including statutes and custom, were naturally occurring phenomena that could be studied scientifically. Such analysis would yield principles that were arranged in a hierarchy of ever greater abstraction, generalization, and applicability. Classification and definition were essential to this system, giving it order and coherence. The legal scientist sought abstraction as the physicist sought mathematical expression of physical laws, but for different reasons.

The pandectists came to view their definitions as being in themselves expressions of truth. They assumed, rather than proved, the validity of their concepts (e.g., liberty of contract, a concept known to the civil law as well as the common). The legal scientists were indifferent to the emergent social sciences like economics, though they were much taken by comparative philology and tried to emulate its techniques as a model for their own work. They believed that justice was not a proper goal of their systematizing. The pandectists exemplified Alan Watson's controversial theory of legal development, in which law is made by a legal elite, largely cut off from its society, functioning under the rulers' benign indifference about substantive policy, developing law by borrowing and adaptation of precedent, whose highest goal is internal conformity of the system, rather than adaptation to society's needs.[130]

Critics like Jhering dismissed such an approach as *Begriffsjurisprudenz*, a "jurisprudence of concepts" (rather than of, say, human experience or the ideals of justice and morality). Legal science nevertheless held sway longer in Europe than it did in the New World. It produced the globally influential German Civil Code of 1896, parent of numerous other codes, and imprinted a pattern on the teaching of civil law that persists today.

Legal science on both continents provided a suitable vehicle for realizing the values cherished by classical liberal economics: individual freedom and autonomy of the individual will. European and American legal scientists persuaded themselves that because their system was scientifically derived, it was ideologically neutral, an expression of universal human values.

Americans did not have Roman law as the foundation of their legal order, so they had to work out scientific systematization for themselves from scratch. As with the pandectists, definition and classification were for Americans the essential procedures of this systematization, recapitulating the early stages of the natural sciences, where scientists first concerned themselves with classification, categorization, and ordering (as Linnean classification was the beginning of modern biology or as the periodic table lay at the heart of nineteenth-century chemistry). In this connection, it was not a coincidence that America's foremost legal scientist, Christopher C. Langdell, was an amateur botanist.[131] For that matter, Roscoe Pound, in his own way a legal scientist though ultimately an opponent of Langdell's method, was a botanist in his first career. His classification of Nebraska phyla, *Phytogeography of Nebraska* (1898), remains authoritative today.[132] *Phytogeography* was a pioneering effort in the nascent science of ecology. In it, the young lawyer and part-time botanist displayed impatience with mere taxonomy and revealed an inclination to experimental empiricism, traits that in a decade would replicate themselves in his legal work.

The reasoning of legal classicism was categorical, holding that if problems could be assigned to their proper conceptual pigeonholes, solutions would predictably follow. The categories themselves were products of abstract reasoning. Legal categories were conducive to thought processes that were both hierarchical and deductive.

We might form a just appreciation of classical legal science by thinking of it as an aspiration to universality, certainty, and truth, achieved through techniques of systematic investigation and inductive reasoning. Before the Civil War, private law had been particularized. Contract law, for example, tended to analyze contractual relations in functionally specific terms, so that there was, for example, a law of carriers for hire,[133] which provided the foundation for early railroad law. The law of property was a luxuriant growth of specificity and localist particularity. Classical law rejected such compartmentalizing functionality and instead aspired to state legal rules in general terms so as to achieve scientific universality.

Legal science strikes the modern mind as an intellectual curiosity. It was non-experimental and, though originally deductive in method, had become inductive.[134] Law, proclaimed the eminent classical practitioner James C. Carter, is an "Inductive Science engaged in the observation and classification of facts."[135] By Langdell's day, the legal scientist proceeded by induction, gathering rules from decided cases, generalizing to principles, harmonizing those principles into a system by classifying them, then descending from the doctrinal system to rules that would resolve particular cases impartially, justly, and consistently.

Legal scientists were ignorant of real sciences, except for the evolutionary thought of Charles Darwin.[136] For many of its practitioners, "legal science" was science more in the medieval and Aristotelian spirit of Roger Bacon (d. 1294?) than in the experimental and inductive approach of Francis Bacon (d. 1626). But by the late nineteenth century, classical thought was moving from the deductive mode of Euclidean geometry to inductive reasoning based on scientific ideals articulated by the later Bacon.[137] His stress on induction from experiments as the basis of scientific inquiry would have struck a responsive chord in the legal mind.

It seems paradoxical that something that so emphatically proclaimed itself to be scientific could be as indifferent to the real thing as it was, but such a conclusion misunderstands the spirit of classicism. The legal scientists did not think of themselves as chemists or mathematicians manqués (as apparently many economists regard themselves today), that is, as scientists who happened to work with case reports rather than laboratory apparatus. Rather, they claimed absolute, objective, universal validity for their methods and the results produced by those methods. They were scientists only in the sense that Karl Marx or Mary Baker Eddy were, rather than as Louis Agassiz or Josiah Willard Gibbs were. Which was just as well: had they been more alert to the progress of experimental science in their day, they would have seen their conceptual world eroding away under their feet. Lacking that disabling knowledge, they enjoyed a certitude in their beliefs that we in our day cannot hope to recapture for ours.

The glory of legal science, in the self-regarding eyes of its *devotees*, was that it structured a legal order that was natural, neutral, and necessary. Because legal rules were determinate and objective, they produced just, predictable, and uniform results. Taken to an extreme, law's claim to objectivity could be dangerously misleading. A later figure, Senator Arthur Vandenberg, defended the Supreme Court's conservative activism in the 1930s by arguing that "when an act of Congress is thus rejected, it is the Constitution which is speaking. . . . The Supreme Court, in such instance, is only the Constitution's voice."[138] Such an attitude encouraged the delusion that the judge's ideological predisposition and policy preference played no role in shaping judicial opinions.

"Law is a science of principles, by which civil society is regulated and held together," proclaimed the future Justice Joseph Bradley in 1865.[139] The late-nineteenth-century legal order conformed, hand in glove, with a classical-liberal economic system and with the social structure that legal elites deemed desirable. The conceptual fit between law, economy, and society was one of its greatest strengths — but one that could be sustained only so long as nonlawyers were willing to accept that the economy was guided by liberal economic principles and society by Darwinian laws of competition and survival.

Legal science prided itself on being apolitical, above parties, beyond partisanship, indifferent to passing interest-group advantage. Thus it regarded with aloof disdain all political attacks on its results, politics being, in the eyes of the law and the men who expounded it, little better than shadows on the walls of the cave, vulgar, often corrupt, always sordid, beneath the dignity of those called to a nobler profession. Once again, the law-politics distinction proved crucial.

Thomas C. Grey contends that American legal science successfully met four challenges it set itself. It was comprehensive, resolving every case in its purview; complete, consisting of norms that provide a correct answer for every case; and formal, driven by reason and logic. Finally, American legal science was conceptually ordered: "[I]ts substantive bottom-level rules can be derived from a small number of relatively abstract principles and concepts, which themselves form a coherent system."[140] Law was "grounded in certain first principles existing in the nature and fitness of things."[141]

The era's leading legal science theoretician was Langdell. G. Edward White has observed that Langdell's "legal science was revolutionary in the methods of acquiring knowledge it espoused, but static in [its] dogmatic orthodoxy."[142] Langdell's method (more accurately, that of his sponsor, Harvard University president and chemist Charles W. Eliot) abandoned the theological and ethical foundations of earlier legal science and substituted for them modern assumptions strongly influenced by biology and Darwinian evolutionary theory. Law and its fundamental doctrines displayed one salient characteristic, growth. This growth could be studied inductively, by examining the data of law. Here, American legal science differed radically from continental, for the "data" of common law legal science were to be found in the reports of cases, whereas judicial decisions were of little significance to the pandectist. (Returning the compliment, the common law legal scientist dismissed the decrees of the prince or juristic writings as an alien, dangerous basis for a free legal order.)

Appointed dean at Harvard from practice at 1870, Langdell devised the basic tool of modern legal education in 1871, the casebook.[143] In his preface to this pioneering innovation, *A Selection of Cases on the Law of Contracts*, Langdell laid out the postulates of modern legal science. "Law, considered as a science, consists of certain principles or doctrines." Mastering these is the mark of a lawyer. Doctrines are a product of long and slow growth, which "is to be traced in the main through a series of cases." But most cases are "useless and worse" for extracting doctrine. "The number of fundamental legal doctrines is much less than is commonly supposed"; they simply recur in slightly different articulations. Therefore the duty of the law teacher–scientist is "to select, classify, and arrange all the cases which had contributed in any important degree to the growth, development, or establishment of any of its essential doctrines."[144] James C. Carter lauded law as "the Science of Human Conduct": reported cases were the records of that conduct and properly amenable to scientific analysis.[145] "If law be not a science, a university will consult its own dignity in declining to teach it," Langdell loftily proclaimed.[146]

His contemporary, William Markby, a law professor at Oxford and judge of the High Court of Judicature at Calcutta, lecturing to Indian law students, endorsed the same ideology that the Harvard dean was propounding in the United States, demonstrating that the conception of legal science was not exclusively American. Markby insisted in 1871, as Langdell was beginning his revolution, that the only reason law should be taught in a university was that it is a science, or at least a body of learning "considered as a collection of principles capable of being systematically arranged, and resting, not on bare authority, but on sound logical deduction."[147]

Grant Gilmore summed up the "dogmatic orthodoxy" of Langdell's method: "[T]he basic idea of the Langdellian revolution seems to have been that there really is such a thing as the one true rule of law, universal and unchanging, always and everywhere the same — a sort of mystical absolute."[148] The Socratic method quickly degenerated into mystical obfuscation (in Langdell's hands) or arid scholasticism (in Joseph H. Beale's).[149] Langdell conceived of his innovations as appropriate to the laboratory; we see them rather as the methods of the seminary. "Purity of doctrine may be lost through wrong decisions of courts, thus warping legal principle by bad precedent," Langdell's colleague Joseph H. Beale declared, "but wrong decisions are after all uncommon, and the law is not seriously affected by them."[150] Langdellianism was an effective technique of indoctrination, socialization, and ideological regimentation, nothing more. Through its influence on his student Samuel Williston and then in the Restatements project of the American Law Institute, Langdell's assumption that "correct" principles of law could be identified and discriminated from error lived on well into the twentieth century. It was Langdell's mind-set that Judge Benjamin N. Cardozo had in mind when he admonished that "the demon of formalism tempts the intellect with the lure of scientific order."[151]

LEGAL EDUCATION

Langdell was the founder of modern legal education. In addition to the casebook, he either invented or reinforced most salient characteristics of legal education today: the university law school with its dedicated library, the integrated two- (later three-) year curriculum with its standardized first-year course of study, requirement of entrance exams and a baccalaureate degree for matriculation, narrow professional scope of law school courses, exams and grades, the law review, full-time teaching faculty, and, above all, the Socratic method.[152] The man himself, a reclusive bachelor, remains shrouded in obscurity. Grant Gilmore dismissed him as "an industrious researcher of no distinction whatever either of mind or . . . of style."[153] But no one, not even Story, had as pervasive an influence on legal education in the United States, an influence undiminished in our time.

Contemporary opinions of Langdell's teaching were mixed, but predominantly negative: most of his students thought him boring and his Socratic technique incomprehensible (apparently another of his lasting contributions to legal education). But with Langdell, legal science found a home in the university law school; cases were its specimens, the library its laboratory, legal academics its scientist-practitioners. Langdell took his scientistic pretensions literally: "[T]he library is the proper workshop of professors and students alike; . . . it is to us all that the laboratories of the university are to the chemists and physicists, the museum of natural history to the zoologists, the botanical garden to the botanists."[154]

The university law school and the Harvard Socratic/casebook pedagogy were allied with the movement toward professionalization in the bar.[155] The English visitor James Bryce, retracing the steps of Tocqueville a half-century earlier, noted "a latent and sometimes and open hostility between the better kind of lawyers and the impulses of the masses."[156] Toward the end of the nineteenth century, the bar's elite, concerned for the previous century about its own status, began to form bar associations. The American Bar Association, for example, was created in Saratoga Springs, New York in 1878, two years after the founding of the New York State Bar Association; state counterparts sprung up everywhere. By the 1890s, the leaders of the ABA were imbued with the classical outlook and its underlying ideological foundations.[157]

Old fears of pettifoggers, expressed in classic form by John Adams, took on an ethnic coloration in the late nineteenth century, as the WASP elite, dominating large firms with corporate practices, looked down with disdain on the *nouveaux* Irish, Italian, and Jewish attorneys. Many of the lawyers who represented poor or working-class clients were products of unorthodox legal education, such as the YMCA night law schools that flourished in the era, or unregulated apprenticeships. The contingent fee, a novelty of the period, provided an entrée to the judicial system for undesirable plaintiffs and their equally undesirable counsel. Determined to marginalize or crush this demimonde bar, the bar associations adopted canons of ethics as an early step in the process of professionalization. The emergent university law schools identified candidates for hiring by the elite firms, then legitimated the process by asserting that they produced an aristocracy of talent, not an elite defined by race, religion, ethnicity, class, or gender.

The bar associations and the elite bar busied themselves with projects for identifying and classifying the principles of the law, but this came to nothing until the end of World War I. In the meantime, treatise writers and the Harvard-influenced law schools elaborated principles aplenty in books and classes. After the war, the ABA joined forces with the Association of American Law Schools (founded 1900), to create the American Law Institute in 1923. Its stated purpose, "to promote the clarification and simplification of the law," was to be achieved by "restatements" of rules and principles, in literally black-letter (i.e., boldface) format. The first series of Restatements, published between 1932 and 1941, attempted to summarize the principles of contracts, agency, conflicts, trusts, restitution (quasi contracts), torts, judgments, and property. Challenged from the outset by skeptics like Holmes and Learned Hand, the first generation of Restatements succumbed to fundamental revisions within two decades. The revisions were necessary because the first series of Restatements was, in Morton Horwitz's judgment, an "attempt to reassert the formalism and conceptualism of the legal thought of the old order;"[158] in other words, classicism *redivivus*.[159]

TREATISES

The treatise proved to be the ideal vehicle for expounding a structure of thought like legal classicism. The treatise writer assumed the existence of fundamental principles that were susceptible of systematic exposition. His oeuvre, the treatise, undertook that exposition, reinforcing the belief in principles.[160]

The output of treatises kept pace with the growth of American law throughout the century. Since the time of Dane and Story, enterprising lawyers published treatises, case collections, and guides on subjects as broad as the Constitution and as microcosmic as utility wires. These publications reflected dominant legal ideas and the prepossessions of their eras. Thus it comes as no surprise to find that shortly after the Civil War, treatises began to expound the ideas of legal classicism. Three of the most influential were *Cooley on Constitutional Limitations, Dillon on Municipal Corporations,* and *Tiedeman on Limitations of Police Power.*[161]

Cooley's tome, first published in 1868, enjoyed the longest life and most extensive influence of the three.[162] At the time his treatise appeared, Thomas M. Cooley was a judge of the Michigan Supreme Court and professor of law at the University of Michigan. He later became one of the first members of the Interstate Commerce Commission and then its chairman.[163] Cooley was concerned with the limits that state constitutions placed on state legislative power, and how these might be enforced by courts. He sought to identify "implied limitations" on state legislative and regulatory authority. He devoted whole chapters to the due process/law of the land clauses, to taxation, and to eminent domain. (In 1876, he expanded the tax chapter into a full-blown treatise.)[164]

Cooley was one of the first to attempt an explicit definition of substantive due process. He wrote that the concept depended on "principles . . . and not any considerations of mere form," and drew on a precocious suggestion that Justice William Johnson of the Supreme Court made in 1819 that the law-of-the-land clause of the Maryland Constitution was "intended to secure the individual from the arbitrary exercise of the powers of government, unrestrained by the established principles of private rights and distributive justice."[165] Cooley had little direct influence on the Supreme Court and the exposition of the federal Constitution,[166] but he was widely cited as authoritative on issues involving the state constitutions.

Cooley was a Jacksonian conservative, but not a laissez-faire reactionary;[167] his service as chairman of the federal government's first administrative regulatory body, the Interstate Commerce Commission, attests to his progressive outlook. Nevertheless, in *Constitutional Limitations* he emphasized restrictions on the states' police powers. Anyone hoping to inhibit state regulation would find in his treatise a trove of authority limiting power in the service of liberty.

John F. Dillon had a career parallel to Cooley's: both were products of New York's Burned-Over District, that remarkable incubator of ideas that changed the nation;[168] both migrated to frontier districts in the upper Midwest (Dillon to Iowa); both served on the supreme courts of their states; and both were among the most influential legal thinkers of the late nineteenth century. Dillon went on to serve on the United States Circuit Court for the Eighth Circuit, then to a brief academic appointment at Columbia Law School, an affluent railroad practice, and the presidency of the American Bar Association.

Dillon's treatise[169] added no substantive doctrines to Cooley's; its influence lay in Dillon's insistence on textual constitutional limits on the taxing powers of municipalities. He shared the rising anxieties of America's professional elites about dangerous classes, ideas, and the violence that both seemed to engender. He warned that "property is attacked openly by the advocates of the various heresies that go under the general name of socialism or communism."[170] But worse than socialist attacks was the political pressure of "the despotism of the many" — that is, of the majority, which "generally takes the insidious, more specious, and dangerous shape of an attempt to deprive the owners — usually corporate owners — of their property by unjust or discriminating legislation in the exercise of the power of taxation, or of eminent domain, or of that elastic power known as the police power . . . regulating the owner out of its full and equal enjoyment and use."

On the rubber chicken circuit of the era, Dillon extended his academic discussion of taxation into jeremiads against redistribution. The nation was founded on the "right of every man to enjoy personal liberty, to work out in his own way, without State domination, his individual destiny, and to enjoy, without molestation or impairment, the fruits of his own labor."[171] He condemned the speculative theories of "communists, socialists, anarchists," among them one "Karl Mark" [*sic*], and all those who promoted schemes of progressive income taxation or inheritance taxes. When taxes are "designed as a forced contribution from the rich for the benefit of the poor, and as a means of distributing the rich man's property among the rest of the community — this is class legislation of the most pronounced and vicious type; in a word, confiscation and not taxation . . . essentially revolutionary."

But Dillon's postprandial rhetoric pales when compared with that of Christopher Tiedeman. Unlike Cooley and Dillon, men of the world and the closest the American legal order has come to producing the equivalent of Roman jurisconsults, Tiedeman was a cloistered but industrious academic.[172] He made his reputation instantly with *A Treatise on the Limitations of Police Power*, published providentially in that year of social crisis, 1886.[173] His doctrinal contributions did not go beyond Cooley's, either. Instead, he blared a tocsin to arouse the bar:

> Contemplating these extraordinary demands of the great army of discontents, and their apparent power, with the growth and development of universal suffrage, to enforce their views of civil polity upon the civilized world, the conservative classes stand in constant fear of the advent of an absolutism more tyrannical and more unreasoning than any before experienced by man, the absolutism of a democratic majority.[174]

Tiedeman anachronistically supported a doctrine of natural rights similar to that of Justice Chase in *Calder v. Bull* a century earlier. With Cooley, he extolled the power of the judiciary to enforce unwritten constitutional norms. "In these days of great social unrest," he wrote in 1890, "we applaud the disposition of the courts" to apply unwritten natural law doctrines of the *Calder* sort "to lay their interdict upon all legislative acts which interfere with the individual's natural rights, even those these acts do not violate any specific or special provision of the Constitution."[175]

Tiedeman came closest of the figures surveyed here to espousing a truly laissez-faire outlook: "[S]ociety, collectively and individually, can attain its highest development by being left free from governmental control, as far as this is possible, provision being made by the government only for the protection of the individual and of society by the punishment of crimes." The heart of his natural-rights philosophy was "a freedom from all legal restraint that is not needed to prevent injury to others . . . or to employ the language of Herbert Spencer, 'Every man has a freedom to do aught that he wills, provided he infringes not the equal freedom of any other man.' The prohibitory operation of the law must be confined to the enforcement of the legal maxim, *sic utere tuo ut alienum non laedas.*"[176]

Legal Classicism: Substantive Content

Individual Liberty

Legal science confirmed many of the dominant assumptions of classicism. It complemented nineteenth-century political economy in constructing a web of norms predicated on human liberty. People must be free to follow their inclinations, especially in economic activities, up to the point where a preexisting norm inhibited their behavior for the purpose of protecting a like liberty in another individual. In this sense, it was an anti-Orwellian world: all that was not forbidden was permitted; little could legitimately be forbidden; and that was the essence of human liberty. The only exception made to this pervasive dogma was for considerations of public policy: an individual's liberty could properly be restricted in the service of some legitimate public purpose.

Herbert Spencer's "law of equal freedom" posited that all men were free to do what they liked, provided it did not trench on a like freedom of another.[177] American lawyers echoed the sentiment: James C. Carter, their epitome, wrote in his magnum opus that the highest end of law was "to secure to each individual the utmost liberty which he can enjoy consistently with the preservation of the like liberty to all others."[178]

Therefore all — which is to say, all adult white males — were jural equals in the eyes of the law. But the question of equality posed a particular challenge to classical thought. Liberty and equality have often been seen as antagonistic principles. The equality ideal itself was a new and therefore conceptually undeveloped value. The inequality that concerned the Framers in the 1770s and 1780s was what might be termed "privileging inequality": the grant of status, privilege, monopoly rights, franchises, or other benefits to favored individuals or groups.[179] The Fourteenth Amendment introduced a radically different concept. The equal protection clause prohibited "disadvantaging inequality": burdening groups by harmful discrimination. Not only was there no mainstream consensus about what constituted harmful discrimination: many white Americans did not think such discrimination wrong as applied to nonwhites, whatever the Constitution might prohibit.

Thus the classical legal conception of equality was stunted. The law could not impute or recognize juristic inequality, as, for example, by extending special protection to the weaker party in a contractual relationship. By definition, neither party was weaker, or at least the legal process could not determine in a neutral and disciplined way which was weaker and how. (Usury laws were a necessary but logically fatal exception to this reluctance to recognize real-world inequality.) Aside from that formal equality of legal status, however, classical lawyers shared the prevalent assumption of actual inequality in ability, merit, achievement, deserts, and rewards.

Formal jural equality worked to preserve the substantive inequality of wealth and power. Judges easily fell into the error of false symmetry: both parties in a bargaining relationship were presumed equal, especially in the employment context. Commenting on an Illinois Supreme Court decision striking down an eight-hour maximum hours law for women, a writer in the Chicago *Times-Herald* observed: "Dives demands protection. The court accedes to his demand, but pleads that it acts in the interest of Lazarus."[180] Justice John M. Harlan wrote in 1908 that "the right of a person to sell his labor upon such terms as he deems proper is, in its essence, the same as the right of the purchaser of labor to prescribe the conditions upon which he will accept such labor from the person offering to sell it."[181] Where liberty is the prime value, inequality (masked by formalistic equality) is inevitable.

The Rule of Law

Classical lawyers and jurists strove to realize the rule of law, elevated and abstracted into a universal philosophical principle. The English constitutional authority Albert Venn Dicey, remote successor to William Blackstone in the Vinerian Chair at Oxford, gave the concept its authoritative formulation, and even coined the phrase "the rule of law" itself, in his celebrated *Law of the Constitution* (1885).[182] He identified the rule of law as comprising three related principles, which he had discovered in operation in the American legal system during a tour that he made in 1870. In Dicey's formulation, the rule of law required the supremacy of law over arbitrary power; the subjection of all people, including rulers, to the authority of "ordinary tribunals"; and the derivation of public from private law (and not the other way around). American jurists resonated with this vision because it subordinated state to society.

The modern exemplar of nineteenth-century liberalism, Friedrich von Hayek, has explained the appeal of the rule of law:

> The conception of freedom under the law . . . rests on the contention that when we obey laws, in the sense of general abstract rules laid down irrespective of their application to us, we are not subject to another man's will and are therefore free. It is because the lawgiver does not know the particular cases to which his rules will apply, and it is because the judge who applies them has no choice in drawing the conclusions that follow from the existing body of rules and the particular facts of the case, that it can be said that laws and not men rule. . . . This generality is probably the most important aspect of that attribute of law which we have called its "abstractness."[183]

Classicist lawyers regarded law as apolitical and neutral among parties, classes, and interest groups. This was both a normative and a descriptive assertion: law *should be* neutral and apolitical; and it *was*. The judge was obliged to see that it stayed that way. Law was chaste and autonomous, separated from earthy politics by a judicially policed moat. It was self-contained, evolving through its own inner logic, coherent and consistent (except for anomalies, which were to be disregarded). Law was the inner core of liberty.

Classical jurists tended to assume that "law" meant, above all, common law, judge-made law. This would have puzzled a layperson, to whom law denoted all norms backed by the power of the state: common law to be sure, but also statutes, constitutions, and, as the century turned, administrative orders. But to the lawyer, law originating in legislative command was suspect, representing Will, the exercise of power by democratic majorities, the product of "the passion and prejudices of a popular election," producing "government by unreason."[184] It was no surprise that statutes came freighted with a troubling potential for expropriating the property of the wealthy. Only common law, the product of Reason, discerned by legal science, could rise above class interest and dispense impartial justice. In this avatar, it was a mystery monopolized by hieratic order of the bench and bar. The trope of a legal priesthood was not some critic's slur; rather it was proudly claimed by some classical lawyers themselves. Joseph H. Beale, a faculty member at the Harvard Law School who did much to extend classical thought into the twentieth century, lectured his students that law "requires a scientific knowledge on the part of a legal caste, thus coming back to a character of the most ancient times, where it was in the knowledge of a priestly caste."[185]

James C. Carter, doyen of the turn-of-the-century bar, provided a jurisprudential summary of this outlook in *Law: Its Origins, Growth, and Function*, a book that culminated the historicist tradition in American law.[186] Society's customs were the dominant source of law, particularly private law.[187] Law was, he wrote elsewhere, "the mere jural form of the habits, usages and thoughts of a people."[188] Legislation could only supplement and confirm that custom. Thus judges find the rules of law in custom. Law, "being tantamount to the custom enforced by society, is an existing fact, or body of facts, and . . . courts do not make it, or pretend to make it, but . . . find and ascertain it, acting upon the true assumption that it already exists." "There is already existing a rule by which the case must be determined," he insisted; "the true rule must be somehow found." It is the office of law to mark the boundary between state and society, delimiting the state's power to intrude into private arrangements.

Written law — that is, legislation or constitutional amendment — should not try to modify or direct custom. Carter chose two examples to demonstrate why: antitrust and black suffrage. He regarded both as failures, mischievous attempts by legislators to thwart objectives that the relevant groups in society, investment capitalists and white supremacists respectively, were determined to achieve. Enfranchisement of the freedmen was, to Carter, "tyranny" in its attempt to force or disappoint custom, in this case, oppression of the freedpeople. The liberty promoted by law sought "to leave each man to work out in freedom his own happiness or misery, to stand or fall by the consequences of his own conduct."

Judges, like their mistress the law, were to be neutral and impartial. Because authority for enforcing the rule of law was entrusted to them, they "may truly be said to have neither Force nor Will, but merely judgment," as Alexander Hamilton had put it aphoristically a century before.[189] This deceptively modest view of the judges' role was necessary to the legitimacy of judicial review and to the role of courts in modernizing American society. That legitimacy ultimately depended on popular support. A. Lawrence Lowell, a prominent conservative political theorist (and later president of Harvard), expressed this paradox when he cautioned that if at any time the people conclude that constitutional law, as interpreted by lawyers, is absurd or irrational, the power of the judiciary will inevitably vanish, and a great part of the Constitution will be irretrievably swept away. Our constitutional law depends for its force upon the fact that it approves itself to the good sense of the people; and the power of the courts is held upon condition that the precedents established by them are wise, statesmanlike, and founded upon enduring principles of justice which are worthy of the respect of the community.[190]

To the classical jurist, the corpus of the law was comprehensive and, at the level of principle, largely complete.[191] While law might, indeed must, adapt to the changing conditions of society, its foundations were invariant. Justice Henry Brown confidently proclaimed in 1898 that "the cardinal principles of justice are immutable," and no one contradicted him.[192] There was little room for judges to elaborate new norms; their role was to find existing norms and apply them to the case at hand. This gave a hermetic and static cast to classical law: the possibilities of change and growth were slight — though classicists proclaimed otherwise.

Though judges had, in this sense, a constrained role in reshaping private law, they assumed a broad, expansive, activist role in interpreting public law. On the private law side, judges often asserted that statutes in derogation of the common law were to be narrowly construed.[193] The public law counterpart of that attitude was a readiness to void statutes that judges thought inconsistent with the spirit of the Constitution, even if they did not conflict with any specific constitutional provision. An extreme example of this attitude, on the eve of the classical era, was Chief Justice Salmon P. Chase's opinion in *Hepburn v. Griswold* (1870),[194] where he managed to apply the contracts clause of Article I, Section 10, as a constraint on the federal government, though in terms it limits only the states. Chase did not let mere constitutional text divert him from the result he wanted to reach. "Those who framed and those who adopted the Constitution," he wrote, "intended that the *spirit* of this prohibition should pervade the entire body of legislation."

The Chief Justice's attitude was founded on a view of the courts' role that derived from John Marshall's postulates in *Marbury v. Madison*. In the triumphalist moment of the late nineteenth century, marked by the successive centennials of national independence, adoption of the Constitution, and establishment of the Supreme Court, the judicial role was closely linked to the preservation of social stability and the status quo of the distribution of power. A jurist generally progressive in his outlook, Stanley Matthews, explained at the constitutional centennial that judicial review in the *Marbury* sense was

the logical necessity of liberty secured by written constitutions of governments unalterable by ordinary acts of legislation. If the prohibitions and limitations of the charters of government cannot be enforced in favor of individual rights, by the judgments of the judicial tribunals, then there are and can be no barriers against the exactions and despotism of arbitrary power; then there is and can be no guarantee or security for the rights of life, liberty, or property.[195]

Into this spacious conception of judicial review, judges incorporated traditional attitudes toward common law adjudication. The primary criterion for the validity of discovered law was its consistency with the existing body of law, not its relevance to social needs or public policy. In the decision that contemporaries considered the most notorious example of the classicist mentality, *Ives v. South Buffalo Railway Co.* (1911),[196] Judge William Werner of the New York Court of Appeals declared that "in a government like ours theories of public good or necessity are often so plausible or sound as to command popular approval, but courts are not permitted to forget that the law is the only chart by which the ship of state is to be guided."

To endow law with the flexibility and applicability necessary to its universal application, its principles had to be articulated at a high level of generalization and in abstract form. Law's essential characteristics, according to the late-classical authority Joseph H. Beale, included generality, universality, comprehensiveness, continuity, predictability, regularity, and a constantly modulating accommodation between certainty and flexibility.[197] Judges often seemed to be trying to remove their decision as far as possible from the specific facts and circumstances of the case. They would characteristically speak of the parties in their procedural roles as appellant or petitioner, or in their substantive role as employee or agent, or simply as A and B. Law dealt with parties "as if they were unknown," boasted one of classicism's votaries, "mere abstract representations of principles."[198] It was precisely that human quality, appealing to the emotions or the sense of justice of juries, that had to be insulated from the application of principles, lest those principles be contaminated, deflected, or ignored. Thus insulated from the real world, the principles of law could appear absolute, undeviating in the face of appeals to sympathy or justice.

Another consequence of classicism's tendency toward abstraction was its indifference toward the specific facts and circumstances of particular cases. This was only natural, since classicism tended toward generalization and away from concrete particulars. But it paid a price for this aspiration to universality, and that was its ever more apparent divorce from reality. John Chipman Gray, one of the intellectual giants of the era largely exempt from classicism's pull, disparaged this tendency:

> Langdell's intellectual arrogance and contempt is astounding. One may forgive it in him or Ames, but in an ordinary man it would be detestable. The idols of the cave which a school bred lawyer is sure to substitute for the facts, may be much better material for intellectual gymnastics than the facts themselves and may call forth more enthusiasm in the pupils, but a school where the majority of the professors shuns and depises the contact with actual facts, has got the seeds of ruin in it and will and ought to go to the devil.[199]

In classical lawyers' thought, the distinction between public and private law was vital.[200] In one of the prominent precedents of the nineties, the Arkansas Supreme Court spelled out one of the most important consequences of the public-private distinction: "[W]hen the subject of a contract is purely and exclusively private, . . . there is no condition existing upon which the legislature can interfere for the purpose of prohibiting the contract or controlling the terms thereof."[201] Taken to such an extreme, the presumed natural order of society was by its very existence a prophylactic against the power of the state. By 1891, this distinction was so well developed that a committee of the American Bar Association could confidently propose a schematic classification of all law that divided domestic (as opposed to international) law into only two branches: public and private. Public law included constitutional, legislative, administrative, and criminal law, while private law comprised substantive (property, contracts, torts, etc.) and "adjective" law, an early term for procedure.[202] This general classificatory arrangement remained unofficially in vogue for half a century.

A principal function of public law was to administer the processes by which the state could take away a person's life, liberty, or property. Jurists hedged the state about with restrictions on its power to preserve the hallowed Lockean triad. Private law concerned itself with the interaction of individuals, where the only state involvement consisted of providing courts to adjudicate their disputes. Its modal bodies of substantive law were contracts, commercial law, property, and those comparative newcomers, torts and agency. By the late nineteenth century, judges were systematizing all these bodies of law, unifying them from disparate sources that dealt with particular relationships: negotiable instruments, sheriffs' duties, sales, railroads, future interests, and so on. Private law was dedicated to protecting the exercise of individual will. It served as a buffer between the public realm, represented by the power of the state, and the private, represented by society.

Classical developments in the law of contracts and property influenced public law developments, as lawyers and judges carried over assumptions and principles across the chasm that separated private and public law, adapting the operative principles that drove private law development into public law doctrines as well. Contracts and property were at the heart of the classical vision. Their doctrines established some of classicism's most potent dogmas and paradigms.

Contracts

Before the nineteenth century, contract scarcely existed as a discrete, unified body of law. Blackstone hardly deigned to take notice of it. Joseph Story wrote nine monumental treatises, and none of them dealt with contract. An image of what the law of contracts looked like before the classical age appeared in Story's 1837 proposal for codification to the Massachusetts General Court, where he spoke not of a law of contracts as such, but of "the law of agency, of bailments, of guaranty, of suretyship, of bills of exchange, or promissory notes, of insurance, and of partnership [and of] the law of navigation and shipping and maritime contracts."[203] Before the middle of the century, contracts was what Lawrence Friedman has called a "residual" body of law: it was what was left over after judges and legislatures carved out specialized bodies of law that controlled more particular economic relationships, such as the law of negotiable instruments, the law of sales, the law of master and servant, the law of railroads or public utilities, and so on.[204] And is has become residual again in the later twentieth century, after classical contract theory deflated and legislatures intervened to provide positivistic rules for such matters as labor relations and commercial law.

At the beginning of the century, John Marshall elevated contract rights to a preconstitutional status, resting on natural law. Contract "evince[d] the idea of a preexisting intrinsic obligation which human law enforces." Their "original and preexisting principles are, like many other natural rights, brought with man into society; and, although they may be controlled, are not given by human legislation."[205]

This confirmed a supraconstitutional status for contract appropriate for the role Marshall envisioned for it in the contracts clause, of providing a judicial check on state legislation that modified contractual obligations.

Beginning in the middle of the century, and in fact with the work of Story's son, William Wetmore Story,[206] commentators began to construct a unified body of contract law and embedded within it a theoretical skeleton that gave it coherence and dimension. This new, generalized law of contracts, the creation of English and American judges, exalted the wills of the contracting parties as the fundament of contractual obligation.[207] The particular contract gave expression to the self-interested pursuit of individual advantage by each of the parties; it was, in effect, a microcosmic "law" governing the economic relationship of the parties *pro hac vice*.[208]

Classical contract theory was founded on three assumptions. The parties were free to choose the terms of their agreement. Parties of full age were competent to enter into contracts. Contract was clearly demarcated from tort. While those postulates seem bland to the point of banality, they had powerful operative effects. Statutes mandating safe workplaces, for example, fell under the interdict of all three principles. Two further conclusions followed from these premises: the public good was best served by a regime of the utmost contractual freedom, and private ordering could usually displace governmental regulation, leaving the only necessary function of government to be the enforcement of contracts and provision of national and internal security.[209]

Given the centrality of individual will in contract, consent and consideration moved to the fore as key components of obligation. Quasi contracts and contracts-implied-in-law became suspect, because they represented the state's intrusion into a relationship (actually, a nonrelationship) that was supposed to have been formed by the parties' mutual assent (the "meeting of the minds"). Consideration and consent became the foci of what was emerging as a grand theory of contractual obligation.

Yet legal developments of the late nineteenth century worked at cross-purposes, because lawyers recognized only objective manifestations of the parties' assent and rejected subjective intent and expressions of that intent that did not meet the objective criteria. Theophilus Parsons articulated this "objective theory" of obligation in his treatise *The Law of Contracts* in 1855: "[T]he court will give to the contract the construction which will bring it as near to the actual meaning of the parties as the words they saw fit to employ, when properly construed, and the rules of law, will permit."[210] This powerful tradition of objectivity was endorsed by Holmes in the late nineteenth century and lived on well into the twentieth. One of the clearest statements of the objective theory was Judge Learned Hand's widely noted opinion in *Hotchkiss v. National City Bank* (1911): "A contract has, strictly speaking, nothing to do with the personal, or individual intent of the parties. A contract is an obligation attached by the mere force of law to certain acts of the parties, usually words, which ordinarily accompany and represent a known intent." The testimony of "twenty bishops" to an inconsistent intent would be unavailing.[211]

Thus, paradoxically, in the name of giving effect to the parties' wills, the law resolutely ignored what those wills might actually have been in a particular case and imposed on the parties an exterior standard that had the effect sometimes of forcing one or both of them into a relationship that they did not want or perhaps even anticipate. This paradox is crucial to legal classicism in several ways, the most important being that it constituted a major and destabilizing anomaly that disturbed the paradigmatic status of contract law.

The late-nineteenth-century law of contracts, like the rest of classical law, operated at a high degree of abstraction. Its unspecific nature made it a natural complement to classical liberal economic theory. Classical contract law and liberal economics rose and fell together in the nineteenth century. The "pure law of contract" that Friedman has identified could work only in a frictionless market of equal and freely bargaining parties, that phantasm of the liberal economists' imaginations.

The goal of classical contract theory was a law that was certain and predictable, enabling entrepreneurs to make business plans with the assurance of a stable legal foundation. But perversely, classical contract law frustrated business expectations. Karl Llewellyn noted that "sense, the ways of men with words, the ways of businessmen in dealing, these are irrelevant and literally inadmissible: they do not get into the hall, to be heard or considered. Generations of law students were introduced to their profession by way of these strange ideas, and courts have in consequence made actual decisions in their image . . . leav[ing] hundreds of good business promises no legal container but the garbage can."[212]

Such stability as the law might have provided came at a price. As the objective theory forced judges to subordinate the parties' actual intentions to some "intent" imputed by the law, it displaced individual will with an externally imposed, judicially chosen goal of public policy. A parallel on the public law side of contract law was the assumption of jural equality among parties to a contract.

Because no legal system can leave reality behind too far or for too long, "pure contract law" was unstable, riddled with inconsistencies, continuously liable to be ignored in favor of the specific facts of a particular case. This in turn forced judges to acknowledge reality either by creating exceptions that threatened to eat away the rule or to swallow it up, or to impose the rule with an indifference to facts and just outcomes, in the name of adherence to doctrinal consistency and rigor. While this dilemma permeates all fields of law, it became especially acute in contract law because of the related stresses of industrialization and development of a national market. Injustice and rigidity, on the one hand, or inconsistency and opportunism on the other, might be prices that judges were willing to pay in an occasional case. But the necessity of constantly choosing between them became intolerable when capricious judicial choice deranged large impersonal commercial markets.

At the same time, contract, property, and tort tended toward convergence as judges created liability for tortious interference with contractual relationships.[213] Judges came to think of contract as creating property rights that might claim protection from disturbance by a third party. Contract naturally included employment relationships, and judges found this a useful doctrine for browbeating unions that called for strikes, boycotts, or a closed shop.[214] The reach of the new doctrine became all the more powerful when it was extended to prospective contracts.

Ironically, at the time when the qualities of rigidity and abstraction might have consigned classical contract law to the attic of outmoded legal doctrine, Langdell resurrected contract theory with his *Contracts* casebook. Like some zombie whose life was unnaturally prolonged, the pure law of contract thereafter lived on in casebooks, law schools, and the Socratic method. Langdell and Holmes imprinted their vision of contracts on Langdell's student Samuel Williston, whose name became synonymous with contracts for the first half of the twentieth century.[215] Thence pure theory passed into the first *Restatement of Contracts* (1932), especially its section 75 on consideration. Thus artificially revivified, contract allied itself with ideology to inhibit policy initiatives by legislatures, especially in the realm of labor law.

Property

Property occupied a special but ambiguous place in classical thought. Property was the paradigm of eighteenth-century legal thought, as contracts became for the nineteenth century. It dominated the concerns of the men who framed the state and federal constitutions.[216] The nationalists who promoted adoption of the Constitution of 1787 sought to balance the republican principles of self-government and majority rule against protection for minorities.[217] They identified minorities principally in terms of property ownership and therefore tried to secure the rights of owners against legislative majorities. In doing so, they shielded property ownership with special constitutional protections (due process, just compensation), while political rights, such as participation in governance through voting and office-holding, were left contingent, dependent on such things as ownership of real property.

The result of the Framers' solicitude for property was a stunted development of constitutionalism in the new nation, privileging property ownership over popular control of public policy. "In a conflict between the rights of the people to implement their will through their representatives and the independent rights of property," Jennifer Nedelsky has concluded, an "implicit priority" of the Constitution gave "precedence to property . . . over the republican principles of government by consent."[218]

A concern for "vested rights," such as that displayed by Justice Chase in *Calder v. Bull*, did not disappear in the nineteenth century, but it was displaced in the judicial mind by other concerns. These included the growing influence of contracts as the paradigmatic legal concept that ordered private relationships, plus a reluctant or unacknowledged judicial recognition that the very concept of property was contingent. In the eighteenth century, Americans thought of property as tangible and physical; they regarded rights in it as absolute. Nineteenth-century economic developments eroded both those characteristics of property.[219] At the same time that judges were coming to think of property in terms of its value and its earning capacity rather than its intrinsic "worth," they also recognized the legally constructed nature of rights in it. With hindsight, we can see that the idea of property as a Hohfeldian "bundle of rights" was looming just over the intellectual horizon. Thus lawyers began, willy-nilly, to think of the rights of property owners as subject to revision by the legislature to conform to changing concepts of public policy, evolving instrumentally to meet new economic needs.[220]

Two examples illustrate these trends. First, the legal conception of property had to expand to include intangible forms of property, such as the rights, whatever they might be, of a shareholder in a corporation. The legal system had to recognize new economic relationships, such as the expectation of an increase in property values, speculative activity (especially in emergent national and regional commodities markets), and the capitalization of future income streams.

Second, nineteenth-century lawyers had to mediate the conflict *among* competing property interests. This was highlighted in the evolution of statutory and common law involving milldams. How freely should legislatures and courts permit individuals (including partnerships and corporations) to erect dams to flood upstream lands for a floodpool that captured potential hydraulic energy? Such flooding would constitute a taking of the upstream owner's land and require compensation under the Fifth Amendment and its state constitutional counterparts. To whom might the legislature extend this condemnation power, and for what purposes? How far would the judiciary supervise legislatures in their redistribution of wealth involved in this sort of taking? These evolving changes strained static, traditional conceptions of property and vested rights.

Conceptual difficulties arose when American jurists recognized that the classical conception of property rights articulated by William Blackstone was inadequate to the rapidly developing commercial and industrial economy of Jacksonian America. Blackstone defined property as "that sole and despotic dominion which one man claims and exercises over the external things of the world, in total exclusion of the right of any other individual in the universe."[221] His view stressed two dominant characteristics of property: the object was physical things, and the owner's right was absolute. If either of these elements was challenged, the structure of property law would wobble. Both elements were to come under attack in the early twentieth century.

The greatest stress on the privileged status of property appeared in the struggle over slavery. Abolitionists scored some of their most persuasive points with northern audiences when they framed the issue in terms of the right of enslaved persons to the fruits of their own labor, endowing *them* with property rights that had been expropriated by those who enslaved them. Abraham Lincoln inerrantly identified the status of labor as the crux of the sectional struggle over slavery and economic policy. The Republican Party made this idea its raison d'être in its free labor plank. The abolition of slavery, that great act of uncompensated expropriation, destroyed any lingering idea of the absolute nature of property interests. But that moral achievement was unsettling. If the national and state governments could wipe out $4 billion of capital investment, taking it from A the slaveowner and transferring it without compensation to B the formerly enslaved person, what security would there be for other forms of property when challenged by other claims with a high moral priority, such as a right to a living wage, or the right to the necessities of life?

After the war, federal and state courts confirmed these trends, thereby subverting traditional conceptions of property relationships, unwittingly or not.[222] They also expanded the concept of property. Justice Noah Swayne proposed a global definition of property in his *Slaughterhouse Cases* dissent (1873): "[P]roperty is everything which has an exchangeable value."[223] Justice Field, in his dissent in *Munn v. Illinois* (1877), insisted that the due process clauses' protections of property extended "to the use and income of the property, as well as to its title and possession."[224] Thus broadly defined to include incorporeal forms and expectations, property took on protean forms. Despite these transformations in the legal conception of property, the Lockean role of property in a capitalist republic became ever more important to classical jurists. Property, John F. Dillon assured the New York bar, was part of the "essential foundations of our social fabric."[225]

The stage was set for a drama of volatile legal development. Jurists exalted a set of interests already endowed by the federal and state constitutions with extraordinary status. But these rights were being so transformed in the new industrial, financial, and commercial climate that they bore only an attenuated resemblance to the concept of property rights that Blackstone described in the second volume of his *Commentaries*.[226]

Class Legislation and the Republican Ideal

Since 1975, historians have mounted a major reinterpretation of classical legal thought, rejecting earlier treatments that, they claim, identified class bias or economic outlook as the determinant of judicial endeavor.[227] This reinterpretation does not coalesce around a single thesis, but it is possible to sketch the broad contours of an alternative "revisionist" view of classical legal thought from several of its foremost exemplars.[228]

A sketch of this new interpretation would emphasize these points: classicist judges were not actuated by anything so sordid as the prejudices of their class, or by a determination to impose their own economic views on the Constitution. Rather, they were dedicated to a cluster of moral ideals coeval with the Constitution. Drawing on the commonwealth idea, the American constitutional tradition condemned what classical judges called "class legislation": statutes enacted specifically to benefit one group in society or burden another. Rather, all legislation had to promote the general welfare (the constitutional phrase encapsulating the commonwealth ideal). The Framers and classical jurists feared that one group would attempt to use the power of government to promote its own interests at the expense of others. This was "special legislation." The archetype of class legislation was monopolies. In their antipathy to monopoly and special privilege, Jacksonian Democrats reaffirmed the constitutional bar to "partial" legislation.

In place of such evils, classical jurists sought to substitute "equality of right," the equal status of all individuals before the law, none privileged above the others, none debased below. This was the essence of American liberty, the goal of classical jurisprudence. To achieve this equality of status, the state had to be neutral among individuals and interest groups, favoring none, oppressing none. Governmental impartiality was the necessary condition of formal equality. Government must be disciplined to neutrality in the service of individual liberty.

Let one of these revisionist scholars, Howard Gillman, speak for all: "[T]he goal was to prohibit the government from passing laws designed merely to promote the interests of certain classes at the expense of their competitors, to impose special burdens and benefits on particular groups without linking these burdens and benefits to the welfare of the community as a whole."[229]

In support of this position, Gillman invokes high authority, Justice Stephen J. Field, who wrote in an 1883 opinion that

[s]uch legislation has been regarded everywhere else as inconsistent with civil liberty. That exists only where every individual has the power to pursue his own happiness according to his own views, unrestrained except by equal, just, and impartial laws. . . . [Section 1 of the Fourteenth Amendment] was, among other things, designed to prevent all discriminating legislation for the benefit of some to the disparagement of others. . . . [States may] legislate to promote health, good order, and peace, to develop their resources, enlarge their industries, and advance their prosperity. It only inhibits discriminating and partial enactments, — favoring some to the impairment of the rights of others. The principal, if not the sole, purpose of its prohibitions is to prevent any arbitrary invasion by state authority of the rights of person and property, and to secure to every one the right to pursue his happiness unrestrained, except by just, equal, and impartial laws.[230]

As a description of one component of the classical outlook, the revisionist interpretation is valid beyond cavil. But there was more to classical legal thought than hostility to class legislation. Further, this one segment of judicial thinking diverted the judges' attention from the real impact of their holdings. It is this larger result, rather than dedication to a single republican ideal, that accounts for the enduring significance of classical legal thought. The revisionist interpretation is not wrong, but merely narrow and incomplete. This study aspires to fill out the larger picture.

Lawyers and judges of the classical era clung to values that they inherited from a century-old tradition of American constitutionalism. On the rights side of the constitutional equation that balanced power versus liberty, these values included the sanctity of contractual obligation and property, which occupied a privileged place in the hierarchy of American liberties. Basic liberties, which Americans had come to think of as rights adhering to the individual, reflected the underlying values of individualism and the role of will (as opposed to status). Thus liberty to contract, including the ability to contract for one's labor, and entrepreneurial liberty ranked as high among the values protected by the constitutional order as did property rights.

On the power side of the equation, the constitutional tradition enshrined a preference for limited government. That tradition, however, had been altered by the Civil War, which taught Americans, in the North at least, the need for forceful governmental response to problems that threatened stability and order. The war thus left a tension unresolved: the traditional preference for local control contended with ' the recently vindicated reliance on national power. After the war, some of the most basic issues of the American constitutional order were in a state of fluid evolution.

The Police Power

It was obvious to all after 1865 that the American constitutional order had changed in profound ways, but these changes seemed to be as unclear as they were potentially far-reaching. The war and the defeat of the states'-sovereignty constitutional vision had changed the balance of federalism. Union victory discounted antebellum Democratic state-power claims and exalted national power. The American people had spoken emphatically but cryptically in the Thirteenth, Fourteenth, and Fifteenth Amendments, saying that "Congress shall have power to enforce this article by appropriate legislation."[231] What was to be the new structure of federalism that was to confront the problems of industrialization? Was anything left of the Democratic state-centered constitutional vision? Who was to have ultimate authority to answer these questions? Congress? The Supreme Court?

The Slaughterhouse Cases

Reconstruction was a matter in part of reestablishing the relationship of the seceded states to the national government, and in part of defining the civil and political rights of the freedpeople who were now citizens of the states and nation. By 1872, it was settled that Congress that would have the final say over the substantive policies of Reconstruction. The Supreme Court ratified the congressional Republican assertion of authority in *Texas v. White* (1869)[232] and *White v. Hart* (1872).[233]

But constitutional amendments, statutes, and judicial decisions resolved the question of Reconstruction only in a narrow sense. The broader question left unsettled was whether the changes brought about by the war had created a new constitutional order. A century's perspective makes it clear to us that the Reconstruction Amendments did in fact create a new nation, under a new constitutional order, in which the rights of individuals were to be protected by national power, especially the federal courts, against state degradation.[234] But that was not obvious to contemporaries, and a majority of the Supreme Court, in the *Slaughterhouse Cases* (1873),[235] shrunk the Fourteenth Amendment's nationalizing potential by the narrowest possible reading of Reconstruction's effect.

Slaughterhouse is conventionally read,[236] and correctly so, as an interpretation of Reconstruction in the narrow sense, particularly as it pertained to the status of African American citizens. But there is another vantage from which to look back on this classic case. Stripped (unnaturally) of its relevance to blacks, the debate between Justice Samuel F. Miller for the majority in *Slaughterhouse* and the four dissenters centered on federal authority over state regulatory power.

The litigation was begun by a group of white butchers who objected to being forced to do their slaughtering in an abattoir given monopoly privileges by the state legislature. The statute was steeped in the quotidian corruption of Louisiana politics and reflected the political struggle that was then convulsing the state: Republican favorites benefited from the monopoly, while the butcher-plaintiffs were Democrats. But the constitutional justification for the monopoly grant was unimpeachable. At common law, government traditionally had power to control abattoirs as public nuisances, a power confirmed by the antebellum police power doctrine.

Justice Miller easily upheld the validity of the monopoly on broadly conservative federalism grounds. "Was it intended to bring within the power of Congress the entire domain of civil rights heretofore belonging exclusively to the States?" he asked rhetorically. He provided his own answer: it if did, the Supreme Court would become "a perpetual censor upon all legislation of the States, on the civil rights of their own citizens."

In a peroration on federalism, Miller resisted significant change to the federal system, and rejected the possibility that the people had established a new constitutional order: "[W]hen, as in the case before us, these consequences are so serious, so far-reaching and pervading, so great a departure from the structure and spirit of our institutions; when the effect is to fetter and degrade the State governments by subjecting them to the control of Congress, in the exercise of powers heretofore universally conceded to them of the most ordinary and fundamental character; when in fact it radically changes the whole theory of the relations of the State and Federal governments to each other,"[237] it would require a clearer statement of Framers' intent to do so than Miller discerned in the record of congressional debates. Politically, Miller was a Republican. He was not trying to cling to antebellum Democratic state-power ideology. He simply could not accept the possibility that a radically different constitutional order had opened before him.

The result of the *Slaughterhouse Cases* was to leave intact state police power as it had been broadly defined by *Commonwealth v. Alger*, and to limit the ability of the federal government to supervise the exercise of that power. But that seeming reaffirmation of antebellum legislative power soon proved illusory. The case was decided by a five-to-four vote, and the radically different vision of two of the dissenters, Justices Field and Joseph P. Bradley, would overturn its narrow perspective in less than twenty years.

Munn v. Illinois

The Supreme Court returned to the issue of the states' police powers four years later in *Munn v. Illinois* (1877)[238] and again upheld state regulatory authority. The Grange, originally a farmers' social organization, had moved into politics during the 1870s as a body speaking for farmers in the states of the upper Midwest (Illinois, Wisconsin, Minnesota, Iowa). It pressured state legislatures to regulate the rates charged by railroads and grain elevators. Chief Justice Morrison R. Waite, writing for the majority, dismissed an elevator owner's challenge to the constitutionality of the Illinois rate statute. Waite grounded his opinion on the *sic utere* maxim, upholding "laws requiring each citizen to so conduct himself, and so use his own property, as not unnecessarily to injure another," identifying that principle as "the very essence of government." At common law, legislatures had regulated special occupations, including ferries and innkeepers, and such regulation did not deprive an owner of his property rights. Such economic activities, known to the common law as "the common callings," were "businesses affected with a public interest," and thus subject to regulation. Waite imputed consent to such regulation from the owner's decision to dedicate the business to public service. The legislature could regulate the rates charged by such businesses. "For protection against abuses by legislatures the people must resort to the polls, not to the courts."

After *Slaughterhouse* and *Munn*, state regulatory authority under the police power appeared secure. *Commonwealth v. Alger* seemed to remain the dominant paradigm of the balance between governmental power and individual liberty. *Munn* endured as authority for state rate-setting powers through the 1892 decision of *Budd v. New York*.[239]

But this seemingly robust scope of the police power was illusory. In *Slaughterhouse*, Justices Field and Bradley filed dissents that heralded the juridical future. Field included among the privileges and immunities of American citizenship an "equality of right, with exemption from all disparaging and partial enactments, in the lawful pursuits of life, throughout the whole country."[240] His reliance on the new privileges and immunities clause of the Fourteenth Amendment proved to be a dead end, but his inclusion of occupational choice among constitutionally protected rights opened up a vista on the future. It was Bradley who identified the vehicle, the due process clause, that protected "fundamental rights," including the "right to choose one's calling," both a liberty and a property right.[241]

In *Munn*, Field again dissented, insisting that property was taken in the constitutional sense by regulations that diminish its profitability: "[A]ll that is beneficial in property arises from its use, and the fruits of that use; and whatever deprives a person of them deprives him of all that is desirable or valuable in the title and possession."[242] Field identified occupations and business opportunities as property rights protected by the Fourteenth Amendment. Thus the *Munn* majority principle was "subversive of the rights of private property," assuring that "all property and all business in the State are held at the mercy of a majority of its legislature."

The depression that began in 1873, the railroad strikes of 1877, and the formation of the Knights of Labor made Field's and Bradley's doctrines all the more appealing to the American legal elite. The conflict between governmental regulatory authority and individual liberties took on a new urgency when the nation experienced the wrenching social dislocations brought on by industrialization. Social turmoil hit the nation at a time when the state and federal governments' administrative capacities were, to say the least, underdeveloped. Elected officials could not respond effectively to the social impact of industrialization: nothing in their experience had prepared them to understand its problems, and they did not have at hand the administrative apparatus to implement whatever solutions they might have conceived. Governments' response to industrialization took place, not in a vacuum of power, but at a time when public administrative capacities scarcely existed.

Americans were learning to value the potential of administration in governmental affairs.[243] The disastrous experience of western railroad development, which took place in an unregulated climate where Congress proved itself incapable of enacting stable legislative policy while the executive branch was unable to supply effective administration,[244] convinced many that traditional forms of policy making and policy implementation had to be supplemented by the administrative process. A young political scientist, Woodrow Wilson, hailed a new era of public administration.[245] Good-government advocates promoted civil service reform, and achieved some success with enactment of the Pendleton Act in 1883, which began the professionalization of the federal civil service. Progressives like Herbert Croly called for expertise in administration, nonpartisan and above politics, capable of impartially discerning the public welfare and pursuing it without the corruptions of elective politics.[246] Graduates and faculty of the new university programs in the social sciences offered expertise to the governmental process.

At the state level, the states created administrative agencies to supervise railroads. The Granger states pioneered what have come to be called "strong" commissions, which had rate-setting and enforcement powers, while the "weak" commissions of the eastern states had only information-gathering powers.[247] The Supreme Court inhibited the authority of the strong commissions in the *Wabash Case* of 1886,[248] striking down Illinois rate regulation having an out-of-state impact on the grounds that it interfered with interstate commerce. Justice Miller delivered a broad hint to Congress: "[T]his species of regulation is one which must be, if established at all, of a general and national character, and cannot be safely and wisely remitted to local rules and local regulations." Congress took the hint, enacting two broad regulatory measures, the Interstate Commerce Act of 1887 and the Sherman Antitrust Act of 1890. In doing so, it asserted a claim for *federal* police power potentially rivaling the traditional state police power ratified by the *Alger* decision.

The philosophical assumptions and ideological orientation that constituted the foundation of legal classicism influenced the Supreme Court from 1890 through the Great Depression. Classicism did not foreordain a monolithic or even coherent outcome in all constitutional decisions of those years. On the contrary: after 1900, the Court developed inconsistent lines of precedent on both side of any significant issue. But the fears and beliefs of the classical jurists provided the single most important determinant of Supreme Court constitutional adjudication in that period. Legal classicism thereby produced a body of doctrine that dominated the work of the Court in the first third of the twentieth century.

Legal classicism grew out of the tension between two poles of republican aspiration: the power of government to regulate, on one hand, and the liberty of individuals, on the other. James Madison had given this tension its classic expression in *Federalist* Number 37, where he called for "combining the requisite stability and energy in Government, with the inviolable attention due to liberty, and to the Republican form."[249] All Justices of the Supreme Court in the last third of the nineteenth century agreed with Madison that the fundamental challenge of American constitutionalism was mediating between the power of government and the liberty of the individual. Public law had to control power to secure the individual's liberty.

Notes

1. The following enumeration is drawn partly from Martin J. Sklar, "Studying American Political Development in the Progressive Era, 1890–1916," in Sklar, *The United States as a Developing Country: Studies in U.S. History in the Progressive Era and the 1920s* (1992), 37, 39.

2. United States Congress, House of Representatives, Committee on Banking and Currency, *Money Trust Investigation: Investigation of Financial and Monetary Conditions in the United States . . .* (1913).

3. Sklar, *United States as a Developing Country*, 48.

4. Alvin Toffler, *Future Shock* (1970).

5. Bruce Ackerman, *We the People: Foundations* (1991), 34–130; quotations 44, 59, 92, 104, 108.

6. 304 U.S. 144, 152 (1938).

7. Gerald Garvey, *Constitutional Bricolage* (1971).

8. William M. Wiecek, "The Great Writ and Reconstruction: The Habeas Corpus Act of 1867," *Journal of Southern History* 36 (1970), 530.

9. William J. Novak, *The People's Welfare: Law and Regulation in Nineteenth-Century America* (1996). See also Frank Bourgin, *The Great Challenge: The Myth of Laissez-Faire in the Early Republic* (1989).

10. From the wealth of secondary sources on the Gilded Age and the Progressive era, the finest single-volume survey is, in my opinion, Nell Irvin Painter, *Standing at Armageddon:*

United States, 1877–1919 (1987), while the most persuasive interpretive study is Alan Dawley, *Struggles for Justice: Social Responsibility and the Liberal State* (1991). Morton Keller's trilogy integrates legal issues into the larger picture: Keller, *Affairs of State: Public Life in Late Nineteenth Century America* (1977); *Regulating a New Economy: Public Policy and Economic Change in America, 1900–1933* (1990); *Regulating a New Society: Public Policy and Social Change in America, 1900–1933* (1994).

11. Alfred D. Chandler, *The Visible Hand: The Managerial Revolution in American Business* (1977).

12. George Fitzhugh, *Sociology for the South; or, The Failure of Free Society* (1854); Fitzhugh, *Cannibals All!; or, Slaves without Masters* (1857).

13. Stephens quoted in Norman Ware, *The Labor Movement in the United States, 1860–1895: A Study in Democracy* (1929), 74.

14. Quoted in Kim Voss, *The Making of American Exceptionalism: The Knights of Labor and Class Formation in the Nineteenth Century* (1993), 88.

15. William Cohen, *At Freedom's Edge: Black Mobility and the Southern White Quest for Racial Control, 1861–1915* (1991).

16. Stuart W. Bruchey, *Enterprise: The Dynamic Economy of a Free People* (1990), 310–311.

17. Daniel Yergin, *The Prize: The Epic Quest for Oil, Money, and Power* (1991), 19–113.

18. Thomas Jefferson, *Notes on the State of Virginia*, (1781; 1st American ed. 1788), 175.

19. *The Independent* (a New York Protestant paper), quoted in Paul S. Boyer, *Urban Masses and Moral Order in America, 1820–1920* (1978), 126; see pp. 123–132 generally on middle-class anxieties.

20. Ignatius Donnelly, *Caesar's Column: A Story of the Twentieth Century* (1892).

21. Painter, *Standing at Armageddon*, xx, citing Charles B. Spahr, *An Essay on the Present Distribution of Wealth in the United States* (1896).

22. Frank H. Easterbrook and Daniel R. Fischel, *The Economic Structure of Corporate Law* (1991).

23. Herbert Hovenkamp, *Enterprise and American Law, 1836–1937* (1991); Morton J. Horwitz, "*Santa Clara* Revisited: the Development of Corporate Theory" (1985), reprinted in revised form in Horwitz, *Transformation II*, 65–108.

24. Ronald Coase, "The Nature of the Firm," 4 *Economica* 386 (1937) (the significance of this article was recognized by the award of the Nobel in economics to the author in 1993).

25. Olivier Zunz, *Making America Corporate, 1870–1920* (1990).

26. Adolf A. Berle and Gardner C. Means, *The Modern Corporation and Private Property* (1932).

27. Louis K. Liggett Co. v. Lee, 288 U.S. 517, 548 (1933) (Brandeis, J., dissenting).

28. Grant Gilmore applied the phrase to the period after the Gilded Age: *The Ages of American Law* (1977), 68. W. H. Auden appropriated it for a later era: *The Age of Anxiety* (1947), and Leonard Bernstein gave Auden's usage musical expression in his Second Symphony. But it seems most apt as a descriptor for the Gilded Age.

29. See generally Stephen Brier et al., *Who Built America? Working People and the Nation's Economy, Politics, Culture, and Society* (1992), vol. 2, 7–213; David Montgomery, *The Fall of the House of Labor: The Workplace, the State, and American Labor Activism, 1865–1925* (1987), 1–257.

30. Christopher L. Tomlins, *Law, Labor, and Ideology in the Early American Republic* (1993).

31. Sean Wilentz, *Chants Democratic: New York City and the Rise of the American Working Class, 1788–1850* (1984).

32. Quoted in Bruce Levine et al., *Who Built America? Working People and the Nation's Economy, Politics, Culture, and Society* (1989), vol. 1, 333.

33. Anthony Woodiwiss, *Rights v. Conspiracy: A Sociological Essay on the History of Labour Law in the United States* (1990), 19–69.

34. John R. Commons et al., *History of Labour in the United States* (1918), vol 1, 404–412.

35. Commonwealth v. Pullis (Philadelphia Mayor's Court, 1806); People v. Melvin (N.Y. Ct. Gen'l Sess., 1809), reprinted in John R. Commons et al., eds., *A Documentary History of American Industrial Society* (1910–11), vol. 3, 250.

36. Robert J. Steinfeld, "The Philadelphia Cordwainers' Case of 1806: The Struggle over Alternative Legal Constructions of a Free Market in Labor," in Christopher L. Tomlins and Andrew J. King, eds., *Labor Law in America: Historical and Critical Essays* (1992), 20.

37. 14 Wend. 9, 18 (N.Y. Ct. Corr. Errors, 1835).

38. Robert J. Steinfeld, *The Invention of Free Labor: The Employment Relation in English and American Law and Culture, 1350–1870* (1991), 3–54.

39. The Knights have been well served by excellent historical treatments: Leon Fink, *Workingmen's Democracy: The Knights of Labor and American Politics* (1983); Voss, *The Making of American Exceptionalism.*

40. Alexander Saxton, *The Indispensable Enemy: Labor and the Anti-Chinese Movement in California* (1971).

41. Robert V. Bruce, *1877: Year of Violence* (1959).

42. Sidney Lens presents a popular history of labor violence in *The Labor Wars: From the Molly Maguires to the Sitdowns* (1973).

43. Philip S. Foner chronicled the railroad strikes and the formation of the Marxist Workingmen's Party in *The Great Labor Uprising of 1877* (1977).

44. Painter, *Standing at Armageddon*, 18–24; T. J. Jackson Lears, *No Place of Grace: Antimodernism and the Transformation of American Culture, 1880–1920* (1981), 28–32.

45. Karl Marx and Friedrich Engels, *Writings on the Paris Commune*, ed. Hal Draper (1971), 78.

46. David R. Roediger, "America's First General Strike: The St. Louis 'Commune' of 1877," *Midwest Quarterly* 21 (1980), 205.

47. Thomas Durfee, *Oration Delivered at the Dedication of the Providence County Court House* (1879), 34.

48. Quoted in Brier et al., *Who Built America?*, vol. 2, 119.

49. Francis A. Walker, "What Shall We Tell the Workingclasses," *Scribner's* 2 (1887), 626–627.

50. Alexander Winchell, "Communism in the United States," *North American Review*, 136 (1883), 456–457.

51. People v. Wilzig, 4 N.Y. Cr. 403, 425 (1886).

52. Samuel F. Miller, "The Conflict in This Country between Socialism and Organized Society" (1888), reprinted in Charles N. Gregory, *Samuel Freeman Miller* (1907), 143, 154–155, 166, 168. I thank Dean Richard Aynes for assistance in locating this source.

53. James H. Haynie, "Socialistic and Other Assassinations," *Atlantic Monthly* 46 (1880), 466.

54. Paul Avrich, *The Haymarket Tragedy* (1984).

55. Christopher L. Tomlins, *The State and the Unions: Labor Relations, Law, and the Organized Labor Movement in America, 1880–1960* (1985), 3–60.

56. 33 *Alb. L.J.* 342 (1886). See Daniel R. Ernst, *Lawyers against Labor: From Individual Rights to Corporate Liberalism* (1995).

57. 4 Met. (45 Mass.) 45 (1842); see Leonard W. Levy, *Law of the Commonwealth and Chief Justice Shaw* (1957; rpt. 1987), 183–206.

58. Quoted in Brier et al., *Who Built America?* vol. 2, 125.

59. Holmes, "Law and the Court" (1913) (speech to Harvard Law School Assn. of New York), in Sheldon M. Novick, ed., *The Collected Works of Justice Holmes: Complete Public Writings and Selected Judicial Opinions* (1995), vol. 3, 507.

60. Paul Krause, *The Battle for Homestead, 1880–1892: Politics, Culture, and Steel* (1992).

61. The Homestead Case, 1 Pa. Dist. Rpts. 785 (1892) (charge to grand jury per Paxson, C.J.).

62. Carlos A. Schwantes, *Coxey's Army: An American Odyssey* (1985).

63. See generally C. Vann Woodward's classic, *Origins of the New South, 1877–1913* (1951).

64. John G. Sproat, *The Best Men: Liberal Reformers in the Gilded Age* (1968).

65. Thomas K. McCraw, *Prophets of Regulation: Charles Francis Adams, Louis D. Brandeis, James M. Landis, Alfred E. Kahn* (1984).

66. Lawrence Goodwyn, *Democratic Promise: The Populist Moment in America* (1976); Robert C. McMath, *American Populism: A Social History, 1877–1898* (1993).

67. On the first, see Robert C. McMath, *Populist Vanguard: A History of the Southern Farmers' Alliance* (1975).

68. The St. Louis Platform of 1892, reprinted in Donald B. Johnson, comp., *National Party Platforms*, rev'd ed. (1978), vol. 1, 89–91.

69. See especially the work of David P. Thelen: *The New Citizenship; Origins of Progressivism in Wisconsin, 1885–1900* (1972); *Robert M. La Follette and the Insurgent Spirit* (1976); *Paths of Resistance: Tradition and Dignity in Industrializing Missouri* (1986).

70. The substance of Progressive thought and its impact on legal development will be examined below in ch. 4.

71. See above, prologue for an introductory overview of the contents of classical legal thought.

72. Phillip S. Paludan, "The American Civil War Considered as a Crisis in Law and Order," *American Historical Review* 77 (1972), 1013.

73. Harold M. Hyman, *A More Perfect Union: The Impact of the Civil War and Reconstruction on the Constitution* (1973), 229–232.

74. On the bond cases, see Charles Fairman, *Reconstruction and Reunion, 1864–88* (vol. 6 of the *Holmes Devise History of the Supreme Court of the United States*) (1971–1987), part 1, pp. 918–1116.

75. 1 Wall. (68 U.S.) 175, 206–207 (1864); see also its sequel, Von Hoffman v. Quincy, 4 Wall. (71 U.S.) 535 (1867).

76. John N. Pomeroy, *An Introduction to Municipal Law* (1864). This was a systematic exposition of American law written for college students, much like Blackstone. "Municipal law" in this context meant national law, not law relevant to cities. See Phillip S. Paludan, *A Covenant with Death: The Constitution, Law, and Equality in the Civil War Era* (1975), 222.

77. John F. Dillon, *Commentaries on the Law of Municipal Corporations*, 3rd ed. (1881), §§ 520–525.

78. 16 Pet. (41 U.S.) 1 (1842).

79. Richard J. Bernstein, *Beyond Objectivism and Relativism: Science, Hermeneutics, and Praxis* (1983), 18–19. (Bernstein was writing about relativism and what he terms the "Cartesian Anxiety" generally, and not about classical legal thought.)

80. Anon. [Oliver Wendell Holmes], "Book Notices", [review of Langdell, *A Selection of Cases on the Law of Contracts*, 2nd ed. (1879)], 14 *Am. L. Rev.* 233–236 (1880). Holmes recycled the logic/experience aphorism into *The Common Law* (1881), reprinted in Novick, ed., *Collected Works of Holmes*, vol. 3, 109. On philosophical idealism generally, see George A. Kelly, *Idealism, Politics and History: Sources of Hegelian Thought* (1969).

81. Lochner v. New York, 198 U.S. 45, 61 (1905).

82. Holmes to M. C. Otto, 26 Sept. 1929, reprinted in *Journal of Philosophy* 38 (1941), 391.

83. Michael H. Hoeflich, "Law and Geometry: Legal Science from Leibniz to Langdell," 30 *Am. J. Legal Hist.* 95 (1986).

84. Cyrus Northrop, *The Legal Profession as a Conservative Force in Our Republic* (1892), 8.

85. Hampton L. Carson, "The Relation of the Judiciary to Unconstitutional Legislation," *Proceedings of the Thirtieth Annual Meeting of the Missouri Bar Association, 1912,* 88.

86. Anatole France, *Le Lys Rouge* (1894; rpt. 1968), 95 (my translation).

87. James Bryce, *The American Commonwealth* (1888), vol. 2, 421.

88. Francis Wayland, *The Elements of Political Economy,* 5th ed. (1853), 114.

89. Arthur L. Perry, *Elements of Political Economy,* 3rd ed. (1867), 136, 126.

90. Quoted in Steinfeld, *Invention of Free Labor,* 147.

91. Herbert Spencer, *Social Statics* (1850), 354–355.

92. William Graham Sumner, *What Social Classes Owe to Each Other* (1883).

93. Oswald Spengler later bespoke their anxieties in *The Decline of the West* (English trans. 1926).

94. Despite Holmes's implication that they had, in his dissent in Lochner v. New York, 198 U.S. 45, 75 (1905).

95. On the general influence of Sumner in the United States, see Robert G. McCloskey, *American Conservatism in the Age of Enterprise, 1865–1910* (1951), 22–71; Richard Hofstadter, *Social Darwinism in American Thought,* rev'd ed. (1955); and Donald Fleming, "Social Darwinism," in Arthur M. Schlesinger Jr. and Morton White, eds., *Paths of American Thought* (1963), 123. But see Robert C. Bannister, *Social Darwinism: Science and Myth in Anglo-American Social Thought* (1979), a corrective to Hofstadter's view.

96. Holmes again: "The secret isolated joy of the thinker, who knows that, a hundred years after he is dead and forgotten, men who never heard of him will be moving to the measure of his thought . . .": "The Profession of the Law" (1886), in Novick, ed., *Collected Works of Justice Holmes,* vol. 3, 473.

97. Sumner quoted in Hofstadter, *Social Darwinism in American Thought,* 51.

98. See generally Alan Trachtenberg, *The Incorporation of America: Culture and Society in the Gilded Age* (1982); T. J. Jackson Lears, *No Place of Grace: Antimodernism and the Transformation of American Culture, 1880–1920* (1981), 4–26.

99. Francis Parkman, "The Failure of Universal Suffrage," *North American Review* 20 (1878), 1, 20.

100. Quoted in Joseph Dorfman, *The Economic Mind in American Civilization: 1865–1918* (1949), 48.

101. John F. Dillon, "Property — Its Rights and Duties in Our Legal and Social Systems," 29 *Am. L. Rev.* 161, 188 (1895).

102. Quoted in translation in Charles Tilly, "Collective Violence," in Hugh D. Graham and Ted R. Gurr, eds., *Violence in America: Historical and Comparative Perspectives* (1979), 12.

103. Josiah H. Benton, *Influence of the Bar in Our State and Federal Government* (1894), 11.

104. Durfee, *Oration Delivered at the Dedication of the Providence County Court House,* 31.

105. Speech of 1890, quoted in Howard Gillman, *The Constitution Besieged: The Rise and Demise of Lochner Era Police Powers Jurisprudence* (1993), 99.

106. Quoted in Robert W. Rydell, *World of Fairs: The Century-of-Progress Expositions* (1993), 45.

107. Christopher G. Tiedeman, *A Treatise on the Limitations of Police Power in the United States* (1886; rpt. 1971), vi–viii.

108. David J. Brewer, "The Nation's Safeguard," 47 *Proc. N.Y. St. Bar Assoc.* 38–41 (1893).

A more appreciative reading of this after-dinner speech is Owen M. Fiss, *Troubled Beginnings of the Modern State, 1888–1910* (vol. 8 of the Holmes Devise *History of the Supreme Court of the United States* (1993), 53–57.

109. David A. Wells, "The Communism of a Discriminating Income Tax," *North American Review* 130 (1880), 236; Simon Sterne, *Suffrage in the Cities* (1878), quoted in Michael Les Benedict, "Laissez-Faire and Liberty: A Re-evaluation of the Meaning and Origins of Laissez-Faire Constitutionalism," 3 *Law & Hist. Rev.* 293, 307 (1985).

110. Choate's argument is reprinted in Joseph H. Choate, *Arguments and Addresses of Joseph Hodges Choate* (1926), 419, 422.

111. Pollock v. Farmers Loan and Trust Co. (the First Income Tax Case), 157 U.S. 429, 607 (1895) (Field, J., concurring).

112. Holmes, "The Path of the Law" (1897), reprinted in Novick, ed., *Collected Works of Justice Holmes*, vol. 3, 398.

113. Gordon, "Legal Thought and Legal Practice," 88.

114. Eric Foner, *Free Soil, Free Labor, Free Men: The Ideology of the Republican Party before the Civil War* (1970).

115. C. B. Macpherson, *The Political Theory of Possessive Individualism: Hobbes to Locke* (1962), 3.

116. Quoted in Wilentz, *Chants Democratic*, 242.

117. Quoted in John R. Commons et al., *A Documentary History of American Industrial Society* (1910–1911), vol. 6, 232.

118. Boaventura de Sousa Santos, *Toward a New Common Sense: Law, Science, and Politics in the Paradigmatic Transition* (1995), ix, 7.

119. Friedrich Kessler, "Contracts of Adhesion—Some Thoughts about Freedom of Contract," 43 *Colum. L. Rev.* 629 (1943).

120. This was the central thesis of Justice Brewer's address, "The Nation's Safeguard."

121. Act of 9 April 1866, ch. 31, 14 Stat. 27.

122. Edward Gibbon, *The Decline and Fall of the Roman Empire* (1776–1788; rpt. n.d. [Modern Library edition]), vol. 2, 687.

123. On this quest for systematization, see James E. Herget, *American Jurisprudence, 1870–1970: A History* (1990), 63–116.

124. West began publishing the *Century Digest* in 1897, and the first *Decennial Digest* in 1906. Its famous key made its appearance in the *Second Decennial Digest* (1917).

125. Daniel J. Boorstin, *The Mysterious Science of the Law: An Essay on Blackstone's Commentaries, Showing How Blackstone, Employing Eighteenth-Century Ideas of Science, Religion, History, Aesthetics, and Philosophy, Made of the Law at Once a Conservative and a Mysterious Science* (1941), 11–24.

126. Christopher G. Tiedeman, "Methods of Legal Education," 1 *Yale L.J.* 150, 153 (1892).

127. On the antecedents of nineteenth-century legal science, see Harold J. Berman, "The Origins of Western Legal Science," 90 *Harv. L. Rev.* 894, 930–941 (1977); Berman, *Law and Revolution: The Formation of the Western Legal Tradition* (1983), 151-164; Berman and Charles J. Reid, "The Transformation of English Legal Science: From Hale to Blackstone," 45 *Emory L.J.* 437 (1996); and Manlio Bellomo, *The Common Legal Past of Europe, 1000–1800*, trans. Lydia G. Cochrane (1995).

128. Mathias Reimann, "Nineteenth Century German Legal Science," 31 *B.C. L. Rev.* 837 (1990).

129. John H. Merryman, *The Civil Law Tradition: An Introduction to the Legal Systems of Western Europe and Latin America*, 2nd ed. (1985), 62–66. "The Pandects" was Justinian's alternative title for the Digest: *Digesta seu Pandectae*. The word comes from Greek roots meaning "all works."

130. Alan Watson, *Slave Law in the Americas* (1989), 1–10.

131. Laura Kalman, *Legal Realism at Yale, 1927–1960* (1986), 11.

132. David Wigdor, *Roscoe Pound: Philosopher of Law* (1974), 23–26, 49–67.

133. With its own early treatise, *Jeremy on Carriers*: Henry Jeremy, *The Law of Carriers, Inn-keepers, Warehousemen, and Other Depositories of Goods for Hire* (1816).

134. William Keener, "The Inductive Method in Legal Science," 17 *A.B.A. Rep.* 473 (1894).

135. James C. Carter, *The Ideal and the Actual in the Law* (1890), 17.

136. Cf. Berman and Reid, "Transformation of English Legal Science," 440, who caution against a ready comparison of legal science with the natural sciences: "This is a contemporary Anglo-American usage; in most other languages, 'science' (in German, *Wissenschaft*, in French, *science*, in Russian, *nauka*) has retained its older, broader meaning of a coherent, systematic body of knowledge, combining particular facts with general principles, and is applied not only to the exact natural sciences, but also to the less exact social and other humane sciences including the science of the law."

137. Paul H. Kocher, "Francis Bacon on the Science of Jurisprudence," *Journal of the History of Ideas* 18 (1957), 3O. On the influence of "Baconian philosophy" among American intellectuals generally, see Theodore D. Bozeman, *Protestants in an Age of Science: The Baconian Ideal and Ante-bellum American Religious Thought* (1977), 3–31. Bacon had been one of the most eminent lawyers of his age, as well as a scientist, having served as attorney general and lord chancellor in the reign of James I. Daniel R. Coquillette, *Francis Bacon* (1992).

138. Quoted in *New York Times*, 3 March 1936, 11.

139. Quoted in William D. Lewis, ed., *Great American Lawyers: The Lives and Influence of Judges and Lawyers . . .* (1907–1909), vol. 6, 402.

140. Thomas C. Grey, "Langdell's Orthodoxy," 45 *U. Pitt. L. Rev.* 1, 6–8 (1983).

141. Northrop, *Legal Profession as a Conservative Force*, 7.

142. G. Edward White, *Tort Law in America: An Intellectual History* (1980), 26.

143. On linkages between legal science and legal education, see G. Edward White, "The Impact of Legal Science on Tort Law, 1880–1910," 78 *Colum. L. Rev.* 213–232 (1978).

144. Christopher C. Langdell, *A Selection of Cases on the Law of Contracts* (1871), viii–ix.

145. James C. Carter, *Law: Its Origin, Growth, and Function* (1907), 338–339.

146. Quoted in William C. Chase, *The American Law School and the Rise of Administrative Government* (1982), 29.

147. William Markby, *Elements of Law Considered with Reference to Principles of General Jurisprudence*, 6th ed. (1905; 1st ed. 1871), x.

148. Grant Gilmore, *The Death of Contract* (1974), 97–98.

149. Much more generous evaluations of Langdell's legal science, stressing its lasting, largely beneficial effects, are: Dennis Patterson, "Langdell's Legacy," 90 *Nw. U. L. Rev.* 196 (1995) and W. Burlette Carter, "Reconstructing Langdell," (forthcoming, *Ga. L. Rev.*)

150. Joseph H. Beale, *A Treatise on the Conflict of Laws*, 1st ed. (1916), 135.

151. Benjamin N. Cardozo, *The Nature of the Judicial Process* (1921), 66.

152. On Langdell's contribution, see White, *Tort Law in America*, 20–38, the best brief survey of late legal science in America; Neil Duxbury, *Patterns of American Jurisprudence* (1995), 11–25; William P. LaPiana, *Logic and Experience: The Origin of Modern American Legal Education* (1994), the most recent study exploring the Harvard Law School's impact on the way lawyers are indoctrinated. More critical views of Langdell and the Harvard enterprise are Paul D. Carrington, "The Missionary Diocese of Chicago," 44 *J. Legal Ed.* 467–518 (1994) and Pierre Schlag, "Law and Phrenology," 110 *Harv. L. Rev.* 877 (1997).

153. Gilmore, *Death of Contract*, 13.

154. Christopher C. Langdell, "Harvard Celebration Speeches," 3 *L.Q. Rev.* 123, 124 (1887).

155. Jerold S. Auerbach, *Unequal Justice: Lawyers and Social Change in Modern America* (1976), 3–73.

156. James Bryce, *The American Commonwealth* (1888), vol. 2, 488.

157. Norbert Brockman, "Laissez-Faire Theory in the Early American Bar Association," 39 *Notre Dame Law.* 270 (1964).

158. Horwitz, *Transformation II*, 183.

159. N. E. H. Hull offers a more favorable evaluation of the *Restatement* project, judging it wholly "progressive" in origins and spirit: "Restatement and Reform: A New Perspective on the Origins of the American Law Institute," 8 *Law & Hist. Rev.* 83 (1990). See also G. Edward White, "The American Law Institute and the Triumph of Modernist Jurisprudence," 15 *Law & Hist. Rev.* 1 (1997).

160. A. W. B. Simpson, "The Rise and Fall of the Legal Treatise: Legal Principles and the Forms of Literature," 48 *U. Chic. L. Rev.* 672 (1981).

161. See generally Clyde E. Jacobs, *Law Writers and the Courts: The Influence of Thomas M. Cooley, Christopher G. Tiedeman, and John F. Dillon upon American Constitutional Law* (1954), a book less about the treatises and their writers than about the substantive due process doctrines that they spawned.

162. Thomas M. Cooley, *A Treatise on the Constitutional Limitations Which Rest upon the Legislative Power of the States of the American Union* (1868).

163. On Cooley generally, see Alan R. Jones, *The Constitutional Conservatism of Thomas McIntyre Cooley: A Study in the History of Ideas* (1987; photoreproduction of the author's 1960 Ph.D. dissertation).

164. Cooley, *The Law of Taxation* (1876).

165. Cooley, *Constitutional Limitations*, 355–356; Bank of Columbia v. Okely, 4 Wheat. (17 U.S.) 235, 244 (1819) (Johnson, J.; dictum).

166. For a contrary view see Phillip S. Paludan, "Law and the Failure of Reconstruction: The Case of Thomas M. Cooley," *Journal of the History of Ideas* 33 (1972), 597.

167. Phillip S. Paludan, *A Covenant with Death: The Constitution, Law, and Equality in the Civil War Era* (1975), 249–273; Alan Jones, "Thomas M. Cooley and Laissez-Faire Constitutionalism: A Reappraisal," *Journal of American History* 52 (1967), 751.

168. See Whitney R. Cross, *The Burned-Over District; The Social and Intellectual History of Enthusiastic Religion in Western New York, 1800–1850* (1950).

169. John F. Dillon, *Treatise on the Law of Municipal Corporations* (1872).

170. John F. Dillon, *The Laws and Jurisprudence of England and America* (1895), 204–205. This book was an expanded version of the 1892 Storrs lectures at Yale Law School.

171. John F. Dillon, "Property — Its Rights and Duties in Our Legal and Social Systems," 29 *Am. L. Rev.* 161, 162 (1895).

172. Besides the works noted here, he published treatises on real property, personal property, bills and notes, sales, commercial paper, and municipal corporations, an output all the more prodigious in view of his untimely death at age forty-six. See David N. Mayer, "The Jurisprudence of Christopher G. Tiedeman: A Study in the Failure of Laissez-Faire Constitutionalism," 55 *Mo. L. Rev.* 93 (1990) and Louise A. Halper, "Christopher G. Tiedeman, 'Laissez-Faire Constitutionalism' and the Dilemmas of Small-Scale Property in the Gilded Age," 51 *Ohio St. L.J.* 1349 (1990) (contending that Tiedeman was not a laissez-faire reactionary either, but, in his later years at least, concerned about preserving small property holdings against the onslaught of consolidation).

173. Christopher G. Tiedeman, *A Treatise on the Limitations of Police Power in the*

United States (1886); revised as A *Treatise on State and Federal Control of Persons and Property in the United States* (1890).

174. Tiedeman, *Limitations of Police Power*, vi–vii.

175. Christopher G. Tiedeman, *The Unwritten Constitution of the United States* (1890), 81.

176. Tiedeman, *Unwritten Constitution*, 76. The embedded Spencer quote is from *Social Statics* (1850), 121.

177. Spencer, *Social Statics*, 121.

178. James C. Carter, *Law: Its Origin, Growth, and Function* (1907; rpt. 1974), 337.

179. See, e.g., Virginia Declaration of Rights (1776), art. 4: "[N]o man, or set of men, are entitled to exclusive or separate emoluments or privileges from the community, but in consideration of publick services." In William F. Swindler, comp., *Sources and Documents of United States Constitutions* (1973–1979), vol. 10, 49; U.S. Const. art. I, secs. 9, 10 (prohibiting the federal and state governments from conferring "any Title of Nobility"). The list could be multiplied indefinitely into the Jacksonian era.

180. Quoted in "Notes of Recent Decisions," 29 *Am. L. Rev.* 767–768 (1895) (comment on the unreported case of *Tilt v. People*).

181. Adair v. United States, 208 U.S. 161, 174 (1908).

182. A. V. Dicey, *Introduction to the Study of the Law of the Constitution* (1885; rpt. 1982), 107–122.

183. Friedrich A. von Hayek, *The Constitution of Liberty* (1960), 153–154.

184. Northrop, *Legal Profession as a Conservative Force*, 9.

185. Quoted in Warren J. Samuels, "Joseph Henry Beale's Lectures on Jurisprudence, 1909," 29 *U. Miami L. Rev.* 260, 292 (1975). Beale was referring to the Egyptian priesthood's monopoly of astronomy, essential to predicting the floodtimes of the Nile, which was literally vital to the survival of the lower kingdom.

186. Carter, *Law: Its Origin, Growth, and Function*, 85–87 (first quote; ital. omitted), 135, 212–217, 337 (second quote). Carter, a major figure among the classical lawyers, was a student of Savigny's student Luther Cushing, and cited Savigny frequently. His resistance to David Dudley Field's codification proposals paralleled Savigny's condemnation of Anton Thibaut's call for codification of German law. See the discussion in Herget, *American Jurisprudence*, 120–130, and in Reimann, "Nineteenth Century German Legal Science." Carter was a founder of the Association of the Bar of the City of New York and president of the American Bar Association in 1895.

187. On historicism in American law, see Stephen A. Siegel, "Lochner Era Jurisprudence and the American Constitutional Tradition," 70 *N.C. L. Rev.* 1, 66–78 (1991); Siegel, "Historism [*sic*] in Late Nineteenth Century Constitutional Thought," 1990 *Wis. L. Rev.* 1431.

188. James C. Carter, *The Ideal and the Actual in the Law* (1890), 13.

189. Jacob E. Cooke, ed., *Federalist* No. 78, 523.

190. A. Lawrence Lowell, *Essays on Government* (1897), 128.

191. See the tabular summary of characteristics in Robert S. Summers, *Instrumentalism and American Legal Theory* (1982), 157–158.

192. Holden v. Hardy, 169 U.S. 366, 387 (1898).

193. Shaw v. Railroad Co., 101 U.S. 557, 565 (1879); see the authorities collected at 50 Am. Jur. *Statutes* §§ 402, 346.

194. 8 Wall. (75 U.S.) 603, 623 (1870) (emphasis added).

195. Speech of Stanley Matthews, printed in Hampton L. Carson, ed., *History of the Celebration of the One Hundredth Anniversary of the Promulgation of the Constitution of the United States* (1889), 371.

196. 201 N.Y. 271, 294–295 (1911) (holding New York's workers' compensation statute unconstitutional as a deprivation of the employer's property interests without due process).

197. Joseph H. Beale, *A Treatise on the Conflict of Laws* (1935), vol. 1, 45–48.

198. Northrop, *Legal Profession as a Conservative Force*, 8.

199. Gray to Charles W. Eliot, 8 Jan. 1883, quoted in Mark De Wolfe Howe, *Justice Oliver Wendell Holmes: The Proving Years, 1870–1882* (1963), 158.

200. Carter, *Law: Its Origin, Growth and Function*, 86–87.

201. Leep v. St. Louis, Iron Mountain, and Southern Ry, 58 Ark. 407, 421 (1894) (holding unconstitutional in part a statute requiring payment of accrued wages in full at the time of an employee's discharge.)

202. American Bar Association, "Report of the Committee on Classification of the Law," 14 A.B.A. *Reports* 379 (1891).

203. Story, "A Report of the Commissioners . . . 1837," in William W. Story, ed., *The Miscellaneous Writings of Joseph Story* (1852), 730–731.

204. Lawrence M. Friedman, *Contract Law in America: A Social and Economic Case Study* (1965), 15–26.

205. Ogden v. Saunders, 12 Wheat. (25 U.S.) 203, 244 (1827).

206. William W. Story, *A Treatise on the Law of Contracts not under Seal* (1844).

207. For the English side of this story: P. S. Atiyah, *The Rise and Fall of Freedom of Contract* (1979), 219–570; and for a synopsis, Atiyah, *An Introduction of the Law of Contract*, 4th ed. (1989), 8–17. There is no work of comparable scope for the American side, but see J. Willard Hurst, *Law and Economic Growth: The Legal History of the Lumber Industry in Wisconsin, 1836–1915* (1964). I have relied on the following for this subchapter: Friedman, *Contract Law in America*; Horwitz, *Transformation II*, 33–39; Gilmore, *Death of Contract*.

208. For an exposition of what might be considered "neoclassical principles" of contract law, emphasizing the necessity of giving effect to parties' willed commitments, see Charles Fried, *Contract as Promise: A Theory of Contractual Obligation* (1981).

209. W. David Slawson, *Binding Promises: The Late 20th-Century Reformation of Contract Law* (1996), 3–21.

210. Theophilus Parsons, *The Law of Contracts* (1855), 6.

211. 200 Fed. 287, 293 (S.D.N.Y. 1911).

212. Karl N. Llewellyn, *The Common Law Tradition: Deciding Appeals* (1960), 39.

213. Note, "Tortious Interference with Contractual Relations in the Nineteenth Century: The Transformation of Property, Contract, and Tort," 93 *Harv. L. Rev.* 1511 (1980).

214. Old Dominion Steamship Co. v. McKenna, 30 Fed. 48 (1887); Barr v. Essex Trades Council, 30 A. 881 (N.J. Ch. 1894).

215. Samuel Williston, *A Treatise on the Law of Contracts* (1926).

216. On the pervasiveness of property concerns in Revolutionary-Era thought, see James W. Ely Jr., *The Guardian of Every Other Right: A Constitutional History of Property Rights* (1992), 26–58; John P. Reid, *Constitutional History of the American Revolution: The Authority of Rights* (1986), 27–46, 98–102.

217. See generally Jennifer Nedelsky, *Private Property and the Limits of American Constitutionalism: The Madisonian Framework and Its Legacy* (1990).

218. Nedelsky, *Private Property*, 7.

219. Kenneth J. Vandevelde, "The New Property of the Nineteenth Century: The Development of the Modern Concept of Property," 29 *Buff. L. Rev.* 325 (1981).

220. On antebellum developments in property law, see Horwitz, *Transformation I*, 31–84.

221. William Blackstone, *Commentaries on the Laws of England* (1765), vol. 2, 2.

222. On postbellum developments, see Horwitz, *Transformation II*, 145–159.

223. 16 Wall. (83 U.S.) 36, 127 (1873).

224. 94 U.S. 113, 143 (1877).

225. Dillon, "Property — Its Rights and Duties in Our Legal and Social Systems," 162.

226. See A. W. B. Simpson's introduction to this volume in William Blackstone, *Commentaries on the Laws of England* (1765; rpt. 1979), vol. 2, iii–xv.

227. For a review of this interpretation, see the appendix to this volume, "Historiography and the Supreme Court."

228. In chronological order, these exemplars are: Michael Les Benedict, "Laissez-Faire and Liberty: A Re-evaluation of the Meaning and Origins of Laissez-Faire Constitutionalism," 3 *Law & Hist. Rev.* 293 (1985); Owen M. Fiss, *Troubled Beginnings of the Modern State, 1888–1910* (vol. 8 of the Holmes Devise *History of the Supreme Court of the United States*) (1993); Howard Gillman, *Constitution Besieged: The Rise and Demise of Lochner Era Police Powers Jurisprudence* (1993); James W. Ely, *The Chief Justiceship of Melville W. Fuller, 1888–1910* (1995).

229. Gillman, *Constitution Besieged*, 61.

230. Butchers' Union Slaughter-House & Livestock Landing Co. v. Crescent City Live-Stock Landing & Slaughter-House Co., 111 U.S. 746, 758–759 (1884) (Field, J., concurring).

231. U.S. Const. amend. XIII, § 2. Sections 5 of the Fourteenth Amendment and 2 of the Fifteenth Amendment contained the same formula couched in minor and nonsignificant verbal variations.

232. 7 Wall. (74 U.S.) 700 (1869).

233. 13 Wall. (80 U.S.) 646 (1872).

234. This is the conclusion of Ackerman, among others: *We the People: Foundations*, 81–103 and *passim*.

235. 16 Wall. (83 U.S.) 36 (1873). On the case, see Charles Fairman, *Reconstruction and Reunion, 1864–88: Part One* (vol. 6 of the *Holmes Devise History of the Supreme Court of the United States*) (1971), 1320–1364. On the spokesman for the majority, see Fairman, *Mr. Justice Miller and the Supreme Court, 1862–1890* (1939).

236. E.g., Harold M. Hyman and William M. Wiecek, *Equal Justice under Law: Constitutional Development, 1835–1875* (1982), 475–482.

237. 16 Wall. 78.

238. 94 U.S. 113, 124, 134 (1877).

239. 143 U.S. 517 (1892).

240. 16 Wall. 109–110. Chief Justice Chase joined in Field's dissent; Justice Swayne filed a brief dissenting opinion for himself. Stephen A. Siegel provides an excellent analysis of Field's thought in "Lochner Era Jurisprudence," 90–99.

241. 16 Wall. 116.

242. 94 U.S. 141, 113, 140.

243. Stephen Skowronek, *Building a New American State: The Expansion of National Administrative Capacities, 1877–1920* (1982); William E. Nelson, *The Roots of American Bureaucracy, 1830–1900* (1982).

244. Wallace D. Farnham, "'The Weakened Spring of Government': A Study in Nineteenth-Century American Economic History," *American Historical Review* 68 (1963), 662.

245. Woodrow Wilson, "The Study of Administration," *Political Science Quarterly* 2 (1887), 197.

246. Herbert D. Croly, *The Promise of American Life* (1909).

247. Thomas K. McCraw, *Prophets of Regulation: Charles Francis Adams, Louis D. Brandeis, James M. Landis, Alfred E. Kahn* (1984).

248. Wabash, St. Louis & Pacific Ry. v. Illinois, 118 U.S. 557, 577 (1886).

249. Cooke, ed., *Federalist* No. 37, 233.

Chapter Three

Classicism Ascendant,
1880–1930

*F*ew of the Justices who served on the Supreme Court in the half-century after 1890 were untouched by the *mentalité* of classical legal thought. And even those few — Brandeis, Cardozo, Stone, Holmes (to a degree) — had to contend with it among their brethren. Classicism informed everything that the Court did, above all its constitutional adjudication.

Here we return to a familiar story, a tale thrice told.[1] For it was in the constitutional decisions of the "*Lochner* era" and beyond that the influence of the classical outlook was most ponderous. The story of the Court's public law adjudication in this half-century can be told from various perspectives; the approach of this study is not the only valid one. Of itself, this account is incomplete, and must be supplemented with other analytical or narrative approaches. But every story must be told from some standpoint, and the standpoint of this study is classical orthodoxy.

Reading the Court's opinions between 1886 and 1937 as specimens of classical legal thought helps explain much that would otherwise be puzzling. Such a reading obviates the need to explain case outcomes by a political, results-oriented interpretation (an approach sometimes attributed, wrongly, to the Progressives). It accounts for the viewpoints of some of the Justices entirely, and for others partially.

Classical constitutional adjudication developed in three phases. The first, which began around 1886, the year of the "Great Upheaval," and crested with *Lochner* in 1905, marked the ascendancy of substantive due process and liberty of contract. The next period, lasting through the Great War, saw those dogmas challenged on and off the Court. Alternate approaches to constitutional adjudication appeared, and produced reasoning and results inconsistent with earlier classicist cases. Finally, the 1920s and 1930s experienced a regression back to the regnant dogmas of the first phase, but with the difference that now those results confronted constant challenge.

The Emergence of Substantive Due Process
and Liberty of Contract

The doctrinal credos of the classical period were substantive due process and its off-spring, liberty of contract.[2]

The antebellum tradition of higher law remained adrift after the Civil War, lacking a textual anchor. Some courts, even the Supreme Court, occasionally relied on social compact reasoning in an echo of *Calder v. Bull*. Justice Noah Swayne, in his *Slaughterhouse* dissent, referred to "rights and privileges . . . which, according to the plainest considerations of reason and justice and the fundamental principles of the social compact, all are entitled to enjoy."[3] As the postbellum Court's enthusiast for the atextual contractarian approach, Swayne condemned a homestead exemption that had the effect of withdrawing real property from a judgment lien as "contrary to reason and justice, and to the fundamental principles of the social compact."[4] Though an antislavery Republican, he sustained the enforceability of a pre-Emancipation contract for sale of an enslaved person because a contrary result would be "forbidden by the fundamental principles of the social compact."[5] Justice Samuel F. Miller relied on "limitations on [governmental] power which grow out of the essential nature of all free governments. Implied reservations of individual rights [are necessary to] the social compact."[6]

Had this approach attracted adherents besides Swayne, it might have been un-necessary for judges to create the new doctrine of substantive due process. But the vitality of the higher law tradition in its pure, nontextual *Calder* form was exhausted by the Civil War, and these occasional echoes were nothing more than doctrinal throwbacks. Higher law in the modern era required some textual home.

Before the war, the New York Court of Appeals had identified the due process clause as that home in *Wynehamer v. The People* (1856).[7] Relying on the joint law-of-the-land and due process clauses of the New York constitution, Judge George F. Comstock struck down a prohibition statute destroying rights in extant stocks of liquor because the owner "is deprived of [property] within the spirit of a constitutional provision intended expressly to shield private rights from the exercise of arbitrary power."

The Supreme Court flirted with this approach on three occasions before 1890, but two of those were not precedents that inspired confidence. In 1856, Justice Benjamin R. Curtis ambiguously proposed the possibility of a substantive reading of the Fifth Amendment's due process clause, suggesting in dicta that it "is a restraint on the legislative as well as on the executive and judicial powers of the government, and cannot be so construed as to leave congress free to make any process 'due process of law,' by its mere will."[8] Justice Curtis assumed that the due process clause was the equivalent of the law-of-the-land clauses of the early state constitutions and, through them, of their ancestor, the *per legem terrae* clause of Magna Charta's Article 39.[9] The law-of-the-land clauses had a stronger substantive connotation.[10]

The next year, Chief Justice Taney gave the clause a substantive interpretation in the *Dred Scott Case* (1857):[11] "an act of Congress which deprives a citizen of the United States of his liberty or property, merely because he came himself or brought his property [slaves] into a particular Territory of the United States, . . . could hardly be dignified with the name of due process of law." His successor Salmon P. Chase toyed with the concept in the first *Legal Tender Case* (1870),[12] voiding wartime greenback statutes making fiat money legal tender.

Justice Samuel F. Miller flatly rejected this substantive interpretation in *Slaughterhouse* (1873): "[U]nder no construction of that provision [the due process clause] that we have ever seen, or any that we deem admissible, can the restraint imposed by the State of Louisiana upon the exercise of their trade by the butchers of New Orleans be held to be a deprivation of property within the meaning of that provision."[13]

But it was Justice Joseph P. Bradley and not Miller who spoke for the future in *Slaughterhouse*. He and Field, who dissented separately, elevated the antebellum concept of free labor to constitutional status. Field relied on what proved to be a constitutional dead end, the privileges-and-immunities clause of the Fourteenth Amendment.[14] Bradley on the other hand emphasized the due process clause of the Fourteenth Amendment, and thereby inaugurated the constitutional tradition that would endure until 1937.

Substantive due process was the enduring core of legal classicism. Bradley identified "fundamental rights that can only be taken away by due process of law," which included "the right to choose one's calling"; this was "a man's property and right." It followed that "a law which prohibits a large class of citizens from adopting a lawful employment, or from following a lawful employment previously adopted, does deprive them of liberty as well as property, without due process of law."[15] At the same term, even Justice Miller, redoubtable foe of the substantive interpretation, acknowledged that if a case were to come before the Court alleging that a prohibition statute had deprived an individual of extant property rights in liquor without due process, it would "require the most careful and serious consideration."[16]

Substantive due process did not capture the imagination of the entire Court and made way only slowly. Five years after *Slaughterhouse*, Miller grumped that "there exists some strange misconception of the scope of this provision [the due process clause] as found in the Fourteenth Amendment." Yet even then he conceded in dictum that, in an extreme case, an arbitrary legislative property transfer of the taking-from-A-giving-to-B sort could amount to a violation of due process.[17]

Similarly, in *Loan Association v. Topeka* (1875), Chief Justice Morrison R. Waite relied on the old *Calder* formula as a limitation on state legislative power. "There are such rights in every free government beyond the control of the State." He condemned redistribution: "[W]here the purpose for which the tax was to be issued could no longer be justly claimed to have [a] public character, but was purely in aid of private or personal objects, the law authorizing it was beyond the legislative power, and was an unauthorized invasion of private right," citing Cooley and Dillon.[18] In the *Civil Rights Cases* (1883), Justice Bradley reasserted his *Slaughterhouse* dissent's claim that a statute "denying to any person, or class of persons, the right to pursue any peaceful avocations allowed to others [or other] class legislation would . . . be obnoxious to the prohibitions of the Fourteenth Amendment."[19]

The Court edged closer to fusing the two concepts of higher law and due process, subsuming the former into the latter, in *Stone v. Farmers Loan & Trust Co.* (1886).[20] There, Chief Justice Waite upheld a state rate-setting statute, but he cautioned that "this power to regulate is not a power to destroy. . . . Under pretense of regulating fares and freights, the state cannot require a railroad corporation to carry persons or property without reward; neither can it do that which in law amounts to a taking of private property for public use without just compensation, or without due process of law."

The next year in *Mugler v. Kansas* (1887),[21] the Court again sustained a state prohibition statute that declared breweries and distilleries to be public nuisances. But Justice John M. Harlan warned that if "a statute purporting to have been enacted to protect the public health, the public morals, or the public safety, has no real or substantial relation to those objects, or is a palpable invasion of rights secured by the fundamental law" or if "it is apparent that its real object is not to protect the community, or to promote the general well-being, but, under the guise of police regulation, to deprive the owner of his liberty and property, without due process of law," the Court would strike it down. By introducing the substantial relation test, and opening up judicial inquiries into the legislature's "real" motive, Harlan went a long way toward undermining his own position of strong support for the police power.

State Court Developments

Meanwhile, as the Supreme Court lumbered ponderously toward substantive due process, state jurists sprinted ahead as the avant-garde of classicism in public law. There was a chronological incidence to these state due process cases that has been overlooked. Nearly all of them, with a few notorious exceptions, were decided between 1885 and 1900. By the turn of the century, state legislatures began to intervene extensively in the issues that furnished the grist of the classicist cases. This unprecedented legislative involvement diverted judicial trends in two ways. First, when legislatures made clear and firm public policy decisions that rebuffed earlier judicial ventures, courts avoided further confrontation, respected lawmakers' authority, and accepted the legislative initiatives. Second, clear and forceful legislative determination of policy, such as the creation of workers' compensation, took responsibility for making public policy out of the judges' hands, and the courts acquiesced.

Courts had assumed policy-making responsibility in the 1885–1900 period *faute de mieux*, as it were. In postwar America, with its undeveloped administrative capacity and near total absence of regulatory tradition, courts filled a vacuum of governance, implicitly assuming that as long as no one else was taking charge of policy making, judges might as well do so. This persistence of the antebellum regime receded once legislatures saw the need for firmer governance and stepped in to provide it by statute and administrative delegation. The paradigmatic example in this period was provided by railroad finance. Federal courts withdrew from supervising railroad receiverships as the Interstate Commerce Commission and its state regulatory counterparts began to assume new roles in financial oversight.

Courts did not persist in long-standing resistance to the legislatures' determination to assume their rightful role as the branch of government responsible for policy making. Indeed, it was the unusual and anomalous persistence of the Supreme Court in that obstructive role in the 1930s that brought on the constitutional crisis of 1937 and the downfall of legal classicism.

But in the closing decades of the nineteenth century, state courts resisted legislative policy initiatives. State judges, in one scholar's opinion, "competed with one another for the starkest application of freedom of contract and the truest belief in laissez-faire ideology."[22] The New York Court of Appeals (that state's highest court), opened the era with *In re Jacobs* (1885) and closed it out with *Ives v. South Buffalo Railway Co.* (1911).

In *Jacobs*,[23] Judge Robert Earl for a unanimous court struck down a state statute that prohibited cigar manufacturing in tenement houses, an urban cottage industry of the era. The employment contract was governed by "the fierce competition of trade and the inexorable laws of supply and demand." In "the unceasing struggle for success and existence which pervades all societies of men," the prohibition of tenement sweatshops may deprive the worker "of that which will enable him to maintain his hold, and to survive." The statute interfered with the profitable use of real property by both owner and lessee, "and thus in a strictly legitimate sense, it arbitrarily deprives him of his property and of some portion of his personal liberty."

"Such governmental interferences disturb the normal adjustments of the social fabric, and usually derange the delicate and complicated machinery of industry and cause a score of evils while attempting the removal of one." Judge Earl imposed a means-ends test to be superintended by courts, requiring legislative means to have "some relation" to legitimate ends. "Under the mere guise of police regulations, personal rights and private property cannot be arbitrarily invaded, and the determination of the legislature is not final or conclusive."

The New York Court of Appeals revisited the issues of *Munn v. Illinois* four years later in *People v. Budd* (1889).[24] A majority of the court upheld state administrative regulation of the rates of warehouses and grain elevators along the Erie Canal. (The regulation would soon prove to be pointless, since the canal had undergone a steep decline in use because it was obsolete for the shipping technology of the day, and would be abandoned by 1900.) Judge Rufus Peckham, shortly to be elevated to the Supreme Court, delivered himself of an unbuttoned dissent denouncing all rate legislation, which simply provided "the most frequent opportunity for arraying class against class" and threatened to introduce "competition for the possession of the government." (A reader might have thought that this was the purpose of democratic politics, but perhaps that was Peckham's point.) Peckham condemned "the disposition of legislatures to interfere in the ordinary concerns of the individual." The court "should not strain after holding such species of legislation constitutional," he opined. "It is so plain an effort to interfere with what seems to me the most sacred rights of property and the individual liberty of contract that no special intendment in its favor should be indulged in." Rate regulation is "vicious in its nature, communistic in its tendency, and in my belief wholly inefficient to permanently attain the result aimed at . . . , an illegal effort to interfere with the lawful privilege of the individual to seek and obtain such compensation as he can for the use of his own property."

Perhaps cheered by such judicial rant, Budd, the warehouseman, appealed the decision to the Supreme Court, where he was disappointed again, when the Court, for the last time, broadly affirmed *Munn*. He had to derive what consolation he could from Justice David J. Brewer's dissent, which contained the famous *cri du coeur*, "The paternal theory of government is to me odious." The indignant dissenters explained: "[T]he utmost liberty to the individual, and the fullest possible protection to him and his property is both the limitation and duty of government."[25]

In re Jacobs led a procession of cases decided in the next fifteen years that drew on general concepts of higher law, or the due process and takings guarantees in the state and federal constitutions, to void state regulation of labor. In *Godcharles v. Wigeman* (1886),[26] Justice Isaac G. Gordon of the Pennsylvania Supreme Court condemned a statute that declared a ton for steel-making purposes to be the statutory 2,000 pounds, rather than the 2,240 pounds imposed by the companies as an industry "custom"; some steelworkers were paid by the ton, so the companies' policy simply squeezed more work out of them. Because this "prevent[ed] persons who are sui juris from making their own contracts," it was an "insulting attempt to put the laborer under a legislative tutelage, which is not only degrading to his manhood, but subversive of his rights as a citizen of the United States." Justice Gordon did not bother to specify which right or which constitutional provision was implicated; he seemed to think the source of the right was so obvious that it did not need to be identified.

The Illinois Supreme Court, along with its New York counterpart, led the state judiciaries in developing this line of thought. In *Millett v. People*,[27] decided the same year as *Godcharles*, the Illinois court voided a statute requiring coal coming out of a mine to be weighed on a track scale. Miners were paid by the ton, and the companies' practice of cheating their miners by weighing coal light was notorious. Judge John Scholfield maintained that the statute was "partial," not "general" legislation binding on all. He rejected the defense of the statute based on the police power, contending that the statute was not enacted to protect the safety of the miner or his property. This was logically inconsistent, because it identified a miner's right to contract for his labor in the future as a property right but not his claim to be paid for work that he had already done.

Judge Scholfield wrote again for the court in *Frorer v. People* (1892),[28] rejecting a statute that prohibited mining companies from keeping company stores or paying their miners in scrip or anything but legal tender. The right of both employer and employee to contract with each other was "both a liberty and a property right." To subject miners and not other kinds of employees to a restriction on their contractual capacity would degrade them, because "theoretically there is among our citizens no inferior class."

Judge Benjamin D. Magruder built on these precedents in the decision that capped Illinois's labor-hostile decisions, *Ritchie v. People* (1895),[29] which voided a statute limiting women's labor in the needle trades to eight hours a day, and forty-eight hours a week. "Labor is property," Judge Magruder reasoned, and the laborer has a right to sell it like any other property, explicitly confirming law's commodification of labor. He confined the legislature's police power categorically, anticipating the United States Supreme Court by thirty years.[30] The statute was partial, and was a "purely arbitrary restriction on the fundamental right of the citizen to control his or her own time or faculties." Gender aside, the imputed bargaining equality between employer and employee was undercut by decisions everywhere, including Illinois, upholding the validity of usury laws (one of Magruder's permissible categories) on the grounds that usurious lenders took advantage of the borrower's necessity.[31]

With an irony that must have galled women's rights advocates, Magruder affirmed the legal equality of women with men by citing an 1872 Illinois statute prohibiting gender discrimination in employment opportunities (a statute that did Myra Bradwell no good when she unsuccessfully sought admission to the Illinois bar.)[32] He also cited *Minor v. Happersett* (1875)[33] to the effect that women were both persons and citizens for purposes of their contractual capacity — but neglected to mention that the Supreme Court in that case held that states could nevertheless exclude them from the ballot. In a sense, such reasoning, and its echo on the United States Supreme Court in *Adkins v. Childrens Hospital* (1923), was congruent with contemporary attitudes toward women workers, who at that time comprised about a quarter of the industrial labor force.[34] Based on the assumptions about formal equality that characterized classical legal thought, plus gender-specific attitudes about women as potential mothers, public policy alternated between protective paternalism and a nominal but empty egalitarianism. Either way, though, women workers could be certain that their treatment at the hands of legislatures and judges would be disadvantageous to their employment status.

Finally, to cap a thoroughly regressive decision, Magruder held in dictum that the state's police power could not be exercised to protect the workplace safety or health of the employee. In his view, it could protect only the public at large: "[I]t is questionable whether [the police power] can be exercised to prevent injury to the individual engaged in a particular calling."[35] After the legislature reasserted its determination to regulate the conditions of labor, the Illinois court accepted a modified statute in 1910.[36]

An economic interpretation of these cases would suggest that it was no accident that the courts of the leading industrial states, Massachusetts, New York, and Illinois, assumed leadership in developing doctrines that limited employers' obligations to their employees or that gave them a free hand in imposing terms of labor. But the courts of nonindustrial states developed the same doctrines too. The West Virginia Supreme Court of Appeals provided one of the most widely cited precedents, *State v. Goodwill* (1889).[37] President Adam C. Snyder held unconstitutional a statute that required payment of wages in money, not scrip, for mining and manufacturing enterprises, on the grounds that it was "partial legislation" since it did not also include, for example, railroad employees. "The natural law of supply and demand is the best law of trade," Snyder thought. Legislation like the antiscrip statute was "a species of sumptuary legislation which has been universally condemned, as an attempt to degrade the integrity, virtue, and manhood of the American laborer, and foist upon the people a government of the most objectionable character, because it assumes the employer is a knave, and the laborer is an imbecile."

Snyder presented a synopsis of the ideology underlying these decisions, quoted here at length because it provides a clear and forthright exposition of the judicial vision of the era:

> The property which every man has in his own labor, as it is the original foundation of all other property, so it is the most sacred and inviolable. The patrimony of the poor man lies in the strength and dexterity of his own hands, and to hinder him from employing these in what manner he may think proper, without injury to his neighbor, is a plain violation of this most sacred property. It is equally an encroach-

ment both upon the just liberty and rights of the workman and his employer . . . for the legislature to interfere with the freedom of contract between them. . . . A person living under the protection of this government has the right to adopt and follow any lawful industrial pursuit, not injurious to the community, which he may see fit. . . . The emjoyment [*sic*] or deprivation of these rights and privileges constitutes the essential distinction between freedom and slavery; between liberty and oppression.

Felix Frankfurter later dismissed this line of reasoning epigrammatically, noting "the futility of freedom *of* contract in the absence of the freedom *to* contract."[38]

The Massachusetts Supreme Judicial Court returned anachronistically to the intellectual environment of *Calder v. Bull* to strike down a statute prohibiting employers from fining weavers for imperfections in their work. In *Commonwealth v. Perry* (1891),[39] Justice Marcus P. Knowlton held that this deprived employers of "certain fundamental rights." A statute encroaching on such rights was unconstitutional "even though the enactment of it is not expressly forbidden" by the Constitution. This provoked Justice Oliver Wendell Holmes in dissent to caution that courts must find some textual basis for the creation of rights. A judge should not overrule legislation "unless [he] thought that an honest difference of opinion was impossible, or pretty nearly so."

Five years later, Massachusetts justice Charles Allen enjoined labor picketing as "private nuisance" because it constituted "moral intimidation" and was an actionable "conspiracy." This decision, *Vegelahn v. Guntner* (1896),[40] provoked Holmes to dissent again, but this time with a more sophisticated and deeper analysis of underlying legal relationships.[41] Holmes insisted that organized labor's contests with employers, along with the tactics they employed, including the picketing involved in this case, were privileged at law, in the same way that ordinary economic competition among merchants or rival technologies was privileged. The absolute rights imagined by Justice Allen and the majority were a chimera. Not all judges were persuaded by Holmes's aperçu, though. A decade later, Illinois judges continued to enjoin picketing as being per se coercive and illegal. To them, it was obvious that "peaceful picketing" was an oxymoron.[42]

The New York Court of Appeals persisted in its dedication to substantive due process and the ideology that was its matrix long after they were discarded elsewhere.[43] Like the Illinois court, the New York judges thought that the near-equality of women with men removed any justification for special legislative solicitude for female workers. Striking down a statute prohibiting night labor by women,[44] Judge John C. Gray in *People v. Williams* (1907) condemned such legislation as "discriminative against female citizens, in denying them equality with men in the same pursuit."[45] Not content with enunciating a norm of law and a construction of the state's constitution, Judge Gray offered this observation on the course of early-twentieth-century social legislation:

> [W]hen it is sought under the guise of a labor law, arbitrarily, as here, to prevent an adult female citizen from working at any time of the day that suits her, I think it is time to call a halt. It arbitrarily deprives citizens of their right to contract with each other. The tendency of legislatures, in the form of regulatory measures, to interfere with the lawful pursuits of citizens is becoming a marked one in this country, and it behooves the courts, firmly and fearlessly, to interpose the barriers of their judgments.

The New York court elaborated classical doctrines in both labor-related cases and in decisions dealing with nonlabor economic regulation, to frustrate exercise of the state's police power.[46] It capped this line of decisions with a coda to the concerto of state-court substantive due process and liberty of contract in the 1911 case of *Ives v. South Buffalo Railway Co.*[47] Throughout the first decade of the twentieth century, state legislatures had struggled to enact workers' compensation, over dogged opposition from employers and their abettors in the legal profession. In *Ives*, the New York Court of Appeals struck down a New York workers' compensation statute enacted in 1910. The statute abrogated the common law doctrines of contributory negligence and assumption of risk in the employment context, making employers absolutely liable for workplace injuries, on the theory that they could insure against such risks, while employees for all practical purposes could not. Employers could pass the charges on to the consumer, thus internalizing the costs of industrial accidents. Under the extant regime of common law (non)liability, such costs were externalized, foisted off first on the employee and his family or survivors, with the remainder being passed on to the community at large.

Even though the doctrines of contributory negligence and assumption of risk were only two generations old,[48] Judge William E. Werner treated them as immemorial, fundamental, and as the legal equivalents of the law of gravity:

> [C]an [property] be taken from [the employer] by the mere assertion that this statute only reverses the common law doctrine that the employee assumes the risk of his employment? It would be quite as logical and effective to argue that this legislation only reverses the laws of nature, for in everything within the sphere of human activity the risks which are inherent and unavoidable must fall upon those who are exposed to them.

Judge Werner railed against legislative schemes looking to "a more equal distribution of wealth." Such redistribution was prohibited by the due process clauses of the federal and state constitutions, which he read in both a substantive and a procedural sense. Underlying the due process guarantees, he believed, was a classical conception of property rights, which rest "not upon philosophical or scientific speculations nor upon the commendable impulses of benevolence or charity, nor yet upon the dictates of natural justice. The right has its foundation in the fundamental law. That can be changed by the people, but not by legislatures." He dismissed the elaborate legislative groundwork that had gone into formulation of public policy supporting workers' compensation: "[I]n a government like ours theories of public good or necessity are often so plausible or sound as to command popular approval, but courts are not permitted to forget that the law is the only chart by which the ship of state is to be guided."

That led Werner to substitute his own conception of the philosophical justification for maintaining the existing distribution of wealth:

> If the legislature can say to an employer, "you must compensate your employee for an injury not caused by you or by your fault," why can it not go further and say to the man of wealth, "you have more property than you need and your neighbor is so poor that he can barely subsist; in the interest of natural justice you must divide with your neighbor so that he and his dependents shall not become a charge upon the State?"

Having bottomed the discourse on this fundamental ground, Judge Werner then simply returned to *Calder* higher law doctrines: "[I]n its final and simple analysis that is taking the property of A and giving it to B, and that cannot be done under our Constitutions."

Chief Judge Irving Lehman, looking back on his predecessors on the New York Court of Appeals in 1939, offered a sympathetic evaluation of the mindset that produced *Ives*. The 1911 judges were not reactionaries, Lehman believed, but "they had adopted the social philosophy of the classical liberals of the nineteenth century, and consciously or unconsciously they were swayed by that philosophy."[49]

Ives shocked the nation. In New York, Werner, a Republican, was defeated in his bid for election to the chief judgeship the next year, and the people promptly ratified a constitutional amendment giving the legislature the power *Ives* denied them.[50] Nationally, Teddy Roosevelt made it a campaign issue in his run for the presidency on the Progressive ticket in 1912. Even the sitting president, the eminently conservative William Howard Taft, deplored the decision as an "individual instance[] of a hidebound and retrograde conservatism on the part of courts in decisions which turn on the individual economic or sociological views of the judges."[51] *Ives* only momentarily deflected the irresistible movement toward workers' compensation. In 1917, the Supreme Court sustained the constitutionality of a subsequent New York workers' compensation statute.[52] But *Ives* did demonstrate the continuing hold of classical premises on the judicial mind.

The general revulsion to the *Ives* decision produced one unanticipated salutary result. The Judiciary Act of 1914[53] corrected an anomalous loophole in federal jurisdiction created by the Judiciary Act of 1789. Under the celebrated section 25 of the 1789 statute, a state court decision involving a state statute challenged as violative of the federal Constitution could be appealed to the Supreme Court only if that decision *upheld* the measure. Thus, if *Ives* had involved a federal rather than state constitutional challenge, it could not be appealed to the Supreme Court. The 1914 measure permitted appeals of decisions either upholding or striking down state legislation. Given the compatibility of state and federal judicial attitudes, that provided little succor at the time to proponents of Progressive legislation, but the expansion of federal jurisdiction would in time prove valuable.

Progressives were disheartened by the power of state and federal courts to stymie social welfare legislation. "The greater number of our state courts are illiberal," complained Walter F. Dodd, a prominent Progressive political scientist, in 1913.[54] The Columbia economist Henry R. Seager, president of the American Association for Labor Legislation, noted that the "fear that . . . legislation might be declared unconstitutional has been a constant bugaboo paralyzing efforts" of social reform advocates and accounted for the American states being "behind progressive European countries in the field of social and labor legislation . . . because of this [judicially erected] constitutional barrier."[55]

Seager's observation caught only part of a larger picture. The obstructive ideology of classical legal thought, privileging abstract conceptions of bargaining equality and property rights, constituted a major part of the explanation for the unique and peculiar structure of American welfare legislation as compared with other modernizing industrialized states. As Dodd implied, the United States lacked the general social insurance (including unemployment compensation) and old age pensions then provided by some European states. Instead, it provided a national system of veterans' pensions that went a long way toward a selective but cross-class program of old age maintenance, and then erected a ramshackle structure of "mothers' pensions," protecting women and children, again across lines of class and ethnicity. The absence of a political Left and powerful trades unions, Samuel Gompers's self-denying attitude toward political involvement, and the individualist foundations of American political culture assured that the abortive "maternalist welfare state," as Theda Skocpol terms it, would be as far as American social welfare experimentation could go, given the junkyard dog mentality of classical jurists patrolling the boundaries of property and contracts, vigilant to suppress unions and worker-protective legislation.[56]

William E. Forbath has compiled an enumeration of decisions that either struck down or upheld state legislation affecting the interests of working people and unions in the classical era.[57] (The cases voiding laws in the nineteenth century outnumbered those upholding them, seventy-six to twenty-six.) These cases involved the following topics: forbidding "yellow-dog" contracts or lesser forms of employer inhibition of union membership; weighing coal as the basis for miners' wages; requiring periodic payment of wages; prohibiting payment of wages in scrip or requiring payment in money; prohibiting or regulating company stores; regulating hours, in governmental, public-works, or private-sector employment, covering men and/or women; prohibiting manufacture in tenements; prohibiting or regulating labor injunctions; modifying the criminal conspiracy doctrine; prohibiting child labor; providing written statements of the reasons for firing an employee; requiring labeling of convict-made goods; inhibiting emigrant-agents (who were a threat to quasi-unfree condition of black labor in the southern states); creating mechanics' liens; requiring union labor in public works; forbidding blacklists; regulating the conditions, usually hours, of women's work; taxing alien labor; mandating minimum wages and workplace inspection; granting antitrust exemptions for unions; and statutes requiring jury trials for contempt proceedings following violation of a labor injunction.

Surveying his enumeration, Forbath concludes that the classical legal order treated "workers . . . like commodities, or like property at someone else's disposal, not only because of the law of the labor injunction (and of the anti-union violence it encouraged), but also because of many other social and economic inequalities"[58]— inequalities protected by classical judges in the name of liberty and the sanctity of property.

The United States Supreme Court

After resisting the trend for nearly two decades, the United States Supreme Court finally embraced substantive due process in the Milwaukee Road Case of 1890, but it did so opaquely.[59] Responding to Granger demands, the Minnesota legislature had created a "strong" railroad commission with rate-setting powers. Justice Samuel Blatchford for the Court's majority[60] held that this process for setting rates took the railroad's property without due process of law because it denied the company the opportunity to have some court review the commission's orders. The reasonableness of the rate set "is eminently a question for judicial investigation, requiring due process of law for its determination. If a company is deprived of the power of charging reasonable rates . . . , it is deprived of the lawful use of its property, and thus, in substance and effect, of the property itself, without due process of law."

In this passage, the Supreme Court for the first time made the fateful transition from the noncontroversial tradition of procedural due process to a substantive reading of the clause. All persons (including corporations, those fictive persons in the eyes of the law) now had a constitutionally protected but vaguely and expansively defined right to use their property. Blatchford's opinion invited judges to second-guess utility commissions, imposing judicial conceptions of reasonableness for rate determinations made through the political and administrative process.

Four years later, the Supreme Court, at the urging of John F. Dillon as counsel, held that a court sitting in equity could find administratively set rates "unjust and unreasonable." In this case, *Reagan v. Farmers Loan and Trust Co.* (1894),[61] Justice David J. Brewer held that the "equal protection of the laws which, by the Fourteenth Amendment, no State can deny to the individual, forbids legislation, in whatever form it may be enacted, by which the property of one individual is, without compensation, wrested from him for the benefit of another, or of the public." "Justice demands that everyone should receive some compensation for the use of his money or property," he insisted, and "the obligations of justice" require that corporations be given an opportunity to make a profit in the market.

This transition to substantive due process blurred a previously crucial distinction, gravely wounding the states' police powers. Under prior doctrine, a "taking" of property required compensation under the Fifth Amendment's takings clause and its state analogues, but police power regulations did not. The power of the state to regulate, as, for example, by controlling nuisances like tanneries, was deemed antecedent to any property rights that might be affected, and so noncompensable. Substantive due process conflated these two doctrinal categories, and thus went a long way toward erasing the difference between regulation and takings, to the detriment of the public authority.

The Court then held, logically enough, that the due process clause of the Fourteenth Amendment incorporated the Fifth Amendment's takings clause, thereby requiring states to pay compensation when they took property by condemnation: "[C]ompensation for private property taken for public use is an essential element of due process of law as ordained by the Fourteenth Amendment." In this case, *Chicago, Burlington and Quincy Railroad v. Chicago* (1897),[62] the Justices added another layer of constitutional protection for property rights. The due process, equal protection, and takings clauses now stood in formidable array against administrative regulation. Apart from its significance in the story of classical legal thought, this decision was also the first instance where the Court in a holding incorporated the guarantees of the Bill of Rights via the Fourteenth Amendment as a constraint on the states. This began the process of selective incorporation that became such an important theme of twentieth-century constitutional history.

With these decisions, the Court transmuted the due process guarantees of the Fifth and Fourteenth Amendments from assurances of fair procedure into a requirement that the substantive content of the statute be "reasonable," with courts retaining ultimate authority to decide on reasonableness. The substantive due process decisions of the Supreme Court contained an implicit theory of political economy, derived from classical economics, which was rapidly becoming discredited among economists.[63] Substantive due process embalmed classical liberal economics in the appellate reports, however, and thus extended its influence preternaturally as pseudo-legal doctrine. The mummified dead hand of the Manchester School was to lie on American public law for another generation.

The new doctrine ushered in an era of judicial activism. According to one count,[64] in the period before 1898, the Supreme Court invalidated a total of twelve federal statutes and 125 state laws, while in the single generation after 1898, it trebled those figures (fifty federal and 400 state.) Another analysis, done by Felix Frankfurter in 1930, suggested that the Court vetoed social and economic legislation in a quarter of the due process cases it decided between 1913 and 1920, and in a third of the cases during the 1920s.[65]

The Supreme Court implemented its new oversight power in *Smyth v. Ames* (1898),[66] where it decided that railroad rates set by a state legislature were so low that they were unreasonable and therefore deprived the railroad of due process. To reach this conclusion, the Court arrogated to itself the power to resolve technical accounting issues that constituted the basis of rate-setting determinations. This mired the Court in a half-century of resolving ever more esoteric issues of accounting. The Justices eventually extricated themselves from this unwonted role of being an accounting superreview board in 1942 and 1944 by overruling *Smyth*.[67]

Substantive due process assumed protean forms. It soon generated a daughter doctrine, liberty of contract, that vindicated the Field and Bradley *Slaughterhouse* dissents. Contractual freedom as a social ideal permeated Anglo-American law in the late nineteenth century. In 1875, Sir George Jessel, Master of the Rolls, set the tone when he proclaimed that "if there is one thing which more than another public policy requires it is that men of full age and competent understanding shall have the utmost liberty of contracting, and that their contracts when entered into freely and voluntarily shall be held sacred and shall be enforced by Courts of justice. Therefore, you have this paramount public policy to consider — that you are not lightly to interfere with this freedom of contract."[68]

In *Allgeyer v. Louisiana* (1897),[69] Justice Rufus Peckham for a unanimous Court approvingly cited Bradley's *Slaughterhouse* dissent and echoed Jessel in holding that the due process clause protects an individual's right to make a contract (in this case, for insurance). With individual contractual capacity thus elevated to constitutional status, the Court was poised as the century turned to strike down state statutes regulating the conditions of labor on the grounds that they interfered with the employers' and employees' liberty of contract.

An unlikely observer offered a remarkable judgment on the new judicial doctrines and their consequences. The English jurisprudent Henry Sumner Maine, who had popularized the notion of progress from status to contract, observed that the prosperity of the United States "reposes on the sacredness of contract and the stability of private property, the first the implement, and the last the reward, of success in the universal competition." The consequences of this reign of contract and property were, however, severe: "[T]here has hardly ever before been a community in which

the weak have been pushed so pitilessly to the wall, in which those who have succeeded have so uniformly been the strong, and in which in so short a time there has
arisen so great an inequality of private fortune and domestic luxury."[70]

1894–1896: Crisis and Resolution

The years 1895–1896 could have been one of those constitutional moments that are
the subjects of Bruce Ackerman's interpretation.[71] The financial panic of 1893, followed by the violence of the Pullman strike and the nonviolent march of Coxey's
"army" in 1894, convinced America's overclass that a nationwide social and economic
crisis was at hand.

With that class angst as background, the Supreme Court produced a remarkable succession of opinions that, taken collectively, attempted to impose restrictions
on the regulatory powers of the federal and state governments; to prevent the redistribution of wealth; to reassert the traditional balance of federalism in questions of
race; and to clear the way for uninhibited deployment of armed force to suppress
striking workers and the marching poor. These decisions began with *Reagan v. Farmers Loan and Trust*; reached a climax in the great triad of 1895 decisions, *United
States v. E. C. Knight Co.* (1895), *In re Debs* (1895), and *Pollock v. Farmers Loan and
Trust Co. I and II* (1895); and concluded with a racial anticlimax, *Plessy v. Ferguson*
(1896). Judicial reaction was confirmed by the presidential election of 1896, which
arrayed capitalism against reform. Capitalism won, resoundingly. Yet we do not look
back on 1895–1896 as a constitutional moment because the Court's initiatives eventually failed.

Redistribution: The Income Tax Cases

Before 1894, classical legal thought had encountered only indirect kinds of wealth
redistribution, such as maximum-hours legislation. But in that year, redistribution
showed its Gorgon's head directly, in the form of a federal tax on incomes. Congress
enacted a flat-rate income tax of 2 percent on all incomes over $4,000 derived from
whatever source. The $4,000 exemption meant that only 2 percent of the American
population would pay the tax. To the febrile imaginations of conservatives, this conjured up the specter of wealth redistribution that the Framers had sought to forestall
a century earlier. In reality, the progressive aspect of the 1894 tax was merely a token
or symbolic offset to the existing inequality of federal taxation, which until then consisted exclusively of a tariff (except for a brief interlude during the Civil War). The
tariff, being a consumption tax, was regressive, placing a relatively heavier burden
on poor and working Americans than on the comfortable minority. Further, given
the extreme inequality in the distribution of wealth in America at the time (with the
top 12 percent of American families owning 86 percent of the nation's wealth), the
impact of federal taxation fell even more disproportionately on the poor. Thus the 2
percent tax on incomes above $4,000 was actually a modest effort to shift a part of the
tax burden onto those who had largely evaded it.

Robert Stanley has reinterpreted the *Income Tax Cases* in a critique of the dominant Progressive interpretation of the episode.[72] Far from being a Populist-driven effort to redistribute income, Stanley argues, the federal income tax of 1994 was "a powerful example of the use of law to constrain significant change in a rapidly developing society." The Fuller Court attempted to preserve "statist capitalism" and a "centrist" political order from challenges emanating from both the right and the left ends of the political spectrum. Stanley posits a late-nineteenth-century political economy in which the state supported capitalist enterprise by a regressive tax (the tariff) and subsidies of various sorts to entrepreneurs. Sensing a serious threat to this system in the social disorders of the 1880s, the federal government threw a symbolic sop to the aggrieved middle classes, an insignificant, "nonallocative" gesture of progressive taxation. It was, in the words of one of its supporters, Missouri congressman Uriel Hall, "a measure to kill anarchy and keep down socialists."

This provoked two contrary reactions. Conservatives sought to banish forever the goal of tax progressivity, however symbolic it might seem, and to remove as much of property — all, if possible — from the reach of federal taxation. At the other end of the political spectrum, Populists and others demanded true progressivity and a redistribution of wealth. The center sought merely stability and continuity with tradition.

The Fuller Court's response to these pressures, Stanley continues, was fragmented. Fuller and the bare majority he managed to scrape together to void the income tax sought to redirect "the course of centrism away from aggregated, federally sheltered, economic power — whether in the form of big government, big business, or growing labor — and the creation of legal conditions whose animating vision seemingly was not the protection of the silk-hatted tycoon but of the village blacksmith."

Failing to forfend a symbolic progressive tax in the political arena, opponents turned to the courts in collusive litigation seeking to have the tax held unconstitutional.[73] This suit, *Pollock v. Farmers Loan & Trust Co.* (1895), attracted some of the most eminent members of the Supreme Court bar of the day: Richard Olney, who was United States attorney general, and James C. Carter for the tax; George F. Edmunds, William D. Guthrie, and Joseph Choate in opposition. Choate, contending the tax was unconstitutional because unapportioned,[74] labored under the disadvantage of having two precedents flatly against him: *Hylton v. United States* (1796)[75] and *Springer v. United States* (1881).[76] An old lawyers' cliché says: when the facts are against you, argue the law. When the law is against you, argue the facts. When the facts *and* the law are against you, pound on the table.

Pound on the table Choate did. He denounced the income tax as "communistic in its purposes and tendencies, and . . . defended here upon principles as communistic, socialistic — what shall I call them — populistic as ever have been addressed to any political assembly in the world."[77] It was "a confiscation under the forms of law." He insisted that "one of the fundamental objects of all civilized government was the preservation of the rights of private property . . . the very keystone of the arch upon which all civilized government rests." It was the most momentous case he had ever argued, Choate claimed, because it involved "the preservation of the fundamental rights of private property and equality before the law." The conservative *Albany Law Journal* seconded Choate, warning that if Congress could tax some and not others, as it had by the 1894 act, it would be "encouraging anarchists and socialists, recognizing the vast body of communists and those who believe in confiscating enough from the rich to properly support their shiftless and useless existences."[78] Progressive taxation, John F. Dillon insisted, was "the most insidious, specious, and therefore dangerous" form of attack by "communists, socialists, and anarchists" on private property, nothing less than "pillage" achieved by "universal suffrage."[79]

Half the Court resonated with such pleas. In its first decision in *Pollock v. Farmers Loan and Trust Co.* (*Pollock I*) (1895), the Court divided four to four on a crucial issue, the terminally ill Howell Jackson having gone home to Tennessee to die. But in holding that a tax on rents was in reality a tax on real property, and thus must be apportioned, Chief Justice Melville W. Fuller let the mask slip a bit, contending that "inequality [among taxpayers of different states, and, by extension, inequality among taxpayers generally] must be held to have been contemplated [by the Framers of 1787], and was manifestly designed to operate to restrain the exercise of the power of direct taxation to extraordinary emergencies, and to prevent an attack upon accumulated property by mere force of numbers." The requirement of apportionment was "one of the bulwarks of private rights and private property."[80]

Justice Stephen J. Field was roused out of his dotage to voice the fear that agitated the propertied classes: "[W]here is the course of usurpation to end? The present assault upon capital is but the beginning. It will be but the stepping-stone to others, larger and more sweeping, till our political contests will become a war of the poor against the rich, — a war constantly growing in intensity and bitterness."[81]

The mostly inconclusive result in *Pollock I* satisfied no one. Jackson was recalled, literally from his deathbed, and in *Pollock II* (1895),[82] the Court held the entire tax unconstitutional because it was not apportioned among the states. In the sort of pedestrian, feebly reasoned opinion characteristic of him, Chief Justice Fuller held that taxes on income from personal property like stocks (dividends) and bonds (interest) were "direct" and, because they had not been apportioned, unconstitutional.

Justice Edward D. White in dissent spoke movingly for tradition and continuity: "[T]he conservation and orderly development of our institutions rests on our acceptance of the results of the past, and their use as lights to guide our steps in the future." If settled principles are overturned, as White thought the *Pollock* decision overturned taxation, "the rights of property, so far as the Federal Constitution is concerned, are of little worth."[83]

Fuller denied that he was resolving any policy issues, so it was left to Harlan in a passionate dissent to denounce "the decision [which] involves nothing less than a surrender of the taxing power to the moneyed class." He chided the brethren: "[E]ven the spectre of socialism is conjured up to frighten Congress from laying taxes upon the people in proportion to their ability to pay them." Sounding more like Ignatius Donnelly than like a jurist, Harlan concluded that the decision would be "the first step toward the submergence of the liberties of the people in a sordid despotism of wealth." The decision "strikes at the very foundations of National authority" and does a "gross injustice to the many for the benefit of the favored few." Because the decision exempted shareholders, bond owners, and *rentiers* from taxes that working people would have to pay, it would "give to certain kinds of property a position of favoritism," subjecting the majority of the American people "to the dominion of aggregated wealth."[84]

The Income Tax Cases denied the federal government access to what contemporary economists recognized as the principal source of government revenue and thus weakened its power relative to the states. It also barred the federal government from a form of taxation that at least held out the potential of progressivity, leaving it to depend on the regressive tariff, which had discriminated against regions and economic classes since Alexander Hamilton had promoted it as secretary of the Treasury. The decision committed the prestige of the Supreme Court to a thinly disguised campaign against wealth redistribution, verifying Populist criticism that it had become the citadel of wealth. Justice Brewer, one of the majority, in fact endorsed the policy results of the decision in a commencement address three years later.[85] The American people had the final word, however, ratifying the Sixteenth Amendment in 1913, the third occasion up to that time when the people thus rebuked and reversed the Court.[86]

Labor: Debs

The second of the 1895 case triad, *In re Debs*, was the latest confrontation between organized labor, on one side, and a phalanx of management, federal courts, United States attorneys, and armed force on the other.[87] Three features of industrial development in the late nineteenth century determined the contours of this struggle, as well as its rules and its outcome. First, organized labor (as opposed to the individual "workingman") loomed as a threat to stability and property in the social visions of American elites, who saw civilization threatened by the forces of anarchy.[88] Second, state and federal courts assumed responsibility for formulating and administering industrial relations policy, in default of executive, administrative, and legislative will or machinery appropriate to the task. Finally, economists and lawyers promoted doctrines that regulated labor as if it were a market commodity.

General Nelson A. Miles, commander of the troops that put down the railroad strikers in Chicago in 1894, bespoke the fears of the dominant classes in American society when he drew this lesson from the experience: "If the property of a corporation or company in which the laboring men, the capitalists, the widows and orphans, the savings banks, properties in which any or all our people are interested, cannot be respected and protected, then the cottage, the hamlet, and the little personal property of the humblest citizen is in jeopardy, liable at the moment to be confiscated, seized, or destroyed." The railway strike posed in starkest terms a choice between "anarchy, secret conclaves, unwritten law, mob violence, and universal chaos," represented by the unions, and "the supremacy of law, the maintenance of good order, universal peace, absolute security of life and property, the rights of personal liberty," defended by army and courts.[89] This middle-class stereotype of the violent worker and his union permeated the labor cases of the period.[90]

The Pullman strike and boycott forced lawyers to reevaluate the direction of American labor law. Chief Judge Shaw's opinion in *Commonwealth v. Hunt* (1842) had rejected the doctrine that unions were per se actionable conspiracies. He had upheld both the union's ends, a closed shop, and its means, a concerted refusal to work.[91] This diminished the usefulness of conspiracy doctrine as a bludgeon of unions. The prosecution of union organizers and artisans for common law conspiracy receded for a time, but then rebounded vigorously after the Civil War.[92]

Conspiracy prosecutions eventually proved to be an unwieldy way to vex unions, however, because, being criminal proceedings, they guaranteed the defendants a hearing before a sometimes sympathetic jury. Something better was needed from the employers' perspective, more expeditious and not subject to the vagaries of jury nullification. That something proved to be the labor injunction, enforced by proceedings for contempt. Federal judges stumbled across these juryless procedures almost accidentally in the course of discharging their unwonted role as railroad administrators. By 1900, most American railroads had been through receivership in federal courts. In 1893 alone, a sixth of the nation's trackage was being run by court-appointed receivers.[93] During the railway labor unrest of 1877, federal judges tried to break the strikes against roads they were administering by issuing injunctions against striking workers and their unions. The volume of labor injunctions thereafter kept pace with union activity.[94]

Organized labor responded with innovative tactics of its own. Workers supplemented strikes with two new activities. The first was the boycott: a "primary boycott" of employers by the workers themselves, usually mounted to oppose an open shop policy, or a "secondary boycott" in which the workers urged their employer's customers or suppliers to shun the employer. The second tactic was the sympathy strike, in which unions not directly involved in the labor dispute walked out in sympathy with their brethren.

The federal judiciary's attitudes and ideology evolved in response to these developments. One strand of judicial attitudes toward labor consisted of paternalism toward individual workers when judges thought they needed protective intervention. The objects of this judicial solicitude were usually women and adult males employed in extrahazardous occupations. (Judges' concern did not extend to children, because few federal cases involved child labor before 1918. Opponents of child labor looked to legislatures, not courts, to promote their goals.) This component of judicial outlook explained the result in cases like *Holden v. Hardy* (1898),[95] which sustained a Utah eight-hour law for all workers in mines and smelters, and *Muller v. Oregon* (1908),[96] upholding a similar law for all women, whether their employment was dangerous or not.

Another strand of judicial thought resulted from the transformation of free labor ideology. Before the war, free labor had emphasized the autonomy and dignity of the worker. In the late nineteenth century, that outlook had evolved into something different, a contractarian vision of the labor market that imputed equality of bargaining status and power to employer and employee alike. Late-nineteenth-century judges embodied their decisions affecting unions in a formalist logic, abstract and dichotomous, that proved to be endlessly manipulable and circular but that inerrantly arrived at the same result: prosecution of union efforts.[97]

Above all, state and federal judges had not shaken off their unthinking antipathy to unions, regarding them as prima facie suspect associations inimical to freedom and prosperity. Judges thought that organized labor threatened interstate commerce, management's power to direct enterprise, owners' control of property, and investors' expectations of profitable opportunity. At most, judges grudgingly conceded that unions as unincorporated associations might represent their members as individuals. But before the twentieth century, judges denied unions collective contractual capacity, yet inconsistently held them collectively liable for injuries inflicted on managements' interests. For a time in the late nineteenth century, judges nurtured the doctrine that union activity of any sort interfered with the property and contractual rights of employers. A federal Circuit Court, for example, held in 1887 that "all [labor] associations designed to interfere with the perfect freedom of employers in the proper management and control of their lawful business, or to dictate in any particular the terms upon which their business shall be conducted . . . are *pro tanto* illegal combinations or associations."[98]

(One special group of workers did not benefit at all from judicial attitudes, benign or malignant: black workers in the southern states. A complex of statutes, regulations, and common law development repressed African American working people, whether they were field hands, domestics, industrial laborers, or convicts, into a status of servitude that mocked any vision of "free" labor. This reinstated much of the antebellum labor-coercion component of the law of slavery, the Thirteenth Amendment notwithstanding.)[99]

This cluster of attitudes shaped the outcome of judicial reaction to the Pullman strike of 1894, which resulted in the climacteric case of *In re Debs*.[100] Both a secondary boycott and a sympathy strike shut down the Chicago plexus of the national railroad system during the Pullman strike.[101] After a criminal-conspiracy prosecution fizzled, United States attorney general Richard Olney sought injunctions from the federal courts to restrain the striking workers, the American Railway Union (ARU), and its leader Eugene V. Debs. President Grover Cleveland backed up the injunction by dispatching federal troops to break the strike. Debs was convicted for violation of the Sherman Act and of contempt for ignoring the injunctions. He sought a writ of habeas corpus from the Supreme Court.

For a unanimous Court, Justice Brewer denied the writ, and in a sweeping opinion, expanded federal authority dramatically in two ways.[102] In phrases extravagant even for the time, he exalted federal authority to suppress workers' unrest:

> The entire strength of the nation may be used to enforce in any part of the land the full and free exercise of all national powers and the security of all rights intrusted by the constitution to its care. The strong arm of the national government may be put forth to brush away all obstructions to the freedom of interstate commerce or the transportation of the mails. If the emergency arises, the army of the nation, and all its militia, are at the service of the nation, to compel obedience to its laws.

Such rhetoric was all the more striking when compared to other views of the federal commerce power when the object was corporations, not unions (these will be examined shortly). It was not out of character with the jingoist mood of the times, however, as the United States hovered on the edge of its plunge into imperialism. Federal judges no less than other imperialists projected visions of national power based on military/naval force and the industrial infrastructure that armed and transported it.

There were three compelling reasons why the labor injunction should not have issued in this case. No statute authorized it; under traditional equity doctrine, courts could not enjoin criminal acts; and the petitioner had to allege a property interest that the injunction could protect. Brewer brushed aside Debs's objection that injunctive relief was not available against criminal acts: if there are "some interferences, actual or threatened, with property or rights of a pecuniary nature," an injunction may issue. In justifying the use of judicial power to supplement armed force, Brewer adverted to an idea that Alexander Hamilton had originally expressed as the ghost-writer of George Washington's 1796 farewell address: "[I]t is a lesson which cannot be learned too soon or too thoroughly that under this government of and by the people the means of redress of all wrongs are through the courts and at the ballot-box, and that no wrong, real or fancied, carries with it legal warrant to invite as a means of redress the cooperation of a mob, with its accompanying acts of violence." Brewer affirmed the constitutionality of the labor injunction in its broadest sweep. He imputed a property interest of the United States in the mails.

Brewer took care not to limit his opinion to the statutory scope of the Interstate Commerce Act. Federal judges like William Howard Taft had seized on that statute almost before its ink was dry on the pages of the *Statutes at Large* as a new weapon in the antiunion arsenal,[103] but Brewer did not confine the *Debs* doctrine to that legislative straitjacket. Legislative favor was too fickle, given a majoritarian and democratic political system. Instead, the Court grounded its position on the much ampler foundation of equity power, seemingly secure from legislative meddling, potentially limitless in its scope. Why tether judges' power to legislative sufferance when courts had in their hands a weapon that they alone controlled?

The labor injunction had a particularly sinister impact in the circumstances of the time. United States attorneys were often sympathetic to management and colluded openly with them. The most prominent example occurred when Attorney General Olney appointed Edwin A. Walker as special United States attorney to prosecute the ARU and its leaders. Walker was at the time general counsel for the Milwaukee Road and counsel of the General Managers Association, the collective representing the railroads. He retained both practices during his public service. A United States attorney or deputy like Walker would seek out a friendly federal judge who could be relied on, as was true of Judge Peter Grosscup in Chicago, to issue what was called an "omnibus injunction," which forbade not only union activity but also rights protected by the First Amendment, such as communication about the strike or boycott. The injunction issued ex parte, with no opportunity for the union or workers to defend or even appear.

Thus muzzled and prevented from defending themselves, workers who tried to vindicate their rights to speak, assemble, or petition were promptly cited for contempt. In the contempt hearing, they were denied the right to trial by jury (a feature Brewer warmly endorsed), and were sentenced to heavy fines and prison terms. The labor injunction did not so much displace criminal law as provide a speedier and more efficient means of incarcerating men for union activity. Management had behind it not only regular federal troops, state militia, private thugs, and mercenaries but also federal courts with powers to break unions financially and send union leaders to prison after juryless hearings. Debs went to prison a union leader and became converted there to socialism, emerging as the leader of the American socialist movement for the next generation.[104]

When the Supreme Court denied state legislatures the power to protect workers from exploitation, in the name of preserving their manhood, as later did in *Lochner*, it "refeudalized" labor relations, in William Forbath's term.[105] Corporations, partnerships, and sole proprietors had a property right in their business and a contractual right in their freedom to conduct it as they pleased. Property and contract converged to create a new pseudoright of employers to preserve the nonunion status of their workforce. This became apparent in a series of Supreme Court decisions in the next decade that discovered even more inventive ways to suppress unions.

Except for the paternalist decisions in *Holden* and *Muller* (which benefited only individual workers, not labor organizations), the Supreme Court's labor decisions before World War I were disastrous not only for organized labor but for the reputation of the Court itself. The Court laid itself open to the charge of partiality toward capital and hostility to unions. Justice Brewer's suggestion in *Debs* that labor's proper remedy was resort to the courts or to the ballot, not to strikes and boycotts, was an insulting, cynical mockery of labor's cause. American workers discovered that law was a weapon for bludgeoning labor no different from militia bayonets and police truncheons.

Federal Police Power

Another major concern of Supreme Court classical adjudication was the federal police power. Before the Civil War, police power was an attribute of the states' residual sovereignty. Chief Justice Shaw's 1851 opinion in *Commonwealth v. Alger* recognized the police power as almost coextensive with the states' governmental authority. In reaction to this expansive conception regulatory state power, state courts developed substantive due process doctrines. Through *Slaughterhouse* and *Munn*, courts had construed state's police powers broadly, though Cooley's *Constitutional Limitations* rang the tocsin of resistance.

It was not clear whether the federal government had a corresponding police power, and, if it did, whether it was as extensive in the federal sphere as the states' powers were in theirs.[106] Some of John Marshall's plangent assertions in *McCulloch v. Maryland* (1819) suggested that the federal government did in fact have extensive police power authority.[107] The federal "government, entrusted with such ample powers, on the due execution of which the happiness and prosperity of the nation so vitally depends, must also be entrusted with ample means for their execution." This led Marshall to his oft-quoted holding on implied powers: "[L]et the end be legitimate, let it be within the scope of the constitution, and all means which are appropriate, which are plainly adapted to that end, which are not prohibited, but consist with the letter and spirit of the constitution, are constitutional." On the other hand, his later successor, Chief Justice Salmon P. Chase, held in 1869 that a federal "police regulation, relating exclusively to the internal trade of the State, . . . can have no constitutional operation" within a state. Such federal police power as might have existed was limited to areas where Congress had exclusive jurisdiction, such as the District of Columbia.[108]

Responding to widespread popular demands after 1886 that it regulate railroads and the economic networks called "trusts," Congress nevertheless exercised the police power in two ways. First, in 1887 it created the Interstate Commerce Commission, the national government's first permanent administrative body.[109] The ICC had vaguely bounded investigative powers backed up by statutory prohibitions of carriers' specific anticompetitive practices. Second, Congress enacted the Sherman Anti-trust Act in 1890, a legislative prohibition of restraints on trade, to be enforced by the United States attorney general and the fledgling Justice Department (which had been organized in 1871). After Congress acted, it was certain that the Supreme Court would have to rule on the existence and scope of federal police powers.

ANTITRUST: *KNIGHT*

The Sherman Antitrust Act[110] addressed a problem that was as old as the Republic but that was clad in modern garb: monopoly.

Manufacturing enterprises combined vertically and horizontally after the Civil War, sometimes in pursuit of efficiencies or the cost advantages identified by the Coase Theorem, sometimes to rationalize production and marketing, or to escape the competition that produced what manufacturers considered "ruinous" price wars, and sometimes simply to achieve oligopolistic pricing.[111] (Consolidation also had the desirable side effect of weakening unions' relative bargaining position.) John D. Rockefeller's Standard Oil provided the classic example of horizontal combination, while Andrew Carnegie's United States Steel pursued vertical as well as horizontal combination.

Sometimes this integration was achieved through pooling or cartelization among independent firms. But pooling arrangements were unstable, with only weak constraints on individual participants pulling out when it suited their advantage to do so. In pursuit of more binding arrangements, the corporate bar devised intercorporate trusts, in which member firms surrendered stock to a trustee, who managed their joint enterprise. The trust device circumvented policies embedded in state incorporation statutes that prohibited corporations from holding the shares of other corporations. Alternatively, when the states began to discard that prohibition, corporate lawyers created holding companies that controlled the stock of operating companies, usually acquiring them by a simple share exchange. New Jersey led the way with statutes of elegant simplicity in 1888 and 1889, which simply permitted one corporation to hold the stock of another.[112] These momentous statutes earned New Jersey Lincoln Steffens's encomium as the "Traitor State"[113] because it spawned the holding company empires popularly referred to in the era as "The Trusts."

In 1890, Congress confronted widespread popular clamor for destruction or regulation of the trusts. But it faced a dilemma: even the trusts' critics conceded that nationwide industrial consolidation captured efficiencies of production and distribution, resulting in lower costs to the consumer. If there was to be national regulation of the trusts, the question was how to prevent oligopolistic pricing and artificial restraints on market entry, yet preserve the benefits of consolidation for the consumer.[114] Some members of Congress had doubts about the constitutional authority of Congress to regulate at all. After *Slaughterhouse*, the prewar structure of federalism remained largely intact. This meant that states retained primary if not exclusive power over corporations, their creatures under state-issued charters.[115] The police powers of the states over corporate activity were constrained to some unknown degree by the United Sates Constitution ever since the Supreme Court in 1886 had held that corporations were persons for purposes of the Fourteenth Amendment.[116]

But that limitation on state power did not confer regulatory authority on Congress over corporate activity.

In the face of these uncertainties, Congress enacted the Sherman Antitrust Act in 1890, which drew on common law doctrines barring the restraint of trade. It struck at both monopolization and exclusionary practices, prohibiting "every contract, combination in the form of trust or otherwise, or conspiracy, in restraint of trade or commerce among the several States." Unlike the Interstate Commerce Act, the Sherman Act did not create an administrative body to enforce the statute's provisions. Instead, Congress gave federal courts responsibility for fleshing out the meaning of the broad, vague terms of the statute and left it to the executive branch to initiate antitrust prosecutions. This provided the Supreme Court an opportunity to convert a diffuse and incoherent political gesture into constitutional doctrine.

The first major test of the Sherman Act's meaning and reach came in *United States v. E. C. Knight Co.* (1895).[117] The Justice Department brought an action to break up the American Sugar Refining Company, which proposed an acquisition that would give it control of over 90 percent of sugar manufacture in the United States. Chief Justice Fuller, for the Court, rejected this antitrust effort on the basis of binary and abstract tests not found anywhere in the Constitution. This technique was common in classicist adjudication since the days of John Marshall: judges relied little on textual and historical analysis, preferring to articulate broad principles and then deduce conclusions from them. Fuller denied that a monopoly of manufacturing constituted a monopoly of commerce: "[T]he power to control the manufacture of a given thing involves, in a certain sense, the control of its disposition, but this is a secondary, and not the primary, sense. . . . Commerce succeeds to manufacture, and is not a part of it." Restraint of trade would only be an "indirect result" of the monopoly. There was no "direct relation" between manufacture and interstate commerce.

Fuller's manufacturing-commerce distinction, implausible though it appears to the modern mind,[118] was not altogether unprecedented. Seven years earlier, another conservative jurist, Lucius Q. C. Lamar, had asserted in dicta that federal commerce regulatory power did not extend to the control of manufacturing.[119] Fuller merely took Lamar's musings and elevated them to the status of constitutional doctrine. Sixteen years later, though, the Court would reject the *Knight* distinction between commerce and "production of commodities" as "unsound."[120]

The manufacturing-commerce dichotomy provided Fuller with an opportunity to set off the power to regulate commerce against the concept of the police power, implying that while the Constitution gave Congress the former, it denied it the latter:

> It is vital that the independence of the commercial power and of the police power, and the delimitation between them, however sometimes perplexing, should always be recognized and observed, for while the one [commerce power] furnishes the strongest bond of union, the other [police power] is essential to the preservation of the autonomy of the States as required by our dual form of government; and acknowledged evils, however grave and urgent they may appear to be, had better be borne, than the risk be run, in the effort to suppress them, of more serious consequences by resort to expedients of even doubtful constitutionality.

Knight, despite its sweeping approach, did not stymie all antitrust prosecution. The Court sensed that different policies might guide application of the Sherman Act to mergers, to price-fixing, and to exclusionary agreements. For sixteen years after Fuller's *Knight* opinion, the Court gave the Sherman Act a literal reading, permitting its application to break up all combinations in restraint of trade. It may be that the judges were torn between a producer-capitalist past and the corporate-capitalist future, hesitating on the threshold of the modern state.[121] Or, less grandiosely, a simpler explanation may be found in changes in the Court's personnel. Rufus Peckham succeeded Howell Jackson in 1895, and brought with him a visceral fear that large economic combinations would devour small entrepreneurs. Much more than his ideological kin Fuller and Brewer, Peckham was prepared to accept almost anything that would restrain multistate corporate power.[122]

Whatever the explanation for its changing position between 1895 and 1911, the Court upheld the Sherman Act against liberty-of-contract challenges,[123] permitted use of the Sherman Act against railroad pooling,[124] and against price-fixing.[125] Peckham wrote feelingly about corporate Goliaths that might crush his cherished small business people, "driving out of business the small dealers and worthy men whose lives have been spent [in trade], and who might be unable to readjust themselves to their altered surroundings. Mere reduction in the price of the commodity dealt in might be dearly paid for by the ruin of such a class, and the absorption of control over one commodity by an all-powerful combination of capital."[126]

The Court began to edge away from Fuller's formalistic and formulaic binary distinctions in *Northern Securities Co. v. United States* (1903) and *Swift & Co. v. United States* (1905),[127] defining interstate commerce broadly in the latter case to encompass everything in the "current" or "stream" of commerce. Finally, in *Standard Oil Co. v. United States* (1911),[128] the Court adopted the so-called rule of reason, construing the Sherman Act to prohibit only unreasonable restraints of trade.

Antitrust was not the only area where the Court came to acknowledge a federal police power. Just after the turn of the century, the Court upheld federal police power under the commerce clause when used to ban lotteries,[129] and under Congress's taxing powers to suppress oleomargarine by a tax.[130] Subsequent cases upheld federal power to strike at interstate prostitution (and even noncommercial transport for sexual purposes),[131] the Pure Food and Drug Act,[132] and the Adamson eight-hour law.[133] Thus Fuller's effort to deny the federal government a regulatory power similar to the states' quickly proved futile. Classical legal thought was beginning to quaver under its inconsistencies and false starts.

RAILROADS: THE INTERSTATE COMMERCE COMMISSION

Popular pressure for regulation of railroad rates prodded Congress to enact the Interstate Commerce Act of 1887.[134] Congress created the first federal regulatory/administrative body, the Interstate Commerce Commission, modeled after the "weak" commissions of the eastern states. It had investigative powers, but could not set rates. The statute prohibited specific marketing abuses, such as pooling and rebates, but ambiguously required that all rates be "reasonable and just," leaving the definition of those terms to the ICC.

The ink was scarcely dry on the measure when the process of regulatory "capture" began. The ICC was first influenced, then overwhelmed, by the industries it was supposed to be regulating. A prominent railroad lawyer, soon-to-be attorney general of the United States, predicted and described the capture phenomenon in remarkably prescient advice to a railroad executive client. Richard Olney cautioned the railroads against trying to abolish the ICC. Instead, the commission

> is, or can be made of great use to the railroads. It satisfies the popular clamor for a government supervision of railroads, at the same time that the supervision is almost entirely nominal. Further, the older such a commission gets to be, the more inclined it will be found to be to take the business and railroad view of things. It thus becomes a sort of a barrier between the railroad corporations and the people and a sort of protection against hasty and crude legislation hostile to railroad interests. . . . The part of wisdom is not to destroy the Commission, but to utilize it.[135]

Not being as astute or worldly-wise as Olney, the Supreme Court at first reacted negatively to this new branch of government. Viewing the corporation as a natural entity in its own right (rather than as the aggregate of its shareholders' identities) and having come around to Justice Field's corporate liberalism that centered on the public-private distinction, the Court was at first hostile to administrative rate-setting and independent fact-finding.[136] The major constitutional issue for the Court was not whether the federal government had regulatory authority, but rather the way in which Congress delegated and structured that authority. The ICC seemed to blend the functions of all three branches of the traditional governmental triad: adjudicatory (it could hear complaints), legislative (it could issue quasi-legislative administrative orders having the effect of law), and executive (it looked like a bureau of the executive branch when it enforced a law or order). The Supreme Court reacted first by holding that the ICC lacked rate-setting powers[137] and then denied finality to the commission's fact-finding, making all ICC fact-finding reviewable *de novo* by federal courts.[138] These holdings left the ICC toothless at the turn of the century.

In something of a dialogue with the justices, Congress responded to the Court's hesitant negativism first by reinforcing the powers of the ICC in the Hepburn Act of 1906,[139] a murky statute that seemed to authorize the Supreme Court to review the finality of commission orders. Then in the Mann-Elkins Act of 1910,[140] Congress seemed to give the ICC original rate-setting power. The Court acceded to such less-than-lucid statements of congressional intent in *ICC v. Illinois Central Railroad Co.* (1910), restricting judicial review to the question of whether the ICC had power to make its order.[141]

In *United States v. Grimaud* (1910),[142] the Court finally accepted the fundamental legitimacy of legislative delegation to administrative agencies. "In the nature of things," Justice Joseph R. Lamar held, "it was impracticable for Congress to provide general regulations for these various and varying details of management" of grazing lands in a forerunner of a National Forest. Where "Congress has legislated and indicated its will," it could delegate to administrative agencies or officials "power to fill up the details by the establishment of administrative rules and regulations." This did not constitute an improper delegation of legislative power. *Grimaud* thus validated the essential function of bureaucracies in the modern administrative state.

The Supreme Court acknowledged the legitimacy of a federal regulatory apparatus that provided the administrative mechanism through which Congress could exercise police power on an ongoing basis, at least over one sector of the economy.

And there the matter rested for a time, federal police power seemingly validated in its administrative mode. But the Supreme Court would have second thoughts in the 1920s, when it reopened the whole question of federal police power exercised through regulatory commissions, this time with respect to the Federal Trade Commission.

ECONOMIC FEDERALISM

After the Civil War, the Court undertook a new responsibility made necessary by development of the national market: policing economic federalism. In numerous cases, it drew lines identifying what areas remained within the reach of traditional state police and tax powers, while it struck down state taxes and regulation that impeded interstate commerce. There was no overarching direction or theory to these cases. The Court patrolled the boundaries of federalism on a case-by-case basis, drawing ad hoc lines that attempted to apportion state and federal regulatory power, never essaying grand theory. These decisions complemented the better known cases involving state police power. By the twentieth century, the Court had established itself as the umpire of federalism in matters of taxation and interstate commerce. But this accession to its authority came at a cost.

The Court assumed its new responsibility right after the war. In 1869, it affirmed state authority by upholding a municipal sales tax as applied to goods brought in from out of state,[143] and confirmed traditional state police powers over the insurance industry, holding that the sale of insurance did not constitute interstate commerce immune from state regulatory power.[144] Yet it struck down a state's capitation tax on people leaving the state, which functioned as a sort of fiscal *ne exeat*, seeing in it an interference with interstate migration, implicitly identifying that right or privilege as a personal liberty.[145]

In the mid-seventies, the Court struck down a state tax on freight passing through the state as an interference with interstate commerce,[146] while upholding a gross receipts tax on railroads.[147] It also voided a license tax on peddlers as it applied to individuals selling goods produced out of state.[148] In the spirit of John Marshall's decision in *Gibbons v. Ogden*, it invalidated a state telegraph monopoly that would have had the effect of excluding competition authorized by Congress.[149] It voided a state statute requiring inspection of meat within twenty-four hours of slaughter as a disguised discrimination against meat brought into the state through interstate commerce.[150] The Court also affirmed John Marshall's "original package doctrine,"[151] applying it to the more varied and complex commercial patterns of the late nineteenth century.[152]

The Court did not seek to monopolize for itself all responsibility for policing the boundaries of economic federalism, however. In the *Wabash Case* of 1886,[153] it invited Congress to take a hand in demarcating the zones of state and federal authority, and in particular to establish federal supervision of the interstate aspects of railroad regulation. In *Wabash*, the Court struck down state prohibition of discrimination in short- and long-haul railroad tariffs, and hinted to Congress that control of such matters "must be of that national character, and the regulation can only appropriately exist by general rules and principles, which demand that it should be done by the Congress of the United States under the commerce clause of the Constitution." Congress responded the next year with the Interstate Commerce Act.

The Court welcomed this congressional initiative and cemented the judicial-legislative partnership by enunciating a new doctrine, the "dormant commerce power." This emanation from the commerce clause had been broadly implied in the Taney Court's only successful attempt to deal with federal commerce power, in the 1851 case of *Cooley v. Board of Wardens*.[154] But it was left to Justice Bradley, in *Robbins v. Shelby County Taxing District* (1887),[155] to draw out the implications of a federal power left unexercised by Congress. Bradley invalidated a tax on drummers as it fell on goods produced out of state. (A drummer was a traveling sales representative of wholesalers, often one who sold by sample.) He again hinted that Congress should act, but stated that until it did, its silence was to be construed as an implicit assertion of its intent that interstate commerce should be left unfettered and unregulated by the states. The dormant commerce power doctrine remains a staple of commerce clause law today.

By 1899, the Court had struck down twenty-nine state tax or regulatory statutes on the grounds that they interfered with interstate commerce.[156] Sensing the need for national uniformity in the regulation of commerce, trade groups sought national legislation, possibly a national code of commercial law.[157] This was a doomed effort, given doubts about Congress's regulatory powers induced by *Knight*. The elite national bar, in cooperation with the states, then took matters into its own hands, creating the National Conference of Commissioners on Uniform State Laws in 1892. The NCCUSL promulgated various uniform acts for state adoption, including a negotiable securities act, a negotiable instruments act, a warehouse receipts act, a sales act, and so on. This trend culminated half a century later in promulgation of the Uniform Commercial Code.

While these economic federalism cases yielded few general principles besides the dormant commerce power doctrine, they disclosed a disturbing predicament for classical lawyers. The Court was unable to formulate general, politically neutral principles of universal applicability to provide guidelines for policing the allocation of regulatory and taxing authority between the national government and the states. This called into question the existence or even possibility of principled, apolitical adjudication, threatening the distinction between law and politics that lay at the core of the classical tradition.

MINORITIES

The Court's handiwork affecting women and racial minorities in the classical era was peripheral to the concerns of legal orthodoxy. But these decisions reflected the social assumptions of classical legal thought and reinforced the regime of law that it created. By the turn of the century, the Court remitted entire groups of people to a status invisible to the Constitution. These groups were unable to claim the Constitution's protections either because the Court deemed them outside its provisions or because it accorded their status merely nominal or formal recognition, requiring only the pretense of protection.

Classicist lawyers and judges were not sexist or racist to a greater degree than other elites. They were merely in accord with the dominant assumptions of their era, which consigned women to the homemaking and nurturing roles dictated by the ideology of "separate spheres." Similarly, lawyer elites shared in the contemporary Euro-American loss of confidence that African Americans could assume a status of equality in American society. Classical judges readily relinquished black Americans to domination by southern white supremacists, who, after all, had accumulated a certain expertise in the matter of racial control.

Women were the first to be categorically excluded from the protections of the Fourteenth Amendment. In *Minor v. Happersett* (1875),[158] the Court unanimously held that a woman's right to vote was not secured by the privileges-and-immunities clause of the Fourteenth Amendment. (The American people "reversed" the Court on this matter in the Nineteenth Amendment.)

The Justices also determined that women could assert no constitutional right that would compel a state to admit them to the bar. In *Bradwell v. State* (1873),[159] Justice Bradley, concurring, invoked supernatural sanction for the Justices' social and economic views. He expressed an untroubled confidence in divine establishment of Victorian-era gender relationships:

> The constitution of the family organization, which is founded in the divine ordinance, as well as in the nature of things, indicates the domestic sphere as that which properly belongs to the domain and functions of womanhood . . . . The paramount destiny and mission of woman are to fulfill the noble and benign offices of wife and mother. This is the law of the Creator.[160]

(Most late nineteenth-century jurists contented themselves with less transcendent sources of law.) The Court reaffirmed its thoughts on the matter in 1894, when Belva Lockwood sought admission to the Virginia bar. Not much had changed for women's constitutional status in twenty years. The cultural dominance of the "cult of true womanhood," as historians have termed it, exerted too powerful a pull on Victorian sensibilities to be easily dislodged. Moreover, given the middle-class anxieties over social dislocation that had been building since 1877, the Court was not inclined to impose social innovation on an angst-ridden bar. Chief Justice Fuller in a conclusory opinion typical of him (unimaginative scissors-and-paste recitation of authorities, no reasoning, leaden prose) found nothing in the Fourteenth Amendment to disturb the results of earlier gender cases.[161]

As the Supreme Court extended the protections of the Fourteenth Amendment to new groups and even to new legal entities, such as corporations, by a sad irony it abandoned the people for whom the amendment's protections had been created in the first place, African American citizens. Black American males may have been enfranchised, and a few fortunates like John Rock admitted to the bar, but in all other respects they fared worse than women did at the hands of the Court.

The process of stripping away the freedpeople's constitutional status began in *Slaughterhouse*, which abandoned them to the racist Democrat-Redeemers coming into power in the southern states, who both dictated the definition of the rights of black people and controlled the (non)enforcement of those rights. Though Justice Miller claimed that the "one pervading purpose" of the Reconstruction Amendments was the security of those rights,[162] his opinion gutted their substance.

Redeemer regimes reimposed Jim Crow in the southern states and, beginning in 1890, adopted the Mississippi Plan to deprive black citizens of the suffrage. The Court approved the Mississippi Plan in *Williams v. Mississippi* (1898).[163] It anointed whites' subjugation of black Americans in *Plessy v. Ferguson* (1896),[164] endorsing the doctrine of separate but equal. Justice Henry Brown's opinion was a specimen of the formalist reasoning typical of the classical style, and reflected racial assumptions almost universal among whites.[165] "In the nature of things," the Fourteenth Amendment "could not have been intended to abolish distinctions based upon color." The states' police power may not have been adequate to assure miners that their employers would not cheat them in weighing coal, but it was potent enough to enable states to impose universal racial degradation. Such laws "do not necessarily imply the inferiority of either race to the other." To those blacks who had the temerity to object to such degradation, Brown noted that "it is not by reason of anything found in the act, but solely because the colored race chooses to put that construction upon it." The Court "cannot accept th[e] proposition . . . that social prejudices may be overcome by legislation." Nature itself ordained racial difference, and "legislation is powerless to eradicate racial instincts or to abolish distinctions based upon physical differences." *Plessy's* hint that the states could extend Jim Crow to education was borne out in *Berea College v. Kentucky* (1908).[166]

The Court's treatment of Asians, whether citizens, resident aliens, or nonresident immigrants, was mixed. In *Yick Wo v. Hopkins* (1886),[167] the Court relied on the equal protection clause to strike down race-based discrimination and went behind a facially neutral ordinance to void its application. But what succor the Court extended to alien Asians in *Yick Wo* it snatched away in a series of cases upholding the power of Congress to exclude Chinese and authorize deportation of resident Chinese aliens.[168]

In the series of decisions known collectively as the *Insular Cases* (1901–1914),[169] the Court, drawing on racist presuppositions, held that the nonwhite inhabitants of the island possessions seized in America's 1898 outburst of imperialism — "alien races, differing from us in religion, customs, laws, methods of taxation and modes of thought" — were not entitled to the full protection of the Bill of Rights. Congress might extend those protections to them if it so chose, but otherwise, in the popular phrase of the time, the Constitution did not follow the flag. Meanwhile, the natives need not worry: "[T]here are certain principles of natural justice inherent in the Anglo-Saxon character," Justice Brown reassured anti-imperialists, "which need no expression in constitutions or statutes to give them effect or to secure dependencies against legislation manifestly hostile to their real interests."

The Court similarly confirmed the fate of the indigenous peoples in the continental United States. Comparable racial prepossessions drove the results in these cases as they would in the *Insular Cases*; in fact, the two were mutually reinforcing. Anticipating the *Insular Cases*, the Court held in *Talton v. Mayes* (1896)[170] that the protections of the Bill of Rights do not extend to Indian tribes. In *Ex parte Crow Dog* (1883),[171] the Court held that Indians were subject to federal laws, not as citizens (which most were not), nor as individual members of independent political communities, but rather as "a dependent community in a state of pupilage," a damaging extension of John Marshall's concept of "domestic dependent nations."[172] This condition of "dependence" demanded that Congress exercise a "trust relationship" over Indian affairs. Rather than being benign, however, *Lone Wolf v. Hitchcock* (1903)[173] revealed that the trust power of Congress was plenary in a destructive sense, and thus permitted Congress to abrogate Indian treaty rights unilaterally and by statute. The Court thus joined as an active participant in the degradation of indigenous peoples, providing a juridical supplement to the legislative land-grab of the Dawes Act (1887) and the occasional genocidal rampages of militia and regular army.

The Apogee of Classical Legal Thought

The case of *Lochner v. New York* (1905) is unique as the only decision that has given its name to a period ("the *Lochner* era") or to an ideological tendency in Supreme Court adjudication ("*Lochner* jurisprudence").[174] Its prominence is not honorable: along with *Dred Scott* and *Plessy v. Ferguson*, it would appear on almost everyone's list of the worst decisions the Supreme Court has perpetrated in two centuries. No case other than *Dred Scott* and *Plessy* has been as widely condemned in modern times. The three are yoked together, especially by conservative jurists, as leading specimens of judicial malfunction.[175] For almost all commentators, including the ideological descendants of its author Rufus Peckham, it epitomizes the abuse of judicial power. Yet in its day, *Lochner* was the capstone of substantive due process and liberty of contract, providing a platform from which the Court would later cantilever extensions of those doctrines into the 1930s.

A troublesome question persists: just what was it about Justice Peckham's opinion in *Lochner* that was so wretched? Substantive due process itself? A misconception of liberty, or of contract? Bad sociology? Outdated economics? Judicial hubris? Indifference to fact and/or reality? Mishandling the ends-means equation?[176] Whatever the critic's choice, for most people, *Lochner* is synonymous with judicial power badly abused. It is the focal point for criticism — or, recently, defense[177] — of substantive due process generally. It may fairly be taken to be what is known in contract law as a "fair sample" of classical adjudication.

Some explanations for the decision may be found in the character of the judge himself.[178] Peckham resembled Fuller in many ways. Both were antebellum Democrats who never abandoned either their party affiliation or its ideology, antique though it had become a half-century after Jackson. Neither man was very bright. One of Holmes's law clerks, Dean Acheson, asked Holmes "What was Justice Peckham like, intellectually?" "Intellectually?" scoffed Holmes. "I never thought of him in that connection. His major premise was, 'God damn it!' But he was a good judge."[179] (In one who did not suffer fools gladly, Holmes's affection for Fuller and Peckham is inexplicable.) Peckham and Fuller were relics of the era of entrepreneurial capitalism, incapable of comprehending an economy dominated by corporate capitalism, judicial woolly mammoths frozen in the ice of a Jacksonian Democratic worldview.

The *Lochner* case itself involved a New York statute, the "Bakeshop Act" of

1895[180] that prohibited the employment of bakers for more than sixty hours a week or ten hours a day. The statute also contained provisions regulating the sanitation of bakeries in such things as plumbing, flooring, ventilation, toilets, and living facilities. (Many bakers of the era lived in their workplaces, sleeping under or on the kneading tables.) From affirmance of his conviction for working a baker beyond the statutory maximum, Joseph Lochner appealed to the Supreme Court. Justice Peckham wrote for a bare majority of five justices[181] striking down the statute.

Peckham cast the issue in the case as a simple dichotomy: "[I]s this a fair, reasonable and appropriate exercise of the police power of the State, or is it an unreasonable, unnecessary and arbitrary interference with the right of the individual to his personal liberty or to enter into those contracts in relation to labor?"[182] He defined both sides of the dichotomy. Citing his own opinion in *Allgeyer*, Peckham noted "the general right to make a contract in relation to his business is part of the liberty of the individual protected by the Fourteenth Amendment," including "the right to purchase or to sell labor." Opposed to this was the police power, the state's sovereign authority to adopt measures that "relate to the safety, health, morals and general welfare of the public." "Both property and liberty are held on such reasonable conditions as may be imposed by the governing power of the State in the exercise of those powers, and with such conditions the Fourteenth Amendment was not designed to interfere." But "it must, of course, be conceded that there is a limit to the valid exercise of the police power by the State."

That limit Peckham found in the character of bakers and baking as an occupation. Bakers and their bosses were "persons who are sui juris (both employer and employee)." He found no reason to believe "that bakers as a class are not equal in intelligence and capacity to men in other trades or manual occupations, or that they are not able to assert their rights and care for themselves without the protecting arm of the State." Nor was baking especially unhealthy: "It may be true that the trade of a baker does not appear to be as healthy as some other trades, and is also vastly more healthy than still others. To the common understanding the trade of a baker has never been regarded as an unhealthy one." If the work of baking was not particularly dangerous to bakers' health, it had no relation at all to public health, including that of the people who ate the bread: "[C]lean and wholesome bread does not depend upon whether the baker works but ten hours per day."

The right to contract was a limitation on the states' police powers, and the role of the judiciary was to monitor the exercise of those powers to determine whether legislation was "fair, reasonable and appropriate." Peckham found no "direct relation" between a proper legislative end and the means chosen (hours limitation).

Having destroyed the police power rationale for the law, to his satisfaction anyway, Peckham felt himself free to go searching for the real motive of the legislature. "It is impossible for us to shut our eyes to the fact that many of the laws of this character, while passed under what is claimed to be the police power for the purpose of protecting the public health or welfare, are, in reality, passed from other motives." He had no trouble discerning that "the real object and purpose were simply to regulate the hours of labor between the master and his employes (all being men, sui juris), in a private business, not dangerous in any degree to morals or in any real and substantial degree, to the health of the employes."

The difficulty with Peckham's position, as both dissents pointed out, was that the legislature had determined otherwise. Peckham was not impressed: "[W]e do not believe in the soundness of the views which uphold this law." Peckham rebuffed the imputation that he was "substituting the judgment of the court for that of the legislature." But he became carried away emotionally by his own *argumentum ad horrendum*: "If this statute be valid, there would seem to be no length to which legislation of this nature might not go," potentially embracing tinsmiths, cabinetmakers, and lawyers' clerks. Because of some trifling occupational hazards, "are we all, on that account, at the mercy of legislative majorities?" Peckham concluded spaciously: laws that limit the hours of "grown and intelligent men . . . are mere meddlesome interferences with the rights of the individual."

The effect of his opinion was to preserve the status quo, any status quo, as natural; to mandate government neutrality in anything affecting that status quo; to preserve the extant allocation of wealth, rights, and power; and to assume the common law regime as a supralegislative norm. He could not conceive of the employment relationship as being a legal construct.

Peckham has suffered the deathless misfortune of having Holmes, writing at his most aphoristic, skewer those underlying premises. Holmes permanently fixed all subsequent understanding of the decision by his not wholly relevant observation that "the Fourteenth Amendment does not enact Mr. Herbert Spencer's Social Statics" and his suggestion that the majority thought the Constitution embodied the principles of laissez-faire. Harlan, speaking for himself and Justices White and William R. Day in a separate dissent, challenged the majority on the facts, reviewing the legislature's proffered evidence concerning health conditions in bakeries and finding it possible at least that reasonable legislators had some rational basis for the policy choice they made. He did, however note that the enactment may have been based on the legislative perception "that employers and employes . . . were not upon an equal footing, and that the necessities of the latter often compelled them to submit to such exactions."

Lochner was a blow to state regulatory power.[183] It construed state police powers narrowly and assumed an activist role for courts in supervising legislators' policy judgments. Even if considered as an exceptional case, it had an *in terrorem* effect on legislative action, warning that judges might capriciously overturn the results of democratic processes at any time by substituting their own judgments about policy for that of the legislature.

The Court followed *Lochner* up with a line of decisions that interposed the due process clauses as filters for any legislation that attempted to better workers' conditions. In *Adair v. United States* (1908),[184] Justice Harlan fused the doctrines of *Lochner* and *Debs* to strike down the federal Erdman Act of 1898,[185] which prohibited yellow-dog contracts for railroad employees, as well as firing or blacklisting them for joining unions. (A yellow-dog contract provided that an employee would not join or organize a union, and that doing so would be grounds for being fired.)[186] Harlan's holding rested on two grounds: liberty of contract and lack of congressional commerce-regulatory authority over the subject. In affirming the employee's liberty of contract, Harlan claimed that in negotiating about employment, "employer and the employee have equality of right." He imputed the doctrines of liberty of contract under the Fourteenth Amendment's due process clause to the due process clause of the Fifth Amendment, subjecting the federal government to the same limitations the Court had contrived to bind the states. In order to sustain the statute as an exercise of the federal commerce power, there had to be "some real or substantial relation" between interstate commerce and union membership, a relationship that he thought was obviously lacking.

An attorney of the day, reading *Adair* against the background of the *Knight* case and the Tenth Amendment, might have thought that in default of federal power, the states would have regulatory authority over the problem of yellow-dog contracts. *Coppage v. Kansas* (1915) belied that assumption.[187] The Kansas legislature had enacted a yellow-dog statute in 1903, applicable to all forms of employment, which obviated the "class legislation" objection.[188] A switchman on the Frisco Line, referred to in the opinion of the Supreme Court merely as "one Hedges," refused to sign a yellow-dog contract. The railroad's superintendent then fired him and was convicted under the statute. The Kansas Supreme Court upheld the conviction and the statute.[189]

On the superintendent's appeal to the Supreme Court, Justice Mahlon Pitney, for a six-member majority, held the statute unconstitutional as a deprivation of liberty of contract.[190] His opinion relied on the due process half of the *Adair* opinion, insisting that its limitation on federal authority applied equally to the states. He extolled the principle of liberty of contract as "fundamental and vital," an indispensable part of "the right of personal liberty and the right of private property." In the first of the opinion's several instances of reasoning by false symmetry,[191] Pitney insisted that "the right is as essential to the laborer as to the capitalist, to the poor as to the rich." Abstractly put: if A seeks to do X and B also seeks to do X, then the relationship of A and B to the action must be identical, and A and B must stand on the same footing toward it. If the employer wishes to contract, and the employee wishes to contract, then each bears the same relationship to the employment relation, and each stands on the same footing with respect to it.

An attenuated free labor ideal appeared in Pitney's opinion. The employee was a "free agent, in all respects competent, and at liberty to choose what was best from the standpoint of his own interests." Pitney conceded the existence of the police power but stated that in the conflict between government power and individual rights, rights trump power. "What possible relation" he asked rhetorically, could the statute have to the police power? None, obviously, for strengthening unions could not be a legitimate purpose of legislation that curtailed the constitutionally protected rights of employer and employee.

Finally, Pitney identified underlying values with unsurpassed candor. He framed the issue of inequality of bargaining power between employer and employee as a question of "coercion." In his political and judicial career, Pitney had been a conservative Republican,[192] and his socioeconomic outlook made it impossible for him to see any employment contract as coercive:

> No doubt, wherever the right of private property exists, there must and will be inequalities of fortune; and thus it naturally happens that parties negotiating about a contract are not equally unhampered by circumstances. This applies to all contracts, and not merely to that between employer and employee. Indeed, a little re-

flection will show that wherever the right of private property and the right of free contract coexist, each party when contracting is inevitably more or less influenced by the question whether he has much property, or little, or none. . . . And, since it is self-evident that, unless all things are held in common, some persons must have more property than others, it is from the nature of things impossible to uphold freedom of contract and the right of private property without at the same time recognizing as legitimate those inequalities of fortune that are the necessary result of the exercise of those rights.

"From the nature of things," economic inequality had to be legitimate. The alternative was communism.

Holmes again dissented pithily, reaffirming his positions in *Lochner* and *Adair* that a legislature could reasonably act to protect union membership "in order to establish the equality of position between the parties in which liberty of contract begins." Whether anti-yellow-dog legislation is desirable "is not my concern." Nothing in the Constitution forbids them.[193]

Coppage died along with the rest of the classical corpus.[194] "This Court . . . has steadily rejected the due process philosophy enunciated in the . . . Allgeyer-Lochner-Adair-Coppage constitutional doctrine," wrote Justice Hugo Black in 1949.[195]

But in the heyday of classicism, *Coppage* was paired with *Adair* to modify the doctrine that constitutional scholars refer to as "dual federalism." Dual federalism as a concept traces back to the Taney era. It posited a model of the federal system in which the federal government and the states each have their appropriate spheres. The boundary between them, established by the Tenth Amendment, is fixed, definite, and impermeable. If something falls within federal authority, it cannot be regulated by the states. Conversely, if something falls within state authority, it is beyond federal power. Such a model of the federal system underlay *Knight* and other decisions constraining the commerce power.

Adair and *Coppage*, read together, wrenched apart the spheres of federal and state authority to create a constitutional no-man's-land. The trope of the no-man's-land derived from a military phrase descriptive of what German soldiers in the Great War called *Grabenkrieg*, "grave warfare" ("trench warfare," in the more euphemistic English). *Adair* denied federal authority over yellow-dog contracts on commerce and Fifth Amendment due process grounds; *Coppage* denied state authority on Fourteenth Amendment due process grounds. The yellow-dog contract was sited in a no-man's-land where the employer's power enfiladed the legal terrain. For the worker, it was a free-fire zone, and he was the target.

The Decline of Classical Legal Thought

"The Allgeyer-Lochner-Adair-Coppage constitutional doctrine" that Justice Black referred to in 1949 reached its apogee with *Coppage*. A generation later, when Black wrote, it was a discredited historical memory. What happened in that generation to bring down so awesome an ideological edifice? How did the certitude of 1915 become the laughingstock of 1949?

Classical legal thought succumbed to sterility within and attacks from without.

The remainder of this chapter describes its impotence to sustain further intellectual development; external assaults are the topic of the next.

Classical thought suffered the usual fate of ideas that evolve from heresy (c. 1873) to orthodox dogma (c. 1915). On the eve of World War I, the underlying values that had given rise to classical doctrine were no longer fertile; they were incapable of stimulating creative thought. After classical dogma had been perfected between 1905 and 1915, it could only be iterated over and over again by some of the Justices. Its growth principle had withered; its ideas became ever more brittle and desiccated. This loss of inner vitality and dynamism left classical thought vulnerable to the charge that it had become out of touch with reality.

As indeed it had. The values of classical legal thought had incubated in the culture of entrepreneurial capitalism, in a producer economy of local economic networks, in an era when the typical workplace was still a small shop occupied by master, journeymen, and apprentices. It became irrelevant in the world of industrial and finance capitalism, dominated by massive corporations coordinated by interlocking directorates and trust instruments, an economy of oligopolistic combination, where the workplace had degenerated into William Blake's "dark satanic mills."

In this transformed economic environment, the doctrinal superstructure of classical legal thought gradually became dissociated from the values that it sat atop. An outlook responsive to the Paris Commune, the railway strikes of 1877, the Great Upheaval of 1886, the Homestead and Pullman strikes had become quaintly antique, like muttonchop whiskers and bustles. This left legal doctrine dangerously disconnected from its value system. The continued application of its dogmas seemed ever more an attempt to squeeze the economic and social realities of the twentieth century back into a nineteenth-century flask.

In time, classical ideology would be updated, as German or Austrian refugee intellectuals like Friedrich von Hayek, Ludwig von Mises, and Leo Strauss rethought, or at least restated, classical values and tutored a new generation of lawyers and political philosophers in their relevance to legal development. But before this infusion of fresh thought, obsolescent legal doctrine ruled an industrial world far removed from journeymen bootmakers in the 1830s or striking trainmen in 1877. Classicism's most effective later spokesmen, jurists like William Howard Taft and George Sutherland, could do no more than repeat its shopworn truths and hold the line "to prevent the Bolsheviki from getting control," as Taft put it.[196]

Damaging consequences followed from this disjuncture of values, doctrine, and reality. The most grave was the law's incoherence. Even that paragon of the American bar, Elihu Root, had to concede in 1923 that "the confusion, the uncertainty [of the law], was growing from year to year", and that "the law was becoming guesswork."[197] It was precisely because of what it diagnosed as "The Law's Uncertainty and Complexity" that the newly founded American Law Institute embarked on its futile quest to reduce law's principles to finite and definite form.[198] But notwithstanding the ALI's efforts, classical thought proved unable to deliver on its basic promise: to provide objective, neutral, and principled distinctions that could guide judges' choices between the dichotomies of police power versus individual rights, businesses affected with a public interest versus entrepreneurial liberty, state power versus federal authority. The application of doctrine to resolve these problems came to seem arbitrary and unprincipled. Critics alleged, with reason, that judges were applying their own personal economic biases, not the impartial rule of law. With the rule of law itself thus threatened, the game could no longer be played without violating its fundamental rules. Law had turned on itself. The latent self-destructive potential of dogma was about to be realized.

Two related inconsistencies marked the post-*Lochner* years. First, in simple quantitative terms, the Supreme Court upheld most federal and state regulatory legislation coming before it, despite the seemingly incompatible pressures of classical doctrine. The legal historian Charles Warren made a count of 790 state police power and tax decisions handed down by the Supreme Court between 1889 and 1918 and discovered that only 53 voided police-power regulations, and of them, only 14 involved what he called "the general rights and liberties of individuals."[199] Though high-visibility cases like *Lochner* and its ilk dismayed Progressives, quantitatively they were the exception, not the norm.

Second, in the major regulatory cases between 1905 and 1930, the Court developed two inconsistent streams of precedent for both federal and state police-power cases, one stream upholding federal and state regulatory authority, the other striking it down.[200] As a result, law was beginning to appear incoherent, in a literal sense: it could not hang together. The center was not holding. In 1930, a lawyer attempting to advise a client could only come away bewildered by the corpus of Supreme Court classical jurisprudence.

The inconsistent streams of major precedent might best be seen first in a bird's-eye-view tabular format (see table 3.1). This tabulation oversimplifies, of course. It notes only major precedents and overrides minor distinctions that a more disciplined chronological approach would reveal. It merely presents a graphic illustration of the growing incoherence of results that characterized legal classicism in the years of its ascendancy.

The course of the federal police power before the Supreme Court was uneven. The Justices upheld Congress's power to prohibit the shipment of lottery tickets and narcotics in interstate commerce[201] and the transportation of women in commerce for immoral purposes.[202] Perhaps such results might be explained by the influence of Edwardian-era moralism, which might have somewhat narcotized the Court's sensitivity to concerns of federalism or substantive due process. But the Court also sustained a federal tax that imposed a competitive disadvantage on oleomargarine.[203] In doing so, the Justices declared legislative motive irrelevant where legislative power existed. The Supreme Court acceded to federal regulation of food and cosmetic quality.[204] It devised doctrines — metaphors, really — of a "throat" or "stream" or "current" of commerce that corroded *Knight's* mechanistic manufacturing-commerce distinction.[205]

Despite *Adair*, the Supreme Court did not adamantly oppose all federal regulation of railroad labor, either on commerce or on liberty-of-contract grounds. The first Federal Employers' Liability Act of 1908[206] abrogated the fellow-servant rule and restricted the defense of contributory negligence, which had the effect of expanding the liability of interstate common carriers for industrial accidents. The Court held the statute unconstitutional on the grounds that its coverage extended into intrastate commerce.[207] Congress reenacted the measure, lopping off the objectionable coverage, and the Court then unanimously upheld it.[208]

Table 3.1. *Federal Police Power (mostly under the commerce clause)*

Striking Down	Upholding
First FELA Case	*Champion v. Ames*
Hammer v. Dagenhart	*McCray v. U.S.*
Bailey v. Drexel Furniture	*Second FELA Case*
FTC v. Gratz	*Stafford v. Wallace*
FTC v. Curtis Publishing Co.	*Loewe v. Lawlor*
	Duplex v. Deering

State Police Power (substantive due process/liberty of contract)

Striking Down	Upholding
Adkins v. Childrens Hospital	*Muller v. Oregon*
Truax v. Corrigan	*Noble State Bank v. Haskell*
Wolff Packing Co.	*Bunting v. Oregon*
Pennsylvania Coal v. Mahon	*NYC R.R. v. White*
	Euclid v. Ambler Realty

But when Congress relied on its commerce-regulatory authority to abolish child labor, the Supreme Court balked in *Hammer v. Dagenhart* (1918), on two grounds that seemed specious to most observers.[209] (Justice David Souter may have had these in mind when he referred to "cases applying highly formalistic notions of 'commerce' to invalidate federal social and economic legislation.")[210] First, Justice William R. Day, writing for the majority, declared that federal commerce power extended only to things harmful in themselves; here, the furniture that had been produced by children was harmless. There was, of course, no textual authority in the Constitution for this distinction. Second, by invading a subject of state police authority, Congress had crossed dual federalism's Tenth Amendment boundary. Day's enthusiasm for this conclusion led him to misquote the Tenth Amendment, injecting the word "expressly" that the Framers in the First Congress had deliberately left out: "[T]o [the states] and to the people the powers not expressly delegated to the National Government are reserved".

Congress immediately returned to the subject, this time using its tax powers in an attempt to suppress child labor. The Court once again struck the statute down, going behind Congress's avowed purpose (taxation) to find an improper motive (invasion of state police powers).[211] Shocked and frustrated, Congress launched a constitutional amendment along the lines of the Sixteenth. It was never ratified, though by 1930 a majority of Americans thought it had been.

In cases involving organized labor, the Court invariably upheld federal regulatory authority, less out of dedication to federal police power than from hostility to unions.[212] In *Debs*, the Court had avoided the question whether labor was covered by the Sherman Antitrust Act,[213] instead finding power to enjoin the railway strike in the broad, traditional equity powers of federal courts. There was no clear statutory language or unambiguous legislative history indicating that Congress had intended antitrust policy to reach unions, but antitrust was too attractive a weapon for bludgeoning labor to be long ignored by federal judges. The Court wielded it in the *Danbury Hatters Case, Loewe v. Lawlor* (1908).[214]

Chief Justice Fuller, writing for the majority, avoided sweeping pronunciamentos of conservative ideology, but the effect of his holding, which subjected unions to the Sherman Act, added another powerful weapon to the federal arsenal for combating labor organization.[215] *Danbury Hatters* provided a striking contrast with *Knight*. The circumstances of the cases were similar, and Fuller wrote both opinions. In *Knight*, he found no commerce power, yet in *Danbury Hatters* he extended the Sherman Act to prohibit secondary boycotts because, he wrote, "the acts must be considered as a whole." The breadth of his conception of federal commerce powers was as sweeping as Brewer's had been in *Debs*, and all the more striking for its contrast with the shrunken federal commerce authority in *Knight*.

Fuller's *Danbury Hatters* opinion marked the persistence of nineteenth-century individualist assumptions into an era of modern law when interest-group pluralism was becoming dominant. The opinion was not so much reactionary as out of touch, the product of a vision of the legal order antedating the dominance of groups in American society. In Fuller's Jacksonian legal world, the law recognized only individuals as actors: Dietrich Loewe and his proprietary hat factory on one hand, the individual members of the Hatters Union on the other. (This proved useful for instrumental reasons: union members were saddled as individuals with ruinous fines.) Fuller simply could not comprehend an economic world dominated by large multistate corporations and collectivities like unions. Less than two years later, death released him from his losing effort to understand a world that had become alien to the antebellum social vision.

Danbury Hatters ought to have convinced union leaders that nothing was going to soften the malevolence of federal judges toward their cause. If they missed the point, *Gompers v. Buck's Stove & Range Co.* (1911) provided a reminder.[216] The American Federation of Labor organized a boycott of Buck's products. The company got an injunction against the boycott, but the AFL published the company's name anyway in its "Don't patronize" list in *The American Federationist*. The company then secured criminal contempt citations against the AFL and its president, Samuel Gompers. The Supreme Court overturned the convictions on a technicality, but Justice Joseph R. Lamar's opinion for a unanimous court made it plain that the First Amendment would be no barrier to the labor injunction, and no refuge for unions or workers.

Hoping to moderate the Court's antiunion bias a little, Congress then tried to abolish the labor injunction by the Clayton Act of 1914.[217] Section 6 provided that labor was not "a commodity or article of commerce," in an ambiguous and indirect effort to block enforcement of the antitrust laws against unions. Section 20 contained a toothless antiinjunction provision: no injunction should issue "unless necessary to prevent irreparable injury to property, or to a property right." Since the first half of the formula merely restated the traditional equitable basis of injunctive relief, it said, in effect: no federal court shall issue a labor injunction unless it wants to do so. The second half of the formula implicitly backed up the courts' expansion of property concepts.

The Court's zeal for antiunion injunctions was not to be deflected by such hesitant and uncertain statutory language.[218] It promptly authorized injunctions against unions, first to enforce a yellow-dog contract,[219] then to stop a secondary boycott,[220] then to prohibit picketing of a struck employer,[221] and then to halt a union's refusal to work on materials produced by nonunion labor.[222] It also subjected unions to the civil damages provisions of the Sherman Act.[223] Lest these cases be read merely as evidence of the Court's newfound enthusiasm for an antitrust policy that just happened to encumber unions, the Court also overturned a state statute that prohibited injunctions against peaceful picketing.[224] Chief Justice Taft, that redoubtable foe of unions, held that even peaceful and legitimate picketing potentially threatened management's property, and therefore could be enjoined. "Peaceful picketing is a contradiction in terms," he insisted.[225] Taft's enthusiasm for the labor injunction had earned him Gompers's encomium in the 1908 presidential race, "the Father of Injunctions."[226]

The same incoherence that marked federal police-power decisions characterized cases involving the states' police powers between 1905 and 1920. The Court sometimes sustained and sometimes rejected state legislation on no perceptible or consistent principle, not even hostility to union labor.[227] The Supreme Court reaffirmed state police power in several major cases. It sustained various state worker-protective laws, as in *Muller v. Oregon* (1908),[228] where it upheld a ten-hour limitation on women's working day, and in *Bunting v. Oregon* (1917),[229] sustaining legislation that imposed maximum hours on both men and women and that regulated wages by mandating overtime pay.

Procedural developments enhanced the powers of federal courts even as the substance of their decisions compounded incoherence. Three years after *Lochner*, Peckham reinforced the substance of that decision in the case of *Ex parte Young* (1908).[230] Through a contorted evasion of the Eleventh Amendment, the Court permitted a federal judge to enjoin a state's attorney general from enforcing a state rate-setting statute on the ground that in doing so the state official was acting in his private capacity and not as an officer of the state. Antic though such a conclusion appears as a matter of logic, the holding in *Young* has been supported in modern times as a necessary means of assuring state compliance with the federal Constitution, especially in civil rights cases.[231]

Taft, the most influential and activist Chief Justice since John Marshall, did not confine his activities to adjudication. He politicked tirelessly to secure the appointment of jurists he considered "sound" to offset the "Bolshevik" views of Brandeis and the dangerously unreliable Holmes. His supreme achievement, though, was the Judiciary Act of 1925,[232] popularly known as "the Judges' Bill" because of Taft's activist lobbying. Taft was determined to cut back the Court's mandatory jurisdiction and to increase its discretionary review authority, and he largely succeeded. The overhaul of federal jurisdiction achieved by the 1925 act greatly enhanced the power of the Court, rendering its control over state statutes and state supreme courts firmer than ever. Joseph Story would have been pleased. In Peter Fish's judgment, "the Supreme Court was transformed [by the 1925 act] from a forum that primarily corrected errors arising in ordinary private litigation to a constitutional tribunal that resolved public policy issues of national importance."[233]

As the political era of Normalcy dawned, orthodox doctrine reigned, but it was in disarray. Classical legal thought seemed to have lost its grip on the judicial mind, yet its monuments —*Lochner, Adair, Coppage,* and the rest — stood intact. The Justices who formed the core of the *Lochner* bloc —Fuller, Brewer, Peckham — were gone. A new Chief Justice, William Howard Taft, known to be an ideological conservative[234] yet a political pragmatist, had achieved his life's ambition with appointment to the center seat. Would he be able to restore coherence to doctrine? Could he clarify what, if anything, was left of classical premises?

The Reaction of the 1920s

The Taft Court dashed assumptions that *Lochner-Adair-Coppage* had been the aberration and the *Muller* line of cases the norm.[235] After World War I, most knowledgeable observers of the Court, and even its new Chief, assumed that the day of *Lochner* had passed. The lawyer-historian Charles Warren wrote of that case in 1922 that "if not now practically overruled, [it] is certain in the near future to be disregarded by the Court."[236] Even to impeccable conservatives like Warren and Taft, *Lochner's* principles and result appeared retrogressive. *Adkins v. Children's Hospital* (1923) thus came as a shock when it struck down a minimum-wage statute for women.[237]

Justice George Sutherland, who spoke for the five-to-four majority in *Adkins*, had been a student of Thomas M. Cooley at Michigan and had imbibed his principles of limited government. *Adkins* signaled a regression in the Court's thinking and an attitude toward the police power even more hostile than *Lochner* had been. Sutherland extended freedom-of-contract reasoning to women, citing their recent political empowerment, unconsciously mimicking the discredited precedent of *Ritchie v. People* (Illinois, 1895). Holmes in response scoffed that "it will need more than the Nineteenth Amendment to convince me that there are no differences between men and women, or that legislation cannot take those differences into account."

Sutherland exalted liberty of contract as "the general rule and restraint the exception." Legislation inhibiting it "can only be justified by the existence of exceptional circumstances." He then specified four categories, apparently exclusive, into which the exceptions might fit (*Munn*, public works, antiscrip, and hours legislation), precisely tailored to accommodate existing precedent like *Muller* and *Bunting* but nothing more.

Sutherland offered an ethical premise for his result: the "right of every worker, man or woman, to a living wage may be conceded . . . but the fallacy of the proposed method of attaining it is that it assumes that every employer is bound at all events to furnish it." He injected a "moral requirement" into the Constitution, a "relation of just equivalence" between work and pay. He airily dismissed social science data on the impact of poverty on women, and with it the influence of the Brandeis Brief, as "interesting but only mildly persuasive."

Chief Justice Taft was aghast at the result in *Adkins*, and his dissent there expressed the same dismay at judicial reaction that he had voiced twelve years earlier in the Arizona Enabling Bill veto. He had "always supposed that the *Lochner Case* was thus overruled *sub silentio*" by *Muller* and *Bunting*.[238] Taft emphasized the inequality of bargaining status between employer and employee, especially when the workers were women "and in their necessitous circumstances are prone to accept pretty much anything that is offered," leading to "the evils of the sweating system." Strong words from so firm a conservative, which he reinforced by insisting that "it is not the function of this Court to hold congressional acts invalid simply because they are passed to carry out economic views which the Court believes to be unwise or unsound."

Munn, which had acclimated the police power to the Court's outlook, lingered as an authority unwelcome to conservatives because it legitimated some state regulation. Though more extreme conservatives like Brewer and Peckham had called for its outright reversal, they could never muster a majority to do so, and had to settle for the next best thing, confining it straitly. The Taft Court achieved that in the *Wolff Packing Company* case of 1923,[239] holding unconstitutional a statute authorizing a state commission to set wages in vital industries, such as food, fuel, and clothing. Taft held that such industries were not automatically "affected with a public interest" and thus subject to the police power. He adopted a categorical approach, confining *Munn*-type businesses to those historically subject to regulation.

Committed to this narrow vision of state regulatory power, the Court then handed down a series of decisions inimical to the police power, usually on due process grounds. These cases denied states power to control the size of bread sold at retail; require minimum wages on public works projects, regulate the quality of materials in bedding, and prohibit corporations from owning pharmacies.[240] Later decisions forbade the states from regulating ticket scalping, employment agencies, and retail sales of gasoline and ice.[241] Included among these were two precedents involving non-economic liberties, *Meyer v. Nebraska* (1923) and *Pierce v. Society of Sisters* (1925) that were the only Old Court classical precedents to survive the slaughter of substantive due process after 1937.[242]

In the most lastingly influential of these due process cases, *Pennsylvania Coal Co. v. Mahon* (1922),[243] Holmes held unconstitutional a statute prohibiting removal of subjacent support in mining operations, as applied to extant mineral leases, as a deprivation of property without due process. He laid down what was for him an uncharacteristically sloppy "general rule": "[W]hile property may be regulated to a certain extent, if regulation goes too far it will be recognized as a taking." Imprecise though this was, it constitutes the slender foundation for modern "regulatory takings" doctrine.[244]

Some contemporary trends in property law seemed inconsistent with these doctrinal tendencies. The Court voiced no objection to government enterprise. When the Non-Partisan League came to power in North Dakota, it used public funds to create state-owned and -operated mills, grain elevators, warehouses, a state bank, and even home-building associations. The Court dismissed a taxpayers' challenge to this Prairie socialism in *Green v. Frazier* (1920),[245] acknowledging that the state's taxing and spending powers were being used for a public purpose. The Court also dismissed taxpayers' suits challenging the spending (rather than the raising) of public funds, thereby establishing a precedent that lies at the base of modern standing doctrine.[246]

The Taft Court sustained a far-reaching interference with property rights in *Euclid v. Ambler Realty* (1926),[247] which validated the constitutionality of municipal zoning. The cynic might observe that zoning does not involve wealth redistribution of the sort that troubled classicist jurists, but rather just imposed regulation of one form of property for the benefit of another, and in any event has only an *in futuro* impact. Yet the author of *Euclid* was none other than Justice Sutherland, whose *Adkins* opinion established him as the premier voice of conservatism on the Taft Court, and he sustained the police power in terms so sweeping that the *Euclid* opinion might have been written by Brandeis. He cited public health, fires, suppression of "disorder," traffic, noise, congestion, residential density, even the provision of children's play space, as legitimate reasons for inhibiting the uses of urban property. Sutherland blandly observed, as if uttering a commonplace, that "the maxim 'sic utere tuo ut alienum non laedas,' which lies at the foundation of so much of the common law of nuisances, ordinarily will furnish a fairly helpful clew" to the legitimacy of such an exercise of the police power.

The Court was similarly inconsistent in decisions involving federal regulatory authority. After Congress created the Federal Trade Commission in 1914 to police unfair trade practices, the Court responded to the administrative state negatively again, retracing the steps of its original resistance to the ICC in the nineties. First, in *FTC v. Gratz* (1920),[248] it arrogated to the judiciary, rather than the agency, power to determine what constituted an unfair trade practice. Then in *FTC v. Curtis Publishing Co.* (1923),[249] the Court denied finality to commission fact-finding.

In contrast with these FTC cases and its decisions invalidating state police powers, the Court supported federal police power under the commerce clause, approving the sweeping federal controls imposed on the national railroad system by the Transportation Act of 1920.[250] It sanctioned intrastate rate-setting by the ICC[251] and permitted a forced subsidization of weaker lines by the stronger,[252] seemingly oblivious to the *Calder* principle forbidding the government from taking from A and giving to B. Having been president, the Chief Justice entertained a more expansive vision of federal authority, and his commerce clause decisions reflected that experience.[253]

Thus the Supreme Court, on the eve of the Great Depression, had established two bodies of doctrine on questions of state and federal police powers, on the amorphous contours of property law, on substantive due process and liberty of contract. Only strained and unpersuasive logic-chopping, a reification of distinctions without differences, could enable these doctrinal inconsistencies to coexist much longer. American public law was ripe for a paradigm shift, and it was not long in coming.

Notes

1. The appendix, "Historiography and the Supreme Court," recounts the three tellings: contemporary (Progressive), neo-Progressive, and modern revisionist.
2. Frank R. Strong provides an idiosyncratic survey of the subject: *Substantive Due Process of Law: A Dichotomy of Sense and Nonsense* (1986).
3. The Slaughterhouse Cases, 16 Wall. (36 (83 U.S.) 36, 129 (1873) (Swayne, J., dissenting).
4. Gunn v. Barry, 15 Wall. (82 U.S.) 610, 623 (1873).
5. Osborn v. Nicholson, 13 Wall. (80 U.S.) 654, 662 (1871).
6. Loan Association v. Topeka, 20 Wall. (87 U.S.) 655, 663 (1875).
7. 13 N.Y. 378, 398 (1856).
8. Murray v. Hoboken Land and Improvement Co., 18 How. (59 U.S.) 272, 276 (1856). Curtis's language lent itself as plausibly to a purely procedural interpretation, however, and the hint of substantive due process may have been inadvertent.
9. Keith Jurow rejects this equivalence in "Untimely Thoughts: A Reconsideration of

the Origins of Due Process of Law," 19 *Am. J. Legal Hist.* 265 (1975), but American courts have generally followed or shared Justice Curtis's assumption.

10. Robert E. Riggs, "Substantive Due Process in 1791," 1990 *Wis. L. Rev.* 941.

11. Dred Scott v. Sandford, 19 How. (60 U.S.) 393, 450 (1857).

12. Hepburn v. Griswold, 8 Wall. (75 U.S.) 603, 624 (1870).

13. 16 Wall. 81.

14. 16 Wall. 109–110.

15. 16 Wall. 116, 122.

16. Bartemeyer v. Iowa, 18 Wall. (85 U.S.) 129, 134 (1873).

17. Davidson v. New Orleans, 96 U.S. 97, 104, 102 (1878).

18. 20 Wall. (87 U.S.) 655, 662 (1875).

19. 109 U.S. 3, 23–24 (1883).

20. 116 U.S. 307, 331 (1886).

21. 123 U.S. 623, 661, 669 (1887).

22. Aviam Soifer, "The Paradox of Paternalism and Laissez-Faire Constitutionalism: United States Supreme Court, 1888–1921," 5 *Law & Hist. Rev.* 249, 254 (1987).

23. 98 N.Y. 98, 104–115 (1885).

24. 117 N.Y. 1, 68–71 (1889).

25. Budd v. New York, 143 U.S. 517, 551 (1892).

26. 113 Pa. St. 431, 437 (1886).

27. 117 Ill. 294, 301 (1886).

28. 141 Ill. 171, 181, 186–187 (1892).

29. 155 Ill. 98, 104, 108, 112, 114 (1895).

30. Wolff Packing Co. v. Court of Industrial Relations, 262 U.S. 522 (1923). The Illinois court's categories were: (1) the *sic utere* principle, (2) property affected with a public interest (*Munn*), (3) common law cases of public necessity like fire-stops, (4) fraud, (5) lack of capacity (minors, but not women), and (6) usury.

31. E.g., for Illinois: Frorer v. People, 141 Ill. at 185.

32. Bradwell v. Illinois, 16 Wall. (83 U.S.) 131 (1873).

33. 21 Wall. (88 U.S.) 163 (1875).

34. A large body of literature reviews women's protective legislation of this era. See: Theda Skocpol, *Protecting Soldiers and Mothers: The Political Origins of Social Policy in the United States* (1992); Susan Lehrer, *Origins of Protective Labor Legislation for Women, 1905–1925* (1987); Vivien Hart, *Bound by Our Constitution: Women, Workers, and the Minimum Wage* (1994), 67–107; Alice Kessler-Harris, *Out to Work: A History of Wage-Earning Women in the United States* (1982); Judith A. Baer, *The Chains of Protection: Judicial Response to Women's Labor Legislation* (1978), 3–106.

35. *Accord: In re* Morgan, 26 Colo. 415 (1899) (statute mandating eight-hour workday for miners unconstitutional because it was not related to public health).

36. Ritchie v. Wayman, 244 Ill. 509 (1910) (the later statute was restricted to women who worked in "mechanical establishments," factories, or laundries, and imposed a ten-hour maximum).

37. 33 W. Va. 179, 182–184, 186 (1889).

38. Felix Frankfurter and Nathan Greene, *The Labor Injunction* (1930), 110 (emphasis in orig.).

39. 155 Mass. 117, 121, 124 (1891).

40. 167 Mass. 92, 98, 106–109 (1896).

41. On Holmes's *Vegelahn* dissent, see Horwitz, *Transformation II*, 133–134, and G. Edward White, *Justice Oliver Wendell Holmes: Law and the Inner Self* (1993), 287–289.

42. Franklin Union, No. 4 v. People, 121 Ill. App. 647 (1905), aff'd 220 Ill. 355 (1906).

43. The only modern history of the Court disappointingly fails to offer any suggestions about why this might have been so: Francis Bergan, *The History of the New York Court of Appeals, 1847–1932* (1985).

44. See Alice Kessler-Harris, "The Paradox of Motherhood: Night Work Restrictions in the United States," in Ulla Wikander et al., eds., *Protecting Women: Labor Legislation in Europe, the United States, and Australia, 1880–1920* (1995), 337.

45. 189 N.Y. 131, 135 (1907).

46. Besides *Wynehamer, Jacobs, Williams,* and other cases noted in text: People v. Marx, 99 N.Y. 377 (1885) (statute prohibiting the manufacture or sale of oleomargarine); People v. Gillson, 109 N.Y. 389 (1888) (statute prohibiting retail premium offers); Colon v. Lisk, 153 N.Y. 188 (1897) (statute providing for seizure of vessels interfering with oystering); People v. Hawkins, 157 N.Y. 1 (1898) (statute requiring labeling of "convict-made" goods); Beardsley v. New York, Lake Erie, & Western R.R., 162 N.Y. 230 (1900) (statute compelling railroads to offer "books" entitling purchaser to ride 1,000 miles within specified time); People v. Orange County Road Construction Co., 175 N.Y. 84 (1903) (statute mandating eight-hour day in public works contracts); People v. Marcus, 185 N.Y. 257 (1906) (statute prohibiting yellow-dog contracts).

47. 201 N.Y. 271, 305, 294–296, 300 (1911).

48. Having been enunciated first in England in Priestly v. Fowler, 3 Mees & Welsby 1, 105 Eng. Rep. 1030 (1837), and in the United States in Farwell v. Boston & Worcester R.R., 4 Metc. (45 Mass.) 49 (1842).

49. Irving Lehman, "Judge Cardozo on the Court of Appeals," 52 *Harv. L. Rev.* 368 (1939).

50. Bergan, *History of New York Court of Appeals,* 246.

51. President Taft's message to Congress accompanying his veto of the Arizona Enabling Bill, 22 Aug. 1911, in James D. Richardson, comp., *A Compilation of the Messages and Papers of the Presidents* (1917), vol. 18, 8023.

52. New York Central R.R. v. White, 243 U.S. 188 (1917); see also Mountain Timber Co. v. Washington, 243 U.S. 219 (1917).

53. Act of 23 Dec. 1914, ch. 2, 38 Stat. 790.

54. W. F. Dodd, "Social Legislation and the Courts," *Political Science Quarterly* 28 (1913), 1, 5.

55. Henry R. Seager, "The Constitution and Social Progress in New York" (1915), quoted in Skocpol, *Protecting Soldiers and Mothers,* 261.

56. Skocpol, *Protecting Soldiers and Mothers.*

57. William E. Forbath, *Law and the Shaping of the American Labor Movement* (1991), 177–192.

58. Forbath, *Law and the Shaping of the American Labor Movement,* 168.

59. Chicago, Milwaukee & St. Paul Ry. Co. v. Minnesota, 134 U.S. 418, 457 (1890). See James W. Ely Jr., "The Railroad Question Revisited: Chicago, Milwaukee & St. Paul Railway v. Minnesota and Constitutional Limitations on State Regulations," *Great Plains Quarterly* 12 (1992), 121.

This case is sometimes referred to as the "Minnesota Rate Case," but that runs the risk of confusing it with the decision that is known as the "Minnesota Rate Cases," 230 U.S. 352 (1913) (which is never referred to by its proper title, Simpson v. Shepherd). To avoid this confusion, I propose that the case either be cited by its formal but awkward title, or by the popular name of the railroad itself, the Milwaukee Road.

60. Bradley, Gray, Lamar, JJ., dissented on the grounds that the majority was, in effect, overruling *Munn v. Illinois.*

61. 154 U.S. 362, 398, 412 (1894).

62. 166 U.S. 226, 235, 234 (1897).

63. Herbert Hovenkamp, *Enterprise and American Law, 1836–1937* (1991), 1–7, 171–182.

64. Gary L. McDowell, *Curbing the Courts: The Constitution and the Limits of Judicial Power* (1988), 3.

65. Felix Frankfurter, "The Supreme Court and the Public," *The Forum* (June 1930), 333.

66. 169 U.S. 466 (1898).

67. FPC v. Natural Gas Pipeline Co., 315 U.S. 575 (1942) (questioning *Smyth v. Ames* and restoring the authority of *Munn v. Illinois*); FPC v. Hope Natural Gas Co., 320 U.S. 591 (1944).

68. Printing and Numerical Registering Co. v. Sampson, 19 L.R.-Eq. 462 (1875), quoted approvingly in Diamond Match Co. v. Roeber, 106 N.Y. 473, 482–483 (1887).

69. 165 U.S. 578 (1897).

70. Henry Maine, *Popular Government* (1886), 51. I have inverted the order of the quotations. Maine was untroubled by the severity of competition in the United States because he regarded the opportunity for "perpetual emigration" to the West as a relief valve for population growth that would otherwise render the law's consequences intolerable. Seven years later, Frederick Jackson Turner announced that the relief valve had been shut and would soon be bolted down. "The Significance of the Frontier in American History" (1893), reprinted in Turner, *The Frontier in American History* (1920).

71. Bruce Ackerman, *We The People: Foundations* (1991), *passim*.

72. Robert Stanley, *Dimensions of Law in the Service of Order: Origins of the Federal Income Tax, 1861–1913* (1993), ix, 139, 136–175 *passim*; Hall quoted at 254. See also Owen M. Fiss, *Troubled Beginnings of the Modern State, 1880–1910* (vol. 8 of the *Holmes Devise History of the Supreme Court of the United States*) (1993), 75–100. Cf. Arnold M. Paul, *Conservative Crisis and the Rule of Law: Attitudes of Bar and Bench, 1887–1895* (1960), 185–220 and Edward S. Corwin, *Court over Constitution: A Study of Judicial Review as an Instrument of Popular Government* (1938; rpt. 1957), 177–209. The modern Progressive-influenced interpretation has been Sidney Ratner, *American Taxation: Its History as a Force in Democracy* (1942).

73. Owen Fiss contends that the suit was not collusive, *Troubled Beginnings of the Modern State*, p. 76, but by every modern criterion, it was. The Supreme Court had held that it had no jurisdiction over collusive suits in Lord v. Veazie, 8 How. (49 U.S.) 251 (1850), and had reaffirmed that holding as recently as 1892: Chicago & Grand Trunk Ry. Co. v. Wellman, 143 U.S. 339, 345 (1892). Collusive litigation has been responsible for some of the Court's most disastrous errors, including *Prigg v. Pennsylvania* (1842), the *Income Tax Cases*, and *Carter v. Carter Coal Co.* (1937). With that kind of a record, the wisdom of the ban is obvious.

According to rumors published in the Cincinnati press, Wall Street attorney William D. Guthrie's involvement in originating the litigation verged on the common-law offenses of barratry or maintenance. At the very least, and by his own admission, Guthrie was the moving spirit behind the suits, approached the nominal clients, and acted initially to promote his professional reputation: Robert T. Swaine, *The Cravath Firm and Its Predecessors* (1946–48), vol. 1, 518–520, 535–536.

74. As required by U.S. Const., art. I, § 2, cl. 3, and § 9, cl. 4.

75. 3 Dall. (3 U.S.) 171 (1796).

76. 102 U.S. 586 (1881).

77. Pollock v. Farmers' Loan and Trust Co., 157 U.S. 429, 533, 534, 553 (1895).

78. 51 *Alb. L.J.* 209 (1895).

79. John F. Dillon, "Property — Its Rights and Duties in Our Legal and Social System," New York State Bar Association *Proceedings*, 18 (1895), 33, 35, 46–48.

80. 157 U.S. at 583.

81. 157 U.S. at 607 (Field, J., dissenting).

82. Pollock v. Farmers' Loan & Trust Co., 158 U.S. 601 (1895) (*Pollock II*).

83. 158 U.S. at 650–651.

84. 158 U.S. 671, 685 (Harlan, J., dissenting).

85. David J. Brewer, *The Income Tax Cases and Some Comments Thereon* (1898).

86. The prior two instances were the Eleventh Amendment, which reversed Chisholm v. Georgia, 2 Dall. (2 U.S.) 419 (1793), and the Fourteenth Amendment, which reversed *Dred Scott*. The Supreme Court reversed that part of its *Pollock* holding exempting interest on state bonds from federal taxation in South Carolina v. Baker, 485 U.S. 505 (1988).

87. Christopher L. Tomlins, *Law, Labor, and Ideology in the Early American Republic* (1993); Tomlins, *The State and the Unions: Labor Relations, Law, and the Organized Labor Movement in America, 1880-1960* (1985), 10–95. On contemporaneous but not parallel developments in Great Britain, see John V. Orth, *Combination and Conspiracy: A Legal History of Trade Unionism, 1721–1906* (1991).

88. For an almost sympathetic effort to treat this vision respectfully, see Fiss, *Troubled Beginnings of the Modern State*, 53–74.

89. Nelson A. Miles, "The Lesson of the Recent Strikes," *North American Review*, Aug. 1894, 180, 186–187. For other reactions to the strike, see Carl S. Smith, *Urban Disorder and the Shape of Belief: The Great Chicago Fire, the Haymarket Bomb, and the Model Town of Pullman* (1995).

90. Dianne Avery, "Images of Violence in Labor Jurisprudence: The Regulation of Picketing and Boycotts, 1894–1921," 37 *Buff. L. Rev.* 1 (1988).

91. 4 Metc. (45 Mass.) 45 (1842).

92. Victoria C. Hattam, "Courts and the Question of Class: Judicial Regulation of Labor Under the Common Law Doctrine of Criminal Conspiracy," in Christopher Tomlins and Andrew J. King, eds., *Labor Law in America: Historical and Critical Essays* (1992), 44; Hattam, *Labor Visions and State Power: The Origins of Business Unionism in the United States* (1993), 30–75.

93. Morton Keller, *Affairs of State: Public Life in Late Nineteenth Century America* (1977), 425–427.

94. See generally Frankfurter and Greene, *The Labor Injunction*.

95. 169 U.S. 366 (1898).

96. 208 U.S. 412 (1908).

97. Ellen M. Kalman, "American Labor Law and Legal Formalism: How 'Legal Logic' Shaped and Vitiated the Rights of American Workers," 58 *St. Johns L. Rev.* 1 (1983).

98. Old Dominion Steam-Ship Co. v. McKenna, 30 Fed. 48, 50 (C.C.S.D.N.Y. 1887).

99. William Cohen, *At Freedom's Edge: Black Mobility and the Southern White Quest for Racial Control, 1861–1915* (1991); Daniel A. Novak, *The Wheel of Servitude: Black Forced Labor after Slavery* (1978); Pete Daniel, *The Shadow of Slavery: Peonage in the South, 1901–1969* (1972); Alex Lichtenstein, *Twice the Work of Free Labor: The Political Economy of Convict Labor in the New South* (1996).

100. On the case generally, see Daniel A. Novak, "The Pullman Strike Cases: Debs, Darrow, and the Labor Injunction," in Michal R. Belknap, *American Political Trials* (1981, rpt. 1994), 119–138.

101. On the strike generally, see Almont Lindsey, *The Pullman Strike: The Story of a Unique Experiment and of a Great Labor Upheaval* (1942; rpt. 1964).

102. *In re* Debs, 158 U.S. 564, 582, 593, 599 (1895).

103. Toledo, A.A. & N.M. Ry. v. Pennsylvania Co., 54 Fed. 730 (1893).

104. David R. Papke, "Eugene Debs as Legal Heretic: The Law-Related Conversion, Catechism, and Evangelism of an American Socialist," 63 *U. Cin. L. Rev.* 339 (1994).

105. Forbath, *Law and the Shaping of the American Labor Movement*, 88.

106. In 1995, Justice Clarence Thomas wrote flatly that "the Federal Government has nothing approaching a police power." United States v. Lopez, 115 S. Ct. 1624, 1642 (1995) (Thomas, J., concurring).

107. 4 Wheat. (17 U.S.) 316, 407, 421 (1819).

108. United States v. Dewitt, 9 Wall. (76 U.S.) 41, 45 (1869).

109. The earliest federal commission, the Freedmen's Bureau, was temporary.

110. Sherman Antitrust Act, ch. 647, 26 Stat. 209 (1890).

111. Naomi R. Lamoreaux, *The Great Merger Movement in American Business, 1895– 1904* (1985).

112. Act of 4 April 1888, ch. 269, 1888 N.J. Laws 385; Act of 9 May 1889, ch. 265, 1889 N.J. Laws 412; Act of 8 Mar. 1893, ch. 67, 1893 N.J. Laws 121, all discussed as elements of the state's "chartermongering" policy in Christopher Grandy, *New Jersey and the Fiscal Origins of Modern American Corporation Law* (1993), 42–43.

113. Lincoln Steffens, "New Jersey: A Traitor State," *McClure's Magazine*, 25 (May 1905), 41.

114. On the origins of antitrust policy generally, cf. William Letwin, *Law and Economic Policy in America: The Evolution of the Sherman Antitrust Act* (1965) with: Hans B. Thorelli, *The Federal Antitrust Policy: Origination of an American Tradition* (1954); Robert H. Bork, *The Antitrust Paradox: A Policy at War with Itself* (1978); Martin J. Sklar, *The Corporate Reconstruction of American Capitalism, 1890–191: The Market, the Law, and Politics* (1988); James May, "Antitrust in the Formative Era: Political and Economic Theory in Constitutional and Antitrust Analysis, 1880–1918," 50 *Ohio St. L.J.* 257 (1989); and Fiss, *Troubled Beginnings of the Modern State*, 107–154.

115. On the vexed problem of the changing status and nature of corporations in this period, see Morton J. Horwitz, "*Santa Clara* Revisited: The Development of Corporate Theory," in *Transformation II*, 65–107. On the states' role in regulating corporations, see Charles W. McCurdy, "The Knight Sugar Decision of 1895 and the Modernization of American Corporation Law, 1869–1903," *Business History Review* 53 (1979), 304.

116. Santa Clara County v. Southern Pacific R.R., 118 U.S. 394 (1886). This case involved the equal protection clause. Its doctrine was extended to the due process clause in Minneapolis & St. Louis Ry. v. Beckwith, 129 U.S. 26 (1889) (dictum).

117. 156 U.S. 1, 12, 16, 13 (1895).

118. But not to Thomas, J., concurring in United States v. Lopez, 115 S. Ct. at 1643, where he hints that he would return to the *Knight* distinction between commerce and manufacturing: "As one would expect, the term 'commerce' was used in contradistinction to productive activities such as manufacturing and agriculture."

119. Kidd v. Pearson, 128 U.S. 1, 20 (1888).

120. Standard Oil Co. v. United States, 221 U.S. 1, 68 (1911).

121. Sklar, *Corporate Reconstruction of American Capitalism*, 86–175.

122. William F. Duker, "Mr. Justice Rufus W. Peckham: The Police Power and the Individual in a Changing World," 1980 *B.Y.U. L. Rev.* 47.

123. United States v. Joint Traffic Assn., 171 U.S. 505 (1898).

124. United States v. Trans-Missouri Freight Assn., 166 U.S. 290 (1897).

125. Addyston Pipe and Steel Co. v. United States, 175 U.S. 211 (1899).

126. United States v. Trans-Missouri Freight Assn., 166 U.S. at 323.

127. 193 U.S. 197 (1903); 196 U.S. 375 (1905).

128. 221 U.S. 1 (1911).

129. Champion v. Ames, 188 U.S. 321 (1903).

130. McCray v. United States, 195 U.S. 27 (1904).

131. Hoke v. United States, 227 U.S. 308 (1913); Caminetti v. United States, 242 U.S. 470 (1917).

132. Hipolite Egg Co. v. United States, 220 U.S. 45 (1911).

133. Wilson v. New, 243 U.S. 332 (1917).

134. Interstate Commerce Act, ch. 104, 24 Stat. 379 (1887).

135. Olney to Charles C. Perkins, 28 Dec. 1892, excerpted in James M. Smith and Paul L. Murphy, eds., *Liberty and Justice: The Modern Constitution: American Constitutional Development Since 1865*, rev'd ed. (1968), 292–293.

136. Gerald Berk, *Alternative Tracks: The Constitution of American Industrial Order, 1865–1917* (1994), 104–112.

137. ICC v. Cincinnati, New Orleans, and Texas Pacific Railway Co., 167 U.S. 479 (1897).

138. ICC v. Alabama Midland Ry., 168 U.S. 144 (1897).

139. Ch. 3591, 34 Stat. 584.

140. Ch. 309, 36 Stat. 584.

141. 215 U.S. 452 (1910).

142. 220 U.S. 506, 516–517 (1910).

143. Woodruff v. Parham, 8 Wall. (75 U.S.) 123 (1869).

144. Paul v. Virginia, 8 Wall. (75 U.S.) 168 (1869). *Paul's* authority was weakened by Allgeyer v. Louisiana, 165 U.S. 578 (1897) (discussed below in another context) and it was effectively overturned in Polish National Alliance v. National Labor Relations Board, 322 U.S. 643 (1944), and United States v. Southwestern Underwriters Assn., 322 U.S. 533 (1944).

145. Crandall v. Nevada, 6 Wall. (73 U.S.) 35 (1868), a case that anticipated *Slaughterhouse* in the definition of rights of national citizenship.

146. The Case of the State Freight Tax, 15 Wall. (82 U.S.) 232 (1873).

147. The Case of the State Tax on Railway Gross Receipts, 15 Wall. (82 U.S.) 284 (1873). (The Reporter of the Court, John William Wallace, adopted his own conventions for naming cases. Fortunately, his successors did not imitate him.) In this spirit, the Court later upheld a tax on property of railroads within the state, even if such property (rolling stock, for example) was used in interstate commerce: Pullman's Palace Car Co. v. Pennsylvania, 141 U.S. 18 (1891).

148. Welton v. Missouri, 91 U.S. 275 (1876).

149. Pensacola Telegraph Co. v. Western Union Telegraph Co., 96 U.S. 1 (1877).

150. Minnesota v. Barber, 136 U.S. 313 (1890).

151. Brown v. Maryland, 12 Wheat. (25 U.S.) 419 (1827).

152. Brown v. Houston, 114 U.S. 622 (1885) (tax upheld); Leisy v. Hardin, 135 U.S. 100 (1890) (tax struck down).

153. Wabash, St. Louis, and Pacific Ry. v. Illinois, 118 U.S. 557, 577 (1886).

154. 12 How. (53 U.S.) 299 (1851).

155. 120 U.S. 489 (1887).

156. Keller, *Affairs of State*, 418.

157. On the desire of business groups for national regulation, see Gabriel Kolko, *The Triumph of Conservatism: A Re-interpretation of American History, 1900–1916* (1963); Kolko, *Railroads and Regulation, 1877–1916* (1965).

158. 21 Wall. (88 U.S.) 162 (1875).

159. 16 Wall. (83 U.S.) 130, 141–142 (1873).

160. Bradwell v. State, 16 Wall. (83 U.S.) 130, 141 (1873) (Bradley, J., concurring).

161. *In re* Lockwood, 154 U.S. 116 (1894).

162. 83 U.S. at 71.

163. 170 U.S. 213 (1898).

164. 163 U.S. 537, 544, 551 (1896).

165. On Plessy, see Charles A. Lofgren, *The Plessy Case: A Legal-Historical Interpretation* (1987).

166. 211 U.S. 45 (1908).

167. 118 U.S. 356 (1886).

168. Chae Chan Ping v. United States, 130 U.S. 581 (1889); Fong Yue Ting v. United States, 149 U.S. 698 (1892); Yamataya v. Fisher, 189 U.S. 86 (1903) (the last involving a Japanese rather than Chinese alien).

169. Chiefly, Downes v. Bidwell, 182 U.S. 244, 286, 280 (1901).

170. 163 U.S. 376 (1896).

171. 109 U.S. 556 (1883).

172. Cherokee Nation v. Georgia, 5 Pet. (30 U.S.) 1 (1831).

173. 187 U.S. 553 (1903). On *Lone Wolf*, and especially its relevance for imperialist and racist thought, see Blue Clark, *Lone Wolf v. Hitchcock: Treaty Rights and Indian Law at the End of the Nineteenth Century* (1994).

174. The secondary writings on Lochner are extensive. To cite only the most recent of important studies: Paul Kens, *Judicial Power and Reform Politics: The Anatomy of* Lochner v. New York (1990); Howard Gillman, *The Constitution Besieged: The Rise and Demise of Lochner Era Police Powers Jurisprudence* (1993); Fiss, *Troubled Beginnings of the Modern State*, 155–165; Matthew S. Bewig, "Lochner v. The Journeymen Bakers of New York: The Journeymen Bakers, Their Hours of Labor, and the Constitution: A Case Study in the Social History of Legal Thought," 38 *Am. J. Legal Hist.* 413 (1994).

175. Planned Parenthood of Southeastern Pennsylvania v. Casey, 505 U.S. 833, 944, 979 (1992) (Rehnquist, C.J., and Scalia, J., concurring in the judgment but dissenting in part).

176. Gerald Gunther considers these questions and others in *Constitutional Law*, 12th ed. (1991), 444–449. Cass Sunstein also addresses the issue in "Lochner's Legacy," 87 *Colum. L. Rev.* 873 (1987).

177. Principally, Bernard H. Siegan, *Economic Liberties and the Constitution* (1980), and Richard A. Epstein, *Takings: Private Property and the Power of Eminent Domain* (1985). For a survey of the pro-*Lochner* literature, see Michael J. Phillips, "Another Look at Economic Substantive Due Process," 1987 *Wis. L. Rev.* 265–324.

178. There is scant biographical work on this important figure. See Richard Skolnick, "Rufus Peckham," in Leon Friedman and Fred L. Israel, eds., *The Justices of the United States Supreme Court: Their Lives and Major Opinions* (1995), vol. 3, 832–852; and three articles by William F. Duker: "Mr. Justice Rufus W. Peckham: The Police Power and the Individual in a Changing World"; "The Fuller Court and State Criminal Process: Threshold of Modern Limitations on Government"; "Mr. Justice Rufus W. Peckham and the Case of *Ex parte Young: Lochnerizing Munn v. Illinois*," in 1980 *B.Y.U. L. Rev.* 47, 275, 539 respectively.

179. Dean Acheson, *Morning and Noon* (1965), 65.

180. "An act to regulate the manufacture of flour and meal food products," ch. 518, 1895 N.Y. Laws 305.

181. Peckham's position may have originally been the minority position, with some unknown member of the Court switching his vote; see Fiss, *Troubled Beginnings of the Modern State*, 165, fn. 32.

182. Lochner v. New York, 198 U.S. 45, 53–63, 69, 75 (1905).

183. Paul Kens, "The Source of a Myth: Police Powers of the States and Laissez Faire Constitutionalism, 1900–1937," 35 *Am. J. Legal Hist.* 70 (1991).

184. 208 U.S. 161, 175, 178 (1908).

185. Ch. 370, 30 Stat. 424.

186. For a specimen of a boilerplate and artfully euphemistic yellow-dog contract, im-

posed by Yale & Towne Mfg. Co. on its hires in the 1890s, see Stanley I. Kutler, ed., *Looking for America: The People's History*, 2nd ed. (1979), vol. 2, 152–153.

187. On the reverberations of this decision into our own time, see Kenneth Casebeer, "Teaching an Old Dog Old Tricks: *Coppage v. Kansas* and At-Will Employment Revisited," 6 *Cardozo L. Rev.* 765 (1985).

188. Kansas Laws 1903, ch. 222.

189. State v. Coppage, 87 Kan. 752, 125 Pac. 8 (1912).

190. Coppage v. Kansas, 236 U.S. 1, 14, 16, 9, 17–18 (1915).

191. Others are at 236 U.S. 13, 20.

192. Fred L. Israel, "Mahlon Pitney," in Friedman and Israel, eds., *The Justices of the United States Supreme Court*, vol. 3, 996–1005.

193. 236 U.S. at 27. Justice William R. Day wrote a lengthier dissent, in which Charles Evans Hughes joined, defending the police power and insisting on the relevance of bargaining inequality.

194. Overruled in Phelps Dodge Corp. v. NLRB, 313 U.S. 177 (1941).

195. Lincoln Federal Labor Union v. Northwestern Iron & Metal Co., 335 U.S. 525, 535–536 (1949).

196. Taft to Horace Taft, 14 Nov. 1929, quoted in Henry F. Pringle, *The Life and Times of William Howard Taft* (1939), vol. 2, 967.

197. "Address of Elihu Root in Presenting the Report of the Committee" (1923), *Proc. Am. Law Inst.*, vol. 1, part 2 (1923), 48–49.

198. The quoted phrase is the title of the report of the ALI's organizational committee: *Proc. Am. Law Inst.*, vol. 1, part 1 (1923), 66.

199. Charles Warren, *Supreme Court in United States History* (1922; rev'd ed. 1926), vol. 2, 741. See also Warren, "The Progressiveness of the United States Supreme Court," 13 *Colum. L. Rev.* 290 (1913) and "A Bulwark to the State Police Power—The United States Supreme Court," 13 *Colum. L. Rev.* 667 (1913). His conclusions have been confirmed more recently by Melvin Urofsky: "Myth and Reality: The Supreme Court and Protective Legislation during the Progressive Era," *1983 Yearbook* of the Supreme Court Historical Society, 53; see also Urofsky, "State Courts and Protective Legislation during the Progressive Era: A Reevaluation," *Journal of American History* 72 (1985), 63. Cf., however, the figures cited by Kermit Hall, *The Supreme Court and Judicial Review in American History* (1985), 27: "Between 1890 and 1937 the Court set aside 232 state laws under the due process provision of the Fourteenth Amendment," and a total of about 380 altogether.

200. Michael E. Parrish, "The Great Depression, the New Deal, and the American Legal Order," 59 *Wash. L. Rev.* 723, 729 (1984).

201. Champion v. Ames, 188 U.S. 321 (1903); United States v. Doremus, 249 U.S. 86 (1919).

202. Hoke v. United States, 227 U.S. 308 (1913).

203. McCray v. United States, 195 U.S. 27 (1904).

204. Hipolite Egg Co. v. United States, 220 U.S. 45 (1911); Pittsburgh Melting Co. v. Totten, 248 U.S. 1 (1918).

205. Swift & Co. v. United States, 196 U.S. 375 (1905); Stafford v. Wallace, 258 U.S. 495 (1922). On *Swift*, see David Gordon, "*Swift & Co. v. United States*: The Beef Trust and the Stream of Commerce Doctrine," 28 *Am. J. Legal Hist.* 244 (1984).

206. Ch. 149, 35 Stat. 424.

207. The [First] Employers' Liability Cases, 207 U.S. 463 (1908).

208. Mondou v. New York, New Haven & Hartford R.R., 223 U.S. 1 (1912), generally known as the *Second Employers' Liability Cases*; Arizona Employers' Liability Cases, 250 U.S. 400 (1919).

209. Hammer v. Dagenhart, 247 U.S. 251, 275 (1918).

210. United States v. Lopez, 115 S. Ct. 1624, 1652 (1995) (Souter, J., dissenting).

211. Bailey v. Drexel Furniture, 259 U.S. 20 (1922).

212. On the Court's antiunion animus, see Irving Bernstein, *The Lean Years: A History of the American Worker, 1920–1933* (1960), 190–243.

213. In the hearing below, the United States Circuit Court had held that the Sherman Act did cover labor unions: United States v. Debs, 64 Fed. 724 (1894).

214. 208 U.S. 274, 309 (1908).

215. Daniel R. Ernst, *Lawyers against Labor: From Individual Rights to Corporate Liberalism* (1995), passim; Ernst, "The Danbury Hatters Case," in Tomlins and King, eds., *Labor Law in America*, 180.

216. 221 U.S. 418 (1911).

217. Ch. 323, 38 Stat. 730.

218. Stanley I. Kutler, "Labor, the Clayton Act, and the Supreme Court," *Labor History* 3 (1962), 19.

219. Hitchman Coal and Coke Co. v. Mitchell, 245 U.S. 229 (1917).

220. Duplex Printing Press Co. v. Deering, 254 U.S. 443 (1921).

221. American Steel Foundries v. Tri-City Trades Council, 257 U.S. 184 (1921).

222. Bedford Cut Stone Co. v. Journeymen Stone Cutters Ass'n, 274 U.S. 37 (1927).

223. United Mine Workers v. Coronado Coal Co., 259 U.S. 344 (1922).

224. Truax v. Corrigan, 257 U.S. 312, 340 (1921).

225. *Accord*, Atchison, Topeka & Santa Fe Ry. v. Gee, 139 Fed. 582, 584 (C.C.S.D. Iowa, 1905).

226. Quoted in Avery, "Images of Violence," 73.

227. Felix Frankfurter compiled a useful list of all cases in which the Supreme Court invalidated state legislation between 1877 and 1938 (a total of 233 instances, most of them involving the due process clause in its substantive aspects): Felix Frankfurter, *Mr. Justice Holmes and the Supreme Court* (1938), 97–137.

228. 208 U.S. 412 (1908). Nancy S. Erickson views *Muller* and the Brandeis Brief critically in "Muller v. Oregon Reconsidered: The Origins of a Sex-Based Doctrine of Liberty of Contract," *Labor History* 30 (1989), 228.

229. 243 U.S. 426 (1917).

230. 209 U.S. 123 (1908); see Duker, "Mr. Justice Peckham and the Case of Ex parte Young."

231. See Erwin Chemerinsky, *Federal Jurisdiction* (1994), 390–394.

232. Act of 13 Feb. 1925, ch. 229, 43 Stat. 936.

233. Peter G. Fish, "Judiciary Act of 1925," in Kermit L. Hall et al., eds., *The Oxford Companion to the Supreme Court of the United States* (1992), 477.

234. See William H. Taft, *Popular Government: Its Essence, Its Permanence and Its Perils* (1913).

235. Thomas Reed Powell published a book-length review of the Taft Court's performance as "The Supreme Court and State Police Power, 1922–1930," 17 *Va. L. Rev.* 529, 653, 765 (1931); 18 *Va. L. Rev.* 270, 379, 481, 597 (1932).

236. Warren, *The Supreme Court in United States History* vol. 2, 741. He entertained the same opinion of *Coppage*.

237. 261 U.S. 525, 570, 546, 558, 560 (1923). Though enacted by Congress, the statute was the functional equivalent of a state statute because Congress was acting in its capacity as the municipal government for the District of Columbia. Furthermore, since *Adair* (1908), Fifth and Fourteenth Amendment due process limitations had been interchangeable.

238. 261 U.S. at 562, 564 (1923)(Taft, C.J., dissenting).

239. Wolff Packing Co. v. Court of Industrial Relations, 262 U.S. 522 (1923).

240. Jay Burns Baking Co. v. Bryan, 264 U.S. 504 (1924); Connally v. General Construction Co., 269 U.S. 385 (1926); Weaver v. Palmer Bros. Co., 270 U.S. 402 (1926); Liggett Co. v. Baldridge, 278 U.S. 105 (1928).

241. Tyson v. Banton, 273 U.S. 418 (1927); Ribnik v. McBride, 277 U.S. 350 (1928); Williams v. Standard Oil, 278 U.S. 235 (1929); New State Ice Co. v. Liebmann, 285 U.S. 262 (1932).

242. 262 U.S. 390 (1923) and 268 U.S. 510 (1925), invalidating state statutes that prohibited teaching foreign languages in elementary schools and outlawing parochial schools, respectively. See William G. Ross, *Forging New Freedoms: Nativism, Education, and the Constitution, 1917–1927* (1994).

243. Pennsylvania Coal Co. v. Mahon, 260 U.S. 393, 415 (1922). See Lawrence M. Friedman, "A Search for Seizure: Pennsylvania Coal Co. v. Mahon in Context," 4 *Law & Hist. Rev.* 1 (1986).

244. Dolan v. Tigard, 114 S. Ct. 2309 (1994).

245. 253 U.S. 233 (1920). In recent times, the Court has reaffirmed its acceptance of state enterprise and actually loosened constitutional controls on the state as "market participant": Reeves, Inc. v. Stake, 447 U.S. 429 (1980) (involving a South Dakota cement-manufacturing plant).

246. Frothingham v. Mellon, 262 U.S. 447 (1923).

247. 272 U.S. 365, 387 (1926) (Van Devanter, McReynolds, and Butler, JJ., dissenting without opinion).

248. 253 U.S. 421 (1920).

249. 260 U.S. 568 (1923).

250. Also known as the Esch-Cummings Act: Ch. 91, 41 Stat. 456.

251. Railroad Commission of Wisconsin v. Chicago, Burlington, and Quincy R.R., 257 U.S. 563 (1922).

252. Dayton-Goose Creek Ry. v. United States, 263 U.S. 456 (1924).

253. Stanley I. Kutler, "Chief Justice Taft, National Regulation, and the Commerce Power," *Journal of American History* 51 (1965), 651.

Chapter Four

Classicism Contested,
1893–1932

By 1930, the tenets of legal classicism seemed to reign triumphant as the legitimating juristic ideology that justified the role of the Supreme Court in American life. For half a century, traditionalist-minded jurists had enjoyed an untroubled confidence that the legal order was an autonomous, determinate, natural, neutral, necessary, objective, and apolitical structure of principles and norms, grounded in an authentic reading of American experience. The social myth that dominated both American society and its law permitted classical jurists to "enforce hierarchical assumptions of property rights, male domination, and white supremacy," in Alan Dawley's judgment.[1]

Nearly all judges believed law's rules to be objective, favoring no economic, social, or racial class, providing a just resolution of legal disputes. Judges applied these rules impartially, through an abstract logic that Sir Edward Coke three centuries earlier had called "the artificial reason . . . of the law."[2] Judges, constrained by the legal order, were independent guardians of the rule of law, who did not (or at least should not) hand down rulings based on their personal biases. Chief Justice William Howard Taft provided the most apt image of his Court, that of a priestly college, entrusted with America's secular Ark of the Covenant, the Constitution.[3]

Or so it seemed. If we analogize classical legal thought to a structure, it appeared as permanent and majestic as the marble temple that would house the hierophants in 1935. The actual building was soundly constructed, but a closer inspection of the metaphorical edifice of the law would reveal that its foundation was sinking and its facade was cracked. It came under attack from within by judges and scholars and from without by mobilized political groups.[4] These attacks were so telling that in 1937, the structure would shudder and collapse into a pile of rubble.

How did something as seemingly powerful, as comprehensive, and as perduring as legal classicism weaken over a generation and then disintegrate? The attack and decay took place in three phases, and from three different sources. During the first phase, in the closing years of the nineteenth century, a few scholars, jurists, and political groups began to criticize specific doctrines or decisions. At the same time, private law doctrine displayed the kinds of stresses and inconsistencies that suggested that a paradigm shift might be in the offing. During the middle phase, which lasted the first two decades of the twentieth century, the academic challenges gained strength, the Court and its power came under attack in the political arena, and a few of the Justices themselves began to question classical dogma. In the final phase, the 1920s, the attacks consolidated, gathered force in the 1924 election, but were repulsed by the seeming solidity of classical ideology. For a time, criticism appeared to ebb.

The Populist Era, 1880–1900

Academic Critique

At the same Chicago World's Fair of 1893 where Frederick Jackson Turner propounded the frontier thesis, another academic, James Bradley Thayer of the Harvard Law School, delivered an equally momentous paper. Each paper integrated its author's scholarly interests into the events of the day: Turner explored the significance of the frontier's disappearance, while Thayer responded to what he may have prophetically seen as an emergent judicial activism. In "The Origin and Scope of the American Doctrine of Constitutional Law,"[5] Thayer defended the power of judicial review as "a great and stately jurisdiction," but he cautioned that federal courts cannot overturn congressional legislation merely because they think it is unconstitutional. They may do so only when legislators "have not merely made a mistake, but have made a very clear one — so clear that it is not open to rational question." Called in modern times "rationality review," Thayer's standard was deferential to legislative judgment and constituted one of the earliest calls for judicial self-restraint.

Obviously, Thayer could not have been criticizing the barrage of policy-driven judicial vetoes after 1895, which were two years in the future as he spoke. As a former abolitionist, he may have been disturbed by the result of *The Civil Rights Cases* (1883),[6] where the Supreme Court held most of the Civil Rights Act of 1875 unconstitutional; or he might have had in mind the Court's troubling flip-flop in the *Legal Tender Cases*.[7] Modern scholars locate his thought in differing contexts,[8] but whatever his motivations, the impact of his essay was extraordinary, and not just because it claimed pride of place. Justice Felix Frankfurter may have exaggerated a little when he claimed that Thayer's ideas were a direct influence on Holmes, the Harvard Law School, and Brandeis, and indirectly through them on Frankfurter and his contemporaries,[9] but he was essentially correct. Thayer's call was the fountainhead of a tradition of skepticism about judicial power that corroded confidence in the authority of classicist orthodoxy.

Elsewhere in the academy, professionals in the newly emergent social sciences began to offer their expertise and critiques to reform the legal order.[10] Classical jurists were indifferent to the rise of economics, anthropology, sociology, social work, and political science. But such intellectual isolation could not endure for long, and before World War I, even the musty, isolated corridors of legal academe were being ventilated by the breezes of empiricism. When that happened, the conceptualist old order began to seem irrelevant.

Classical legal thought became the victim of a web of developments in all fields of thought that we call "modernism." Difficult to define, elusive in both time and space,[11] Modernist trends nevertheless dominated scientific, artistic, and intellectual endeavor after 1890. Like legal classicism itself, modernism was a form of consciousness, but it was not confined to any one domain of thought. It was "a change in sensibility and a change in consciousness comparable with the impact of the Romantic movement, the scientific revolution of the seventeenth century, and the Renaissance."[12] Sharing some values with classicism — including an emphasis on rationality and a veneration of "science"[13] — the spirit of modernism was nevertheless antithetical to the classical approach to law.[14] The modernist impulse spurned dogma and logical systems not grounded in empirical investigation.

Modernists assumed radical "cognitive subjectivity": despairing of epistemological objectivity (defined as "access to reality independent of any particular view of it"),[15] modernism embraced instead the conviction that all knowledge and belief were subjective, a quality in the viewer rather than the viewed object. Modernists concluded that "no foundation for knowledge or value exists outside the meanings that human beings construct for their own purposes."[16] Karl Pearson declared in 1892 that truth, even scientific truth, was not a mirror representation of reality but rather merely a conception formed out of the individual's sense experience.[17]

Political Assault: Populists and Labor

The early political attack on classicism's results was multifocal. The first of the foci was the Populist movement.[18] The Populists assaulted classicism by trying to reconstitute the social and economic organization of Gilded Age America. Emerging at the grass roots among farmers, taking shape out of the welter of 1870s political reform movements — the Grange, the Greenback Party, the Knights of Labor, other industrial unions — the Farmers Alliances were an attempt to create a "cooperative commonwealth" of farmer-producers at the state level.[19] They hoped to establish statewide marketing cooperatives to break the control over agricultural prices wielded by grain elevators, railroads, warehousemen, furnishing merchants, and ultimately eastern banks. Organizing into an effective national Farmers Alliance after 1886, the agrarian movement drafted the 1892 St. Louis platform, with its radical demands for remaking the American political and economic order.

The St. Louis platform suggested that corruption "touches even the ermine of the bench." Angered by the Supreme Court's firm stance against municipal bond repudiation, inhibitions on state regulation of railroad rates, and the federal courts' handling of railroad receiverships, Populist spokesmen and sympathizers like William Peffer, Sylvester Pennoyer, James B. Weaver, and John Peter Altgeld denounced the federal courts and their decisions.[20] For the next four years, Populists proposed various remedies to rein in judicial power, including the elective judiciary, judicial recall, and "recall" of judicial decisions.[21] The triad of 1895 decisions — the *Income Tax Cases*, *Debs*, and *Knight*— drove the party to overt attacks on federal judicial power. Five governors with Populist sympathies issued a joint statement in 1895 claiming that "the federal courts have flagrantly usurped jurisdiction, first, to protect corporations and perpetuate their many abuses, and second to oppress and destroy the powers of organized labor."[22] Populist members of Congress introduced bills to restrict labor injunctions and the federal courts' contempt powers. Pennoyer denounced the Supreme Court as a "judicial oligarchy."

The Populists and classical jurists cherished mirror-image visions of American society. To the judges, democratic government posed a threat to economic power and the distribution of wealth. To Populists, economic power posed a threat to democracy. Each side adopted increasingly confrontational stances toward the other.

The farmers' groups that coalesced in the People's Party reached out to organized labor. Unions had begun to suspect, correctly, that they were encountering a systemic antilabor, antiunion bias among American judges. To cite only one prominent example among hundreds, a decade before he delivered himself of his *Debs* opinion, Brewer, then a judge on the Eighth Circuit, presided over litigation involving railroad workers' complaints about working conditions, including uncompensated overtime, long hours, and late pay. He responded with a patronizing lecture to them, urging them to have consideration for the railroad's profitability, and then dismissed their grievances as "very trivial."[23] Thus his recommendation in *Debs* that workers resort to courts rather than strikes rang hollow to railroad workers. Judges like Brewer simply could not comprehend the thoughts, values, and experiences of working people. Being blind to the reality of working conditions in industrial America, these men substituted a stereotype of their own creation, one that exaggerated the threat to order and stability that was the dominant concern of the age.[24]

Crafts unions organized themselves into a national alliance, the American Federation of Labor, in 1886, the same year that the Farmers Alliances began *their* national organizing. The AFL articulated a philosophy of trade unionism that stressed the unions' powers of self-governance and the collective realization of their members' individual liberty.[25] Not coincidentally, it was in 1886 that state legislatures threw a sop to the labor movement by designating May Day as the nation's first Labor Day.

While unionists regarded their collective efforts as being squarely in the tradition of republican liberty in America,[26] their corporate and judicial enemies reached the opposite conclusion, seeing unions as a menace to that same republican liberty. Judges were frightened by the thought of these working-class *imperia in imperio*, potential rivals to the state's claim to the monopoly of force and coercive authority. Recorder Moses Levy had denounced "a new legislature consisting of journeymen shoemakers" as early as 1806 in the Philadelphia *Cordwainers' Case*. Judge Ogden Edwards of New York asked in 1836 whether "any body of men could raise their crests in this land of law, and control others by self-organized combination."[27] In *Debs*, Brewer denounced unions as self-constituted private sovereigns, guilty of "the attempted exercise by individuals of powers belonging only to government."[28] In light of such judicial attitudes, the Knights of Labor concluded that resort to courts to protect their interests was futile because "the interpretation of law rests largely upon the public sentiment of the wealthy part of the community."[29]

Employers considered their struggle with labor as a contest over who was to control industrial policy: unions or corporate management. They found a sympathetic hearing in American courts, where after 1886 corporations were deemed persons for some Fourteenth Amendment purposes. Nineteenth-century judicial thinking about organized labor was deeply imprinted: the values of individual autonomy, a voluntaristic economic system arranged by contractual ordering, and respect for property rights were hostile to any possibility that judges could ever side with unions in their struggle with management.

Judges converted concepts like corporate control of the workplace, expectations of profit, and access to markets into property rights.[30] The labor reformer Andrew Furuseth provided a capsule summary of this theory: corporate lawyers claim that business has "the land, the appliances, the raw material, and contracts to deliver goods; but, owing to a 'conspiracy' on the party of labor, it is unable to get workmen, and its property — that is, its business — is being destroyed." This argument turned on "the idea that the earning power of property is [itself] property."[31] The Vermont Supreme Court anticipated this view as early as 1887:

> The labor and skill of the workman, be it of high or low degree, the plant of the manufacturer, the equipment of the farmer, the investments of commerce, are all in equal sense property. If men, by overt acts of violence, destroy either, they are guilty of crime. The anathemas of secret organizations of men combined for the purpose of controlling the industry of others [i.e., unions] . . . are quite as dangerous, and generally altogether more effective, than acts of actual violence.[32]

A labor economist later observed that "the law cannot help being in spirit inimical to unionism. Unionism is in its very essence a lawless thing, in its very purpose and spirit a challenge to law."[33]

Unions lobbied for measures that would restrict the equity jurisdiction of the federal courts, in order to eliminate the labor injunction. From state legislatures they sought workers' compensation statutes, as well as legislation modifying the common law doctrines of assumption of risk, contributory negligence, and the fellow-servant rule. Labor got some encouragement from the Democratic and Populist Parties. The 1896 Democratic platform condemned "government by injunction," demanded jury trials in certain contempt hearings, opposed life tenure for the judiciary, and hinted at reconstituting (packing) the Supreme Court.[34]

Labor and Populist attacks on the federal courts peaked in the epochal presidential campaign of 1896.[35] But the results of the 1896 election consigned their criticisms to oblivion, along with the Populists themselves. In the ensuing triumph of reaction, Roman Catholic archbishop John Ireland warned that the Populist "spirit of socialism . . . may light up in the country the lurid fires of a 'commune,'"[36] (a reference to the Paris commune). He crowed that "the personification of law and of order in America is our courts."

Judicial Critique: Holmes

The American judiciary itself contributed to subverting classical thought. Oliver Wendell Holmes, first as a legal theorist, then as a jurist of the Massachusetts Supreme Judicial Court, expressed skepticism that judges could identify any objective criteria for adjudication. At the same time, judges less theoretically inclined than he were evolving doctrines in property, contracts, and torts that exposed classicism's internal inconsistencies.

Holmes's earliest published writings[37] displayed the positivist inclination, skepticism about deductive reasoning, and bleak social Darwinian outlook that characterized his views throughout his life. In 1881, he brought out *The Common Law*, a milestone that marked the end of his career as a lawyer-editor and the beginning of his nineteen years on the Massachusetts high court.[38] The book showcased Holmes's lingering affinities to the formalism of the era. No other writer or judge, for example, seemed to go so far as he in seeking almost to abolish liability in tort: "[T]he general principle of our law is that loss from accident must lie where it falls. . . . There is obviously no policy in throwing the hazard of what is at once desirable and inevitable upon the actor."[39] But the book otherwise subverted classicist premises. Its central insight, the "imaginative leap that changed all legal thinking afterward," in the opinion of a leading Holmes scholar, was that "the organizing principle of the common law was liability, not duty."[40]

Holmes began *The Common Law* by repeating his aphorism of a decade earlier, "[T]he life of the law has not been logic; it has been experience." He went on: "The felt necessities of the time, . . . intuitions of public policy, . . . even the prejudices which judges share with their fellow-men, have had a good deal more to do than the syllogism in determining the rules by which men should be governed. [Law] cannot be dealt with as if it contained only the axioms and corollaries of a book of mathematics."[41] Thomas C. Grey considers this insight, the triumph of experience over logic, to be "the central, if obscure, truth of American legal thought; as Cardozo wrote, 'Here is the text to be unfolded. All that is to come will be development and commentary.'"[42]

Holmes rejected both natural rights and subjective moral states as bases for legal rights or liabilities, because they were unsuited to the conditions of an industrializing, commercial society. In their place, he insisted on objective standards as the basis of liability in contract, tort, and criminal law. He originally believed, with the classicists, that law grew out of custom, which was nothing more than the collective experience of society. The duty of the judge was to ascertain that custom and enforce it.

Holmes confronted the dilemma of modernism in law. In his more stark moods, Holmes conceded that only raw Hobbesian force controlled legal development. "I believe that force, mitigated as far as may be by good manners, is the *ultima ratio* and between two groups that want to make inconsistent kinds of world I see no remedy except force."[43] In more sanguine moments, he emphasized the right of popular majorities to have their way through the political process. Finally, in a purely pragmatic vein, Holmes emphasized the idea that all life was an experiment, never a completed achievement. He rejected pragmatism as an "amusing humbug," but shared some pragmatic insights and attitudes.[44]

Holmes's experience on the Massachusetts bench after his appointment in 1883 tempered these views. His reactions to the labor conflicts of the era inspired his seminal article, "Privilege, Malice, and Intent" (1894).[45] There, he moved beyond societal custom as the basis of law: "[T]he time has gone by when law is only an unconscious embodiment of the common will." Instead, "[T]he ground of decision really comes down to a proposition of policy." Since judges applying legal rules are policy-makers, they must avoid "unconscious prejudice or half conscious inclination," and confront the policy grounds of decision forthrightly. Nothing in the legal order justified treating unions' efforts to pressure employers differently from competition among business firms. Morton Horwitz considers "Privilege, Malice, and Intent" the first instance where "a fully articulated balancing test has entered American legal theory," and therefore marked "the moment we should identify as the beginning of modernism in American thought." "The triumph of the balancing test marks the demise of the late-nineteenth-century system of legal formalism," Horwitz concludes.[46]

Holmes had an opportunity to apply these balancing theories to an actual case coming before him two years after the article was published. In *Vegelahn v. Guntner* (1896),[47] the majority enjoined a union's picketing, a result typical for state courts of the time. Holmes, who had denied the injunction at the trial level, dissented, contending that business "combination . . . is patent and powerful. Combination on the other [i.e., unions] is the necessary and desirable counterpart, if the battle is to be carried on in a fair and equal way. . . . Certainly the policy is not limited to struggles between persons of the same class competing for the same end."

Holmes's position, that the judge was engaged in adjusting competing interests rather than mechanically deriving norm from doctrine, triumphed a generation later, on the eve of formalism's overthrow on the Supreme Court. Justice Harlan Fiske Stone observed that a judge "is often engaged not so much in extracting a rule of law from the precedents, as we were once accustomed to believe, as in making an appraisal and comparison of social values." The end of the law "is to be attained through the reasonable accommodation of law to changing economic and social needs." A judge's choice of rules will "depend upon the relative weights of the social and economic advantages which will finally turn the scales of judgement." Doing this, the judge "performs essentially the function of the legislator, and in a real sense makes law."[48] This marked the obsequies of legal classicism, though a bit prematurely.

Holmes's systematic thought culminated in the closing years of the century. In "The Path of the Law" (1897), a lecture he delivered at Boston University Law School,[49] he uttered his oft-quoted positivist aphorism: "[T]he prophecies of what the courts will do in fact, and nothing more pretentious, are what I mean by the law." He snatched away from his audience of young lawyers any hope that legal logic would lead to objective results: "[C]ertainty generally is an illusion, and repose is not the destiny of man." Instead, judging is a matter of choosing results on competing policy grounds: "[B]ehind the logical form lies a judgement as to the relative worth and importance of competing legislative grounds, [which is] the very root and nerve of the whole proceeding." Morton Horwitz evaluated the impact of these heterodox ideas: "Holmes pushed American legal thought into the twentieth century." It was a moment marking a profound "change in American consciousness . . . a fundamental break with theological and doctrinal modes of thought. It was at this moment that the idea that law is discovered and not made was dealt its most powerful blow."[50]

Holmes's 1897 insights remained incomplete and inadequate, however. Without elaboration, his positivism would have expressed nothing more than the truistic conclusion that those with power impose their will. He redeemed his thought from such triviality two years later by returning to a conviction that law was a science, but not the science of Langdell.[51] Legal science was not theology, mathematics, or anthropology. Its growth derived from "accurately measured social desires instead of tradition." In doubtful cases, "what really is before us [judges] is a conflict between two social desires." In one plangent aphorism, Holmes struck at the heart of classicism: "[J]udges are called on to exercise the sovereign prerogative of choice."

Such quotations might convey the misleading impression that Holmes was a jurisprudential Saint George, who slew the dragon of legal classicism at a blow. (The dragon was Holmes's own metaphor, in "The Path of the Law."[52]) But that would be the form of anachronism that reads history backward. At the time, Holmes was, especially in his own perception, an obscure state court judge, a legal thinker whose vaulting ambition failed to move the world of legal thought much. Experience on the bench forced him to modify his earlier thinking, a point extremely difficult for him to admit.[53] His passionate correspondence at the time with Clare Castletown, with whom he had fallen in love, suggests that he regarded his 1897 work as expressing a pinnacle of his thought.[54] But it was a lonely pinnacle and, at the time, apparently seemed to be a futile effort. The dragon remained secure in its cave.

Private Law Developments

Besides their relative obscurity, Holmes's off-the-bench writings could be ignored as theoretical and academic. Not so ongoing developments in private law, which might have disclosed to a discerning eye the troublesome anomalies that heralded an incipient paradigm shift. In contracts, torts, and property, doctrinal developments revealed instability in some basic concepts of those princely domains of private law.

Contract law developed along two tracks in the nineteenth century. In the realm of public law, the contracts clause of the Constitution's Article I, Section 10, served throughout the century as the principal textual source for limitations that the Supreme Court imposed on state regulatory power. In the 1890s, it was overtaken by the due process clause of the Fourteenth Amendment — and even then, expiring, it left behind it a ghostly influence through *Allgeyer v. Louisiana* (1897), which spawned the protean doctrine of liberty of contract.

On the private law side, contract law, as nurtured by Joseph Story and his son William Wetmore Story, had evolved successfully to serve the needs of a growing antebellum mercantile economy and a national market, validating speculation, futures markets, mercantile substitutes for a national currency, and so on. Yet as it approached classicist ideals in the years between 1870 and 1890, it seemingly distanced itself from such instrumental approaches. After the war, in the intellectual climate reflected in Holmes's *The Common Law*, contract law shed its moralistic trappings and strove to enhance individual autonomy, even at the expense of reliance interests.[55] Grant Gilmore, not entirely tongue in cheek, described "the general theory of Contract," as it evolved through the succession of Holmes-Langdell-Samuel Williston-Learned Hand, as "dedicated to the proposition that, ideally, no one should be liable to anyone for anything." Since that was not practicable, "the compromise solution was to limit liability within the narrowest possible limits. Within those limits, however, liability was to be absolute."[56]

But it was never that simple. Contract law throughout the nineteenth century had always had an air of incoherence about it. A revealing illustration was provided by two cases from the adjacent jurisdictions of Massachusetts and New Hampshire, handed down in 1824 and 1834 respectively, involving the problem of the farm worker who quit his employment before the term of his annual contract was up. New Hampshire allowed recovery on quantum meruit for the time worked[57]; Massachusetts denied it.[58] To the Massachusetts judges, it would have been a "flagrant violation of first principles of justice" to allow recovery, while to the New Hampshire judges, "the general understanding of the community" supported recovery. Rational policy grounds could be found for either result, so neither holding in itself could be said to be irrational or aberrational. But the two decisions, and their underlying policies and doctrines, were incompatible with each other. Jurists of the late nineteenth and early twentieth centuries, as well as academics like Langdell and Williston, resolved this sort of incoherence by assuming that one result or doctrine had to be right, and the other, because of its divergence, wrong. (For the illustrative problem, Williston decided that the Massachusetts line of cases, denying recovery, was founded on "the best rule.")[59] To this kind of juristic *ipse dixit*, Holmes directed his exasperated comment that "the common law is not a brooding omnipresence in the sky."[60]

Holmes in *The Common Law*, Langdell in his *Contracts* casebook, and later Williston in his *Contracts* treatise[61] struggled to impose order, coherence, integration, and objective standards on the law of voluntary agreements, but reality kept bursting through the seams of the doctrinal garment. Quasi contract emerged repeatedly, and in ways that imposed obligations on parties where there had been no agreement in fact. Doctrines of waiver and estoppel similarly intruded into the domain of purely consensual, voluntaristic contract law. Such obligations, which were imposed by law rather than by a meeting of the parties' minds, threatened the elaborate structure of pure doctrine. Taken to an extreme, it could become difficult to discriminate between liability in tort and liability in contract.[62] Tort, contract, and property threatened to merge, like perspectival lines approaching some conceptual vanishing point, into a pseudo–property right, "contractual property," especially when the late-nineteenth-century doctrine of tortious interference with contractual relationships emerged.[63]

At the same time, broader social and economic developments were conspiring to make classical private-law contract doctrine irrelevant. The individualist model of society was ever more beside the point. To whatever extent liberty and equality are incompatible in the economic realm, many Americans were coming to value more the principles of a limited equality. Complexity, size, bureaucratization, statistical reasoning all drove social organizations to a managed state and away from some hypothetical natural liberty. The rise of large organizations like corporations and unions displaced traditional mediating social institutions like church and family. All these trends left the structure of classical contract dogma isolated, cut off from a social reality that had left it a derelict.[64]

Frederick Pollock, the great English legal historian and also an authority on the law of contract, pronounced the obsequies for the classical doctrine of contract in 1921, writing in his *Principles of Contract* (ninth edition) that "[l]earned Americans are still engaged from time to time in valiant efforts to reduce the common law rules of contract, and the doctrine of consideration in particular, to strict logical consistency. That quest is . . . misconceived. Legal rules exist not for their own sake, but to further justice and convenience in the business of human life; dialectic is the servant of their purpose, not their master."[65] Thanks to Williston and the Restatement project, classical doctrine would linger a bit longer, but Pollock had espied the future, and Judge Cardozo was even then ushering it in.

Tort law displayed similar strains in the late nineteenth century.[66] Like the law of contracts, the law of torts was a relatively recent invention. Blackstone took little notice of anything that we moderns recognize as torts. He allotted a mere five pages of his third volume, "Of Private Wrongs," to personal injuries, the staple of modern tort actions, and did not mention "negligence" at all. More significantly, his entire treatment was organized procedurally, around court structure and the forms of action at common law.[67] Not until the middle of the nineteenth century did English and American judges move beyond the old, narrow concept of "neglect" to the broader idea of "negligence." When they did, however, they launched a doctrinal revolution in the law.

This revolution derived from two unrelated sources. First, the forms of action and common law pleading that had structured legal thought and action in Blackstone's day were disappearing by mid-century. At the same time, earlier concepts of "private wrongs," predicated on personal relationships and status, gave way to legal norms that ordered the relationships among strangers who, until the moment of injury, bore no legal relationship to each other. The old cases known to Blackstone that dealt with the liability of sheriffs or physicians were nearly irrelevant to modernizing America. This was due in part to the rise in personal injuries caused by industrialization and the ubiquity of the Machine, but only in part. The new law of torts was a product of academics working through legal science to identify the principles of tort law and to analyze their relationships to decided cases.[68]

The negligence principle triumphed in academic writing by 1873,[69] and on the bench in that same year thanks to one of the nation's most original judicial thinkers, Chief Justice Charles Doe of the New Hampshire Supreme Court, in *Brown v. Collins*.[70] There, building on the innovations of Chief Justice Shaw in the previous generation, Doe extended the doctrine of fault as the basis of liability to a generalized standard of care, a duty owed to all the world rather than one owed to a specific person, which had been the basis of the now antique tort concept of neglect. Tort thereby emerged as a new domain of law, organized around the overarching theory of generalized duty.

Simultaneously, however, judges and legislators were eroding the solidity of fault and its related doctrines. Between 1870 and the First World War, legislatures abrogated or modified the fellow servant rule, assumption of risk, and contributory negligence, while some judges, repelled by the harshness and injustice of the results those doctrines generated, invented exceptions to them. But these common law doctrines died hard, because some judges erroneously regarded them as constitutionally grounded, as, for example, the New York Court of Appeals did in *Ives* (1911).

A more serious erosion of classical tort doctrine occurred when the idea of causality itself began to weaken. The earlier conception of causal relationships, apparently derived from Francis Bacon, assumed a workable distinction between proximate and remote causes, with only the former being a basis of liability.[71] One of Holmes's associates in the Metaphysical Club, Nicholas S. Green, attacked this concept of a chain of causation as "a pure fabrication of the mind"[72] that seduced judges into thinking that their reasoning was based at least on pseudoscience, if not the real thing, while disguising its true foundations: mere judicial policy preference or moral judgment.

More orthodox thinkers like Francis Wharton, a polymath authority in international and criminal law, denounced the implications of such an attack on objective unicausality and chains of causation as "practical communism" because it threatened redistribution of wealth, as juries traced causal connections back to the client with deep pockets, usually corporations. Wharton's indignation was fired at the thought that "the noblest and most meritorious classes of the land" as well as piteous "widows and orphans" might have to bear ultimate financial responsibility for the costs of industrial accidents.[73]

Property was the most unstable of the private law domains. The wonder is not that property law's older categories dissolved in the solvent of twentieth-century critique, but that they managed to cohere as long as they did. The social and economic reality that property law served was changing vertiginously because of the industrial revolution, the rise of the national market, the transportation revolutions, and the impact of new technologies. The United States participated, though late, in the underlying shift away from realty as a source of wealth (characteristic of agrarian societies) to personal and then incorporeal property as the dominant medium of wealth and power. The most stable and well-defined property rules, those relating to future interests, became relatively less significant in a developing nation that treated land as a commodity rather than as a basis for family wealth and continuity. From protecting a right in things, property law came to protect their value, and that in turn often meant an expectation of future income.

Property was especially vulnerable because classical law since the eighteenth century placed impossible expectations on it. Property law became freighted with ideological responsibilities in public law, such as realizing Lockean theories about the role of property in protecting human liberty. One turn-of-the-century treatise, *Smith on Personal Property*, illustrates the extravagant claims of property law: "[T]he right of property is of divine origin derived by title-deed from the universal creator of all things."[74] When Progressive economists and lawyers demonstrated the somewhat more mundane origins of property claims in social convention, classicism seemed embarrassingly like an apologia for the status quo of wealth distribution — which, of course, it was.

Blackstone had defined three rights of English people as "absolute": life (including personal security), liberty, and "property: which consists in the free use, enjoyment, and disposal of all his acquisitions, without any control or diminution, save only by the laws of the land."[75] But even Blackstone recognized that not all rights in property were literally absolute. The problem of defining limits on property rights became aggravated by the expanding commercial activity of the nineteenth century. By 1900, the legal conception of property had lost any determinate meaning it may have had a century earlier. Legal rules were not derived from the nature of property but imposed on the relations among people having claims to it.

Throughout the nineteenth century, property law was a theater of conflicts over wealth redistribution. Joseph Schumpeter identified "the process of creative destruction" as "the essential fact about capitalism" that constantly revolutionized manufacturing processes, the economy, and underlying property relationships.[76] Legal rules that judges developed to mediate these changes inescapably involved a transfer of wealth from one class of property owner to another, with some being forced to bear the costs of legally sanctioned destruction or expropriation. The century's most cataclysmic act of redistribution was the abolition of slavery, by which "owners" of nearly half the South's wealth were abruptly divested of their "property" without compensation.[77]

Compounding the confusion surrounding property law, the Supreme Court was not consistent in its attitudes toward the supposed sanctity of property. Though the Justices deplored "confiscation" through regulation or taxation, when faced with an authentic confiscation, made all the more repellent because it was prompted by religious bigotry, the Court supinely acquiesced with scarcely a nod at the Fifth Amendment. As part of its campaign against polygamy and the Mormons who practiced it, Congress in 1862 annulled the corporate charter of the Church of Latter-Day Saints, and declared all church property forfeit, escheated to the United States, to be disposed of for charitable uses. The church's effort to recoup the confiscated property was unavailing: in 1890, Justice Bradley found no constitutional bar to Congress's property grab.[78] Apparently possessed of a less dormant sense of justice than the Court, Congress later restored the confiscated property.

The valuation of property posed its own sorts of problems. Property could not be valued where no market existed for it, except by undisciplined judicial divination that discovered some "intrinsic" value by methods no more sophisticated than those of the ancient Roman haruspices who peered into fowls' entrails. This led the Supreme Court into accounting and economic depths beyond its abilities, as in *Smyth v. Ames*. Thus when an economist like John R. Commons uttered what is today a truism in regulatory economics, "[M]arket value is the present value of the expected rates,"[79] such an untoward intrusion of economic thought had a destabilizing effect on legal doctrine. Only a few lawyers recognized, with Commons, that a court cannot determine a utility's rates by guessing at its value, because to do so would be conceptually circular.[80]

State courts expanded the concept of property when they began thinking of property not as mere title or possession, but as a "bundle of rights" in real or personal property.[81] The New Hampshire Supreme Court redefined "property" to mean "only the rights of the owner in relation to it."[82] In the same spirit, the Supreme Court gave a more expanded reading to constitutional provisions protecting property rights through the takings clause when it held that the flooding of land by a dam was not mere noncompensable consequential damage. Justice Miller asserted that "a serious interruption to the common and necessary use of property may be . . . equivalent to the taking of it[;] under the [state] constitutional provisions it is not necessary that the land should be absolutely taken."[83] Aside from the redistribution of wealth such a decision caused, it failed to stabilize or reconcile the inconsistencies of nineteenth-century property law, a problem critics were soon to exploit.

An extreme instance of this uncontrolled expansion of property concepts was provided by a federal District Court judge, James G. Jenkins, who in 1894 enjoined railroad employees from quitting their jobs, individually or en masse, because that would threaten the railroad's property interests.[84] Judge Jenkins saw no conflict between liberty of contract, then ascendant, and this new industrial servitude imposed by a labor injunction.

By the turn of the twentieth century, influential voices had questioned judicial review and courts' use of their powers to displace legislative policy making. Holmes had already uttered thoughts that, if accepted, would undermine the classical order. Reformers and labor challenged judicial power in the political arena. While the principles of classical law themselves remained undisturbed for the moment, the doctrinal superstructure of private law was displaying worrisome signs of instability. The center continued to hold for a time, but different ways of thinking about law were asserting themselves and could not be ignored much longer.

The Progressive Era, 1900–1920

The Progressive Outlook

The second phase of the assault on the old legal order was dominated by the congeries of reform efforts collectively known as Progressivism.[85] These movements were heterogeneous and resist generalization, but some commonalities of outlook among them suggest their relevance for legal reform.[86] Progressives considered extant political, intellectual, social, and economic structures obsolete and irrelevant, barriers to the progress made possible by industrial and technological development. They were living through a period of rapid change, especially in communications (telegraph, telephone, wireless), transportation (automobiles, aircraft), and industrial processes (oil, steel, chemicals). Progressives sensed that the traditional, local, small-town, agrarian, individualist society and mores of the nineteenth century were passing away, to be replaced by a national integrated economy driven by technological change. Unlike the Populists, who regarded themselves as victims of this change, Progressives optimistically embraced it. They believed that society must adapt its institutions to the population and technology of twentieth-century America. They resisted not change or modernity, but obsolete impediments to them. They were sensitive to the complexity and interrelatedness of the new economy and social order, and willing to accept its challenges. Like other Americans, Progressives were ambivalent about business and labor collectivism, seeing both of them as inevitable and possibly beneficial, but nevertheless threatening to self-government.

Progressives believed that reform of American politics and social institutions was not only possible but necessary to the preservation of fundamental American values. In contrast with the Populists, however, they were skeptical about the possibilities of collective action and had embarrassing doubts about the potential of democracy — though they backed democratic institutional reforms like the initiative, referendum, recall, primary elections, and the secret ballot. They placed their faith, rather, in suprapolitical expertise, confident that management and planning could eliminate societal ills like slums and epidemics. They were not daunted by bureaucracy and scorned the old Jacksonian belief that any honest man could manage a complex public enterprise. A Jacksonian spoilsman could no more run a gasworks than he could drive a horseless carriage. Progressives believed that traditional structures of government had to be modernized, adapted to the new industrial society around them.

Implicit in this program was the Progressive faith in the possibilities of government, both state and federal. This was exemplified in the "Wisconsin Idea" pushed by Governor Robert M. La Follette, and in Louis D. Brandeis's commitment to activism at the local level. Both called upon expertise to guide enlightened citizen action, La Follette drawing on the magnificent resource of the University of Wisconsin.

Progressivism had its dark side as well. With a few honorable exceptions, Progressives reflected the racism of the era, fearing Asians and shunning African Americans. (The influential Progressive journalist Ida Wells was all the more remarkable in that age for being both an African American and a woman.) Considered the "genteel reformers," many of them were uneasy about the urban masses, fearing especially the unlettered and non-Protestant "New Immigrants" from eastern and southern Europe. Some of them, caught up in the "uplift" spirit of the times, looked to eugenics, with its sinister instrumentalities of intelligence testing and involuntary sterilization, to improve the population.

Progressive social scientists, historians, philosophers, and political commentators had a pervasive impact on legal thought. The romantic age of social science in the nineteenth century had given way to professionalism in the founding of the American Historical Association, and in its counterparts, the American Economic Association, the American Political Science Association, and the American Sociological Association in the mid-1880s.[87] Their practitioners saw themselves as professionals and taught at the great research universities of the era—Wisconsin, Johns Hopkins, Clark, Harvard, Columbia. Philosophers like Charles Peirce, William James, and John Dewey rejected formalistic and conceptualist ways of thinking in favor of approaches that have come to be called pragmatism or instrumentalism. [88] Dewey's preferred term for his outlook and approach was "experimentalism," which nicely captured the spirit of the Progressive intellectuals.[89] The measure of truth was not conformity to a priori postulates, revelation, or logical systems, but its impact on human well-being. James insisted that the ultimate test of truth is the conduct it inspires. He might have been speaking directly to the classical lawyers when he called on thinkers in all fields to turn "away from abstraction, . . . from verbal solutions, from bad a priori reasons, from fixed principles, closed systems, and pretended absolutes and origins."[90]

Peirce and James influenced the outlook of Holmes through their association with him in the Metaphysical Club, a discussion/self-improvement group that met in the late 1860s and early 1870s.[91] In this way, pragmatist assumptions were mainlined directly into American legal thinking, though Holmes remained as skeptical of their pragmatism as he was of other systems. Pragmatist philosophers identified moral and legal norms as the product of human experience and needs, the resultant of evolution and environment, not as absolute or objective. From thence it was but a short step to seeing law itself as the product of human action and will, a human artifact responsive to social needs.

The contribution of historians to Progressive thought was almost as far-reaching as that of the philosophers. With the passing of the Romantic historians, gentleman-amateurs like George Bancroft, James Ford Rhodes, and Francis Parkman, a new generation of professional historians blazed onto the scene, impatient with the nomothetic aspirations and literary narrative techniques of the romantics, yet profoundly skeptical of the scientistic pretensions of their contemporaries.[92] Charles A. Beard, Carl L. Becker, J. Allen Smith, James Harvey Robinson, Vernon L. Parrington and, to a lesser extent, Frederick Jackson Turner dismissed the Rankean ideal of writing history "as it really was" (objectivism again, this time in historical garb). They emphasized the role of economic interests in the shaping of American politics and the legal order.[93] (Beard, however, defended the legitimacy of judicial review in *The Supreme Court and the Constitution* [1912].) Henceforth, legal thought with any pretensions to historical grounding had to contend with this new and unhelpful spirit.

Progressive economists offered no solace to classicist judges, either. Richard T. Ely, John R. Commons, Thorstein Veblen, and Edwin R. A. Seligman rejected classical liberal economics and its assumption that the unregulated market was natural, just, and inevitable. They demonstrated the linkages between conservative economics and its legal expressions, revealing the contingency of legal rules and stripping them of their supposed transcendent and suprapolitical quality. Political scientists like Frank Goodnow and Arthur F. Bentley abandoned abstractions like "sovereignty" in favor of realistic analyses of the play of interests and government's role in mediating them.[94] Another rising political scientist, Woodrow Wilson, showed himself to be intellectual kin to Holmes when he wrote:

> Government is not a machine but a living thing. It falls not under the theory of the universe, but under the theory of organic life. It is accountable to Darwin, not to Newton. It is modified by its environment, necessitated by its tasks, shaped to is functions by the sheer pressure of life. . . . Government is not a body of blind forces; it is a body of men. . . . Living political constitutions must be Darwinian in structure and practice.[95]

Lester Ward and other Progressive sociologists stressed human control over both the natural and the social environment, rejecting passivity in the face of supposed "laws" of human behavior or the economy.

Belief in objective causation was eroding in the physical sciences as well as in philosophy and history. The simple, determinate, Euclidean/Newtonian universe governed by universal laws was giving way in scientific thought to one less tangible and certain. Concepts of causation were one of the first victims of this intellectual revolution. Probability and statistical explanation displaced old, simple Aristotelian and Newtonian theories of cause and effect.[96] "There is no cause nor effect in nature," provocatively declared Ernst Mach, the Austrian physicist and philosopher of science.[97] By 1927, when Werner Heisenberg advanced his uncertainty principle, traditional notions of causality were defunct, undercutting lawyers' assumptions about causal relationships. With causality went uncomplicated certainty. Reality was not fixed, but probabilistic. This new scientific inquiry eroded certitude in religion and what people of the nineteenth century sometimes called "the moral sciences." Orthodoxy was compelled to cede place to nonteleological explanations that claimed to be no more than a search for patterns in indeterminate events.[98]

The Michelson-Morley experiment of 1887, which disproved the concepts of absolute space and absolute motion, stripped away the comforting assumptions that had made the physical universe seem rational to the eighteenth-century mind. With scientific causation undermined, lawyers' views of causality now seemed as unreal as phlogiston or the philosopher's stone. Objectivism went the way of the ether (also disproved by Michelson and Morley), leaving Aristotelian logic, Newtonian physics, and Euclidean geometry intellectual relics of a simpler world.[99] Progressive legal thinkers trumpeted their advance beyond archaic science and logic.[100]

Darwinian thought revolutionized not only the biological sciences but broader fields of thought as well. George Sabine, a Progressive political scientist, observed that the Darwinian intellectual revolution

> swept away the whole apparatus of fixed categories of explanation, such as the species of pre-Darwinian biology, and reduced the so-called self-evident truths and *a priori* principles upon which both science and philosophy [and, he might have added, law] had been supposed to rest to the level of "provisional" rules. And if one asked, "Provisional for what?," a generation that had learned of Darwin could only answer, "Provisional for human action."[101]

In an intellectual world dominated by Darwin, Marx, Freud, Weber, Rutherford, Bohr, Planck, and Einstein, classical lawyers found themselves bewildered and abandoned.

Even in theology, higher criticism challenged the certainties of faith. In reaction to that alarming pretension, successive popes anathematized first liberalism, and then modernism.[102] The Protestant churches were riven by modernist controversies provoked by literal interpretation and scriptural infallibility. Religious humanism disdained orthodoxy, stressing benevolence rather than doctrinal conformity. The Social Gospel, or Christian Socialism as its adherents termed it, left behind individualistic preoccupation with dogmas like salvation and redemption, seeking instead to apply Christ's teachings to ameliorate human ills.

The Progressive outlook was popularized by two influential books, Herbert Croly's *The Promise of American Life* (1909) and Walter Lippmann's *Drift and Mastery* (1908). Croly condemned "the existing concentration of wealth and financial power in the hands of a few irresponsible men," a common Progressive complaint, reflected in the writings of Brandeis and confirmed for Progressives in the findings of the Pujo Committee of 1913. America's excessive individualism had fostered corruption and the maldistribution of wealth. "Economic privilege" produced "the malevolent social influence of individual and incorporated American wealth," a plaint having a curiously Jeffersonian ring.[103] (Croly was a fervent admirer of Hamilton.) Croly's and Lippmann's calls for deliberate human control over social institutions directed toward progressive ends sounded the themes of the Progressive political effort of 1912 that found its voice in Theodore Roosevelt's Bull Moose campaign.[104] Roosevelt decried the fact that the American people had been forced to "surrender to any set of men [i.e., judges] the final right to determine those fundamental questions upon which free self-government ultimately depends."[105]

The legislative achievements of the Progressives were impressive, at both the federal and state levels. They could claim credit for three constitutional amendments — the Sixteenth, Seventeenth, and Nineteenth — involving the federal income tax, direct election of senators, and women's suffrage respectively. The Roosevelt and Wilson administrations recommended the nation's first conservation laws; strengthened the Interstate Commerce Commission (ICC) and created its junior cousin, the Federal Trade Commission; provided for standards or inspection of food, drugs, and cosmetics; created the Federal Reserve System; and strengthened antitrust (including the attempted legislative labor reforms that recognized the legitimacy of unions, exempted them from antitrust prosecution, restricted the labor injunction, sought to legalize strikes and boycotts, and provided for jury trials in contempt proceedings). At the state level, Progressives enacted income taxes and other tax reforms, established regulatory commissions, controlled wages and hours, prohibited child labor and enacted school legislation, promoted public health measures such as inoculation, mandated factory inspection and workers' compensation, established minimum wages, and provided the first public assistance to mothers with children.

But just at the time that the Progressive agenda was achieving its greatest triumphs in state legislation, the election of Woodrow Wilson diverted, then spiked, Progressive energies. The wing of the movement that had supported Roosevelt's "New Nationalism" program in the 1912 campaign followed their leader into increasingly reactionary postures. The Wilson "New Freedom" group achieved some notable legislative triumphs at the federal level, until America's entry into the Great War drained off Progressive commitments at the national level.

Paradoxically, though, the war was responsible for a centralized control of the economy unimaginable a decade earlier. The War Industries Board and the Lever Act (1917) centralized economic planning and fixed commodity prices, while the Webb-Pomerene Act of 1918 promoted cartelization. The War Revenue Act implemented the authority granted by the Sixteenth Amendment by imposing graduated income and excess-profits taxes. The Railroad Administration established national control over the rail system. Unlike rent controls, abandoned soon after the Armistice, the quasi nationalization of the railroads was extended by the Esch-Cummings Act of 1920 to new *dirigiste* heights by diverting revenue from the more profitable roads to maintain the less profitable, a blatant redistribution of wealth that provoked surprisingly little outrage from *devotés* of Manchester school economics.

Academic Critique: Pound

As Progressive academic criticism turned to law and more specifically to the United States Supreme Court, it mounted a sustained challenge to judicial power. The Court itself seems to be have been indifferent to this critique, if indeed its members were even aware of it.

Leading this assault from the academy, Roscoe Pound was a host unto himself.[106] In a remarkable series of law review articles published between 1906 and 1913, Pound first attacked the dominant ideas of classicism, then offered constructive suggestions for alternative judicial approaches. In the titles of these articles he coined two phrases that captured the negative and positive components of his contribution: "mechanical jurisprudence" and "sociological jurisprudence."

Pound was responsible for much of the momentum toward law reform in the early twentieth century. His 1906 wake-up call to the American bar, "The Causes of

Popular Dissatisfaction with the Administration of Justice,"[107] sparked efforts to update and revise American law that ran in both conservative and liberal directions. Pound warned the bar that the people would not long tolerate the divergence between "Law in Books and Law in Action,"[108] but he thought that legislation was a blunt and clumsy method for bringing the two back into sync.

Pound dethroned the classical model of law, which he called "mechanical jurisprudence."[109] He condemned classical thought as a closed system of norms and precedents, where judges fancied themselves as being little more than technicians who input facts and derive an output of neutral results. Pound derided such a self-deceiving attitude as the "slot-machine theory of justice," the reference being not to the modern gambling device but to an early mechanical analog computer. In its place, he proposed a reorientation of American law that was permeated with Progressive assumptions. "The sociological movement in jurisprudence is a movement for pragmatism as a philosophy of law." Law "must be judged by the results it achieves, not by the niceties of its internal structure [and] not by the beauty of its logical processes." Troubled by the widening divergence between social needs and legal doctrine, between what he called "social justice" and "legal justice," Pound reminded his professional brethren that "law is no longer anything sacred or mysterious," but rather merely a means to an end, social justice.[110]

Pound, who read German and French with ease, was influenced by recent continental and English jurisprudential debates. He resonated with Rudolph von Jhering's distinction between a "jurisprudence of conceptions" (*Begriffsjurisprudenz*), which Jhering attributed to Karl F. von Savigny, the foremost figure of the German historical school, and a "jurisprudence of results" (actually, *Wirklichkeitsjurisprudenz*, which would be better translated a "jurisprudence of reality").[111] Pound put this distinction to use in demolishing the liberty of contract cases, demonstrating their artificial character and their divorce from social reality.[112] He thought it obvious that de facto inequality is the condition of individuals in society; why then "do courts persist in . . . forc[ing] upon legislation an academic theory of equality in the face of practical conditions of inequality? . . . Why is the legal conception of the relation of employer and employee so at variance with the common knowledge of mankind?" He answered his own question by suggesting the "individualist conception of justice, which exaggerates the importance of property and of contract, exaggerates private right at the expense of public right, and is hostile to legislation." The liberty-of-contract doctrine exalted private right over the public interest, and the private right only of the employer, at that. He saw liberty of contact as a momentary phase of laissez-faire, an idea whose time had long since come and gone.

In a lengthy historical survey of jurisprudential thought in 1911–1912, Pound concluded that law is "a social institution which may be improved by intelligent human effort," and was to be judged by its results rather than by its "abstract content."[113] From the title of this essay, his early contribution took its name: sociological jurisprudence.[114] Pound did not invent the concept of sociological jurisprudence, though. He was merely the American exponent of an idea that had an international provenance, being earlier expounded by the Austrian Eugen Ehrlich and the French scholar François Gény.[115]

Pound was not alone among Americans in his efforts to bring law into harmony with social needs.[116] Ernst Freund's monumental treatise on the police power (1904) confirmed the place of its topic in the constitutional order, undercutting the ideological animosity that *Lochner* would display the next year to legislative authority.[117] In his magisterial essay *The Nature and Sources of the Law* (1909), John Chipman Gray, whom Pound joined at Harvard in 1910, refuted the idea that judges discovered law.[118] This challenged the nineteenth-century fiction that G. Edward White has called "the oracular theory of judging."[119] Frank Goodnow, a lawyer turned political scientist at Columbia, provided doctrines that federal and state courts could deploy to uphold regulatory legislation.[120]

Morris Cohen, a philosopher and not a lawyer, asserted that judges not only make law, but find ex post rationalizations that justify their policy choices. "It is not unreasonable to suppose," he wrote, "that the minds of most judges work like those of other mortals"; they decide first, then "look for and find reasons or precedents for such decisions."[121] Learned Hand, not yet appointed to the bench, called into question some of the most hallowed of classical premises, including whether "the uncontrolled exercise of the advantages derived from possessing the means of living of other men will also become recognized as giving no social benefit corresponding to the evils which result." Judges, like all other people, are "recruited from a class which has its proper bias." Under the influence of classicism, public law "relapse[d] . . . into a theory of natural rights."[122]

These Progressive criticisms fueled the extended debate on the nature of judicial review that had ignited in 1895. The primary fora of this debate were the scholarly and popular press, with the political arena playing a secondary role. A stream of scholarly articles in law reviews and the popular press, as well as books,[123] attacked[124] and defended[125] the exercise of judicial power.

Edward S. Corwin, who would become the nation's leading academic authority on the Constitution, criticized Beard's defense of judicial review, as did Charles Grove Haines.[126] Both these political scientists brought a realistic and skeptical attitude to their historical review of the Supreme Court's power, which did not bode well for continued veneration of classical doctrine. Gustavus Myers wrote the only history of the Supreme Court written from a socialist perspective.[127] Needless to say, the Marxian view was not congenial to classical orthodoxy, least of all its adulation of private property, but the influence of socialist doctrine was limited in America.

Prominent lawyers and scholars also undermined the Court's pretensions. Louis D. Brandeis supplemented his advocacy with a stream of speeches, legislative testimony, articles, and even a book, *Other People's Money* (1914),[128] condemning corporate giantism and, implicitly, the courts' role in supporting it.[129]

A young Yale law professor, Wesley Hohfeld, challenged the jurisprudential bases of classical adjudication by supplying a theoretical substitute for classical rights doctrine that exposed its incoherent and opportunistic content.[130] Hohfeld introduced Austinian analytical jurisprudence to American legal thought as a means of achieving nothing less than a reconsideration of "the fundamental working conceptions of all legal reasoning."[131] His conceptual scheme had the effect of subverting the dogma of "rights." In the domain of property, Hohfeldian legal analysis reinforced the idea that all property relationships were legally constructed. An employer's property right in his physical plant, for example, could not serve as the basis for enjoining employees' picketing if it was seen as nothing more than a tautology lending the state's monopoly of force to the employer to enable him to dictate the terms of his relationship with his workers.

Judge Benjamin N. Cardozo of the New York Court of Appeals provided an influential explanation of *The Nature of the Judicial Process* in the 1920 Storrs Lectures at Yale.[132] This widely read reflection on the art of judging, replete with citations to Jhering, Gray, and Pound, acclimated once radical ideas to the postwar legal world. "The outstanding truths of life, the great and unquestioned phenomena of society, are not to be argued away as myths and vagaries when they do not fit within our little moulds [of legal doctrine]," Cardozo asserted. "If necessary, we must remake the moulds. We must seek a conception of law which realism can accept as true." Cardozo conceded that judges have discretion to shape law; provocatively, he spoke of "the judge as legislator." But the judge's discretion was narrowly hedged, and determined not by a priori axioms but by the ends of the law. "All that the method of sociology demands is that within this narrow range of choice [the judge] shall search for social justice." That assertion would have been incomprehensible to Fuller and Peckham, flagrantly wrong to Brewer.

Ferment in the academy was echoed in political struggles outside. Progressive journalists, whom Theodore Roosevelt labeled "muckrakers" in one of his reactionary moments, exposed political corruption, corporate exploitation of consumers and workers, and the biases of the legal system that supported both. Lincoln Steffens, Ida Tarbell, Ray Stannard Baker, Brandeis, and even Roosevelt himself (in his occasional Progressive moments), filled pages of *The Independent, The Outlook, McClure's,* and *Collier's* with exposés of monopolistic power, municipal corruption, and deadly working conditions. The photographs of Jacob Riis and Lewis Hine provided unforgettable images of poverty in the cities and the realities of everyday life for working people. The tragedy of the Triangle Shirtwaist fire in 1911, when 146 young women were immolated or leapt to their death to escape the flames, provided a hideous confirmation of the Progressives' condemnation of working conditions. It did not help the repute of American law that the proprietors, who had in effect locked the seamstresses into an unsafe workplace, were acquitted of criminal charges.

The role of the judiciary came into sharply defined political focus in the struggle over Arizona's admission to statehood in 1911. The incipient state's constitution provided for judicial recall. President William Howard Taft vetoed the admission bill because of that provision.[133] Popular control of the judiciary would be "likely to subject the rights of the individual to the possible tyranny of a popular majority." "The government is for all the people," he explained, "and is not solely for a majority of them." "Constitutions are checks upon the hasty action of the majority," and "an independent and untrammelled judiciary" must be able to protect the people's "rights of life, liberty, and property." The territory removed the offending provision, was admitted, and promptly readopted it.

Judicial Critique

Finally, a few members of the Supreme Court itself, chiefly Holmes, rejected the axioms and methods of classical thought. *Lochner* was the most significant focus of confrontation. Holmes's dissent noted that "this case is decided upon an economic theory which a large part of the country does not entertain": classical liberal economics, backed by Darwinian presuppositions about the functioning of society. This introduced his famous aphorisms about the Constitution not enacting Herbert Spencer's *Social Statics* or embodying a particular economic theory.[134] Citing a wide range of regulatory legislation, including antitrust, securities regulation, vaccination, and Sunday closing, as well as bans on usury and lotteries, Holmes pointed out that John Stuart Mills's precept about being free to do whatever you like providing it does not interfere with a like liberty in others is nothing more than a "shibboleth." "General propositions do not decide concrete cases," he continued, echoing himself in "The Path of the Law." "The decision will depend on a judgment or intuition more subtle than any articulate major premise." "The word 'liberty,' in the 14th Amendment, is perverted when it is held to prevent the natural outcome of a dominant opinion." Yet Holmes's skepticism left a wide scope for judicial discretion to determine whether a statute was reasonable and whether it comported with "fundamental principles as they have been understood by the traditions of our people and our law."

Justice Harlan took a different approach, dissenting in the same case.[135] He anticipated the Brandeis Brief and the general Progressive approach of Justice Brandeis by explicitly evaluating the substance of the legislation for its reasonableness. Both he and Peckham for the majority balanced police powers versus individual liberty; they simply came out differently. Harlan did hint, though, that the inequality of bargaining status between employer and employee might have influenced his attitude toward reasonableness. His approach relied on what have come to be called "constitutional facts": a review of the factual (that is, nonlegal) data on which the legislature relied to confirm that the legislative judgment was reasonable.[136] Harlan reviewed the medical data supporting the New York legislation and deferred to the informed judgment of the legislature on the policy issue.

Louis D. Brandeis as counsel for the state in *Muller v. Oregon* (1908) fully realized the potential of the briefing technique that bears his name.[137] In an era when the social sciences had come into their own in informing and directing the course of social policy, and when women entered the field in ever larger numbers,[138] it was natural that Brandeis's sister-in-law Josephine Goldmark and her colleague Florence Kelley should seek his help in sustaining an Oregon statute that limited to ten the hours that women could work in factories or laundries. Goldmark and Kelley did the research legwork, amassing medical and social science authorities, which Brandeis incorporated into the brief. It consisted of a mere fifteen pages of traditional legal argumentation and over a hundred pages of copious citations to the nonlegal medical and socialscience treatise literature. The Brandeis brief was the first example of sociological jurisprudence in action, the instantiation of Pound's call for informing legal judgment with the data of the social sciences.

In submitting such a brief, Brandeis was taking a significant risk.[139] Inviting the Court to review the authorities on which legislative judgment rested flew in the face of the Court's demonstrated willingness to rely on its own uninformed opinions about the basis of legislation, as it had done in *Lochner*. But the gamble paid off. In *Muller*, Justice David Brewer (of all people!) for a unanimous Court[140] upheld the statute.[141] Brewer noted that "in patent cases counsel are apt to open the argument with a dis-

cussion of the state of the art. It may not be amiss, in the present case, before examining the constitutional question, to notice the course of legislation, as well as expressions of opinion from other than judicial sources." He then quoted from the Brandeis
brief in a footnote. The real surprise of the *Muller* opinion came in that seemingly
effortless triumph of Brandeis's effort to educate the judges to social reality.

Doctrinally, *Muller* and *Lochner* were formally compatible, but only by logic-
chopping and a blend of Edwardian-era Darwinian assumptions, paternalism, and
eugenics. "Woman's physical structure and the performance of maternal functions
place her at a disadvantage in the struggle for subsistence." Women need "especial
care" by the courts because "in the struggle for subsistence she is not an equal compe-
titor with her brother." Brewer believed that it was apparently part of the natural order
of things that "woman has always been dependent upon man." Besides, women were
breeders: "[H]ealthy mothers are essential to vigorous offspring," and so woman's
well-being was important "to preserve the strength and vigor of the race."

Muller was not a fluke. *In Bunting v. Oregon* (1917),[142] five Justices upheld a
state statute that imposed a ten-hour workday maximum for both men and women
and mandated a time-and-a-half overtime rate, thus regulating both hours and pay.
Justice Joseph McKenna dismissed the previously powerful class-legislation argument lightly: "[T]hat it is not as complete as it might be . . . is no impeachment of
its legality." *Lochner* thus seemed to have been overruled *sub silentio* — but it would
rise from its grave in *Adkins*.

In that same year, the Court upheld a New York workers' compensation measure, implicitly rebuking the premises of the *Ives* decision.[143] Justice Pitney (the author of the *Coppage* opinion!) casually brushed aside the fellow servant rule, plus
the doctrines of assumption of risk and contributory negligence, as susceptible of
being overridden by state legislative power in the public interest.

In *Noble State Bank v. Haskell* (1911),[144] Holmes cooped up the classical approach to legislation:

> [W]e must be cautious about pressing the broad words of the Fourteenth Amend-
> ment to a drily logical extreme. Many laws which it would be vain to ask the court
> to overthrow could be shown, easily enough, to transgress a scholastic interpretation
> of one or another of the great guarantees in the Bill of Rights. They more or less
> limit the liberty of the individual or they diminish property to a certain extent. We
> have few scientifically certain criteria of legislation, and as it often is difficult to
> mark the line where what is called the police power of the States is limited by the
> Constitution of the United States, judges should be slow to read into the latter a
> nolumus mutare as against the law-making power.

"It may be said in a general way," he concluded expansively, "that the police power
extends to all the great public needs." Since the statute in question, a levy on banks
to support an insolvency fund, involved an A-to-B wealth transfer, this was strong
language.

But the Court was not ready to fling the doors open to unlimited state regulatory authority. Responding to a petition for rehearing in the *Noble State Bank* case,
Holmes was forced to into a semiretraction. He conceded that his "analysis of the
police power, whether correct or not, was intended to indicate an interpretation of
what has taken place in the past, not to give a new or wider scope to the power. The
propositions . . . are rather in the nature of preliminaries."[145]

In a different realm, antitrust, classical premises disintegrated. The *Knight* case of 1895 had begun to lose its deathgrip on antitrust policy almost immediately, as the Court repeatedly declined to erect barriers to antitrust prosecution.[146] In *Standard Oil Co. v. United States* (1911),[147] Chief Justice Edward D. White rejected the simple dualisms of classical thought to hold that the Sherman Act did not prohibit *all* combinations in restraint of trade, but only "unreasonable" ones. The criteria for determining whether violations of the Sherman Act occurred, White wrote in his characteristically involuted prose, "is the rule of reason guided by the established law and by the plain duty to enforce the prohibitions of the act, and thus the public policy which its restrictions were obviously enacted to subserve." This was a balancing test, and one that turned on considerations of public policy. It expanded the discretion of judges, but did so explicitly and without the self-deceptions of *Knight*. In a case decided the same term, *American Tobacco Co. v. United States* (1911),[148] White remanded another big antitrust prosecution without requiring immediate dissolution, instructing the lower court to work out some flexible reorganization plan that would protect public and private interests while complying with the statute. Such flexibility was impossible under the absolutes of *Knight*.

The judicial attack on classical doctrine was marked by a vein of positivism. This emphasis became the occasion for one of Holmes's most memorable aphorisms, uttered in his dissent to a decision holding the New York workers' compensation statute invalid as in conflict with federal admiralty law when applied to a longshoreman working on a ship in international commerce. Justice James McReynolds's opinion for the majority treated federal admiralty law as a sort of universal prophylactic against state police power. Holmes objected: "the common law is not a brooding omnipresence in the sky, but the articulate voice of some sovereign or quasi sovereign that can be identified," he insisted.[149] In classical doctrine, law was the "brooding omnipresence" that Holmes decried, always available to frustrate state public policy through judicial interpretation. In the realm of maritime commerce, *Jensen* in its way was as lethal to the policy behind workers' compensation as *Ives* had been six years earlier. Holmes's criticism encouraged Progressives in their long and partially successful struggle against expansive federal-court jurisdiction, which culminated in Justice Brandeis's attempt to destroy general federal common law in *Erie Railroad v. Tompkins* (1938).[150]

The 1920s

The pall of Republican Normalcy after 1921 did not stifle Progressive criticism of the old legal order. This was especially true in the legal academy, where sociological jurisprudence provided a platform for launching the movement known as legal realism.

Academic Critique: Legal Realism

In 1922, the political scientist Charles G. Haines suggested that since judges engaged in "judicial legislation," the public ought to know something about the political and economic influences on their thinking.[151] This was not a revelation: in 1908 President Theodore Roosevelt had insisted that "the decisions of the courts on economic and social questions depend upon their economic and social philosophy."[152] While that is a commonplace in the late twentieth century, in the climate of legal classicism it was irreverent, an impudent act of peeking under the black robes. Haines relied on recent Supreme Court cases unfriendly to labor[153] to buttress his point that judges deploying vague public law concepts like due process, equal protection, vested rights, or liberty of contract exercise unrestrained power.

As Haines was humanizing the function of judging, other academics focused on the results: the ideological structure of both private and public law doctrine. Many of them have been lumped together under the rubric "legal realists."[154] That phrase, though adopted by several of the group's most prominent members, is misleading in several ways. Labeling them that way makes the realists into an ideological monolith and suggests a greater unity of viewpoint and method than ever existed among that disparate, uncoordinated assortment of individuals. It also divides them from their predecessors, sundering their continuity with Holmes, Thayer, and Pound. That continuity is more important than the generational rift that marked the debut of realism in the heedless exchange of 1930–1931 between Karl Llewellyn, in his early realist *enfant terrible* role, and Pound, who was then beginning to lapse into the pontifical mode.[155]

Robert Summers offers an alternative way of thinking about the realists. He rejects the categorization in favor of a different jurisprudential alignment, which he denominates "pragmatic instrumentalism."[156] Summers links Holmes, Dewey, Pound, Gray, Llewellyn, Felix (not Morris) Cohen, Walter W. Cook, Joseph W. Bingham, Jerome Frank, and Herman Oliphant together in a conceptual association that is more illuminating than the merely chronological association of faculty members who taught at Yale and Columbia in the 1920s.[157]

Realist thought was both a continuation of the Holmes-Pound criticism of classical legal thought, and the legal expression of the late-Progressive agenda. Realists ridiculed the classical belief that law was a preexistent, self-contained collection of immutable principles that were objective, neutral, and nonpolitical. They rejected the very concept of a priori principles. "Neither 'liberty' nor 'property' is antecedent to the state or beyond the domain of public control," Walton Hamilton maintained. "Each is but a name for a cluster of prevailing usages . . . which binds the individual to the social order."[158] Llewellyn insisted that the "is" and the "ought" should be temporarily separated for clarity of thought. Others carried that qualified suggestion to perilous extremes. "The ideal of a government of laws and not of men," Hessel Yntema proclaimed, "is a dream."[159] "I deny ethical *right* and *ought* without qualification," Walter Nelles declared.[160] Such insistence that ethical absolutes and objective principles were illusions left realists open to charges of ethical relativism. That, in turn, exposed them a decade later to absurd but lacerating accusations of being protototalitarians.

Realists denied that judges could deduce rules of law impartially from these principles. They spurned the paradigm of syllogistic reasoning in classical law, where the legal norm is the major premise, the facts of the case provide the minor premise, and the conclusion is the outcome of the case. Instead, they saw judges as humans with the usual biases and fallibilities who chose norms and outcomes in the light of what they believed to be desirable social policy.[161] Law, they insisted axiomatically, was not found or discovered or revealed. It was made by human beings, including judges, and the pretense that it was "found" only concealed that human agency. Law is a social construct, and must serve social ends. Legal norms had to respond to human needs and be based on human experience. Law is always a means, an instrument, not an end in itself. Though this sounded provocative in 1930, Holmes had said it all a generation before.

Realists demystified the market, which they saw as no more neutral or apolitical than law itself. The supposedly private market, which classical lawyers assumed was the impersonal and apolitical sum of choices of individuals' wills, was in reality shaped by law and depended for its effect on the force of the state. Law reenforced whatever inequalities parties brought with them into the market.

The realists reserved some of their sharpest critical analysis for the Restatement project undertaken in 1923 by the recently formed American Law Institute. The restaters believed that it was possible to identify *the* rules and principles of a body of law by consensus among leading legal academics, practitioners, and judges. They hoped to capture that formulation in an extended outline, with concise, general principles in boldface (thus, "black letter law"), followed by explanatory commentary. The Restatements would unify whole domains of law, saving them at the same time from the flood of heterogeneous decisions and from statutory reform as well.[162] Realists thought it no coincidence that the *Restatement of Contracts* should have appeared just at the time legislatures were beginning to disaggregate the unitary body of contract law built up by nineteenth-century jurists, which had received its definitive formulation in *Williston on Contracts*. Realists considered the Restatements a futile yet dangerous attempt to mummify legal doctrine and impose it as the central ordering project of American law. Thurman Arnold, a prominent realist, dismissed the ALI and its first Restatements as irrelevant to the present, mired in the conceptualism of the nineteenth century.[163]

It may be true, as Natalie Hull contends,[164] that the real founders of the ALI were law professor progressives, among them William Draper Lewis, Arthur Corbin, and Wesley Hohfeld, and that the intellectual matrix of the organization was a combination of philosophical pragmatism and political Progressivism. The first round of the Restatements themselves,[165] however, were formalist and conceptualist disappointments, from a realist point of view. Grant Gilmore's judgment on the *Restatement of Contracts I* applies to the whole first round: "[T]he Restatement project can be taken as the almost instinctive reaction of the legal establishment of the time to the attack of the so-called legal realists. . . . [I]n the 1920s there was still hope that the revolution [against formalist classical legal thought] could be put down, that unity of doctrine could be maintained and that an essentially pure case law system could be preserved from further statutory encroachment."[166]

The realists continue to elude us today. Though we glibly proclaim that "we are all Realists now,"[167] we avoid their insights by carping on their faults. A freshet of criticism swept away their positivistic separation of morality from law.[168] A more sophisticated legal academy mocks their naive and trivial empiricism.[169] We parody their emphasis on the personal biases of judges as the "alimentary theory of judging," where results are determined by what the judge had for breakfast. Jerome Frank's psychoanalyzing seems sophomoric, while at the same time the attitude of Llewellyn toward Pound appears positively oedipal. Grant Gilmore felt compelled to title what was actually an appreciative retrospective on realist contributions "Legal Realism: Its Cause and Cure".[170]

Such a dismissive attitude is too sophisticated. Seen as a phase in the growing maturity and effectiveness of the challenge to classicism, the realist challenge continued the critique of classicism's premises that had been begun by Holmes and accelerated by Pound and Brandeis. Yet classical thinking lived on in the courts, seemingly impervious to challenge, and attained the heights of its authority as the realists were working to undermine it in the 1920s and 1930s.

Political Assault

In the climate of the 1920s, with the executive branch dominated by the miasma of Harding-Coolidge Normalcy and the Court in the grip of classicism, legal Progressives could not realistically hope to dethrone classical thought. Yet they did enjoy some legislative triumphs at both the state and federal level, as the United States began to take a few hesitant steps toward the social welfare levels achieved by Hohenzollern Prussia forty years earlier.

At the state level, legislatures enacted workers' compensation statutes in most states, which, despite *Ives*, survived assault in the courts. The Supreme Court upheld the constitutionality of these statutes in 1917,[171] laying to rest any possibility of further due process challenges. Whether workers' compensation represented a Progressive victory or a triumph of corporate capitalism, it permanently altered the employment relationship in the United States by socializing industrial risk.[172] Hand in hand with this achievement, Progressive legislators also enacted wages-and-hours legislation for women (struck down by the United States Supreme Court in 1923 and 1936) and child labor statutes, mostly through school attendance laws.

Congress was no laggard in enacting social welfare legislation, either. In addition to the New Freedom measures of the early Wilson years, Congress erected an expansive structure of wartime regulatory measures, such as the Lever Act. After the war, Congress not only continued some centralizing experiments like railroad regulation on a permanent basis, but even struck out in new directions, such as the Sheppard-Towner Act, which provided grants-in-aid to the states to support maternal and child welfare assistance. (The Supreme Court declined an invitation to overturn this legislation on constitutional-procedural grounds, originating the twentieth-century doctrine of standing.[173]) The Grain Futures Trading Act of 1921 began federal regulation of the capital markets.[174]

When Progressives could not defeat conservative initiatives substantively, they scored some successes procedurally. They continued their struggle against the anti-labor biases of the federal judiciary, principally by trimming federal jurisdiction. Reacting to Peckham's opinion in *Ex parte Young* (1908),[175] which permitted a single federal judge to enjoin the actions of state officials, Congress enacted the first of a series of measures requiring a panel of three federal judges to hear petitions for restraining orders.[176] The Johnson Act of 1934[177] withdrew jurisdiction from federal district courts to enjoin compliance with state utility-rate orders, a blow at a much-abused form of collusive litigation. The Tax Injunction Act of 1937[178] prohibited federal courts from issuing injunctions against collection of state taxes. (The 1937 statute was a sop thrown to FDR in the aftermath of his defeat in the court-packing struggle.)

The most important of these jurisdiction-trimming measures was the Norris-LaGuardia Act of 1932,[179] which constrained federal injunctive power in labor disputes (a response to *Truax v. Raich*[180] and *Truax v. Corrigan*[181]) and made yellow-dog contracts unenforceable in federal courts, an indirect effort at legislatively overruling *Adair v. United States*.

In enacting these statutes limiting the equitable powers of the federal courts, Congress reflected the Progressive belief that corporate defendants were abusing federal diversity jurisdiction and federal judicial power generally to evade state regulatory and tax measures and to wear down employee-plaintiffs seeking nonstatutory compensation for workplace injuries.[182] (That Progressive view drove Justice Brandeis to the position he took in *Erie Railroad v. Tompkins* [1938], denying the existence of a general federal common law.)[183] Progressives regarded the federal courts as refuges for large corporations, creditors, and conservative economic interests that were seeking to hold federal and state regulatory legislation unconstitutional under one or another classical doctrine. Progressives of the 1920s and 1930s were not hostile to the powers of federal courts per se. They voted to expand federal judicial power where they thought it would not be used in knee-jerk opposition to reform legislation. Thus, for example, they did not try to block creation of the declaratory judgment,[184] but they did provide that it not be used to thwart collection of federal taxes.[185]

The last hurrah of political Progressivism was the presidential campaign of 1924, in which Wisconsin senator Robert M. La Follette and Democratic senator Burton Wheeler of Montana ran as the Progressive Party candidates. The Progressives had plenty to be unhappy about: the Harding administration was riddled with scandals and influence-peddling, of which Teapot Dome was only the most conspicuous. Treasury secretary Andrew Mellon's fiscal program pushed aggressive upward wealth redistribution through reducing taxes on business while increasing federal financial handouts to it, balancing the budget, maintaining a high protective tariff, deregulating federal supervision of business, and opposing payment of a veterans' bonus. The Progressives denounced this regressively redistributive program, demanded abolition of the labor injunction, and attacked "the control of government and industry by private monopoly." They condemned "the usurpation in recent years by the federal courts of the power to nullify laws duly enacted by the legislative branch of the government" as a "plain violation of the Constitution." La Follette recommended constitutional amendments that would enable Congress to override a judicial veto and that would provide for an elective federal judiciary.[186]

But prosperity proved too powerful a support for the Republican status quo, and the Progressive campaign had nothing to show for its efforts except the satisfaction of chastising the Democrats for nominating the conservative corporation lawyer John W. Davis. Progressive sentiment lingered on in Congress and in the state legislatures, but it was ineffectual to stem the body of classical adjudication that constituted the achievement of the Taft Court in the 1920s.

Judicial Critique: Cardozo and Brandeis

As in politics, so in the judicial realm: conservative thinking remained dominant, while under the surface Progressive and realist ideas were undermining the old legal order in both private and public law. Late-Progressive legal thought did not just tinker with the classical hierarchy of principles-doctrine-norms. Postclassical jurists rejected the entire body of classicism, insisting that law conform to social reality and the nation's democratic aspirations. Law would not dominate society; it must be made to serve social ends.

In the realms of private law, torts, contract, and property were transformed as they were adapted to twentieth-century industrialization and commerce. In public law, orthodoxy reigned on the Supreme Court under the nurturing hand of Chief Justice Taft. But Holmes and Brandeis, usually in dissent, laid the foundations of a different legal order.

Tort law principles and assumptions, derived from nineteenth-century ideas of causality and an elegantly ordered structure of concepts (duty, fault, standard of care), gave way between the wars to a realist vision that regarded tort law as an instrument of public policy.[187] Leon Green, a realist faculty member at Northwestern Law School, challenged established theories of causation in negligence cases, arguing that cause was a factual, not a legal, concept. Formulaic categories of causation only obscured the actual function of torts adjudication, he argued, which was to balance competing social interests and allocate risk. Both were issues of public policy, to be decided on utilitarian considerations, not by metaphysical concepts of causation.[188]

Judge Cardozo's opinion for the New York Court of Appeals in *MacPherson v. Buick Motor Co.* (1916) ignored the old doctrine of privity by making the manufacturer of a defective product (in this case, a wooden-spoked automobile wheel) liable to the ultimate consumer.[189] Cardozo predicated liability on a generalized principle of foreseeability, made necessary by the technology and marketing practices of an advanced industrial society.

The evolving nature of causation was the focus of the landmark 1928 *Palsgraf* case.[190] Cardozo's unsatisfactory majority opinion[191] remained within traditional tort conceptual boundaries of duty and foreseeability, but he did contend that negligence was a relational, rather than an abstract, concept: "[R]isk imports relation," in his often quoted phrase. "Proof of negligence in the air, so to speak, will not do." Judge William Andrews, dissenting, more overtly balanced the interests involved, asking ultimately who was best able to bear the costs of unforeseeable injury in a crowded urban society. "This is not logic," he explained. "It is practical politics. . . . It is all a question of expediency. There are no fixed rules to govern our judgment." Fowler Harper, author of a contemporary torts treatise,[192] concluded that after *Palsgraf*, issues of causation would be resolved on the basis of "considerations of fairness, justice and social policy which are often difficult to explain and frequently have their basis in vague feelings or intuitions of what is proper and desirable."

Modern jurists created new torts, such as intentional infliction of emotional distress, brushing aside old fictions that had impeded their emergence in favor of the realist sense that it was "the business of the courts to make precedent where a wrong calls for redress, even if lawsuits must be multiplied."[193] This frank declaration by

William Prosser, who dominated thinking in the law of torts for a generation, signaled the triumph of realism and a shift in tort law toward a proplaintiff orientation.

Cardozo, abetted by the Yale contracts authority Arthur L. Corbin, did much to overturn classical doctrines in the law of contracts.[194] The core problem of old contract law, as Corbin saw it, was "the illusion of certainty . . . and the delusion that law is absolute and eternal, that doctrines can be used mechanically, and that there are correct and unchangeable definitions."[195] With characteristic diffidence, Cardozo set about modernizing contract law and injecting flexibility into its rigid doctrines. Consideration, bargained-for reliance, hostility to contracts implied by law — all underwent the solvent of Cardozo's gentle skepticism. The doctrine of implied promises provides a good example. In litigation over a five-year employment "agreement," Cardozo concluded that "the whole contract . . . may be 'instinct with an obligation' imperfectly expressed."[196] To hold one of the parties to an informal agency relationship, Cardozo implied an agent's promise to use reasonable efforts to market the principal's services, which were fashion endorsements.[197]

Consideration could be easily found, if not implied. In *DeCicco v. Schweizer* (1917),[198] Cardozo discovered consideration for defendant's obligation to pay an annuity to his engaged daughter in the fact that the daughter married. In the *Allegheny College* case of 1927,[199] Cardozo invented consideration out of thin air, finding in a college's implicit duty to memorialize a benefactor enough consideration to support his obligation to pay a pledge.

One peculiar result of these doctrinal innovations was what Grant Gilmore called the "schizophrenic quality" of the first *Restatement of Contracts* (1932), which had Samuel Williston, a protagonist of classical law, as its chief reporter.[200] Section 75, reflecting Williston's views, expressed classical Holmesian (c. 1881) doctrine in defining consideration as act, forbearance, or promise "bargained for and given in exchange for the promise."[201] No *nuda pacta* here. Yet section 90 makes promises binding if they induce reliance and "injustice can be avoided only by enforcement of the promise."[202] Gilmore commented drolly: "[T]he universe includes both matter and anti-matter. Perhaps what we have here is Restatement and anti-Restatement or Contract and anti-Contract."[203]

Realist critiques also subverted the law of property.[204] Many lawyers, not just the realists, came to recognize that "rights" in property were not unitary, exclusive, or absolute. In itself, that was hardly a revelation: the common law had for centuries recognized multiple rights in a single object of property or contingent claims to it. But as lawyers prepared ever more sophisticated indentures and other real estate or finance instruments, they came to see that claims to property were in reality "bundles of rights." Further, by this time Holmes's insight had sunk in and displaced Blackstone's physicalist conception of property: property "rights" were in reality prescriptive of relations among individuals, not descriptive of the relationship between an individual owner and the owned thing. Here the Hohfeldian classification of jural categories had a corrosive effect on traditional ways of thinking about property, because it demonstrated that rights were in reality a power to exclude others from access to the property or the use of it. It followed that "the law has delegated to [the owner] a discretionary power over the rights and duties of others." This rights-focused conception, liberated from Blackstonian physicality, led some scholars and then judges to view property as a form of state-sanctioned power that enabled one individual to coerce others.[205]

(The conservative bloc on the modern Supreme Court has affirmed this realist conception of rights, but diverted it in an antiregulatory direction. In 1994, Chief Justice William H. Rehnquist held that for a city to require an owner to grant an easement allowing public access on a pedestrian path "would deprive petitioner of the right to exclude others, 'one of the most essential sticks in the bundle of rights that are commonly characterized as property.'"[206] His emphasis on a power that the realists had long ago demonstrated implied state coercion led Justice John P. Stevens in dissent to warn that the modern Court was indulging itself in a "resurrection of a species of substantive due process analysis" tracing back to Lochner and from thence through the Holmes's "regulatory takings" dicta in Pennsylvania Coal, which had "an obvious kinship with the line of substantive due process cases that Lochner exemplified. Besides having similar ancestry, both doctrines are potentially open-ended sources of judicial power to invalidate state economic regulations that members of this Court view as unwise or unfair.")[207]

Twentieth-century judges came to recognize that property rights were not innate in reality, like some inherent metaphysical essences, but rather were social constructs, legally enforceable conventional claims. When Holmes and Brandeis engaged in their seminal debate over the creation of property rights in International News Service v. Associated Press in 1918,[208] Holmes asserted, without challenge, that "property [is] a creation of law," not some function of natural law. The subtext was, of course, that if property rights were created by law, they could be regulated by law. Some putative Lockean natural law basis for property no longer stood as an implicit barrier to regulation, which is simply the enforcement of majoritarian social policy.

To have legal effect, the claims of property owners ultimately had to be backed by the force of the state, as where an owner of real property could resort to legal process to exclude the rest of the world from asserting an easement. The philosopher Morris Cohen elegantly demonstrated that by dissolving the boundary between the Roman-law concepts of dominium and imperium (a distinction crucial to Blackstonian property ideas), modern property was a "sovereign power compelling service and obedience."[209] If property claims were thus inherently coercive, then the state was in the position of enforcing and maintaining fundamental inequalities in access to wealth and power.[210] When the Supreme Court accepted this idea, in the context of racial subordination presented by the 1917 case of Buchanan v. Warley,[211] it struck down racial zoning, but as much to protect the free transferability of property as to pursue an ideal of racial justice.[212] The same insight would lead a later Court to hold that judicial enforcement of racially restrictive covenants constituted the state action that triggered the prohibition of the equal protection clause.[213]

Developments in civil procedure provided an unexpected parallel to these property doctrines. In Pennoyer v. Neff (1877),[214] Justice Field had developed a theory of personal jurisdiction based on physical presence within a state's jurisdiction. This physical requirement (of a human body within the imaginary lines of state boundaries) proved inadequate as a basis of jurisdiction in the twentieth century both for reasons of technological change, such as the transformations wrought by the automobile, and for jurisdiction over intangibles. While not abandoned,[215] the physicalist basis of jurisdiction had to be severely modified, first by imputed consent in the case of out-of-state motorists,[216] then by the Court's rethinking the entire nature of jurisdiction and state power in the modern landmark of *International Shoe Co. v. Washington* (1945),[217] a case that may be considered the supreme realist achievement in the field of civil procedure. Other procedural landmarks influenced by realist thought included *Erie Railroad v. Tompkins* (1938), understandable only in the light of Justice Brandeis's Progressive suspicion of federal judges' sympathies for corporate power, and the Federal Rules of Civil Procedure (adopted in 1938), attributable largely to the efforts of realist Charles E. Clark.

In public law, where state courts had been the earliest venues of classical legal thought in the 1880s, now they led the way in rejecting classical premises. The New York Court of Appeals and Irving Lehman, successor to Cardozo as its chief judge, provide numerous examples. Though not realists like Llewellyn, Lehman and his colleagues were instrumentalist in outlook, deferential to legislative policy judgment, committed to the idea that law must adapt to modern needs, sensitive to the factual circumstances in which rules and precedents were to be applied, and above all, determined that just results should not be sacrificed to consistency in a mindless obeisance to precedent.[218] Thus in *People v. Weller* (1924),[219] the New York court rejected the premises of the *Adkins* opinion of the preceding year: "[A] legislative mandate which regulates the exercise of the compulsive force [resulting from unequal bargaining power or monopolization] may in effect restore and not diminish the liberty of the individual."[220] The New York court was similarly hostile to the labor injunction as a device for inhibiting communication or prohibiting acts that were in themselves legal.[221] In vain they tried to warn conservative activist jurists on the federal bench that "courts are called upon to determine only whether the legislature has acted within its powers in enacting this legislation; the judges have no disposition, and the courts have no right, to pass upon the wisdom of its exercise."[222]

Few federal judges shared that progressive outlook. An occasional case of the post–World War I era might evince a respect for congressional discretion in policy making, as when the Supreme Court upheld the Esch-Cummings Act or reaffirmed the "stream of commerce" doctrine that permitted an expansive reading of Congress's commerce-regulatory powers. But the 1920s was generally a conservative-activist decade, when the Court struck down numerous federal and state regulatory measures: *Bailey v. Drexel Furniture* (1922); *Truax v. Corrigan* (1921), *Duplex Printing Press Co. v. Deering* (1920), *Adkins v. Childrens Hospital* (1923), *Bedford Cut Stone Co. v. Journeymen Stone Cutters' Association* (1926), *New State Ice Co. v. Liebmann* (1932), to mention only the more conspicuous.

Brandeis regularly dissented, often joined by Holmes and the newly appointed Harlan Fiske Stone. Even when Brandeis chose not to release his opinions, they sometimes deflected the Court from a more egregious stance than it took.[223] He attempted to rein in classicist activism that substituted the judges' opinions of sound policy for that of the legislature, calling on his brethren to respect legislative discretion and to accept legislative determinations of policy. Brandeis sought to accomplish this with appeals to judicial professionalism, through an emphasis on procedural constraints. His enumeration of those constraints in *Ashwander v. TVA* (1936)[224] stands today as an enduring reminder for judges to recognize and accept the limits of their power. The Court has often ignored these admonitions, only to return to them after its activist urges have subsided.

Though classical assumptions appeared to dominate as imperturbably as the Chief himself during the Taft years, a close reading of some cases, illuminated by hindsight, reveals an intellectual body so far advanced in senescence that its tottering authority would soon succumb. A relatively minor dormant commerce power case of 1927, *Di Santo v. Pennsylvania*, is illustrative. Justice Butler for the majority struck down a state license fee on agents selling steamship tickets for overseas travel on the grounds that it imposed a direct burden on international commerce. Justice Stone's dissent pointed out that the old direct-indirect distinction had outlived its day, being "too mechanical, too uncertain in its application, and too remote from actualities" to be of value. He then provided a critique of the entire classical method:

> [W]e are doing little more than using labels to describe a result rather than any trustworthy formula by which it is reached. . . . Those interferences [with commerce] not deemed forbidden are to be sustained, not because the effect on commerce is nominally indirect, but because a consideration of all the facts and circumstances, such as the nature of the regulation, its function, the character of the business involved and the actual effect on the flow of commerce, lead to the conclusion that the regulation concerns interests peculiarly local and does not infringe the national interest in maintaining the freedom of commerce across state lines.[225]

Classical legal thought was hostile to legislative judgment in economic affairs but deferential to that same judgment when the object of legislative concern was civil liberties. Thus the Supreme Court sustained congressional and state criminalization of ideas in an undeviating line of cases in the twenties.[226] Brandeis and usually Holmes dissented in all these cases, creating a legacy of libertarian thought in the First Amendment area that was ultimately vindicated a half-century later.[227] In one of these separate opinions (in form a concurrence), Brandeis issued a call to civic courage unique in the *United States Reports*. "Fear of serious injury cannot alone justify suppression of free speech and assembly. Men feared witches and burnt women. It is the function of speech to free men from the bondage of irrational fears."[228] He went on: "[T]hose who won our independence by revolution were not cowards. They did not fear political change. They did not exalt order at the cost of liberty. To courageous, selfreliant men, with confidence in the power of free and fearless reasoning applied through the processes of popular government, no danger flowing from speech can be deemed clear and present," unless it met the stringent Holmes/Brandeis clear-and-present-danger standards. Brandeis's words endured through the second Red Scare and recalled Americans to their better natures.

Legal classicism attained the height of its coherence and influence at the turn of the twentieth century, and from that dominating position controlled the development of American public law for a generation. But classical thought contained within itself the potential for its own disintegration. Its critics saw it to be ever more divorced from social and economic reality, rapt in contemplation of its own internal symmetry and conformity.

Challenges to classical hegemony had come in three waves, coincident with periods of political reform but only loosely affiliated with them. During the Populist decade of the 1890s, then again throughout the Progressive years of the pre–World War I period, and then finally during the autumn of Progressivism in the 1920s, critics accosted orthodox beliefs. Holmes and Pound were only the best known of the many judges, academics, and political figures who mounted a systematic critique of classicism's fundamental premises.

By 1925, however, it appeared that legal classicism had weathered these surges of criticism. Personified in the Chief Justice of the United States, William Howard Taft, classicism presided confidently over a decade of public law adjudication that constrained state and federal regulatory power. The Court itself was a symbol of order and security in a time when values seemed unstable and the nation in transition to an unknown future.[229] Classical jurists assumed that their principles and axioms were unshakable, grounded in fundamental law and elementary logic.

That confidence was buoyant during the decade of Normalcy. But when economic and social conditions deteriorated after 1929, the Supreme Court found that traditional dogmas provided scant shelter against the howling winds of change.

Notes

1. Alan Dawley, *Struggles for Justice: Social Responsibility and the Liberal State* (1991), 23.

2. In the incident Coke reported as "Prohibitions del Roy," 12 Coke Rep. 63, 65, 77 Eng. Rep. 1342, 1343 (1607).

3. Bailey v. Drexel Furniture Co., 259 U.S. 20, 37 (1922).

4. William G. Ross reviews Progressive attacks on the judiciary and proposals for reform in *A Muted Fury: Populists, Progressives, and Labor Unions Confront the Courts, 1890–1937* (1994).

5. 7 *Harv. L. Rev.* 129, 152, 144 (1893).

6. 109 U.S. 3 (1883). For speculation about the influence of this decision, see Jay Hook, "A Brief Life of James Bradley Thayer," 88 *Nw. U. L. Rev.* 1, 6 (1993), part of a centennial symposium sponsored by Northwestern University School of Law on the article that is the subject of this paragraph.

7. Hepburn v. Griswold, 8 Wall. (75 U.S.) 603 (18868), *reversed by* The Legal Tender Cases, 12 Wall. (79 U.S.) 457 (1870), on which see Charles Fairman, *Reconstruction and Reunion, 1864–88, Part One* (vol. 6 of the *Holmes Devise History of the Supreme Court of the United States*) (1971), 677–775.

8. Cf. Mark Tushnet, "Thayer's Target: Judicial Review or Democracy?" 88 *Nw. U. L. Rev.* 9–27 (1993) (Thayer called for greater legislative responsibility to achieve the essentially conservative end of restraining reform legislation), with G. Edward White, "Revisiting James Bradley Thayer," 88 *Nw. U. L. Rev.* 48–83 (1993) (Thayer as "Brahmin legal scientist").

9. Frankfurter to Arthur Schlesinger Jr., 18 June 1963, in Max Freedman, ed., *Roosevelt and Frankfurter: Their Correspondence, 1928–1945* (1967), 25. Wallace Mendelson, "The Influence of James Bradley Thayer upon the Work of Holmes, Brandeis, and Frankfurter," 31 *Vand. L. Rev.* 71 (1978).

10. George M. Fredrickson, *The Inner Civil War: Northern Intellectuals and the Crisis of the Union* (1965), 199–216; Dorothy Ross, *The Origins of American Social Science* (1991).

11. See the essays by Malcom Bradbury, Allan Bullock, and James McFarlane in Bradbury and McFarlane, eds., *Modernism, 1890–1930* (1978), 19–94.

12. Allan Bullock, "The Double Image," in Bradbury and McFarlane, eds., *Modernism*, 68.

13. H. Stuart Hughes, *Consciousness and Society: The Reconstruction of European Social Thought, 1890–1930* (1958; rpt. 1976), 33.

14. G. Edward White, "The First Amendment Comes of Age: The Emergence of Free Speech in Twentieth-Century America," 95 *Mich. L. Rev.* 299, 301–310 (1996).

15. Dorothy Ross, ed., *Modernist Impulses in the Human Sciences, 1870–1930* (1994), 5.

16. Ross, ed., *Modernist Impulses*, 2.

17. Karl Pearson, *The Grammar of Science* (1892), quoted in Ross, ed., *Modernist Impulses*, 176.

18. Lawrence Goodwyn, *Democratic Promise: The Populist Moment in America* (1976); see also his abbreviated version of that study, *The Populist Moment: A Short History of the Agrarian Revolt in America* (1978).

19. Robert C. McMath, *Populist Vanguard: A History of the Southern Farmers' Alliance* (1975).

20. Robert L. Clinton catalogues some of the earliest critiques in "The Populist-Progressive Reinterpretation of American Constitutional History: The Scapegoating of John Marshall, His Court, and the Founding Fathers" (1984) (Ph.D. dissertation, University of Texas (Austin), 25–36, 241–339.

21. Stephen Stagner, "Recall of Judicial Decisions and the Due Process Debate," 24 *Am. J. Legal Hist.* 257 (1980).

22. 29 *Am. L. Rev.* 641 (1895).

23. Frank v. Denver & Rio Grande Ry., 23 F. 757, 759 (C.C.D. Colo. 1885).

24. Robert H. Wiebe, *The Search for Order, 1877–1920* (1967).

25. Christopher L. Tomlins, *The State and the Unions: Labor Relations, Law, and the Organized Labor Movement in America, 1880–1960* (1985), 32–59.

26. Sean Wilentz, *Chants Democratic: New York City and the Rise of the American Working Class, 1788–1850* (1984), 61–103.

27. The cases are reproduced in John R. Commons, ed., *A Documentary History of American Industrial Society* (1910–11), vol. 3, 235, and vol. 4, 323, respectively. The latter is known as *The Case of the Twenty Journeymen Tailors* or *People v. Faulkner* (1836).

28. *In re* Debs, 158 U.S. 564, 592 (1895).

29. George McNeill, "Declaration of Principles of the Knights of Labor" (1886), quoted in Leon Fink, "Labor, Liberty, and the Law: Trade Unionism and the Problem of the American Constitutional Order," *Journal of American History* 74 (1987), 904, 912.

30. Duplex Printing Press Co. v. Deering, 254 U.S. 443, 465 (1921); Truax v. Corrigan, 257 U.S. 312, 327 (1921).

31. Testimony before House Judiciary Committee, 1912, quoted in William E. Forbath, *Law and the Shaping of the American Labor Movement* (1991), 155–156.

32. State v. Stewart, 59 Vt. 273, 9 A. 559 (1887).

33. Robert F. Hoxie, *Trade Unionism in the United States*, 2nd ed. (1923), 238.

34. Donald B. Johnson, ed., *National Party Platforms*, rev'd ed. (1976), 99–100.

35. Alan Westin, "The Supreme Court, the Populist Movement, and the Campaign of 1896," *Journal of Politics* 15 (1953), 3–41. On the culmination of Populist reform, see Robert F. Durden, *The Climax of Populism: The Election of 1896* (1965).

36. Quoted in Westin, "The Supreme Court, the Populist Movement, and the Campaign of 1896," 38.

37. E.g.: "Codes, and the Arrangement of the Law," *Am. L. Rev.* (1870); "The Gas-Stokers' Strike," *Am. L. Rev.* (1873), reprinted in Sheldon M. Novick, ed., *The Collected Works of Justice Holmes: Complete Public Writings and Selected Judicial Opinions of Oliver Wendell Holmes* (1995), vol. 1, 211–221, 323–325, respectively.

38. On Holmes's thought, the following are illuminating but not always compatible with one another: editor's introduction in Oliver Wendell Holmes, *The Common Law*, Mark DeWolfe Howe, ed. (1963), xi–xxvii; Horwitz, *Transformation II*, 109–142; editor's introduction

in Novick, ed., *Collected Works of Holmes*, vol. 1, 18–135; G. Edward White, *Justice Oliver Wendell Holmes: Law and the Inner Self* (1993), 148–195, 215–223; Sheldon M. Novick, *Honorable Justice: The Life of Oliver Wendell Holmes* (1989); Robert Gordon, "Holmes's Common Law as Legal and Social Science," 10 *Hofstra L. Rev.* 719, 727 (1982).

39. "Torts—Trespass and Negligence," *The Common Law*, in Novick, ed., *Collected Works of Holmes*, vol. 3, 163, 164. David Rosenberg minimizes Holmes's formalism in the field of torts, contending that he stood for a principle of "foresight-based strict liability": Rosenberg, *The Hidden Holmes: His Theory of Torts in History* (1995), 6.

40. Sheldon M. Novick, "Holmes's Path, Holmes's Goal," 110 *Harv. L. Rev.* 1028, 1030 (1997).

41. Holmes, *The Common Law*, in Novick, ed., *Collected Works of Holmes*, vol. 3, 115.

42. Thomas C. Grey, "Holmes and Legal Pragmatism," 41 *Stan. L. Rev.* 787, 791 (1989), quoting Benjamin N. Cardozo, "Mr. Justice Holmes," 44 *Harv. L. Rev.* 683 (1931).

43. Holmes quoted in Lloyd Morris, *Postscript to Yesterday* (1947), 341. The Latin phrase means "final argument"; Holmes, consciously or not, was quoting from a common inscription on cannon in the seventeenth century: *ultima ratio regum*, "the final argument of kings."

44. John P. Diggins evaluates Holmes in relation to pragmatist philosophers in *The Promise of Pragmatism: Modernism and the Crisis of Knowledge and Authority* (1994), 342–359; quote on p. 345 (Holmes's comment on William James's book *Pragmatism*).

45. *Harvard Law Review* (1894), in Novick, ed., *Collected Works of Holmes*, vol. 3, 371–380; quotations at 376–377.

46. Horwitz, *Transformation II*, 131.

47. 167 Mass. 92, 108, 107 (1896) (Holmes, J., dissenting).

48. Harlan Fiske Stone, "The Common Law in the United States," 50 *Harv. L. Rev.* 4, 10, 20 (1936).

49. *Harvard Law Review* (1897), in Novick, ed., *Collected Works of Holmes*, vol. 3, 391–406; quotations at 393, 397. The essay is reprinted, along with reflections on its influence by nine different scholars, in "The Path of the Law after One Hundred Years," 110 *Harv. L. Rev.* 991 (1997).

50. Horwitz, *Transformation II*, 142.

51. "Law in Science and Science in Law" (1899), in Novick, ed., *Collected Works of Holmes*, vol. 3, 406–420; quotations at 413, 418–419.

52. Novick, ed., *Collected Works of Holmes*, vol. 3, 399.

53. Mark V. Tushnet concludes that Holmes's state judicial experience left him disappointed with the lack of opportunities to shape law: "The Logic of Experience: Oliver Wendell Holmes on the Supreme Judicial Court," 63 *Va. L. Rev.* 975 (1977); see pp. 1029–1041 on labor cases especially.

54. See the correspondence excerpts in Horwitz, *Transformation II*, 143.

55. Jay M. Feinman and Peter Gabel, "Contract Law as Ideology," in David M. Kairys, ed., *The Politics of Law: A Progressive Critique*, rev'd ed. (1990), 375–385.

56. Grant Gilmore, *The Death of Contract* (1974; rpt. 1995), 14. The Symposium "Reconsidering Grant Gilmore's *The Death of Contract*," 90 *Nw. U. L. Rev.* 1 (1995) raised the questions of how seriously Gilmore meant such provocative statements to be taken, whether he was attempting serious legal history, and whether his theses made any sense. The one proposition all thirteen authors concurred on was that the book has been extraordinarily influential.

57. Britton v. Turner, 6 N.H. 481, 493 (1834).

58. Stark v. Parker, 2 Pick. (19 Mass.) 267, 274 (1824). See Wythe Holt, "Recovery by the Worker Who Quits: A Comparison of the Mainstream, Legal Realist, and Critical Legal Studies Approaches to a Problem of Nineteenth Century Contract Law," 1986 *Wis. L. Rev.* 677.

59. Samuel Williston, A *Treatise on the Law of Contracts* (1920–1922, rev'd ed., 1936–38), § 1478.

60. Southern Pacific Co. v. Jensen, 244 U.S. 205, 222 (1917).

61. Williston, *A Treatise on the Law of Contracts*.

62. See generally Horwitz, *Transformation II*, 33–51.

63. Note, "Tortious Interference with Contractual Relations in the Nineteenth Century: The Transformation of Property, Contract, and Tort," 93 *Harv. L. Rev.* 1151 (1980).

64. P. S. Atiyah provides a lucid account of parallel developments in England in *The Rise and Fall of Freedom of Contract*, 2nd ed. (1979), 571–715.

65. Quoted in Atiyah, *Rise and Fall of Freedom of Contract*, 661.

66. Horwitz, *Transformation II*, 51–63.

67. William Blackstone, *Commentaries on the Laws of England* (1765), vol. 3, 118–123.

68. G. Edward White, "The Intellectual Origins of Torts in America," 86 *Yale L.J.* 671 (1977) and its revision in *Tort Law in America: An Intellectual History* (1980).

69. Oliver Wendell Holmes, "The Theory of Torts," *Am. L. Rew.* (1873), in Novick, ed., *Collected Works of Holmes*, vol. 1, 326, 331 (negligence as failure to conform to "duties of all the world to all the world").

70. 53 N.H. 442 (1873). See John P. Reid, *Chief Justice: The Judicial World of Charles Doe* (1967), 134–139.

71. "In jure non remota causa, sed proxima spectatur": Bacon, *Maxims of the Law* (1630), in J. Spedding et al. eds., *Works of Francis Bacon* (1861; rpt. 1969), vol. 14, 189–193.

72. [Green], "Proximate and Remote Cause," 4 *Am. L. Rev.* 201, 211 (1870).

73. Quoted in Horwitz, *Transformation II*, 55, 58. Wharton penned these phrases in 1874 and 1876.

74. Quoted in Roscoe Pound, "The Need of a Sociological Jurisprudence," 19 *Green Bag* 607, 614 (1907).

75. Blackstone, *Commentaries*, vol. 1, 123–134 (quotation at 134).

76. Joseph A. Schumpeter, *Capitalism, Socialism, and Democracy*, 3rd ed. (1950), 83. For an illustrative application of the Schumpeter thesis to property relationships, see Stanley I. Kutler, *Privilege and Creative Destruction: The Charles River Bridge Case* (1971).

77. "Half the South's wealth": Roger L. Ransom and Richard Sutch, *One Kind of Freedom: The Economic Consequences of Emancipation* (1977), 52–53.

78. The Late Corporation of the Church of Jesus Christ of Latter-Day Saints v. United States, 136 U.S. 1 (1890).

79. John R. Commons, *Legal Foundations of Capitalism* (1924), 196.

80. Gerard C. Henderson, "Railway Valuation and the Courts," 33 *Harv. L. Rev.* 902, 917 (1920).

81. The phrase first appeared in John Lewis, *A Treatise on the Law of Eminent Domain in the United States* (1888), 41, 43, and was later exploited by Wesley Hohfeld and Progressive contemporaries.

82. Eaton v. Boston, Concord & Montreal R.R., 51 N.H. 504, 511 (1872).

83. Pumpelly v. Green Bay Co., 13 Wall. (80 U.S.) 166, 179 (1872).

84. Farmers' Loan & Trust Co. v. Northern Pacific R.R., 60 F. 803 (E.D. Wis. 1894).

85. Another discussion of the Progressive critique will be found in the appendix, "Historiography and the Supreme Court."

86. I have drawn on both classic and recent interpretations of Progressivism for interpretive insights, but the text does not reflect the viewpoint of any one authority. See Richard Hofstadter, *The Age of Reform; From Bryan to F.D.R.* (1955); Samuel P. Hays, *The Response to Industrialism, 1885–1914* (1957); Ray Ginger, *Age of Excess: The United States from 1877 to 1914*

(1965); Robert H. Wiebe, *The Search for Order, 1877–1920* (1967); Morton Keller, *Affairs of State: Public Life in Late Nineteenth Century America* (1977); Keller, *Regulating a New Economy: Public Policy and Economic Change in America, 1900–1933* (1990); Keller, *Regulating a New Society: Public Policy and Social Change in America, 1900–1933* (1994); David P. Thelen, *The New Citizenship: Origins of Progressivism in Wisconsin, 1885–1900* (1972); Alan Dawley, *Struggles for Justice: Social Responsibility and the Liberal State* (1991).

87. Dorothy Ross, *The Origins of American Social Science* (1991); Thomas L. Haskell, *The Emergence of Professional Social Science: The American Social Science Association and the Nineteenth-Century Crisis of Authority* (1977); Mary O. Furner, *Advocacy and Objectivity: A Crisis in the Professionalization of American Social Science, 1865–1905* (1975).

88. The locus classicus is William James, *Pragmatism, A New Name for Some Old Ways of Thinking* (1907). The secondary-source classic is Morton G. White, *Social Thought in America: The Revolt against Formalism* (1949). On the movement in law, see Robert S. Summers, *Instrumentalism and American Legal Theory* (1982), and on its recrudescence in our times, Symposium on the Renaissance of Pragmatism in American Legal Thought, 63 *So. Cal. L. Rev.* 1569 (1990).

89. Alan Ryan provides a warm appreciation of Dewey in *John Dewey and the High Tide of American Liberalism* (1995).

90. *The Writings of William James*, John J. McDermott, ed. (1967), 379.

91. Bruce Kuklick, *The Rise of American Philosophy: Cambridge, Massachusetts, 1860–1930* (1977), 48–54.

92. Peter Novick, *That Noble Dream: The "Objectivity Question" and the American Historical Profession* (1988), 86–167; Richard Hofstadter, *The Progressive Historians: Turner, Beard, Parrington* (1968).

93. Principally: Charles A. Beard, *An Economic Interpretation of the Constitution of the United States* (1913); *The Rise of American Civilization* (coauthor: Mary R. Beard, new ed. [1933]); Carl. L. Becker, *The History of Political Parties in the Province of New York, 1760–1776* (1909); J. Allen Smith, *The Spirit of American Government* (1907).

94. Arthur F. Bentley, *The Processes of Government* (1908). Goodnow's contributions will be noted below.

95. Woodrow Wilson, *Constitutional Government in the United States* (1908), 56–57.

96. I. Bernard Cohen, "Scientific Revolutions, Revolutions in Science, and a Probabilistic Revolution, 1800–1930," in Lorenz Kruger et al., eds, *The Probabilistic Revolution*, vol. 1: *Ideas in History* (1987), 40.

97. Quoted in William A. Wallace, *Causality and Scientific Explanation*, vol. 2, *Classical and Contemporary Science* (1974), 170.

98. Paul J. Croce, *Science and Religion in the Era of William James*, vol. 1: *Eclipse of Certainty, 1820–1880* (1995).

99. For a modern recognition that law must deal with problems not susceptible of Euclidean solutions, see Dennis v. United States, 341 U.S. 494, 525 (1951) (Frankfurter, J., concurring, rejecting "dogmas too inflexible for the non-Euclidian problems to be solved").

100. E.g.: Jerome Frank, "Mr. Justice Holmes and Non-Euclidean Legal Thinking," 17 *Cornell L.Q.* 568 (1932).

101. George H. Sabine, "The Pragmatic Approach to Politics," *American Political Science Review* 24 (1930), 865, 866.

102. Pius IX, *Quanta Cura* (1864) (enumerating the "Syllabus of Errors," a synopsis of liberal principles of government); Pius X, *Pascendi Domini Gregis* (1907) (identifying religious modernism as "the synthesis of all heresies"), in Claudia Carlen, comp., *The Papal Encyclicals* (1981), vol. 1, 381–386, and vol. 2, 71–98.

103. Herbert Croly, *The Promise of American Life* (1909), 23.

104. Edward A. Stettner, *Shaping Modern Liberalism: Herbert Croly and Progressive Thought* (1993), 86–90.

105. Theodore Roosevelt, "The Progressive Party's Appeal," *The Independent* 93 (1912), 73.

106. On Pound's contribution, see David Wigdor, *Roscoe Pound: Philosopher of Law* (1974), 161–206, and N. E. H. Hull, *Roscoe Pound and Karl Llewellyn: Searching for an American Jurisprudence* (1997). I thank Prof. Hull and the University of Chicago Press for their joint courtesy in allowing me to read page proofs of this excellent study before its publication. Edward B. McLean attempts to summarize Pound's ideas in *Law and Civilization: The Legal Thought of Roscoe Pound* (1992).

107. Roscoe Pound, "The Causes of Popular Dissatisfaction with the Administration of Justice," *Am. Bar Ass'n. Ann. Rep.*, 29 (1906) part 1, 395.

108. The title of his reformist essay in 44 *Am. L. Rev.* 12 (1909).

109. Roscoe Pound, "Mechanical Jurisprudence," 8 *Colum. L. Rev.* 605 (1909).

110. Roscoe Pound, "The Need of a Sociological Jurisprudence," 19 *Green Bag* 607, 614, 610, 613 (1907).

111. Pound, "Mechanical Jurisprudence," 610.

112. Roscoe Pound, "Liberty of Contract," 18 *Yale L.J.* 454 (1909).

113. Roscoe Pound, "The Scope and Purpose of Sociological Jurisprudence," 24 *Harv. L. Rev.* 591 (1911); 25 *Harv. L. Rev.* 140, 489 (1912), quotations 516.

114. On the influence of sociological jurisprudence, see G. Edward White, "From Sociological Jurisprudence to Realism: Jurisprudence and Social Change in Early Twentieth-Century America," (1972), rpt. in G. Edward White, *Patterns of American Legal Thought* (1978), 99 at 99–115; Horwitz, *Transformation II*, 188–191; and Hull, *Pound and Llewellyn*.

115. J. M. Kelly, *A Short History of Western Legal Theory* (1992), 361–363.

116. See the compendious statement of early-twentieth-century critique: Joseph W. Bingham, "What Is the Law?" 11 *Mich. L. Rev.* 1, 109 (1912).

117. Ernst Freund, *The Police Power, Public Policy and Constitutional Rights* (1904).

118. John Chipman Gray, *The Nature and Sources of the Law* (1909).

119. G. Edward White, *The American Judicial Tradition: Profiles of Leading American Judges* (1988), 150.

120. Frank J. Goodnow, *Social Reform and the Constitution* (1911).

121. Morris R. Cohen, "The Process of Judicial Legislation," 48 *Am. L. Rev.* 161, 172 (1914).

122. Learned Hand, "Due Process of Law and the Eight-Hour Day," 21 *Harv. L. Rev.* 495, 506, 508, 509 (1908). On the influence of this piece, see Gerald Gunther, *Learned Hand: The Man and the Judge* (1994), 118–123.

123. Alan F. Westin compiled a bibliography of these in his editorial apparatus to the 1962 reprint of Beard's *The Supreme Court and the Constitution* (1912, rev'd ed. 1938, rpt. 1962), 134–139.

124. Among others: Louis B. Boudin, "Government by Judiciary," *Political Science Quarterly* 26 (1911), 238; Walter Clark (a North Carolina state judge who was something of a monomaniac on the issue): "Is the Supreme Court Constitutional?," *The Independent* 63 (1907), 723; Clark, "Back to the Constitution," 50 *Am. L. Rev.* 1 (1916); Clark, "Where Does the Governing Power Reside?" 52 *Am. L. Rev.* 687 (1918); Roscoe Pound, "Courts and Legislation," *American Political Science Review* 7 (1913), 361; Gilbert Roe, *Our Judicial Oligarchy* (1912).

125. Among others: Horace H. Lurton (Justice of the U.S. Supreme Court), "A Government of Law or of Men," *North American Review* 193 (1911), 9; William Howard Taft (president of the United States), *Popular Government: Its Essence, Its Permanence and Its Perils* (1913), 161–168; Charles Warren, "The Progressiveness of the United States Supreme Court," 13 *Col. L. Rev.* 290 (1913).

126. Edward S. Corwin, *The Doctrine of Judicial Review: Its Legal and Historical Basis and Other Essays* (1914); Charles G. Haines, *The American Doctrine of Judicial Supremacy* (1914).

127. Gustavus Myers, *History of the Supreme Court of the United States* (1912).

128. Brandeis's writings are catalogued in Roy M. Mersky, *Louis Dembitz Brandeis, 1856–1941: A Bibliography* (1958).

129. On his advocacy role, see Melvin I. Urofsky, *A Mind of One Piece: Brandeis and American Reform* (1971), 43–68; Urofsky, *Louis D. Brandeis and the Progressive Tradition* (1981), 47–67; Philippa Strum, *Louis D. Brandeis: Justice for the People* (1984), 339–353; Strum, *Brandeis: Beyond Progressivism* (1993), 72–99. But see Clyde Spillenger, "Elusive Advocate: Reconsidering Brandeis as People's Lawyer," 105 *Yale L.J.* 1445 (1996) (expressing reservations about Brandeis's advocacy).

130. Wesley N. Hohfeld, *Fundamental Legal Conceptions as Applied in Judicial Reasoning and Other Legal Essays* (*Yale L.J.* 1913; rpt. 1923). See Joseph Singer, "The Legal Rights Debate in Analytical Jurisprudence from Bentham to Hohfeld," 1982 *Wis. L. Rev.* 975.

131. Quoted from a 1914 address by Hohfeld in Horwitz, *Transformation II*, 152; on Hohfeld's influence, see 151–156.

132. Benjamine N. Cardozo, *The Nature of the Judicial Process* (1921), 127, 137.

133. President Taft's message to Congress accompanying his veto of the Arizona Enabling Bill, 22 Aug. 1911, in James D. Richardson, comp., *A Compilation of the Messages and Papers of the Presidents* (1917), vol. 18, 8018–8020.

134. Lochner v. New York, 198 U.S. 45, 75–76 (1905) (Holmes, J., dissenting).

135. Harlan was joined by Justices White and Day, but not, significantly, by Holmes; nor did the three in the Harlan group sign on to Holmes's dissenting opinion. 198 U.S. 65–74.

136. Jeffrey M. Shaman, "Constitutional Fact: The Perception of Reality by the Supreme Court," 35 *U. Fla. L. Rev.* 236 (1983).

137. For an evaluation of the Brandeis Brief, see David P. Bryden, "Brandeis's Facts," 1 *Constitutional Commentary* 281 (1984). John W. Johnson considers the "penchant for information" symbolized by the Brandeis Brief as a major synthetic key to twentieth-century legal history: *American Legal Culture, 1908–1940* (1981).

138. Ellen F. Fitzpatrick, *Endless Crusade: Women Social Scientists and Progressive Reform* (1990).

139. Urofsky, *A Mind of One Piece*, 30–42.

140. Another surprise, given that most of the *Lochner* majority still sat: Fuller, Peckham, Brewer, and McKenna.

141. 208 U.S. 412, 419, 421 (1908).

142. 243 U.S. 426 (1917).

143. New York Central R.R. v. White, 243 U.S. 188 (1917); see also Mountain Timber Co. v. Washington, 243 U.S. 219 (1917).

144. 219 U.S. 104, 109–110 (1911). *Nolumus mutare*: Lat., "We forbid change."

145. Noble State Bank v. Haskell, 219 U.S. 575, 580 (1911).

146. United States v. Trans-Missouri Freight Association, 166 U.S. 290 (1897); Addyston Pipe and Steel Co. v. United States, 175 U.S. 211 (1899); Northern Securities Co. v. United States, 193 U.S. 197 (1904); Swift and Co. v. United States, 196 U.S. 375 (1905).

147. 221 U.S. 1, 62 (1911).

148. 221 U.S. 106 (1911).

149. Southern Pacific Co. v. Jensen, 244 U.S. 205, 222 (1917).

150. 304 U.S. 64 (1938). Edward A. Purcell Jr. recounts this struggle in *Litigation and Inequality: Federal Diversity Jurisdiction in Industrial America, 1870–1958* (1992) and in his forthcoming monograph, "Constitutional Visions and the Politics of the Federal Courts: Bran-

deis, Erie, and the Judicial Power in Twentieth-Century America." I thank Prof. Purcell for the opportunity of reading this study in ms. before its publication.

151. Charles Grove Haines, "General Observations on the Effects of Personal, Political, and Economic Influences in the Decisions of Judges," 17 *Ill. L. Rev.* 66 (1922).

152. Roosevelt message to Congress, 8 Dec. 1908, in James D. Richardson, comp., *Messages and Papers of the Presidents* (1910), vol. 10, 7594.

153. Hitchman Coal and Coke Co. v. Mitchell, 245 U.S. 229 (1917); Truax v. Corrigan, 257 U.S. 312 (1921).

154. I have drawn on the following valuable studies of the realists: Laura Kalman, *Legal Realism at Yale, 1927–1960* (1986); William L. Twining, *Karl Llewellyn and the Realist Movement* (1973); John H. Schlegel, *American Legal Realism and Empirical Social Science* (1995); Neil Duxbury, *Patterns of American Jurisprudence* (1995), 64–159; Edward A. Purcell, *The Crisis of Democratic Theory: Scientific Naturalism and the Problem of Value* (1973); Purcell, "American Jurisprudence between the Wars: Legal Realism and the Crisis of Democratic Theory," *American Historical Review* 75 (1969), 424; Robert S. Summers, *Instrumentalism and American Legal Theory* (1982); Horwitz, *Transformation II*, 169–212; Wilfrid E. Rumble, *American Legal Realism: Skepticism, Reform, and the Judicial Process* (1968); Gary Aichele, *Legal Realism and Twentieth-Century American Jurisprudence: The Changing Consensus* (1990); G. Edward White, *Patterns of American Legal Thought* (1978), 97–162; Joseph W. Singer, "Legal Realism Now," 76 *Cal. L. Rev.* 465 (1988); William W. Fisher, "The Development of Modern American Theory and the Judicial Interpretation of the Bill of Rights," in Michael J. Lacey and Knud Haakonssen, eds., *A Culture of Rights: The Bill of Rights in Philosophy, Politics, and Law—1791 and 1991* (1991), 266–286. Excerpts of some principal primary sources of realism are collected in William W. Fisher, Morton J. Horwitz, and Thomas A. Reed, eds., *American Legal Realism* (1993).

155. This exchange, often and misleadingly treated as the defining moment of legal realism, was contained in three articles: Karl Llewellyn, "A Realistic Jurisprudence—The Next Step," 30 *Colum. L. Rev.* 431 (1930); Pound, "The Call for a Realist Jurisprudence," 44 *Harv. L. Rev.* 697 (1931); and Llewellyn, "Some Realism about Realism—Responding to Dean Pound," 44 *Harv. L. Rev.* 1222 (1931). See N. E. H. Hull, "Some Realism about the Llewellyn-Pound Exchange over Realism: The Newly Uncovered Private Correspondence, 1927–1931," 1987 *Wis. L. Rev.* 921.

156. Summers, *Instrumentalism and American Legal Theory*. See also N. E. H. Hull, "Reconstructing the Origins of Realistic Jurisprudence: A Prequel to the Llewellyn-Pound Exchange over Legal Realism," 1989 *Duke L.J.* 1302.

157. Cf. a somewhat different list in Horwitz, *Transformation II*, ch. 6, fns. 85–104 (pp. 312–319); and cf. both with Llewellyn's famous list of twenty in "Some Realism about Realism," fn. 18.

158. Walton H. Hamilton, "Property—According to Locke," 41 *Yale L.J.* 864, 879 (1932).

159. Hessel E. Yntema, "The Hornbook Method and the Conflict of Laws," 37 *Yale L.J.* 468, 479 (1928).

160. Walter Nelles, Book Review, 33 *Colum. L. Rev.* 763, 767 (1933).

161. Joseph C. Hutcheson, "The Judgment Intuitive: The Function of the 'Hunch' in Judicial Decision," 14 *Cornell L.Q.* 274 (1929). The author was a United States district court judge in the Southern District of Texas.

162. Thurman Arnold, "Institute Priests and Yale Observers—A Reply to Dean Goodrich," 84 *U. Pa. L. Rev.* 811 (1936); G. Edward White, "The American Law Institute and the Triumph of Modernist Jurisprudence," 15 *Law & Hist. Rev.* 1 (1997).

163. Thurman Arnold, "Leon Green—An Appreciation," 43 *Ill. L. Rev.* 1 (1943).

164. N. E. H. Hull, "Restatement and Reform: A New Perspective on the Origins of the American Law Institute," 8 *Law & Hist. Rev.* 55 (1990).

165. The first-round, late-formalist Restatements were: *Contracts* (1932); *Agency* (1933); *Conflict of Laws* (1934); *Trusts* (1935); *Restitution* (1937); *Torts* (1939); *Security* (1941); *Judgments* (1942); and *Property* (1944).

166. Gilmore, *Death of Contract*, 59.

167. Joseph Singer quotes the cliché in "Legal Realism Now," 503.

168. Inter al., Lon Fuller, "American Legal Realism," 82 *U. Pa. L. Rev.* 429 (1934).

169. Schlegel, in *American Legal Realism and Empirical Social Science*, labors to redeem the realists from the charge that their empirical work was trivial.

170. Grant Gilmore, "Legal Realism: Its Cause and Cure," 70 *Yale L.J.* 1037 (1961).

171. New York Central R.R. v. White, 243 U.S. 188 (1917); Mountain Timber Co. v. Washington, 243 U.S. 219 (1917).

172. Lawrence M. Friedman and Jack Ladinsky, "Social Change and the Law of Industrial Accidents," 67 *Colum. L. Rev.* 50 (1967).

173. Massachusetts v. Mellon and Frothingham v. Mellon, 262 U.S. 447 (1923).

174. Grain Futures Trading Act, ch. 86, 42 Stat. 187, held unconstitutional in Hill v. Wallace, 259 U.S. 44 (1922).

175. 209 U.S. 123 (1908).

176. Act of 3 March 1910, ch. 48, 36 Stat. 1087, also providing appeal as of right from a restraining order issued by the panel; expanded in 1913 and 1925 to cover permanent injunctions and state administrative proceedings.

177. Act of 14 May 1934, ch. 283, 48 Stat. 775.

178. Act of 21 Aug. 1937, ch. 726, 50 Stat. 738.

179. Act of 23 March 1932, ch. 90, 47 Stat. 70; upheld in Lauf v. E. G. Shinner & Co., 303 U.S. 323 (1938).

180. 239 U.S. 22 (1915) (federal injunction against enforcement of a state statute prohibiting employer from hiring more than specified percentage of aliens).

181. 257 U.S. 312 (1921) (holding unconstitutional a state statute prohibiting the use of injunctions to halt picketing). The appellant in this and the preceding case was the same person, William Truax, a restaurateur of Bisbee, Arizona, a fact that suggests that he was making a career or crusade of challenging state legislation regulating employment relationships. Bisbee, not coincidentally, was the site of the infamous Bisbee deportations of 1917, in which hundreds of striking workers were herded onto railroad cars and dropped off to languish in the middle of the New Mexico desert.

182. On the problems of federal diversity jurisdiction and its abuses, see Purcell, *Litigation and Inequality*.

183. 304 U.S. 64 (1938).

184. Declaratory Judgment Act of 1934, ch. 512, 48 Stat. 955; upheld in Aetna Life Insurance Co. v. Haworth, 300 U.S. 227 (1937) with no objection from Justice Brandeis, who would have been sensitive to such a major expansion of federal jurisdiction if it threatened regulatory or reform legislation.

185. Act of 30 Aug. 1935, ch. 829, § 405, 49 Stat. 1014.

186. Progressive Platform, 1924, in Kirk H. Porter, ed., *National Party Platforms* (1973), vol. 1, 252–254.

187. G. Edward White, *Tort Law in America: An Intellectual History* (1980), 92–113.

188. Leon Green, *Rationale of Proximate Cause* (1927), 132–141.

189. 217 N.Y. 382 (1916). For a general evaluation of Cardozo's impact on tort law, see Warren A. Seavey, "Mr. Justice Cardozo and the Law of Torts," 52 *Harv. L. Rev.* 372 (1938).

190. Palsgraf v. Long Island Railroad, 248 N.Y. 339, 344, 341, 352, 354 (1928).

191. John T. Noonan, *Persons and Masks of the Law: Cardozo, Holmes, Jefferson, and Wythe as Makers of the Masks* (1976), 111–151.

192. Fowler V. Harper, *A Treatise on the Law of Torts* (1933), 258.

193. William L. Prosser, *Handbook of the Law of Torts* [1st ed.] (1941), 212.

194. Candor compels me to note that Corbin denied that Cardozo had revolutionized the law of contracts, but had rather merely nudged it along in evolutionary directions: "Mr. Justice Cardozo and the Law of Contracts," 52 *Harv. L. Rev.* 408 (1938). I believe Corbin's evaluation was understated.

195. Arthur L. Corbin, *Corbin on Contracts: A Comprehensive Treatise on the Rules of Contract Law* (1963), vol. 1, § 109.

196. Moran v. Standard Oil Co., 211 N.Y. 187, 198 (1914).

197. Wood v. Lucy, Lady Duff-Gordon, 222 N.Y. 88 (1917).

198. 221 N.Y. 431 (1917).

199. Allegheny College v. National Chautauqua County Bank, 246 N.Y. 369 (1927).

200. Gilmore, *Death of Contract*, 55–72.

201. *Restatement of Contracts* (1932), § 75; Holmes, *The Common Law*, in Novick, ed., *Collected Works of Holmes*, vol. 3, 265 ("reciprocal conventional inducement, each for the other, between consideration and promise").

202. *Restatement of Contracts* (1932), § 90.

203. Gilmore, *Death of Contract*, 61.

204. Horwitz, *Transformation II*, ch. 5, "The Progressive Transformation in the Conception of Property."

205. Robert L. Hale, "Rate Making and the Revision of the Property Concept," 22 *Colum. L. Rev.* 209, 214 (1922); Morris R. Cohen, "Property and Sovereignty," 13 *Cornell L.Q.* 8 (1927). I should note that Morris Cohen (not his son Felix) was a prominent critic of the realists.

206. Dolan v. Tigard, 114 S. Ct. 2309, 2316 (1994), per Rehnquist, C.J., quoting Kaiser Aetna v. United States, 444 U.S. 164, 176 (1979).

207. 114 S. Ct. 2326–2327 (Stevens, J., dissenting).

208. 248 U.S. 215, 246 (1918) (Holmes, J., concurring).

209. Cohen, "Property and Sovereignty," 17.

210. Robert L. Hale, "Coercion and Distribution in a Supposedly Non-Coercive State," *Political Science Quarterly* 38 (1923), 470.

211. 245 U.S. 60 (1917).

212. In Alexander M. Bickel and Benno C. Schmidt Jr., *The Judiciary and Responsible Government, 1910–1921* (vol. 9 of the Holmes Devise *History of the Supreme Court of the United States*), 729–819 (1984), Dean Schmidt emphasizes the ideal of racial justice.

213. Shelley v. Kraemer, 334 U.S. 1 (1948).

214. 95 U.S. 714 (1877).

215. Scarcely: see Burnham v. Superior Court, 495 U.S. 604 (1990), per Scalia, J.

216. Hess v. Pawloski, 274 U.S. 352 (1927).

217. 326 U.S. 310 (1945).

218. William M. Wiecek, "The Place of Chief Judge Irving Lehman in American Constitutional Development," *American Jewish Historical Quarterly* 60 (1971), 280.

219. 237 N.Y. 316 (1924).

220. 237 N.Y. 316, 328 (1924).

221. J. H. & S. Theatres, Inc. v. Fay, 260 N.Y. 315 (1932); Interborough Rapid Transit Co. v. Lavin, 247 N.Y. 65 (1928).

222. People v. Weller, 237 N.Y. at 332.

223. Alexander M. Bickel, ed., *The Unpublished Opinions of Mr. Justice Brandeis: The Supreme Court at Work* (1957).

224. 297 U.S. 288, 341 (1936) (Brandeis, J., concurring).

225. Di Santo v. Pennsylvania, 273 U.S. 34, 44 (1927).

226. Schenck v. United States, 249 U.S. 47 (1919); Frohwerk v. United States, 249 U.S. 204 (1919); Debs v. United States, 249 U.S. 211 (1919); Abrams v. United States, 250 U.S. 616 (1919); Schaefer v. United States, 251 U.S. 466 (1920); Pierce v. United States 252 U.S. 239 (1920); Gilbert v. Minnesota, 254 U.S. 325 (1920); Milwaukee Social Democratic Publishing Co. v. Burleson, 255 U.S. 407 (1921); Gitlow v. New York, 268 U.S. 652 (1925).

227. Brandenburg v. United States, 393 U.S. 948 (1969).

228. Whitney v. California, 274 U.S. 357, 376–377 (1927).

229. Max Lerner, "Constitution and Court as Symbols," 46 *Yale L.J.* 1290 (1937).

Chapter Five

The Collapse of
Legal Classicism,
1930–1942

The constitutional revolution of 1937–1938[1] resembled other revolutions of modern times. At the outset, the *ancien régime* seemed impervious to challenge. The collapse, when it came, was shockingly sudden. The authority of the old order disintegrated almost embarrassingly, and its fragmented resistance was soon mopped up by the new regime. With hindsight, we now see that classical legal thought had advanced far in decay by 1937. But nevertheless, after the seemingly absolute dominance of classical premises in the 1920s, and the succession of cases in 1935–1936 reviewed in this chapter, the abrupt destruction of a dominant way of thinking about law was dramatic.

The story told in this chapter is a familiar one,[2] perhaps grown threadbare in the retelling. But it is still worth our effort to retrace the conflict of ideas as they contended in the armageddon of legal doctrines, where the nineteenth century and its law ways confronted the modern world for the last time.

After an initially hospitable but five-to-four reception of regulatory power to cope with the distress of the Great Depression, the Supreme Court reverted to classicist negativism. The conservative bloc of the Court, Justices George Sutherland, Willis Van Devanter, James McReynolds, and Pierce Butler, repudiated nearly every federal and state initiative that came before them to cope with economic turmoil. In a frenzy of obstruction, they lurched beyond restraint to stymie all economic regulation and to enthrone the mouldering dogmas of *Knight*, *Lochner*, and *Adkins* atop the Constitution once again.

President Franklin D. Roosevelt responded with the politically misbegotten court-packing plan, which was stillborn in the Senate.[3] It is a bit more than a half-truth that he lost the battle but won the war. The Court itself, even before the president reconstituted it, disavowed classicism and all its works. The Roosevelt Court devised new doctrinal approaches to assure that economic substantive due process remained entombed.

The Ride of the Four Horsemen

Early Affirmation of the Police Power

In the 1932 presidential election, American voters rejected what they had come to see as the Hoover administration's ineffectual response to three years of economic depression. The electorate voiced hope, if not confidence, in FDR's vague assurances of action and change. At first, the Supreme Court responded to the resulting initiatives equivocally.

In the 1930 Term, after Hughes and Roberts had replaced Taft and Sanford, the Court handed down several decisions suggesting that the old classical paradigm might be breaking up. It sustained state regulation of fees charged by insurance brokerages,[4] struck down a state ban on display of the red flag as a symbol of opposition to organized government,[5] and voided a state statute prohibiting publication of a "malicious, scandalous and defamatory newspaper."[6]

But by 1932, Justice Owen Roberts displayed his distressing tendency to move unpredictably, if not erratically, in and out of the paradigm, and the Court seemed to revert back to its 1920s trajectory. In March 1932, it struck down an Oklahoma statute prohibiting the state corporations commission from issuing a business license for ice making where an ice company already existed.[7] Justice Sutherland held simply that the enactment was an arbitrary interference with private business activity, apparently assuming that for that reason it violated the due process clause. Brandeis in dissent reviewed the facts of the ice business in Oklahoma at length, a typically Progressive approach to the problem of adjudication. He reminded the Court that it was not free to substitute its opinions about economic conditions in Oklahoma for that of the state's legislature. In one of his most frequently quoted aphorisms, Brandeis repeated his *Whitney* call for civic courage: "[W]e must be ever on our guard, lest we erect our prejudices into legal principles. If we would guide by the light of reason, we must let our minds be bold. . . . There must be power in the states and the nation to remould, through experimentation, our economic practices and institutions to meet changing social and economic needs."

But after November 1932, it seemed for a time as if the Court did indeed follow the election returns. It — or five members of it, at any rate — appeared ready to acknowledge the electorate's demand for responsive and effective government. In doing so, the Court seemed about to venture outside the limits of the classical paradigm again, not so much abandoning it as asserting that other approaches to constitutional governance could coexist with it, as they had since the turn of the century.

The Court first eluded classical confines in *Home Building and Loan Association v. Blaisdell* (1934),[8] where a five-member majority, speaking through Chief Justice Charles Evans Hughes, returned to the spirit of John Marshall's great dictum, "[W]e must never forget that it is a constitution we are expounding, . . . a Constitution . . . to be adapted to the various crises of human affairs."[9] Upholding a state moratorium on mortgage payments, Hughes acknowledged the postclassical world of the twentieth century, in which legislatures and courts must make "a rational compromise between individual rights and public welfare. The settlement and consequent contraction of the public domain, the pressure of a constantly increasing density of population, the interrelation of the activities of our people and the complexity of our economic interests," made state intervention in the economy necessary "to protect the very bases of individual opportunity." In such a changed environment, "the question is no longer merely that of one party to a contract as against another, but of the use of reasonable means to safeguard the economic structure upon which the good of all depends."

Justice Sutherland,[10] speaking for the four dissenters, attributed the nation's economic distress to "public or private extravagance." He insisted that "a provision of the Constitution does not mean one thing at one time and an entirely different thing at another time." Sutherland obtusely quoted and applauded Chief Justice Roger B. Taney's insistence in the *Dred Scott Case* (1857) that

> while the Constitution remains unaltered, it must be construed now as it was understood at the time of its adoption; that it is not only the same in words but the same in meaning, and as long as it continues to exist in its present form, it speaks not only in the same words, but with the same meaning and intent with which it spoke when it came from the hands of its framers, and was voted on and adopted by the people of the United States. Any other rule of construction would abrogate the judicial character of this court, and make it the mere reflex of the popular opinion or passion of the day.[11]

From this, Sutherland drew the conclusion that the meaning of the Constitution is "changeless." He relied on that perennial resort of conservative constitutionalism, "plain-meaning" interpretive strategy, to preserve an ideologically pure approach: the Constitution spoke "in such plain English words that it would seem the ingenuity of man could not evade them."

Hughes dismissed such embalmed constitutionalism as beneath consideration: "[I]f by the statement that what the Constitution meant at the time of its adoption it means to-day, it is intended to say that the great clauses of the Constitution must be confined to the interpretation which the framers, with the conditions and outlook of their time, would have placed upon them, the statement carries its own refutation."

In that same term, the Court, again by a five-to-four margin, upheld the states' police power when exercised to control retail milk prices so as to stabilize competition among producers. In *Nebbia v. New York* (1934), Justice Roberts sustained the police power against vague property and contracts challenges: "[N]either property rights nor contract rights are absolute; for government cannot exist if the citizen may at will use his property to the detriment of his fellows, or exercise his freedom of contract to work them harm. Equally fundamental with the private right is that of the public to regulate it in the common interest."[12] Roberts vindicated the police power in broad terms, greatly extending *Munn*: "[T]here is no closed class or category of businesses affected with a public interest. . . . [That phrase] can, in the nature of things, mean no more than that an industry, for adequate reason, is subject to control for the public good." Roberts denied that courts could pass on the policy of legislation. Justice McReynolds, speaking for the conservatives in dissent, proclaimed otherwise: "[P]lainly, I think, this Court must have regard to the wisdom of the enactment."

The Court also upheld federal monetary power in the group of decisions known collectively as the *Gold Clause Cases* (1935).[13] Chief Justice Hughes sustained Congress's power to suspend specie payments and held that private obligations could be paid off in legal tender, not gold. Because they were not commodity contracts but rather simply required payment in money, such provisions were subject to Congress's monetary powers. Hughes did find the government's abrogation of the specie payment clause in federal obligations unconstitutional, but held that the plaintiff had suffered only nominal damages and would have been unjustly enriched by payment in specie.

Hughes could hardly have ruled otherwise: a holding forcing specie payments under the deflationary conditions of 1935 would have had a catastrophic effect on the national economy. The windfall wealth transfer to the rich would have been achieved at the cost of near-universal bankruptcy of both business and governmental authorities. The dollar amount of ordinary residential mortgage payments would have increased by an estimated 69 percent.[14] But that did not deter the conservatives from denouncing the result, with Justice McReynolds departing from the written text of his dissent to splutter: "[T]he impending legal and moral chaos is appalling. As for the Constitution, it does not seem too much to say that it is gone. Shame and humiliation are upon us now! This is Nero at his worst."[15]

Federal regulatory power enjoyed one last autumnal victory in 1936, when the Court upheld Congress's power to create the Tennessee Valley Authority, finding its authority in the commerce and defense powers. However, Chief Justice Hughes, writing for the Court, made a dangerous procedural concession to those who would challenge any exercise of federal authority, by reaffirming the validity of shareholder suits against officers and directors of a corporation to enjoin them from "yielding . . . to governmental demands which are without warrant of law or are in violation of constitutional restrictions."[16] This was an invitation to conservatives to use the device of stockholder litigation to challenge federal and state regulatory authority. It threatened a proliferation of such suits throughout the United States, overwhelming the capacity of the Justice Department, the solicitor general's office, and the United States attorneys to respond adequately to the flood of litigation.

Brandeis, who while in practice had been one of the nation's leading corporate lawyers, saw this danger and in a concurrence called for judicial self-restraint. He laid out the terms of an authentically conservative constitutional jurisprudence (as opposed to the radical-reactionary course of the anti–New Deal bloc), by enumerating seven prudential rules to control judicial hubris:

- Refuse jurisdiction of collusive suits.
- Do not anticipate constitutional issues before they must be decided.
- Do not devise constitutional rules broader than necessary.
- Do not pass on constitutional questions if a nonconstitutional issue in the case might be dispositive.
- Require plaintiff to show injury.
- Decline relief to a plaintiff who has benefited from the statute challenged.
- Construe statutes in a way that avoids the constitutional question.

Brandeis recited a litany of authorities, including Chief Justice Marshall, to remind his activist brethren that "in no doubtful case, would [the Court] pronounce a legislative act to be contrary to the constitution."[17] Hughes himself, in a 1928 book written between his two terms of service on the Court, had similarly identified "principles which [the Justices] adopted for the control of their exercise of the judicial power." He cautioned the Court not "to aggrandize itself at the expense of either executive or legislature."[18] The conservatives of 1936 were in no mood to heed counsels of restraint, but when legal classicism had been interred, the Supreme Court a decade later affirmed the wisdom of Brandeis's prudential restraints.[19]

The Early New Deal

Conservative lawyers, including the elite of the corporate bar, mounted a comprehensive assault on New Deal governmental regulatory power, drawing on absolutist conceptions of property and contract rights. The Liberty League, its Lawyers' Vigilance Committee and National Lawyers' Committee, and even the American Bar Association itself subsidized briefs, books, pamphlets, and speeches attacking regulatory capability and demanding a return to the eternal verities of classical belief.

America's legal elite was torn in its response to the New Deal, however. They did not oppose state and federal initiatives simply because they were corporate lackeys doing the bidding of their capitalist masters. Rather, as heirs of classical legal thought, they viewed law as neutral, scientific, apolitical. It was created primarily and preferably by judges through common law adjudication. The proliferation of statutes and legislative policy, the rise of the administrative state, and the general air of uncertainty that accompanies serious change were all unsettling to the corporate bar. Thus their response reflected concerns about the place of the legal profession in American society as much as it did ideological resistance to activist government.[20]

A closely coordinated network of the corporate bar produced countless books, wrote articles in both the professional and the popular press, spoke live and on radio, testified before Congress, lobbied, and organized the American Bar Association committees to challenge New Deal initiatives. One of the most widely noted of these attacks was an ABA-sponsored radio address delivered in December 1934 by John W. Davis, former United States solicitor general and 1924 Democratic presidential candidate.[21] Davis laid out criteria by which the constitutionality of New Deal legislation should be judged: The Constitution created a federal government of limited and delegated powers. Separation-of-powers doctrine prohibited delegation of legislative power. Regulation of interstate commerce must be confined to *Knight* limitations. The due process clause of the Fifth Amendment protected individuals from governmental intrusion into their affairs. The power of taxation could not be used for regulatory purposes. Davis's address was a synopsis of classical constitutional doctrine and a shot across the bow of the New Deal. "I do not know of any shelter whatever in the fundamental law of the land, written or unwritten, express or implied, for many of the activities in which the Federal Government is now engaged," he intoned.

A sympathetic, conservative federal judiciary was standing by, eager to implement the Liberty League's agenda and stymie national power. Federal district court judges, predominantly Republican appointees, issued some sixteen hundred injunctions in the October 1935 Term alone, prohibiting enforcement of federal statutes.[22]

In October 1935, the Justices moved out of the old Senate chamber into their recently completed courtroom and chambers in the Marble Palace on First Street.

The majesty of the $10 million facility daunted its new inhabitants. Justice Stone, gazing at the massive Corinthian-columned central portico, with its great bronze doors opening onto the colonnaded hall, commented: "[W]hen I look at that building, I feel that when the Justices go to work, they ought to ride in on elephants." One of his brethren remarked, "I wonder if we will look like nine black beetles in the Temple of Karnak." The first arguments in the new courtroom demonstrated that splendor had its drawbacks, though: acoustics were terrible at first in the chamber. Velvet curtains had to be added to intercept arguments made inaudible by bouncing off the marble-clad walls.[23]

The new Supreme Court building was a physical symbol of the spirit of legal classicism, promoted by its high priest, Chief Justice Taft, who personally chose its architect, the neoclassical exponent Cass Gilbert. The building is impressive, neoclassical in spirit, balanced, dignified, imposing, reverential, symmetrical, majestic, intimidating, dramatic, and above all, awe-inspiring. Its spirit radiates hostility to innovation. The pseudomythological figures flanking the steps and composing the frieze on the pediment symbolize power, authority, law, and, in feminine and subordinated forms, equity and justice.[24] To the extent that the building was a symbol of classical legal consciousness, the move uncannily bore out one of Parkinson's "laws": "[P]erfection of planned layout is achieved only by institutions on the point of collapse."[25] The Marble Palace provided a fitting theater for classicism's grand finale, the two Terms of 1934–1936.

The last act began with the "Hot Oil Case," *Panama Refining Co. v. Ryan* (1935), which vindicated the lawyer-conservatives' challenge to delegation of legislative power.[26] The outcome of the case was unobjectionable: Chief Justice Hughes castigated the sloppy drafting of the petroleum code under the National Industrial Recovery Act. Justices Brandeis and McReynolds[27] excoriated the unavailability of published versions of the oil code, a deficiency immediately remedied by creation of the *Federal Register*. But Hughes's blast at legislative irresponsibility was the first breeze of a storm that would reach tempest levels within the year.

Next, the Court split five-to-four to void the federal Railroad Retirement Pension Act on the grounds that its application to different categories of employees was "arbitrary," a judgment that required Justice Owen Roberts to evaluate the details and reasonableness of the pension scheme.[28] He held that it violated the due process clause and hinted that it might also constitute an unconstitutional taking. Roberts returned to *Knight* conceptions of interstate commerce, holding that railroad employee pensions lacked any real relationship to interstate commerce. Conservatives hailed the decision as the bellwether of holdings that "would smash any social security legislation that may be passed by Congress."[29]

In the same month (May 1935), the Court, again unanimously, struck down one of the two major legislative pillars of the early New Deal, the National Industrial Recovery Act. The results and much of the *ratio decidendi* in *Schechter Poultry Corp. v. United States* (1935)[30] were also unexceptionable. The statute had been hastily drafted.[31] Congress delegated such excessive power to the president and through him to private groups to regulate production segments of the national economy that Cardozo could not be faulted for exclaiming that "this is delegation running riot." The Court's determination that the business in question, a kosher market on Long Island that did its own chicken slaughtering, went on outside the flow of interstate commerce, was sensible and realistic. Yet Hughes's opinion for the Court was redolent of a *Knight*-era conception of commerce, grounded on the metaphysical distinction between direct and indirect effects.

In the second of the so-called Black Monday decisions (all unanimous) handed down on 27 May, *Lousville Bank v. Radford*, Brandeis held that the Frazier-Lemke Farm Bankruptcy Act violated the takings clause of the Fifth Amendment by forcing the mortgagee-bank to accept the mortgagor's repurchase of mortgaged farm property at current appraised value, and to accept payment of less than the full amount of the mortgage.[32] This suggested that the takings clause might bar measures that the Court thought redistributed wealth from creditor to debtor.

FDR was dismayed that even Cardozo and Brandeis had deserted him on Black Monday ("What about old Isaiah?" he wailed to Donald Richberg), and grumbled at his next press conference that the decision had thrust the nation back into "the horse and buggy age."[33] In reality, *Schechter* may well have rescued from him from a grotesque administrative contraption that was fast proving unworkable and unpopular. Viewed on its merits, the National Industrial Recovery Act was an experiment in de facto cartelization of the national economy that had gotten out of hand, surrendering national economic policy-making to the industry leg of the industry-labor-consumer stool that the act had originally envisioned. FDR, understandably, did not see it that way. The journalist George Creel quoted the president as saying that if "the present generation is powerless to meet social and economic problems that were not within the knowledge of the Founding Fathers . . . then the President will have no other alternative than to go to the country with a constitutional amendment that will lift the Dead Hand, giving the people of today the right to deal with today's vital issues."[34]

Though temporarily thwarted, the president urged Congress to enact mini-NIRA legislation for the soft coal industry, "leaving to the courts, in an orderly fashion, the ultimate question of constitutionality. A decision by the Supreme Court relative to this measure would be helpful as indicating with increasing clarity the constitutional limits within which this Government must operate."[35] We need not credit this statement as demonstrating FDR's deference to the Court. Only four months earlier, edgily awaiting the outcome of the *Gold Clause Cases*, he was prepared to threaten, vaguely, that "I shall immediately take such steps as may be necessary" to avoid an adverse holding rather than "to stand idly by and to permit the decision of the Supreme Court to be carried through to its logical, inescapable conclusion."[36] Nevertheless, for the time being, the president's relations with an obstructive Court were guided by his respect for the institution, as well as by the expediency and opportunism usually charged to him.

If there was opportunism in the building confrontation, it lay with the Court's conservative bloc. In *Humphrey's Executor v. United States* (1935),[37] the third of the Black Monday decisions, Justice Sutherland implied that FDR had acted illegally in firing a commissioner of the Federal Trade Commission, though in fact the president thought he was complying with the Court's own 1926 directive on dismissal in the executive agencies.[38] The judge was evidently playing his own political game with the president. Sutherland had no aversion to grossly expanded presidential power as such. His opinion in *United States v. Curtiss-Wright Export Corp.* (1936)[39] constituted a sweeping and dangerous affirmation of the president's power to act without legislative impediment or judicial oversight in the conduct of foreign relations. But Sutherland and the other three classicist judges were determined to frustrate New Deal initiatives in the domestic sphere that threatened the existing configuration of wealth and power.

The Final Triumph of Classicism

This confrontation between the judiciary and the political branches escalated in 1936, as luck would have it a presidential election year. The Court's opening salvo, *United States v. Butler* (1936),[40] blasted away the second major pillar of early New Deal policy, the Agricultural Adjustment Act, and the processing tax that funded the crop-reduction and benefits system designed to raise commodity prices.[41] Justice Roberts's opinion for the six-Justice majority was a peculiar effort: progressive in one respect, a reactionary throwback in all others. Its overall effect was to reaffirm the dominating authority of classical thought.

Roberts began with a trope that shrunk one of John Marshall's magisterial assertions to a reductionist formula. In one of his most frequently-cited passages in *Marbury v. Madison* (1803),[42] Marshall had written that

> It is emphatically the province and duty of the judicial department to say what the law is. . . . If two laws conflict with each other, the courts must decide on the operation of each. So if a law be in opposition to the constitution: if both the law and the constitution apply to a particular case, so that the court must either decide that case conformably to the law, disregarding the constitution; or conformably to the constitution, disregarding the law: the court must determine which of these conflicting rules governs the case. This is of the very essence of judicial duty.

This passage has ever since been the foundation of the doctrine of judicial review. Attempting to reaffirm it over a century later, Roberts produced only a burlesque of Marshall's thought.

Roberts approached the problem of judicial review defensively, noting that "it is sometimes said that the Court assumes a power to overrule or control the action of the people's representatives. This is a misconception." Rather, since *Marbury* it had been established that all statutory law must conform to the principles of the Constitution, which is the supreme law. Therefore

> when an act of Congress is appropriately challenged in the courts as not conforming to the constitutional mandate, the judicial branch of the government has only one duty; to lay the article of the Constitution which is invoked beside the statute which is challenged and to decide whether the latter squares with the former. All the court does, or can do, is to announce its considered judgment upon the question. The only power it has, if such it may be called, is the power of judgment. This court neither approves nor condemns any legislative policy.[43]

This sort of "double-column reasoning," casting judges as nothing more than proofreaders or editors, nicely conveyed the image of classical adjudication. Roberts might have meant only to assert innocuously that the Court is concerned with constitutionality, not policy. But his unfortunate choice of visual image has dogged his reputation ever since. In the same vein, his reminder that "ours is a dual form of government" called up the paradigm of dual federalism that had been stalking through the *United States Reports* from Marshall through Taft.

Turning to substance, Roberts first held that the processing tax was not a tax at all, but rather a "mere instrumentality" to achieve some other end, which he identified as regulating agricultural production. (As authority, Roberts cited *Bailey v. Drexel Furniture*, the second child labor tax case.) If not a tax, then the forced exaction for processors had to be "the expropriation of money from one group for the benefit of another." Put *that* way, the problem with the Agricultural Adjustment Act was transformed into the old *Calder* natural law formula of taking from A and giving to B.

Roberts concluded that "the act invades the reserved rights of the states. It is a statutory plan to regulate and control agricultural production, a matter beyond the powers delegated to the federal government" and reserved to the states under the Tenth Amendment. To bolster this point, Roberts insisted that because the federal government "is a government of delegated powers, it follows that those not expressly granted, or reasonably to be implied from such as are conferred, are reserved to the states." With his choice of the word "expressly," Roberts seemed to be converting the Tenth Amendment into the discredited Article II of the old Confederation,[44] as Justice Day had attempted in the first child labor case, *Hammer v. Dagenhart* (1918). Roberts warned that if the Court's vigilance relaxed, "the United States [would be] converted into a central government exercising uncontrolled police power in every state of the Union, superseding all local control or regulation of the affairs or concerns of the states."

Justice Harlan Fiske Stone was not impressed with such hyperbole of federalism. He opened his dissent with unusually blunt language:

> The power of courts to declare a statute unconstitutional is subject to two guiding principles of decision which ought never to be absent from judicial consciousness. One is that courts are concerned only with the power to enact statutes, not with their wisdom. The other is that while unconstitutional exercise of power by the executive and legislative branches of the government is subject to judicial restraint, the only check upon our own exercise of power is our own sense of self-restraint. For the removal of unwise laws from the statute books appeal lies not to the courts but to the ballot and to the processes of democratic government.

He warned that a

> tortured construction of the Constitution is not to be justified by recourse to extreme examples of reckless congressional spending. . . . Such suppositions are addressed to the mind accustomed to believe that it is the business of courts to sit in judgment on the wisdom of legislative action. Courts are not the only agency of government that must be assumed to have capacity to govern.

The admonition was lost on the conservative bloc, though.

Roberts's *Butler* majority opinion offered one curiously forward-looking concession to federal power, however. He noted the surprising fact that the Supreme Court had never resolved the old debate between Madison and Hamilton over the scope of the general welfare clause.[45] Madison had contended that the phrase merely identified what the public moneys might be spent for, and did not convey an independent substantive power.[46] Hamilton, by contrast, maintained in his 1791 *Report on Manufactures* that "[t]he phrase is as comprehensive as any that could have been used; because . . . this necessarily embraces a vast variety of particulars, which are susceptible neither of specification nor of definition. . . . [W]hatever concerns the general Interests of learning of Agriculture of Manufactures and of Commerce are within the sphere of the national Councils as far as regards an application of Money."[47]

Roberts adopted the Hamiltonian position: "The power of Congress to authorize expenditure of public moneys for public purposes is not limited by the direct grants of legislative power found in the Constitution." This enhanced federal powers, but only potentiality. Moreover, it was incompatible with Roberts's suspicious approach to the processing tax. An interpretation in the spirit of Hamilton's spacious vision might have seen the federal taxing and spending powers as adequate to sustain this redistribution of farm income, since the levy would ultimately be paid by the consumer anyway, with the processor being only a tax conduit.

FDR came up with a remarkably prescient prediction about *Butler's* impact. Quoting an unnamed "prominent historian" (Edward S. Corwin?), Roosevelt wrote

> that fifty years from now the Supreme Court's AAA [Agricultural Adjustment Act] decision will, in all probability, be described somewhat as follows:
> 1) The decision virtually prohibits the President and Congress from the right, under modern conditions, to intervene reasonably in the regulation of nation-wide commerce and nation-wide agriculture.
> 2) . . . The objective of the Court's purpose was to make reasonableness in passing legislation a matter to be settled not by the views of the elected Senate and House of Representatives and not by the views of an elected President but rather by the private, social philosophy of a majority of nine appointed members of the Supreme Court itself.[48]

In their eagerness to extend the rights protected under the federal Constitution against state regulation, the Court's conservatives next revived the comatose privileges-and-immunities clause of the Fourteenth Amendment, which had lain aswoon since Justice Miller first constricted it in his *Slaughterhouse* majority opinion. Under nineteenth-century precedent, insurance was not considered an article of interstate commerce, and thus the insurance industry could not be protected from state regulation by invoking the dormant commerce power.[49] The anti–New Deal coalition needed an alternative if it was to strangle state insurance regulation. In *Colgate v. Harvey* (1936),[50] a tax case, Justice Sutherland found that alternative by declaring that "the right of a citizen of the United States to engage in business, to transact any lawful business, or to make a lawful loan of money in any state other than that in which the citizen resides is a privilege equally attributable to his national citizenship," protected by the newly awakened privileges-and-immunities clause of the Fourteenth Amendment. For a brief moment, Field's *Slaughterhouse* dissent stood vindicated at last. But the career of the reawakened privileges-and-immunities clause was to be brief: after the constitutional reversal of 1937, the new Court overruled *Colgate* and sunk it back into *Slaughterhouse's* poisoned sleep.[51] There it continues to slumber today.

Sutherland next took a gratuitous swipe at the newest of the federal regulatory agencies, the Securities Exchange Commission, and more broadly at the larger concept of administrative regulation. In *Jones v. Securities and Exchange Commission* (1936),[52] an applicant seeking to register a stock issue before the SEC sought to withdraw his application, and thus terminate all proceedings, as soon as the commission began an investigation into whether the registration statement violated the Securities Exchange Act (because it contained false statements). Relying on an invalid analogy to equity proceedings, Sutherland held that the petitioner could do so, and then indulged himself in some florid rhetoric:

> [T]he action of the commission finds no support in right principle or in law. It is wholly unreasonable and arbitrary. It violates the cardinal precept upon which the constitutional safeguards of personal liberty ultimately rest — that this shall be a government of laws — because to the precise extent that the mere will of an official or an official body is permitted to take the place of allowable official discretion or to supplant the standing law as a rule of human conduct, the government ceases to be one of laws and becomes an autocracy. Arbitrary power and the rule of the Constitution cannot both exist. They are antagonistic and incompatible forces; and one or the other must of necessity perish whenever they are brought into conflict.

All this, when the commission was merely pursuing its statutory responsibility of suppressing fraudulent securities issues in an action initiated not by it but by the one who hoped to benefit from the allegedly fraudulent statement. The result of *Jones* was to throw a cloak of immunity around purported violators of the securities acts, the real analogy being letting criminal defendants terminate prosecutions at their election. Sutherland's opinion displayed an inflexible hostility to regulatory agencies, then emerging as a principal means of enforcing federal policy.

In *Carter v. Carter Coal Co.* (1936)[53] Sutherland and the other conservatives, joined by the erratic Roberts, pushed the doctrinal envelope in a retrograde direction. They widened the no-man's-land that judicial conservatives from Fuller to Taft had bulldozed into the Constitution.

Carter struck down a reenacted fragment of the National Industrial Recovery Act, the Guffey Act, which imposed price and labor controls on the bituminous coal industry.[54] Aside from doctrine, several aspects of the case struck a sinister note. The suit was collusive, and hence should have been dismissed for lack of jurisdiction. The conservatives brushed this obstacle aside in their eagerness to foster the shareholder suit perfected by the Liberty League in its challenge to the New Deal. Seven major coal-mining states filed amici briefs urging that the act be upheld, yet Sutherland voided the statute in the name of protecting states' rights. Finally, Congress had gone to great lengths to meet the Court's *Schechter* objections, and stated its intent explicitly that the two major titles of the act, relating to prices and wages, should be severable.[55] Sutherland ignored this directive, stating that Congress could not have intended precisely what it stated it *did* intend. He thus sent a clear signal to Congress that the Court was prepared to disregard all indicia of legislative efforts to comply with judicial demands.

Sutherland began by holding that Congress's options with respect to legislative goals were "rigidly limited to the enumerations of the Constitution." He dismissed the vision of national power as extending to all matters in which the states were incompetent as merely a "proposition, often advanced and as often discredited . . . always definitely rejected by this Court." He, too, tried to import a modern version of the "expressly" clause into the Article I enumerations of congressional powers: "[T]he general purposes [of the statute] are beyond the power of Congress except so far, and only so far, as they may be realized by an exercise of some specific power granted by the Constitution."

Stressing that congressional powers were "enumerated," Sutherland attempted to push back the clock of constitutional development to 1798–1800, when Jefferson and Madison laid the foundations of a states'-rights constitutionalism in the Virginia and Kentucky Resolutions and Madison's Report. The Framers, he argued, "meant to carve from the general mass of legislative powers, then possessed by the states, only such portions as it was thought wise to confer upon the federal government; . . . the national powers of legislation were not aggregated but enumerated — with the result that what was not embraced by the enumeration remained vested in the states without change or impairment."

Having resurrected the states'-rights constitutional tradition from the grave where it had been laid in 1865, Sutherland then fast-forwarded thirty years and reinstated *Knight* conceptions of the federal commerce power, including both the direct/indirect and the manufacturing/commerce distinctions. "The distinction is not formal, but substantial in the highest degree." (Cardozo, dissenting, replied that "a great principle of constitutional law is not susceptible of comprehensive statement in an adjective." Rather, "the power is as broad as the need that evokes it.")

Finally, Sutherland performed a judicial contortionist's act, disregarding Congress's explicit assertion of its intent as if it did not exist. He hypothecated instead a fictive legislative intent, while ignoring the real one. "The conclusion is unavoidable that the price-fixing provisions of the code are so related to and dependent upon the labor provisions . . . as to make it clearly probable that the latter being held bad, the former would not have been passed."

Given his premises, Sutherland might have as easily expended his effort in voiding the price, rather than the wage, provisions of the Guffey Act. By ignoring the severability title, he could have achieved the same end. Was there a significance in his choice of target? By May 1936, when *Carter* was decided, a second round of New Deal legislation was coming up before the Court. More carefully drafted than the first, the work of young lawyers with a less nationalizing outlook, the later legislation included the National Labor Relations Act, the Social Security Act, the Public Utility Holding Company Act, the Securities Act, the Securities Exchange Act, and the Government Contracts Act. The first two in particular, as successors to the National Industrial Recovery Act and the Agricultural Adjustment Act, were foundations for a new economic and regulatory system, potentially more far-reaching than their predecessors. It is likely that Sutherland intended his painstaking effort in *Carter* to recast the foundations of American constitutionalism, his lengthy quotations from precedent, and his considered, backward-looking concepts of federalism, to erect an impregnable fortress against all New Deal innovations and their state counterparts.

This supposition is supported by the last major case in which the conservative bloc tried to cordon off the line of precedents that accommodated state and federal regulatory power, *Morehead v. Tipaldo* (1936).[56] New York enacted a minimum-wage law covering women and children, striving to distinguish it from the statute struck down in *Adkins* by requiring that the state commission take the fair value of services provided into account when setting the minimum wage. Justice Butler, writing for a majority of the four conservatives plus Roberts, disregarded this difference, held the statute indistinguishable from that struck down in *Adkins*, and on a note of judicial triumphalism, reaffirmed the older precedent: "[I]n making contracts of employment, generally speaking, the parties have equal right to obtain from each other the best terms they can by private bargaining. Legislative abridgement of that freedom can only be justified by the existence of exceptional circumstances. Freedom of contract is the general rule and restraint the exception."

Such ideas of individualism, imputed equality of bargaining power, and Darwinian struggle had a distinctly otherworldly quality in the 1930s. It was as if Butler and his colleagues were detached from reality. Anyone not blindered by ideological predisposition would have agreed with Max Weber:

> The formal right of a worker to enter into any contract whatsoever with any employer whatsoever does not in practice represent for the employment seeker even the slightest freedom in the determination of his own conditions of work, and it does not guarantee him any influence on this process. It rather means . . . that the more powerful party in the market, i.e., normally the employer, has the [power] to set the terms, to offer the job "take it or leave it," and, given the normally pressing economic need of the workers, to impose his terms on him. The result of contractual freedom, then, is . . . power over others.[57]

Hughes in dissent attempted to distinguish the two statutes, but Stone called for a reconsideration of *Adkins*, insisting that "it is not for the courts" to choose among economic theories. "The legislature must be free to choose unless government is to be rendered impotent. The Fourteenth Amendment has no more embedded in the Constitution our preference for some particular set of economic beliefs, than it has adopted, in the name of liberty, the system of theology which we may happen to approve."

The significance of *Morehead v. Tipaldo* must be seen in relation to *Carter*, decided three weeks earlier. In *Carter*, Sutherland minimized federal regulatory power over the conditions of labor. *Morehead* achieved the same result for state power. Between them, they reinstated the no-man's-land where neither government could regulate and widened it even beyond the spacious breadth established by the Taft Court in the 1920s. After these two opinions, a reasonable observer might have concluded, no government in the United States could regulate wages or hours.

FDR understood this. In a news conference, he denounced *Morehead*: "[T]he 'no-man's land' where no Government — State or Federal — can function is being more clearly defined. A State cannot do it, and the Federal Government cannot do it."[58] The results of these decisions justified Justice Stone's privately expressed judgment: the 1935–1936 Term was "in many ways one of the most disastrous in [the Court's] history."[59] The corporate bar that had been recruited into the Liberty League cheered the majority's anti–New Deal posture. One of their number, Raoul Desvernine, exulted: "[T]he judiciary has again proved itself to be the bulwark of defense against the subtle and skilful manipulation of democratic processes to achieve unsanctioned theories."[60]

The Wagner Act was then on its way to the Supreme Court for review. If the five-judge *Carter/Morehead* majority were to prevail, it was certainly doomed, given the hostility of classicist jurists to labor unions. Federal and state inability to regulate the terms and conditions of labor would leave labor relations in the world's most advanced industrial power a chaos of massed employer might confronting atomized labor. Meanwhile, in the world beyond First Street, American workers and their unions had achieved unprecedented organization and were about to deploy innovative tactics like the sit-down strike. Like trains approaching each other on a single track, classicist judicial dogma and social reality were speeding toward a head-on collision.

The Court-Packing Struggle

The stasis in government that was imposed by classicist dogmatism frustrated the president and led him to his ill-advised court-packing plan.[61] FDR had been an indifferent law student at Columbia and had not made a significant mark as a lawyer in his three years of private practice. But he followed the Court's decisions keenly and probed the thinking of lawyers and judges for ideas about dealing with the Court's obdurate stance. He had been critical of the Court ever since the 1932 campaign, even before the Justices handed down the line of anti–New Deal decisions that began in 1935. For almost two years, though, he tried to avoid a confrontation with the Justices. Even then, in what might anachronistically be called the period of the phony war, the president and his advisors, principally Attorney General Homer Cummings (who was to play the key role in the Court-packing struggle), considered schemes for expanding the Court or ridding it of superannuated justices. The precedent of Prime Minister Herbert Asquith's 1911 threat to pack the House of Lords surfaced occasionally in speculations.

The confrontation between Court and White House began in earnest with the first of the adverse decisions in January 1935 and then escalated. The favorable result in the *Gold Clause Cases* did little to soothe rising apprehension among the president's intimates, but they could not agree on what to do about the recalcitrant tribunal. The shock of the Black Monday decisions in May 1935 goaded Roosevelt into action. He called a press conference to express his misgivings about the Court's decisions. Dramatically arranging a stack of telegrams from citizens demanding action next to a copy of the *Schechter* decision, FDR criticized the Court's course, spoke in vague terms about restoring federal powers, and said, "[W]e have been relegated to the horse-and-buggy definition of interstate commerce.[62] This statement, which sounds bland today, nevertheless roused a furor of criticism, which may have curbed the president's impetuosity.

The White House considered various constitutional amendments, but after a year's deliberations, the president came to the conclusion that the amendment process would be too slow and too easy to frustrate, especially in the ratification process, where the New Deal's opponents could have readily bought off one house of a quarter of the state legislatures. Congress, meanwhile, stirred with proposals of its own, bills reflecting the various court-curbing schemes that had surfaced in 1912 and 1924. All languished in committee.

The president continued to bide his time, hoping to build up a reservoir of public demand for action to back whatever course he might eventually elect. He planted a trial balloon in the popular magazine *Colliers* via George Creel:

[I]f it is held that one hundred and fifty years have no bearing on the case, and that the present generation is powerless to meet social and economic problems that were not within the knowledge of the founding fathers, and therefore not made the subject of their specific consideration, then the President will have no other alternative than to go to the country with a Constitutional amendment that will lift the Dead Hand.[63]

Urged on by Cummings and Harold Ickes, the president kept consideration of different measures churning, without committing himself to any one particular solution. As 1935 slid into 1936, FDR held back for political considerations imposed by the upcoming presidential campaign: he did not want to appear too radical or too ready to lay profane hands on the sacred institutions of Court and Constitution. Ickes believed that his boss was actually hoping that the Court would sink all the New Deal measures coming before it, expecting that this would produce a popular groundswell for whatever he might eventually propose.[64]

The decisions of 1936 (*Ashwander* excepted) dissipated what little resistance there was left within the administration to some kind of confrontation with the Court. *Morehead v. Tipaldo* persuaded even some conservatives that the Court's course had to be redirected. Herbert Hoover, from his sullen retirement, called for a constitutional amendment empowering the states to legislate, as did the Republican Party in its campaign platform.

After FDR's unprecedented sweep of forty-six states in the November elections, Cummings and Justice Department lawyers worked out the final terms of the court-packing bill. The president clamped tight secrecy on their labors and maintained it until he sent the plan to Congress in February 1937. Its principal provision would have enabled the president to nominate as many as six additional Justices to the Supreme Court, and a total of fifty for all federal courts, for every sitting jurist who reached the age of seventy and did not retire. The proposal contained several other less controversial jurisdictional provisions. One would have authorized direct appeal of district court constitutional holdings to the Supreme Court. Another would have required notice to the Justice Department, and opportunity for participation by federal attorneys, before a district court enjoined enforcement of an act of Congress. This was eventually salvaged from the debacle of the plan and enacted.[65]

The substance of the proposal was flawed, and its political execution bungled. FDR's tight secrecy hurt rather than helped. His refusal to consult with members of Congress was ultimately to prove fatal, politically. Worst of all, it was obvious to everyone that the president was being disingenuous in his original justification for the bill, which claimed that aged jurists were not able to carry on the work of the courts. This was needlessly dishonest and antagonized the elderly Hughes and Brandeis. In a tactless yet weak nod to his real motives, the president asserted in his message accompanying the bill that "lower mental or physical vigor leads men to avoid an examination of complicated and changed conditions. Little by little, new facts become blurred through old glasses fitted, as it were, for the needs of another generation; older men, assuming that the scene is the same as it was in the past, cease to explore or inquire into the present or the future."[66] Maybe, but the president appeared to be dissembling in his emphasis on enfeeblement rather than ideology.

Senate Majority Leader Joe Robinson, likely to be FDR's next nomination to the Court, fought for the bill loyally despite his misgivings about its merits. There was some public support for the measure, but not what FDR had expected. Key congressional Democrats in both houses, including the chairs of the judiciary committees, were opposed. At best, the bill's political prospects were doubtful, and dwindled over time.

Then the Court itself fired two torpedoes into the hull of the bill. On March 29, the five-to-four majority swung around to support of state regulatory power in the *West Coast Hotel* decision,[67] and on May 18, Justice Van Devanter announced his retirement. The Senate Judiciary Committee recommended that the court-packing bill "be so emphatically rejected that its parallel will never again be presented to the free representatives of the free people of America." It was an "invasion of judicial power such as has never before been attempted in this country, . . . a vicious precedent which must necessarily undermine our system."[68]

Despite such opposition, FDR and Robinson kept the bill precariously alive into a hot Washington summer. But when Robinson dropped dead of a heart attack on 14 July 1937, the bill died with him. The Senate voted to recommit, effectively killing it.

FDR himself endorsed the popular cliché of the day, that he may have lost the battle but had won the war. After *West Coast Hotel*, the Court systematically dismantled the entire doctrinal structure of legal classicism. Sutherland and McReynolds followed Van Devanter into retirement; Butler died while still a sitting Justice. Roosevelt ultimately got nine judicial appointments, more than any president since Washington.[69]

But the president's triumph came at an appalling cost. The court-packing struggle dissipated much of the political capital that FDR had amassed by his sweeping second-term victory. A powerful anti–New Deal coalition formed in Congress,[70] and Democrats found it easier to desert the president. After the Court struggle, FDR eked out only one more major enactment of the New Deal, the Fair Labor Standards Act, before being overtaken by foreign-policy crises. Henry Wallace exaggerated in reminiscence, but with some truth: "[T]he whole New Deal really went up in smoke as a result of the Supreme Court fight."[71] The Democratic Party and the New Deal coalition began their long-drawn-out disintegration. Paradoxically and ironically, the Court itself emerged heightened in public esteem.

Contemporaries contemplating the events of 1937 thought that a constitutional revolution had taken place. Edward S. Corwin, the nation's preeminent constitutional authority, entitled his retrospective, *Constitutional Revolution, Ltd.* (1941). Conservatives witnessing the repudiation of legal classicism might be expected to indulge in hyperbole, but the sense that a revolution had taken place was not confined to the right wing of the politicoideological spectrum. With the perspective of a half-century's hindsight, a historian who has pondered this question deeply offers these judgments: "The Constitutional Revolution of 1937 altered fundamentally the character of the Court's business, the nature of its decisions, and the alignment of its friends and foes. . . . In 1937 the Supreme Court began a revolution in jurisprudence that ended, apparently forever, the reign of laissez-faire and legitimated the arrival of the Leviathan State."[72]

Classicism Dismantled

From 1937 to 1942, the Court tore down almost all the doctrinal structure of public law that derived from the premises of legal classicism.[73] What it had taken the Court two generations to construct, it demolished in fewer than five years. The Court finally resolved the conflict between two incompatible lines of precedent by rejecting classical doctrine and validating its antithesis as the correct reading of the Constitution.

Largely unnoticed in the demolition of the doctrinal structure was the fact that the Court bulldozed away the underlying foundation of principles as well, leaving a gaping crater where once a comprehensive legal vision had stood. Earlier understandings about the place of the Court in a democratic society, the function of judicial review, and the nature of law passed into oblivion, not explicitly rejected as the doctrinal superstructure was, but simply abandoned ingloriously, with little notice and less concern. Robert McCloskey noted with great insight that an explicit decision to jettison all substantive due process review of economic legislation "would have compelled the Justices to explain themselves, to examine the basis for their abnegation." But they have never done so, "and this leaves, to say the least, a large gap in the rationale that underlies the structure of modern constitutional law."[74]

Substantive Due Process

First to go among the dogmas of yesteryear was the substantive due process constraint on state regulatory authority. In *West Coast Hotel v. Parrish* (1937),[75] Chief Justice Hughes dismissed liberty of contract as if it had been a bad dream, a phantom of the night. In doing so, he reconfigured the competing values of governmental power and individual liberty:

> The Constitution does not speak of freedom of contract. It speaks of liberty and prohibits the deprivation of liberty without due process of law. In prohibiting that deprivation, the Constitution does not recognize an absolute and uncontrollable liberty. . . . [T]he liberty safeguarded is liberty in a social organization which requires the protection of law against the evils which menace the health, safety, morals, and welfare of the people. Liberty under the Constitution is thus necessarily subject to the restraints of due process, and regulation which is reasonable in relation to its subject and is adopted in the interests of the community is due process.

This turned the classical conception of liberty and the police power on its head — or, to paraphrase what Marx said of Hegel, found it standing on its head and turned it on its feet. Hughes reverted to the conception of police powers sketched by Chief Justice Shaw in 1851, restored its antebellum potential, and incorporated due process within it, not as a straitjacket around it.

Hughes explicitly overruled *Adkins* as "a departure from the true application of the principles" that govern employment relationships. He adverted to his own opinion in a forgotten 1911 case that upheld a state workers' compensation statute: "[F]reedom of contract is a qualified, and not an absolute, right. There is no absolute freedom to do as one wills or to contract as one chooses. . . . Liberty implies the absence of arbitrary restraint, not immunity from reasonable regulations and prohibitions imposed in the interests of the community."[76]

Hughes also disposed of the old *Coppage* dicta about the consequences of bargaining inequality. Quoting from *Holden v. Hardy* (and its prose that had become antique with the passage of time), he affirmed that

> the proprietors of these establishments and their operatives do not stand upon an equality, and that their interests are, to a certain extent, conflicting. The former naturally desire to obtain as much labor as possible from their employes while the latter are often induced by the fear of discharge to conform to regulations which their judgment, fairly exercised, would pronounce to be detrimental to their health or strength. In other words, the proprietors lay down the rules, and the laborers are practically constrained to obey them. In such cases self-interest is often an unsafe guide, and the legislature may properly interpose its authority.[77]

With *Adkins* discarded, *Muller* became the reigning authority on the matter of women's work. Hughes stated that state legislatures were "clearly entitled to consider the situation of women in employment, the fact that they are in the class receiving the least pay, that their bargaining power is relatively weak, and that they are the ready victims of those who would take advantage of their necessitous circumstances. . . . The community is not bound to provide what is in effect a subsidy for unconscionable employers."

Sutherland spoke for the conservative bloc in an elegiac dissent. In *Carter*, he had provided a compendium of the classicist doctrinal position. Now, recognizing that the Court was crossing over a historic divide, descending into the watershed of a new constitutional order, he saluted the old regime in a moving farewell.

He first returned to Stone's *Butler* and Brandeis's *Ashwander* challenges, their calls for judicial self-restraint: "The suggestion that the only check upon the exercise of the judicial power, when properly invoked, to declare a constitutional right superior to an unconstitutional statute is the judge's own faculty of self-restraint, is both ill considered and mischievous. Self-restraint belongs in the domain of will and not of judgment."

With a subtlety so delicate many observers may have missed the point, he rebuked Roberts for his supposed switch. A judge has "a duty imposed upon him, which cannot be consummated justly by an automatic acceptance of the views of others which have neither convinced, nor created a reasonable doubt in, his mind. If upon a question so important he thus surrenders his deliberate judgment, he stands forsworn. He cannot subordinate his convictions to that extent and keep faith with his oath or retain his judicial and moral independence."

Sutherland concluded with a peroration worthy of the great tradition that was passing:

> The meaning of the Constitution does not change with the ebb and flow of economic events. We frequently are told in more general words that the Constitution must be construed in the light of the present. If by that it is meant that the Consti-

tution is made up of living words that apply to every new condition which they include, the statement is quite true. But to say, if that be intended, that the words of
the Constitution mean today what they did not mean when written — that is, that
they do not apply to a situation now to which they would have applied then — is to
rob that instrument of the essential element which continues it in force as the people have made.

The problem lay not in the judges, but in the charter they guarded. "If the Constitution . . . stands in the way of desirable legislation, the blame must rest upon that
instrument, and not upon the court for enforcing it according to its terms. The remedy in that situation — and the only true remedy — is to amend the Constitution."[78]
On that note, an epoch ended.

In the ensuing two decades, the Court redundantly kicked the corpse of substantive due process.[79] Doctrinally, it applied differential levels of scrutiny: the Court
reviewed economic regulation deferentially, while it subjected statutory infringe-
ments on noneconomic liberties to more exacting scrutiny. Such analysis focused
on two elements of legislative policy: ends and means. The Court defined the level
of scrutiny by descriptive adjectives and sometimes adverbs. Eventually, deferential
scrutiny — the kind applied to economic legislation after 1938 — required only
"legitimate" ends and "reasonable" means. Strict scrutiny such as that applied to
racial distinctions, by contrast, demanded "compelling" ends and "narrowly tailored" means. In the case marking the transition between "old" and "new" substantive due process, *United States v. Carolene Products Co.* (1938),[80] Justice Stone articulated the lowest imaginable level of scrutiny for legislative means, amounting
almost to judicial abdication: the Court's "inquiries . . . must be restricted to the
issue whether any state of facts either known or which could reasonably be assumed,
affords support" for the legislative judgment.

The Court was similarly indulgent toward the legislature's identification of ends.
In *Olsen v. Nebraska* (1941),[81] Justice William O. Douglas stated that "we are not
concerned, however, with the wisdom, need, or appropriateness of the legislation."
Reviewing decisions that rested on classical assumptions, Douglas stated that "the
only constitutional prohibitions or restraints . . . suggested for the invalidation of this
legislation are those notions of public policy embedded in earlier decisions of this
Court but which, as Mr. Justice Holmes long admonished, should not be read into
the Constitution. . . . Since they do not find expression in the Constitution, we cannot give them continuing vitality as standards by which the constitutionality of the
economic and social programs of the states is to be determined."

Thereafter the Court seemed to go out of its way to condemn the classical doctrinal tradition. In the *Lincoln Federal Labor Union* case of 1949[82] it upheld states'
right-to-work laws against, ironically, a union's liberty-of-contract challenge. Justice
Hugo Black spurned the invitation to return to what he called "the Allgeyer-Lochner-
Adair-Coppage constitutional doctrine," noting that the Court "has steadily rejected
the due process philosophy enunciated in the Adair-Coppage line of cases."

Justice Douglas treated liberty-of-contract arguments contemptuously. "Our recent decisions make plain that we do not sit as a super-legislature to weigh the wisdom of legislation nor to decide whether the policy which it expresses offends the
public welfare," he observed in 1952."[83] "The day is gone," he reiterated, "when this

Court uses the Due Process Clause of the Fourteenth Amendment to strike down state laws, regulatory of business and industrial conditions, because they may be unwise, improvident, or out of harmony with a particular school of thought."[84] Meanwhile, though, substantive due process lingered on for a while in the state supreme courts, which continued to strike down economic-regulatory legislation on *Lochner* grounds well into the 1950s.[85]

In a 1963 case, Justice Black sustained the Kansas bar's effort to monopolize debt collection despite his doubts about the wisdom of the law. The United States Supreme Court no longer resorted to "the 'vague contours' of the Due Process Clause to nullify laws which a majority of the Court believed to be economically unwise."[86] In a line that intoned the final obsequies for legal classicism, he concluded that "whether the legislature takes for its textbook Adam Smith, Herbert Spencer, Lord Keynes, or some other is no concern of ours."

Labor Legislation

One of the most far-reaching innovations of the New Deal was its comprehensive program of legitimating labor union organization and providing protection for workers, both in retirement and from workplace-related injuries. For that reason, it was also a prime target of conservative opposition and in 1936 was the most vulnerable of the New Deal's programs. Industry despised anything that might legitimate workers' collective action, and the Liberty League pronounced the Wagner Act unconstitutional. Test cases were on their way up to the Supreme Court that conservatives hoped would nullify all federal involvement in labor relations (except, of course, the management-friendly labor injunction).

The centerpiece of New Deal labor policy was the National Labor Relations Act (the Wagner Act) of 1935,[87] which legitimated union organization and made labor relations a federal responsibility. Reversing a century and a half of judicial hostility to unions, the Wagner Act's section 7 affirmed the right of workers to join unions and to bargain collectively with their employers. This put to rest all challenges to the legitimacy of union activity.

The Wagner Act did more than legitimate unions. It defined unfair labor practices by employers, depriving management of some of its cherished techniques of union-busting. The act created the National Labor Relations Board, empowering it to call elections to determine bargaining representatives, to recognize collective-bargaining units, to adjudicate unfair labor practices by employers, and to issue cease-and-desist orders to stop antiunion activities. Aside from its impact on unionization, the NLRB challenged conservatives because of its powers and its blend of governmental functions. Some industrial states complemented the federal statute with so-called little Wagner Acts providing comparable protections at the state level.

The New Deal's solicitude for labor did not stop with protecting unionization. The Norris-Laguardia Act of 1932 (actually a pre–New Deal measure)[88] prohibited federal courts from issuing injunctions to restrain strikes, boycotts, and picketing, and from upholding yellow-dog contracts. This was a congressional effort to kill off the hated labor injunction for good. As if to dance on the grave of the old legal order, section 1 of the statute declared that "the individual worker is commonly helpless to exercise actual liberty of contract and to protect his freedom of labor" without the backing of a union. Later, Congress enacted the Fair Labor Standards Act of 1938,[89] which established a federal minimum wage and maximum hours, and restricted child labor in defiance of *Hammer v. Dagenhart.* The Social Security Act of 1935[90] supplemented state unemployment insurance programs with a joint federal-state unemployment compensation program financed by a payroll tax. The statute also provided for federally administered old age insurance and federal support for state-sponsored old age pensions. Congress created a special program for railroad pensions and, in the Walsh-Healey Government Contracts Act of 1936,[91] required federal contractors to pay the prevailing minimum wage of the locality.

In the palmy days of 1936, conservatives confidently expected the Court to strike down the entire array of labor legislation. And well they might, given the consistent record of judicial enmity up till then to unions and to any governmental regulation of the employment relationship that empowered workers. The Court's *volte-face* of 1937 therefore provided a string of bitter disappointments. (Not that labor triumphed, of course. Management merely turned to legislative venues during and after the war, and succeeded in reversing some of labor's gains through the Taft-Hartley Act of 1947 and state right-to-work legislation.)

In the *Jones & Laughlin* case of 1937, the Supreme Court reversed the entire line of precedents inhibiting federal regulation of labor relationships through the commerce power.[92] With a stroke, Chief Justice Hughes overturned *Knight*-style formalism: "[W]e have often said that interstate commerce itself is a practical conception. . . . [I]nterferences with that commerce must be appraised by a judgment that does not ignore actual experience." He then brought the Court back to Marshallian concepts of interstate commerce: "[T]he fundamental principle is that the power to regulate commerce is the power to enact 'all appropriate legislation'. . . . That power is plenary." He substituted a "close and substantial relation" test to permit congressional control over intrastate activities having an impact on interstate commerce. "The question is necessarily one of degree."[93] Justice McReynolds, speaking for the four dissenters, could only try to summon *Knight, Adair,* and *Carter* from the dead. In four companion cases, the Court applied these general principles to varying factual circumstances that previously would have been held beyond the reach of federal power.[94] After *Jones & Laughlin,* the way was clear for Congress to regulate all aspects of industrial activity.

With that principal issue out of the way, the newly reoriented Court was able to dispose easily of other challenges to the New Deal labor program. The Court held the Norris-Laguardia Act constitutional in *Lauf v. Shinner* (1938), and extended its coverage the same day to a nonunion organization (significantly, a black civil rights group) that was picketing in an employment-related dispute.[95] The Court interpreted New Deal labor legislation to declare that union activity, even if it constrains commerce, is not of itself a violation of the Sherman Act.[96] It held that unions could engage in all the activities permitted them under the Clayton Act without being enjoined under antitrust laws, because the Norris-Laguardia Act was a "harmonizing text" that redefined labor's relationship to the antitrust acts.[97]

Finally, the Court sustained the Fair Labor Standards Act in *United States v. Darby* (1941)[98] and, in doing so, reburied *Knight, Hammer,* and *Carter,* as well as derivative doctrines like dual federalism. It made no difference what Congress's motivation might be for regulating commerce, or that Congress was exercising a power identical to the states' police power. By 1941, such conclusions were no longer remarkable. What was surprising in Justice Stone's *Darby* opinion was his shriveled conception of the Tenth Amendment as a barrier to federal power: it "states but a truism that all is retained which has not been surrendered." The once mighty amendment, the very core of states'-power constitutionalism and the touchstone of the Virginia and Kentucky Resolutions, was now seen as merely "declaratory of the relationship between the national and state governments as it had been established by the Constitution before the amendment." Stone adopted an extremely low scrutiny-level test for validating national authority against federalism challenges: the end must merely be "permitted" and the means "appropriate and plainly adapted" to the end.

Social Welfare Legislation

The other major component of the New Deal to emerge intact was the Social Security program. Conservatives had confidently predicted its demise since 1935, and had classicism retained its potency, they would have been proved correct in the event. In classical political economy, neither state nor federal government had an appropriate role in assuring individuals a modicum of income in case of retirement or disability, or providing for survivors of a deceased breadwinner. Until Wisconsin enacted the nation's first unemployment insurance legislation in 1932, poor relief remained in substance and technique largely what it had been in Elizabeth's day. To those who believed that poverty was the result of moral depravity, and that the wealth of A should not be taken and given to B, that was entirely appropriate. Those attitudes did not long survive on the Court, however. A mere decade later, as conservative a judge as James F. Byrnes could write: "[T]he theory of the Elizabethan poor laws no longer fits the facts. . . . [W]e do not think that it will now be seriously contended that because a person is without employment and without funds he constitutes a 'moral pestilence'. Poverty and immorality are not synonymous."[99]

The Social Security Act of 1935 changed the structure of America's social welfare system, with its provisions for old age pensions, survivors' insurance, and unemployment compensation, financed by withholding taxes collected from joint employer-employee contributions. The Liberty League and its allies in industry promptly challenged the program, and under a restrictive view of federal taxing/spending powers, their prospects would have been bright. They insisted that "the relation of employment is one so essential to the pursuit of happiness that it may not be burdened with a tax."[100] Without endorsing that fanciful argument, the Court in 1935 voided a federally administered pension plan in a specific industry, railroads, as "an attempt for social ends to impose by sheer fiat noncontractual incidents upon the relation of employer and employee, not as a rule or regulation of commerce and transportation between the states, but as a means of assuring a particular class of employees against old age dependency."[101]

But the principal test cases, *Steward Machine Co. v. Davis* and *Helvering v. Davis*, did not reach the Court until 1937, and when they did, the Social Security program survived by five-to-four and seven-to-two margins respectively. With the major constitutional issues of the New Deal already settled in *West Coast Hotel* and *Jones & Laughlin*, it was unnecessary for Justice Cardozo, writing for the new majority, to restate broad principles. He therefore confined himself to the specific challenges to the statute, focusing on the supposed coercion of the states, an argument now easy to rebut. "It confuses motive with coercion," he wrote. To thus assume the carrot was the stick, Cardozo went on, perhaps with tongue in cheek, risks "philosophical determinism by which choice becomes impossible. Till now the law has been guided by a robust common sense which assumes the freedom of the will as a working hypothesis in the solution of its problems."[102] We may only wonder what Justice Sutherland was thinking when he heard himself being accused of determinism; he denounced the invasion of states' powers as a violation of the Tenth Amendment.

In *Helvering v. Davis*,[103] Cardozo upheld the old-age insurance provisions of the Social Security Act. He confirmed *Butler*'s broad reading of the general welfare clause, but emphasized that the concept of welfare does not remain static. Only national power could cope with the nationwide economic crisis. With the expansive portion of *Butler* validated, all that remained was to dispose of the remainder of that opinion, now become anachronistic. Oddly, it was *Butler*'s author, Justice Roberts, who slew his own juridical offspring, in *Mulford v. Smith* (1939).[104] There Roberts upheld the second Agricultural Adjustment Act[105] on commerce clause grounds, drawing a logical but not persuasive distinction from his earlier opinion, which had turned on the general welfare clause.

The Late New Deal

The second Agricultural Adjustment Act was one of a number of measures regulating agriculture that sought to stabilize commodity prices by controlling production. The Supreme Court validated it and the New Deal's broadened conception of federal regulatory power under the commerce clause in *Wickard v. Filburn* (1942).[106] The facts of the case demonstrate how expansive federal commerce-regulatory power had become after 1937. Roscoe Filburn, a farmer in southern Ohio, planted twelve acres of wheat in excess of his marketing quota promulgated under the second Agricultural Adjustment Act, and was accordingly fined. Because he intended to use the wheat on his farm to feed poultry and livestock, to grind into flour for his own use, and for seed, he insisted that federal commerce authority could not reach him. The nonquota produce never left his farm, to say nothing of moving in interstate commerce. Justice Robert Jackson brushed this objection aside. Even if Filburn's specific wheat never made it to an interstate market, the aggregate effect of his actions and that of thousands like him could have an effect on the national market. He discarded for all time the distinction between direct and indirect effects on commerce as well as between production and commerce. Writing off the entire line of precedents headed by *Knight* as "a few dicta," Jackson stated that "the mechanical application of legal formulas [is] no longer feasible. . . . [Q]uestions of federal power cannot be decided simply by finding the activity in question to be 'production' nor can consideration of its economic effects be foreclosed by calling them 'indirect.'" Exit *Knight*.

In 1940, the Court provided a reprise of the sweeping changes that had occurred in a mere three years. The vehicle was a late challenge to the Bituminous

Coal Act of 1937, a reenactment of major features of the [National Industrial Recovery Act] NIRA and the soft coal "little NIRA" that had been invalidated by *Schechter* and *Carter*. In the *Sunshine Coal* case, newly appointed Justice William O. Douglas casually observed, as if it had been obvious all along, that the existence of constraints on federal regulatory power does "not mean that there is a no man's land between the state and federal domains. . . . Congress under the commerce clause is not impotent to deal with what it may consider to be dire consequences of laissez-faire."[107] What had been sanctified truth a mere five years ago was now an evil having dire consequences. The Court upheld congressional price regulations in the soft coal industry, explicitly affirming the Cardozo and Hughes dissents in *Carter*. It sustained a nonrevenue regulatory tax (thereby repudiating *Bailey*), extolled paramount federal authority over interstate commerce, and brushed aside formerly fatal complaints about the delegation of legislative power. It was as if *Schechter* had never been.

In a mere five years, the Supreme Court swept away an entire body of law: principles, doctrine, precedents, dogma. With it went a way of thinking about law and about the place of the Court in a democracy. Flawed and inadequate though the old view may have been, it at least provided *some* comprehensive explanation of what law was and what judges do when they expound it. After 1937–1938, no such encompassing vision of law was left to justify judicial review. Into this vacuum Hugo Black, Felix Frankfurter, and others rushed after the war to provide replacements. Despite their impressive efforts, however, none of them succeeded, and the Court has labored for the remainder of this century under a popular suspicion that its results were bereft of a legitimating jurisprudence that integrated law into the larger social realm.

Notes

1. On the question of whether there *was* a revolution in 1937–1938, cf. William Leuchtenburg, *The Supreme Court Reborn: The Constitutional Revolution in the Age of Roosevelt* (1995), with Richard D. Friedman: "Switching Time and Other Thought Experiments: The Hughes Court and Constitutional Transformation," 142 *U. Pa. L. Rev.* 1891 (1994). See also Barry J. Cushman, "The Structure of a Constitutional Revolution: Nebbia v. New York and the Collapse of Laissez-Faire Constitutionalism," (1995) (Ph.D. dissertation, University of Virginia).

2. But being refreshingly reinvestigated by Friedman, "Switching Time" and "Telling the Story of the Hughes Court," *Law Quadrangle Notes* 39 (1996), 32. Prof. Friedman is the designated author of the Hughes Court volume in the *Holmes Devise History of the Supreme Court of the United States*.

3. For a differing, but compatible, interpretation of the developments recounted in this chapter, see Barry Cushman, "Rethinking the New Deal Court," 80 *Va. L. Rev.* 201 (1994), and accompanying commentary: Eben Moglen, "Toward a New Deal Legal History," 80 *Va. L. Rev.* 265 (1994) and Edward A. Purcell Jr., "Rethinking Constitutional Change," 80 *Va. L. Rev.* 277 (1994).

4. O'Gorman & Young Inc. v. Hartford Fire Ins. Co., 282 U.S. 251 (1931).

5. Stromberg v. California, 283 U.S. 359 (1931).

6. Near v. Minnesota, 283 U.S. 697 (1931. See the discussion of the significance of these cases in Friedman, "Switching Time," 1903–1909.

7. New State Ice Co. v. Liebmann, 285 U.S. 262, 311 (1932).

8. 290 U.S. 398, 442–443, 449–451 (1934).

9. McCulloch v. Maryland, 4 Wheat.'(17 U.S.) 316, 407, 415 (1819).

10. Sutherland was the intellectual center among the four conservatives. Cf. Joel F. Paschal, *Mr. Justice Sutherland, a Man against the State* (1951) (sympathetic but balanced older biography) with Hadley Arkes, *The Return of George Sutherland: Restoring a Jurisprudence of Natural Rights* (1994) (uncritically apologetic).

11. Scott v. Sandford, 19 How. (60 U.S.) 393, 426 (1857).

12. 291 U.S. 502, 523, 536, 556 (1934).

13. Norman v. Baltimore & Ohio R.R., 294 U.S. 240; Nortz v. United States, 294 U.S. 317; Perry v. United States, 294 U.S. 330 (1935).

14. William F. Swindler, *Court and Constitution in the Twentieth Century: The New Legality, 1932–1968* (1970), 35.

15. Because McReynolds delivered his opinion orally and in part extemporaneously, his precise words are a matter of uncertainty. See the following accounts: *New York Times*, 24 Feb. 1935 Section 4, p. 1, col 1; "Justice McReynolds' Dissent in the Gold Clause Cases," 18 *Tenn. L. Rev.* 768 (1945); Alpheus T. Mason, *Harlan Fiske Stone: Pillar of the Law* (1956), 391 n.; Edward S. Corwin, *Constitutional Revolution, Ltd.* (1941), 45–46.

16. Ashwander v. Tennessee Valley Authority, 297 U.S. 288, 319, 347–354 (1936).

17. Dartmouth College v. Woodward, 4 Wheat. (17 U.S.) 518, 625 (1819).

18. Charles Evans Hughes, *The Supreme Court of the United States* (1928), 29, 41.

19. Rescue Army v. Municipal Court, 331 U.S. 549, 568 (1947).

20. Ronen Shamir, *Managing Legal Uncertainty: Elite Lawyers and the New Deal* (1995).

21. William H. Harbaugh, *Lawyer's Lawyer: The Life of John W. Davis* (1973), 348–349 (whence quote below is taken); *New York Times*, 23 Dec. 1934, section 1, p. 1, col 5.

22. Arthur M. Schlesinger Jr., *The Politics of Upheaval* (1960), 447.

23. For reactions of the Justices and the public to the new surroundings, see *Newsweek*, 12 Oct. 1935, 20; *New York Times*, 8, and 13 Oct. 1935 section 1, p. 2, col 1 and section 4, p. 1, col 5; *Time*, 16 Dec. 1935, 17.

24. In the guardian figures flanking the steps and the figures of the west frieze, symbols of Law (*lex*) are masculine, military, and armed, such as the two Roman soldiers who represent Order and Authority on either side of the goddess of Liberty in the center of the east pediment. The female figure on the north side of the steps represents Equity; she holds a miniaturized figure of Justice.

25. C. Northcote Parkinson, *Parkinson's Law and Other Studies in Administration* (1957), 82.

26. 293 U.S. 388 (1935).

27. The oddest of odd couples, given McReynolds' scarcely concealed anti-Semitism.

28. Railroad Retirement Board v. Alton R.R., 295 U.S. 330 (1935).

29. *Business Week*, 11 May 1935, quoted in Leuchtenburg, *Supreme Court Reborn*, 89.

30. 295 U.S. 495, 553 (1935).

31. On the contrasts between legal craftsmanship of the early and the later New Deal, both in statutory drafting and in appellate argument, see Peter H. Irons, *The New Deal Lawyers* (1982), 227.

32. 295 U.S. 555 (1935). Along with *Schechter*, the other Black Monday decision was *Humphrey's Executor* (see n. 37).

33. Franklin Delano roosevelt, "The Two Hundred and Ninth Press Conference, May 31, 1935," in Samuel I. Rosenman, comp., *The Public Papers and Addresses of Franklin D. Roosevelt* (1938–1950), vol. 4, 209.

34. George Creel, *Rebel at Large* (1935), 291.

35. Roosevelt to Rep. Samuel B. Hill, 6 July 1935, in Rosenman, comp., *Public Papers of Roosevelt*, vol. 4, 297–298.

36. Draft of speech, February 1935, in Elliott Roosevelt, ed., *F.D.R.: His Personal Letters, (1928–1945)* (1950), vol. 1, 459–460.

37. 295 U.S. 602 (1935).

38. See Myers v. United States, 272 U.S. 52 (1926).

39. 299 U.S. 304 (1936).

40. 297 U.S. 1, 60–63, 65–67, 77, 87, 78–79 (1936).

41. See generally Paul L. Murphy, "The New Deal Agricultural Program and the Constitution," *Agricultural History* 29 (1955), 160.

42. 1 Cranch (5 U.S.) 137, 177–178 (1803).

43. William Van Alstyne provides a sympathetic reading of this passage in "Interpreting This Constitution: The Unhelpful Contributions of Special Theories of Judicial Review," 35 *U. Fla. L. Rev.* 209, 225–227 (1983).

44. Article II of the Articles of Confederation provided that "Each State retains its sovereignty, freedom, and independence, and every Power, Jurisdiction and right, which is not by this confederation expressly delegated to the United States, in Congress assembled." Philip B. Kurland and Ralph Lerner, eds., *The Founders' Constitution* (1987), vol. 1, 23.

45. U.S. Const. art. I, sec. 8, cl. 1: "The Congress shall have Power To lay and collect Taxes, Duties, Imposts and Excises, to pay the Debts and provide for the common Defence and general Welfare of the United States."

46. Madison's statement in House of Representatives on the Bank Bill, 23 Feb. 1791, in Robert Rutland, ed., *The Papers of James Madison* (1975), vol. 8, 375–376.

47. [Alexander Hamilton], *Report on Manufactures* (1791), reprinted in Harold C. Syrett and Jacob E. Cooke, eds., *The Papers of Alexander Hamilton* (1961–1987), vol. 10, 303.

48. Memorandum of 24 Jan. 1936, quoted in Leuchtenburg, *Supreme Court Reborn*, 99.

49. Paul v. Virginia, 8 Wall. (75 U.S.) 168 (1869), substantially overruled by United States v. South-Eastern Underwriters Assn., 322 U.S. 533 (1944). See Prudential Insurance Co. v. Benjamin, 328 U.S. 408 (1946); Western and Southern Life Insurance Co. v. State Board of Equalization, 451 U.S. 648 (1981).

50. 296 U.S. 404 (1936).

51. Madden v. Kentucky, 309 U.S. 83 (1940).

52. 298 U.S. 1, 24–25 (1935).

53. 298 U.S. 238, 291, 294, 297, 304, 307, 316, 327 (1936).

54. Bituminous Coal Conservation Act, ch. 824, 49 Stat. 991.

55. Bituminous Coal Conservation Act, ch. 824, § 15.

56. Morehead v. New York *ex rel.* Tipaldo, 298 U.S. 587, 610–611, 636 (1936).

57. Max Weber, "Forms of Creation of Rights," in Gunther Roth and Claus Wittich, eds., *Economy and Society: An Outline of Interpretive Sociology*, vol. 2, 729–730 (1968, rpt. 1978).

58. Franklin Delano Roosevelt, "The Three Hundredth Press Conference, 2 June 1936," in Rosenman, comp., *Public Papers of Roosevelt*, vol. 5, 192.

59. Quoted in Schlesinger, *Politics of Upheaval*, 483.

60. Raoul E. Desvernine, *Democratic Despotism* (1936), 182.

61. This account follows Leuchtenburg, *Supreme Court Reborn*, 82–162. An earlier survey is Schlesinger, *Politics of Upheaval*, 447–496. Leonard Baker provides a journalistic account of the political struggle in *Back to Back: The Duel between FDR and the Supreme Court* (1967).

62. Rosenman, comp., *Public Papers of Roosevelt*, vol. 4, 221.

63. Quoted in Leuchtenburg, *Supreme Court Reborn*, 94.

64. Harold Ickes diary entries of 24, 29, 31 January 1936, quoted in Leuchtenburg, *Supreme Court Reborn*, 99, 101.

65. Act of 24 Aug. 1937, ch. 754, § 3, 50 Stat. 751.

66. Rosenman, comp., *Public Papers of Roosevelt*, vol. 6, 55.

67. West Coast Hotel v. Parrish, 300 U.S. 379 (1937).

68. U.S. Senate, Committee on the Judiciary, 75 Cong., 1st Sess., Sen. Rep. 711 (1937), 23, 11, 13.

69. This includes his nomination of Stone to be Chief Justice.

70. James T. Patterson, *Congressional Conservatism and the New Deal: The Growth of the Conservative Coalition in Congress, 1933–1939* (1967).

71. Oral history interview, quoted in Leuchtenburg, *Supreme Court Reborn*, 158.

72. Leuchtenburg, *Supreme Court Reborn*, 235–236.

73. The only surviving remnants were Meyer v. Nebraska, 262 U.S. 390 (1923) and Pierce v. Society of Sisters, 268 U.S. 510 (1925), which carried substantive due process forward into an era when the Court was concerned to protect noneconomic liberties.

74. Robert G. McCloskey, "Economic Due Process and the Supreme Court: Exhumation and Reburial," 1962 *Sup. Ct. Rev.* 34, 40.

75. 300 U.S. 379, 391–392, 398–399 (1937).

76. Chicago, Burlington, & Quincy Ry. v. McGuire, 219 U.S. 549, 565 (1911).

77. Holden v. Hardy, 169 U.S. 366, 397 (1898). This insight applied on the private law side produced the doctrine of contracts of adhesion. See, e.g., Williams v. Walker-Thomas Furniture Co., 350 F.2d 445 (D.C. Cir. 1965).

78. 300 U.S. 401–404.

79. See generally Robert L. Stern, "The Commerce Clause and the National Economy, 1933–1946," 59 *Harv. L. Rev.* 645, 883 (1946); Stern, "The Problems of Yesteryear — Commerce and Due Process," 4 *Vand. L. Rev.* 446 (1951).

80. 304 U.S. 144, 154 (1938).

81. 313 U.S. 236, 246–247 (1941).

82. Lincoln Federal Labor Union v. Northwestern Iron and Metal Co., 335 U.S. 525, 535–536 (1949).

83. Day-Brite Lighting, Inc. v. Missouri, 342 U.S. 421, 423 (1952).

84. Williamson v. Lee Optical, 348 U.S. 483, 487 (1955).

85. Monrad G. Paulsen collected the cases in "The Persistence of Substantive Due Process in the States," 34 *Minn. L. Rev.* 91 (1950); updated in John A. Hoskins and David A. Katz, "Substantive Due Process in the States Revisited," 18 *Ohio St. L.J.* 384 (1952).

86. Ferguson v. Skrupa, 372 U.S. 726, 731–732 (1963).

87. Act of 5 July 1935, ch. 372, 49 Stat. 449; see Karl E. Klare, "Judicial Deradicalization of the Wagner Act and the Origins of Modern Legal Consciousness, 1937–1941," 62 *Minn. L. Rev.* 265 (1978).

88. Act of 23 March 1932, ch. 90, § 1, 47 Stat. 70.

89. Act of 25 June 1938, ch. 676, 52 Stat. 1060.

90. Act of 14 Aug. 1935, ch. 531, 49 Stat. 620.

91. Act of 30 June 1936, ch. 881, 49 Stat. 2036.

92. National Labor Relations Board v. Jones & Laughlin Steel Co., 301 U.S. 1, 41–42, 36–37 (1937). See generally Richard C. Cortner, *The Jones and Laughlin Case* (1970).

93. Cf. the reaffirmation of Hughes's position by Justices Anthony Kennedy and David Souter in United States v. Lopez, 115 S. Ct. 1624, 1635 (Kennedy, J., concurring), 1652 (Souter, J., dissenting) (1995).

94. N.L.R.B. v. Freuhauf Trailer Co., 301 U.S. 49; N.L.R.B. v. Friedman-Harry Marks Clothing Co., 301 U.S. 58; Associated Press v. N.L.R.B., 301 U.S. 103 (sustaining the NLRA

against a First Amendment challenge); and Washington, Virginia, & Maryland Coach Co. v. N.L.R.B., 301 U.S. 142 (1937).

95. Lauf v. E. G. Shinner & Co., 303 U.S. 323; New Negro Alliance v. Sanitary Grocery Co., 303 U.S. 552 (1938).

96. Apex Hosiery Co. v. Leader, 310 U.S. 469 (1940).

97. United States v. Hutcheson, 312 U.S. 219, 231 (1941).

98. 312 U.S. 100, 124 (1941).

99. Edwards v. California, 314 U.S. 160, 174, 177 (1941).

100. Justice Cardozo's paraphrase of opponents' arguments in Steward Machine Co. v. Davis, 301 U.S. 548, 578 (1937).

101. Railroad Retirement Board v. Alton R.R., 295 U.S. 330, 374 (1935).

102. Steward Machine Co. v. Davis, 301 U.S. 548, 589–590 (1937).

103. 301 U.S. 672 (1937).

104. 307 U.S. 38 (1939).

105. Act of 3 June 1937, ch. 296, 50 Stat. 246.

106. 317 U.S. 111, 119, 124 (1942).

107. Sunshine Anthracite Coal Co. v. Adkins, 310 U.S. 381, 396 (1940).

Epilogue

Felix Frankfurter Looks Back

In 1949, Professor-become-Justice Felix Frankfurter provided a donnish reprise of classicism's growth and demise. His concurrence in companion cases upholding the power of the states to enact right-to-work legislation reads oddly as a sort of after-the-fact dissent, as if Frankfurter were composing the opinion *he* would have written if he had been sitting on the *Lochner* Court.

Frankfurter began with a succinct historical sketch of America's industrial experience:

> The coming of the machine age tended to despoil human personality. It turned men and women into 'hands.' The industrial history of the early Nineteenth Century demonstrated the helplessness of the individual employee to achieve human dignity in a society so largely affected by technological advances. Hence the trade union made itself increasingly felt, not only as an indispensable weapon of self-defense on the part of workers but as an aid to the well-being of a society in which work is an expression of life and not merely the means of earning subsistence. But unionization encountered the shibboleths of a premachine age and these were reflected in juridical assumptions that survived the facts on which they were based. Adam Smith was treated as though his generalization had been imparted to him on Sinai and not as a thinker who addressed himself to the elimination of restrictions which had become fetters upon initiative and enterprise in his day. Basic human rights expressed by the constitutional conception of 'liberty' were equated with theories of laissez faire. The result was that economic views of confined validity were treated by lawyers and judges as though the Framers had enshrined them in the Constitution. This misapplication of the notions of the classic economists and resulting disregard of the perduring reach of the Constitution led to Mr. Justice Holmes' famous protest in the Lochner case.[1]

But then Frankfurter turned the historical tables on unions. He pointed out that the abuses of substantive due process had been committed in the cause of crushing unions, "but when the tide turned, it was not merely because circumstances had changed and there had arisen a new order with new claims to divine origin." The new era was one "not of social dogma but of increased deference to the legislative judgment." Then he returned to a curiously anachronistic nineteenth-century notion: "unions are powers within the State" and, as such, within the ambit of permissible state control and regulation. Whether to favor their uninhibited operation or to protect the interests of nonunion workers by right-to-work laws was precisely the kind of legislative judgment that was secured by the demise of substantive due process.

A cynic might observe that now it was Frankfurter who was reading the election returns: Congress had enacted the Taft-Hartley Act over President Harry S Truman's veto less than two years previously. Frankfurter, however, defended the necessary impartiality of results that mandated his position by a lengthy Holmesian discourse on judicial review. Policy issues were beyond judicial ken: "[T]he very limited function of this Court is discharged when we recognize that these issues are not so unrelated to the experience and feelings of the community as to render legislation addressing itself to them willfully destructive of cherished rights." Unbridled indulgence in judicial power "debilitates popular democratic government." Social policy is best evolved by trial and error, not by juristic *diktat*.

"In the day-to-day working of our democracy it is vital that the power of the non-democratic organ of our Government be exercised with rigorous self-restraint," Frankfurter cautioned. The Supreme Court's power was "inherently oligarchic": "[T]he judiciary is prone to misconceive the public good by confounding [the judges'] private notions with constitutional requirements." The Supreme Court's operations are inherently (and properly) undemocratic, but that was all the more reason for preserving the powers of the democratically chosen legislatures to set social and economic policy. The judiciary's power requires "intellectual humility, and such humility presupposes complete disinterestedness." (Felix Frankfurter attributing intellectual humility and disinterestedness to himself was like Falstaff claiming to be modest, but that is another story.)

Frankfurter then expressed some beliefs at the core of his outlook as a judge. If a court were to "yield[] to the popular will," it would thereby "license[] itself to practice despotism, for there can be no assurance that it will not on another occasion indulge its own will. Courts can fulfill their responsibility in a democratic society only to the extent that they succeed in shaping their judgments by rational standards, and rational standards are both impersonal and communicable." Echoing John Marshall, he insisted that policy issues "demand the resolution of conflicts of value, and the elements of conflicting values are largely imponderable." The body to undertake such functions is the legislature, not the judiciary. Legislative "functions can be assumed by this Court only in disregard of the historic limits of the Constitution."

In this remarkable opinion, Frankfurter closed a circle. Pronouncing classicist activism defunct, he returned to the beginnings of judicial review in the thinking of John Marshall, and thereby began anew in seeking a solution to the dilemma of judicial review in a democratic society.

A Retrospective Evaluation

To take up the challenge posed in the prologue of this book: Why did an explanatory and legitimating paradigm of such power, such comprehensive scope, as classical legal thought fail? And why did it succumb as abruptly and completely as it did
in 1937–1938?
　　Classical legal thought had become incompatible with the development of industrial and finance capitalism in the twentieth century. While late-classical judges
clung to the paradigm of individuals bargaining face-to-face in labor or contractual
relationships, the complexities of industrial America demanded new models of employment and commercial relations. These new ways of thinking about the organization of society would have to be responsive to the existence of collective entities
like unions. Classical thought proved itself incapable of generating new and creative
ways of thinking about the economy. In this sense, FDR's homely image of "horse-
and-buggy" constitutional thought was on the mark. The frontier individualism that
underlay George Sutherland's outlook was irrelevant to the modern industrial world
into which it survived.
　　If classical legal thought was ill adapted to the twentieth-century economy, it was
just as out of place as a descriptor of modern social relations. It distanced itself from
its Victorian assumptions about women's spheres only to make women the objects of
employers' rapacity, as in *Adkins*, endowed with a jural equality that fitted them for
exploitation in sweatshops along with the cigarmakers of *Jacobs* and the bakers of
Lochner. Juridical thought was founded on classical notions of political economy,
which had never been descriptive of any reality anywhere but that were certainly
anachronistic in twentieth-century America. By the time of *Lochner*, liberal economic thought was being displaced by institutional economics and marginal utility
theory, so judges like Peckham found themselves wedded to a corpse.[2]
　　Similarly with classicism's understanding of government. Classical thought was
so deeply grounded in the constitutional order of the founding that it was unable to
accommodate itself to post-Reconstruction realities, including national dominance
in economic relations and the rise of the administrative state. The prominence of
antebellum Democrats among the classical jurists, above all Field, Fuller, and Peckham, gave the group a state power orientation that was incongruous in the national
markets of the twentieth century. Their lingering Jacksonian Democratic attachment to state power and their suspicion of the corporate form proved to be a futility
with respect to corporate governance after *Knight*. Their ideology blinded them to
the problem of the no-man's-land they created in such matters as yellow-dog contracts
and women's working hours.
　　Technological development and economic growth left classical thought behind, an antique relic of an earlier political economy no more suited to industrial
America than the buggy whip or the grain flail. Unlike the priesthood of pharaonic
Egypt, who retained a monopoly of useful learning (astronomy, mathematics), the
judicial hierophants served only to obstruct progress with their mysteries.
　　Classical legal thought collapsed as an ideological armature for public law be-
cause it had become obsolete by 1920, if not by 1900. Even modern conservative ju-

rists like Chief Judge Richard A. Posner concede that "the Court's mistake in the liberty of contract cases was to be out of step with dominant public opinion. But this was true only toward the end of the era, and is the reason why the era ended."[3] After 1920, classical thought lived on as a reflex and an abstraction, not as a credible picture of social reality. Even in its youth, in the 1880s, classical thought no longer expressed the realities of the workplace and the market. In its declension, classical thought drew Chief Justice Hughes's scorn: "[W]e are asked to shut our eyes to the plainest facts of our national life and to deal with the question of direct and indirect effects in an intellectual vacuum." Marketplace realities "must be appraised by a judgment that does not ignore actual experience."[4]

Classicism's individualist outlook may have been appropriate for the affluent, but for working people, immigrants, and city dwellers, cooperative and collective action were essential.[5] "The organization of laborers in Trades Unions recognizes the fact that mutualism is preferable to individualism," wrote the union organizer George McNeill in 1899.[6] At the opposite end of the ideological spectrum, Richard Olney, that scourge of unions in the Pullman strike, indignantly wrote, apropos of *Adair,* that "it is archaic — it is a long step back into the past — to conceive of and deal with the relations between the employer in such industries and the employee as if the parties were individuals." Unions, he had come around to see, were "necessary measures of protection and defense" for workers.[7]

The paradigm of individualism might have had some validity in describing the bargaining relationship between a master and a journeyman cordwainer, or between a peddler and a farmwife, in 1810. But it was incongruous as a model structuring employment relationships in the mills and factories of Andrew Carnegie, Henry Ford, or Alfred Sloan. That an immigrant steelworker could be treated as the bargaining equal of the United States Steel Corporation was a legal fiction that could not survive into the twentieth century. A legal order that insisted on presuming such unreal equality was incompatible with a democratic society.

Sensing their lore to be worse than useless, the priesthood of classicism resorted to another craft of their Egyptian ancestors. They tried to embalm the Constitution, converting it to a mummy that retained its eighteenth-century limits intact into the twentieth century. Justice Sutherland proclaimed that the Constitution's "meaning is changeless," fixed before ink dried on parchment and unalterable except by amendment.[8]

Rigidity, no matter how zealously maintained, could not compensate for the confusion and uncertainty that classical premises generated. Langdell's system was unable to furnish plausible rules that were capable of consistently resolving all cases. Instead, judges devised exceptions, counterrules, new doctrines, whatever was necessary to avoid injustice or absurdity in particular cases. Law was incoherent in the literal sense of the word: its doctrinal structure could not hold together. Classical doctrine was incapable of applying its dichotomous principles in a consistent, plausible, convincing way.

Classicism could not deliver on its promises of universality and completeness. It stood embarrassed before the manifold contradictions of its own systematization. For example, all but the most doctrinaire of classical judges accepted the validity of usury laws in both public and private law as a necessary means of protecting the weak against those who would take advantage of them in bargaining relationships. Yet these same judges condemned labor-protective legislation founded on assumptions of inequality of bargaining relationships, without being able to explain how these two situations could be distinguished from each other. Unable to offer a credible explanation, classical thought appeared to justify nothing more than raw policy preferences.

Indeterminacy was the twin of incoherence. The law was unable to generate predictable results, or rules that could realize law's promise of stable and reliable development. When law appeared to ordinary citizens as erratic, unpredictable, and unstable, the rule of law was threatened. One of the republican fundaments of the legal order was that law be known, preexisting, and certain in its application. Classical jurists and their intellectual ancestors reaffirmed this ideal countless times, yet legal development continued to belie their assurances.

Aside from being out of touch with reality, classical legal thought was undemocratic. A distinct attitudinal line runs through such decisions as Taney's in *Dred Scott*; Fuller's in *Knight*, on one hand, and the *Danbury Hatters' Case*, on the other; Peckham's in *Lochner*; Sutherland's in *Adkins* and *Carter*. In all these cases, jurists, often speaking for only half the Court plus one, presumed to halt democratic processes and the realization of majority will in public policy by imposing the judicial veto. If there is a universal lesson in the story of classicism's rise and fall, it is that the judiciary cannot for long attempt to sweep back, Canute-like, the ocean of majority will democratically expressed. Granted that judicial authority must sometimes be countermajoritarian, and that the Framers, or at least some of them plus the Marshall Court, intended it to be; nevertheless, Holmes was correct in reminding his brethren that in the long run, in a republican government the majority must have its way. The bankruptcy of the late classical view was manifest in Justice Sutherland's plaint in his *West Coast Hotel* dissent that the fault lay not with the judges, but with the Constitution itself. Such a view was possible only in a man lost to all sense of democratic constraints on judicial authority. Any long-term judicial effort to stifle democracy is bound to be unsuccessful.

But experience triumphed over logic, life over syllogism. Ultimately, classical legal thought, leaving behind the emotional urgency that gave it birth in the 1880s, lingered on too long as abstract dogma that did not correspond to the reality of changing times. If it was not a crude effort to protect the pelf of the wealthy, it became a creed without believers among ordinary people. It lost resonance with both its historical roots and contemporary experience. Although classical legal thought could legitimately claim roots in the beginnings of the American republic, as it developed by logical abstraction, it became cut off from legitimating origins in the Framers' intent, in the common law, or in revolutionary historical experience. Thus isolated, in its latter days legal classicism appeared to ordinary Americans as nothing more than the policy preferences of a bench and bar subservient to large corporations and investors.

In attenuated form, classical dogma lingered on in placid and prosperous times, partly because the countertradition occasionally relieved its heavy-handed reign. But in a time of prolonged economic and social distress, it became obvious that classical legal thought had lost any capacity it might have ever had to speak to the concerns of American working men and women.

For a century, classical legal thought had attempted to prevent the state from becoming involved in issues of distributive justice, from determining the fairness of society's allocation of resources and burdens. Its ideal was a purely private realm of ordering, where private parties made all essential decisions about who gets what, about where society spends its assets, and on what. Government, both state and federal, was not to make substantive policy decisions that affected the distribution of wealth and power. Classicism presumed that government was no more competent to decide on the fairness of a wage than it was to pass on the truth of reincarnation. In such a view, the law's aversion to monopolies or favoritism, with its roots in the revolutionary and Jacksonian eras, seamlessly evolved into a prohibition of governmental intervention to protect labor or the weaker members of society.

Whether such a division of state and society might ever have proved workable in some hypothetical society is unanswerable and irrelevant. What *is* relevant is that the status quo privileged those who benefited from the extant distribution of wealth and power. At the time of classicism's triumph in the late nineteenth century, the legal and political order was manifestly not neutral: it intervened with lethal force when necessary to protect wealth and privilege. To its critics, law had become the fang and claw of predatory capitalism.

"The [Supreme] Court's power lies . . . in its legitimacy . . . [which] depends on making legally principled decisions under circumstances in which their principled character is sufficiently plausible to be accepted by the Nation," wrote the authors of the joint opinion in *Planned Parenthood of Southeastern Pennsylvania v. Casey* (1992).[9] That was no less true of the classical-era Court. The Justices of the era squandered the Court's legitimacy by seeming to succor one small segment of American society at the expense of the rest. The problem was not that classicist decisions were unprincipled, but rather the opposite: they were *too* principled, based on bloodless abstractions and theories that had no relationship to the real life of most Americans. Classical legal thought failed *Casey's* plausibility requirement. As the law's credibility eroded, so did its legitimacy, until, at the end, all that stood was, to borrow from another *Casey* opinion, "a sort of judicial Potemkin Village, which may be pointed out to passers by as a monument to the importance of adhering to precedent."[10] To an unsympathetic observer, only a façade of doctrine presented itself as the comely appearance of law; behind it lay a hovel of political reality.

Notes

1. American Federation of Labor v. American Sash and Door Co., 335 U.S. 538, 543–544, 549–550 (1949).
2. Herbert Hovenkamp, *Enterprise and American Law, 1836–1937* (1991), 177–182.
3. Richard A. Posner, *Economic Analysis of Law*, 4th ed. (1992), 626. It is not clear when Judge Posner thinks the era ended. See also Rehnquist, J., dissenting in Central Hudson Gas & Electric Corp. v. Public Service Commission, 447 U.S. 557, 592 (1980):"There is no reason for believing that ... the invisible hand will always lead to optimum economic decisions in the commercial market."
4. N.L.R.B. v. Jones & Laughlin Steel Corp., 301 U.S. 1, 40, 42 (1937).
5. David Montgomery, *The Fall of the House of Labor: The Workplace, the State, and American Labor Activism, 1865–1925* (1987), 2–5.

6. Quoted in Montgomery, *Fall of the House of Labor*, 4.

7. Richard Olney, "Discrimination against Union Labor—Legal?," 42 *Am. L. Rev.* 161, 164 (1908).

8. Home Building & Loan Assn. v. Blaisdell, 290 U.S. 398, 451 (1934).

9. 505 U.S. 833, 865–866 (1992).

10. 505 U.S. at 966 (Rehnquist, C.J., dissenting).

Appendix

Historiography and the Supreme Court

Writing and Reading History

For the reader who is not a historian, it might be useful to describe the uses of historiography in historical writing, and to sketch the historiography of the subject of this book.

Historians instinctively think in historiographic terms at some point in any project. Whether we discuss that historiography or not is a matter of taste, convention, or need. But historiography is a basic and essential ancillary activity to all historical writing.

When historians think about a historical subject, either to write about it or to teach it, we first ask what has already been written about it, partly as a way to inventory what is already known and partly to position ourselves in the flow of what has been written. There is no point to writing what has already been written, so we explore the historiography of a topic for gaps, errors, anomalies, inconsistencies, or simply in a search for promising terrains of what early mapmakers labeled *terra incognita*. It is customary to begin books or articles on historical topics with a cursory review of historiography, by way of explaining what we intend to say beyond what is already known.[1] Historiographic review is also a convenient way of opening up a challenge to existing interpretations.

Historiography serves the reader, as well. If you know nothing about the development of historical thinking on a subject, you might not be able to determine whether what you are reading conforms to what has been written and confirms it, or challenges and refutes it. Nonprofessional readers of history underestimate the grip that historical writing has on the way that we think about the past. Commonplace expressions like "History teaches us that . . ." or "We read in the history books that . . ." reflect this view. There is only a weak version of quality control in the writing of history, so that junk can be as enduring as good work in determining what lay people believe about the past.

When historians at the end of the twentieth century write about the role of the Supreme Court, we do so in a tradition of historiography that has developed over a century. That is not an accident, for "professional" history — history written and taught by people who devote full time to the project as a career — is itself just over a century old. Amateurs (no disparagement implied in that word) have been writing about the Supreme Court since the early nineteenth century, and writing some good and/or influential history. (Those, unfortunately, are not always the same thing.) But not until the end of the nineteenth century did historians begin to compile a body of critical, disciplined writing about the Court and its past. That historical writing has sometimes been critical of the Court and judicial review, sometimes more positive in its attitudes. But no historian who writes today, and no reader who "consumes" that historical writing, should ignore the historiography of the Court.

The best general introduction to the history of American historical writing, which has something to say about Supreme Court historiography, is Peter Novick, *That Noble Dream: The "Objectivity Question" and the American Historical Profession* (1988). Some constitutional historians have criticized the ways that one particular group of amateur historians, the Justices of the United States Supreme Court, have misused history: Charles A. Miller, *The Supreme Court and the Uses of History* (1969); Alfred H. Kelly, "Clio and the Court: An Illicit Love Affair," 1965 *Supreme Court Review* 119, and William M. Wiecek, "Clio as Hostage: The United States Supreme Court and the Uses of History," 24 *California Western Law Review* 227 (1988). Richard L. Aynes has provided a case study of what might be called the social construction of history and its manipulation to serve doctrinal and ideological ends on the Supreme Court, in "Charles Fairman, Felix Frankfurter, and the Fourteenth Amendment," 70 *Chicago-Kent Law Review.* 1197 (1995).

A recent one-volume interpretive survey of the Supreme Court's history, which might prove useful as background to the subject of this book, is Bernard Schwartz's *A History of the Supreme Court* (1993). A valuable reference work, providing succinct entries on everything relevant to the Court, is Kermit L. Hall et al., eds., *The Oxford Companion to the Supreme Court of the United States* (1992).

The Historiography of Legal Classicism

People have been writing about lawyers' ideology for almost as long as lawyers have been doing systematic thinking. This is true of legal classicism as well. We can distinguish three different periods in the historiography of the subject. Each was characterized by a prevalent attitude or coherent body of ideas about classical legal thought. This makes generalization possible and justifies treating classicism as a discrete phase of this subset of intellectual history. The labels and dates I adopt below are not wholly arbitrary.

The first period, which I will call "contemporary" or "Progressive," may be dated from 1910 to 1940. It emerged in the midday of classicism's reign and reflected dominant intellectual and ideological trends of the Progressive Era. The foremost figure of this period was the towering Princeton political scientist who was the nation's leading nonlawyer authority on the Constitution, Edward S. Corwin. Progressive historiography was not friendly to classicist premises.

The succeeding period, lasting from 1940 to 1970, might be considered a time of "liberal" or "neo-Progressive" thought. The liberal interpretation condemned the premises of classicism. It constituted the orthodoxy of its time, the post–World War II generation that was characterized by prosperity and insecurity.

The antithesis of the liberal interpretation emerged around 1970 and is currently dominant. This revisionist work on legal classicism rejects most liberal assumptions — or at least ideas imputed to the liberals of the 1950s, fairly or not. While there is no single, dominant interpretive thread in revisionist work, what unites historiography of the last quarter-century about classicism is a determination to relocate classicist figures like Stephen J. Field or Thomas M. Cooley more authentically in the context of their era and to dissociate their ideas from the shorthand caricatures liberal historiography had used to label them. Thus revisionist work is stimulating without being apologist, but it has not yet cohered as a unitary interpretation. It succeeds as critique but has not replaced the liberal tradition.

In the current revisionist era, some scholars continue to write about classicism in ways that reaffirm the enduring insights of the neo-Progressives while incorporating valid elements of the revisionist critique. The book you are now reading was written in that framework.

Contemporary or Progressive Interpretations, 1910–1940

An entrée for thinking about how historians have written about legal classicism might begin with their wider interpretations of the Progressive Era. With some sense of the intellectual currents of the age, the reader will be able to locate classicism and its critics in their time. Anything else runs the risk of reproducing the kind of arid doctrinalism, abstracted from social reality, that has characterized so much legal-historical writing in the past.

There has never been a single authoritative interpretation of Progressivism. Historians have not captured the heterogeneity and dynamism of Progressive-Era thought in a comprehensive, synthetic interpretation. They recognize that there was no canonical "Progressive" creed or set of values.[2] Some are doubtful that it makes any sense even to refer to "Progressivism" and are sure it does not make sense to refer to a "Progressive movement."[3] Reflecting this despair over synthesizing some distilled essence of Progressivism, one of the finest recent surveys of the era does not even refer to it as a discrete subject.[4]

"The Progressive interpretation of . . . ." can be a misleading phrase. When modern authorities speak of "the Progressive interpretation" of some constitutional topic like legal classicism, they usually mean the spirit of skepticism and challenge to orthodoxy represented by the vibrant works of the Progressive historians and their associates. Progressives did not constitute an intellectual monolith, and they did not share a consensus on fundamentals. While most Progressives did condemn *Lochner*, *Adair*, and other ornaments of classicism, contemporary critics of the Court lacked a unity of outlook and method. As there was no single Progressive movement, so there was no unified Progressive critique of the Supreme Court and its ideology. By referring to "Progressive interpretations," I mean to suggest only that scholars, jurists, and publicists who wrote about the court between 1900 and 1940 were influenced in their approaches by the prevailing ideas of the age, chiefly their rejection of classical economics and formalist logic.

Since neither comprehensive synthesis nor unitary interpretation of Progressivism is available, it might be more useful to explore one domain of the Progressive intellectual background, historical writing, as an introduction to the critique of classical legal thought. Progressive historians challenged the formalistic, reverential, and intellectually filiopietist tenor of then-current historical writing.[5] They scoffed at claims of objectivity in historical writing and denied even the possibility of writing history as Leopold von Ranke had demanded, *"wie es eigentlich gewesen"* ("as it really was"). That bad attitude provoked the enduring wrath of more traditionalist-minded contemporaries and later conservatives.[6]

Charles A. Beard was the most influential of the Progressive historians. His *Economic Interpretation of the Constitution* (1913)[7] shocked contemporaries accustomed to revering the document as American civic religion's equivalent of sacred scripture. Beard depicted the drafting of the Constitution and the struggle over its ratification as a conflict of economic interests. The Constitution "was essentially an economic document based upon the concept that the fundamental private rights of property are anterior to government and morally beyond the reach of popular majorities." Beard might have expected that such thoughts would gladden the hearts of the *Adair* and *Coppage* jurists.

Conservatives who denounced Beard's profanation of the secular ark of the covenant were little mollified by the fact that the year before, he had published a study[8] arguing that judicial review was consistent with the intentions of the Framers, who sought to establish a regime of "judicial control" over such democratic initiatives as currency devaluation and meddling with contracts by debtor stay laws.

Justice Holmes was unimpressed with *An Economic Interpretation*: "Except for a covert sneer I can't see anything in it so far," he reported on reading it.[9] But Holmes was unique in his emotional distance from the subject. Many readers reviled the book; all were shaken from their complacency about the Virgin Birth of the American constitutional order. The problem was not that Beard called attention to the play of economic interests; after all, Madison had done just that in *Federalist* Number 10. Rather, it was that Beard's sympathies were clearly with the democratic impulses supposedly suppressed in the constitutional Thermidor of 1787. Bad form, bad timing: it would just not do to invert conventional sympathies and winners' history as the nation was about to plunge into the jingoist frenzy of the Great War and its repressive aftermath, the first Red Scare.

Beard's *Economic Interpretation* had the larger effect of subjecting the entire experience of American constitutionalism to critical review; it set the tone, as it were. Beard and his wife Mary R. Beard, a historian in her own right, repeated the heresy with the 1927 publication of *The Rise of American Civilization*, which provided a compelling interpretation of the entire sweep of the American past as a struggle of economic interest groups.

Beard was seconded by Carl L. Becker, whose 1909 study of prerevolutionary political parties in New York[10] similarly stressed the role of economic conflict in America's past. His later work on the Declaration of Independence[11] remains today an insightful study of political thought, but it was suspect in the eyes of contemporaries because it lacked the appropriate cheerleading spirit. Others, most notably the political scientist J. Allen Smith[12] and the *litterateur* Vernon L. Parrington,[13] similarly extolled democracy and deplored conservative efforts to smother the insurgencies of the lower orders with a legal/constitutional pillow. Frederick Jackson Turner wrote idyllically of frontier democracy and displayed an obvious distaste for the effete, Europe-oriented civilization of the east coast, implicitly denigrating its constitutionally structured legal order.

Beard, Becker, and Turner established the Progressive tradition in American historical writing. With their counterparts in economics, philosophy, and political science, they desanctified the mystique of constitutional debate, making constitutional argument accessible to others outside the hieratic caste of lawyers and judges who treated it as their exclusive preserve. Progressive historiography in its earlier phase tended to a dualistic, almost Manichaean, vision of events that corresponded to the crude Progressive mantra of The People versus The Interests. Progressives optimistically believed that society was moving toward a higher plane of organization and consciousness; they did their bit to nudge it along. As they modernized historical writing, so they hoped their work would help modernize society.[14]

Historical writing on the Constitution during the later nineteenth century had begun to develop a protorealist approach, abandoning a formalistic and theoretical reverence for the Constitution as a static collection of precepts and replacing it with a dynamic interpretation that stressed institutions and interests. Using evolutionary models of explanation, historians and political scientists searched for the real workings and motivations of the constitutional order.[15] Beard even attacked classical legal thought itself: the classicists' "devotion to deductions from 'principles' exemplified in particular cases, which is such a distinguishing sign of American legal thinking, has the same effect upon correct analysis which the adherence to abstract terms had upon the advancement of learning."[16]

This realist approach carried over into the new century, where it flowed into another powerful current of interpretation, one that stressed economic motivations underlying human behavior. This "economic interpretation," associated after 1913 with Beard, rejected the traditional static interpretation of constitutional thought that had focused on concepts, rather than interests. This rivalry created an oscillation between two poles of thought, which the foremost student of constitutional historiography in this era terms "traditional" and "realist."[17] In its most exaggerated form, the "realist" position derided the very idea of the rule of law, dismissing courts as lackeys or "servitors of the ruling economic forces."[18] It is this extreme position, associated either with socialist writings of a vulgar-Marxist bent or with heated Progressive political rhetoric, that is often attributed to the entire Progressive enterprise. In reality, Progressive scholarship was diverse, heterogeneous, and less prone to oversimplification than a pure economic interpretation might suggest.

The oscillation between traditionalist and realist poles continued up to 1940, with enduring works of scholarship being produced by both tendencies. Andrew C. McLaughlin, Charles H. McIlwain, Max Farrand, Charles Warren, Randolph G. Adams, and Benjamin F. Wright wrote in the idealist vein, stressing the importance of constitutional ideas, while Beard, Arthur F. Bentley, J. Allen Smith, James G. Ran-dall, William B. Munro, Louis Boudin, and Walton Hamilton discounted the disembodied force of ideas and stressed the struggle of economic forces.

The Princeton political scientist Edward S. Corwin was the dominant academic figure of Progressive historiography. His writings bracket the era.[19] He began with a piece in 1909 criticizing the Supreme Court's development of due process doctrine[20] and brought this phase of his career to a climax with four books written between 1934 and 1941 that offered a thoroughgoing critique of the Court's posture in the 1930s.[21] All who work in the field of constitutional history today tread in tracks that Corwin blazed. Some of his original insights, such as the concept of class legislation, have been rediscovered recently; others have provided the enduring canon of scholarship throughout the century.

Lawyers too were influenced by the trends of Progressive thought in history and political science. James Bradley Thayer and Oliver Wendell Holmes Jr. had laid the foundations of the Progressive legal critique of classicism in the 1890s, Thayer stressing the finite bounds of judicial review and Holmes offering a radical alternative to classicist assumptions in "The Path of the Law." The writings and speeches of Roscoe Pound between 1906 and 1913 were instinct with Progressive insights. He was the first to define the assumptions and dogmas of classicism. Holmes, Thayer, and Pound demonstrated that public and private law are shaped by struggles among interest groups for their own advantage. Law is thus not some transcendent or immanent product of reason alone. In fact, to the extent that lawyers and judges relied on abstract reason, unenlightened by human experience, law inevitably drifted away from reality. Abstract and artificial doctrines were a sign that judges were pursuing policy ends reflecting their own economic biases rather than the experience of all the parties before them, including working people and their families.

Other legal commentators warned of the expansive potential of due process even before the Supreme Court realized it in the 1890s.[22] In the next decade, scholars and judges denounced substantive due process, as well as the power the Court was arrogating to itself by deploying that doctrine.[23] State court judges[24] and political scientists[25] vied with each other in denouncing these trends, the academics being more decorous and measured in their attacks. Various scholarly criticisms[26] complemented the chest-thumping and self-promoting op-ed pieces by Theodore Roosevelt in *The Outlook*, which peddled various nostrums popular among Progressives clustered around his Bull Moose campaign.[27] These remedies included such structural reforms as requirements of supermajorities on the Court to invalidate federal statutes, congressional override of judicial vetoes, and limited-term appointments for federal judges.

From the socialist band of the political spectrum came two criticisms of judicial power significant for their class-based analysis: Louis B. Boudin's "Government by Judiciary" (1911),[28] the more moderate, and Gustavus Myers's *History of the Supreme Court of the United States* (1912), the only explicitly Marxian presentation of that topic.

Other legal scholars besides Pound made weighty contributions to Progressive thought about classicism. Ernst Freund's *Police Power* (1904)[29] provided an extensive analysis and review of police power doctrine, which could have served as a massive and learned foundation for that line of precedents in the classicist period upholding the exercise of state legislative power. Rodney L. Mott later did the same for the due

process clause, though his treatment was only implicitly critical and more in the nature of a catalogue.[30]

Of course, the Court did not lack for defenders in the Progressive Era, and not
all of them can be dismissed as reactionaries or shills for corporate elites. Charles
Warren, assistant attorney general in the Wilson administration from 1914 to 1918
and one of the twentieth century's most celebrated constitutional historians, demonstrated that the Court upheld legislation more often than it struck statutes down,
leaping from that observation to the questionable conclusion that the Court was
"progressive."[31] For this reason, Warren concluded in his 1925 study, *Congress, the
Constitution and the Supreme Court*, that Progressive proposals to inhibit judicial
review were unnecessary and mischievous. Warren was a staunch conservative,[32] yet
his study of the origins of the 1789 Judiciary Act's section 25 contributed significantly
to cutting back on the Court's power to declare general common law.[33] His *The
Supreme Court in United States History* (1922; rev'd ed. 1926) remains in active use
today, a monument of scholarship in a genre of writing — history — where authors
consider themselves blessed if their books have a shelf-life of ten years. Other eminent jurists, lawyers, and scholars came to the defense of the Court in the Progressive Era: Justice Horace H. Lurton (writing off the bench),[34] future Chief Justice
(and former president) William Howard Taft,[35] the noted historian Andrew C.
McLaughlin,[36] William M. Meigs,[37] and Joseph H. Choate.[38]

These patterns of thought repeated themselves in the second or later Progressive
surge that occurred in the midst of that decade of reaction, the 1920s. Economists[39]
and philosophers[40] continued to undermine the foundations of classical thought,
without overtly attacking the Supreme Court. Max Lerner, however, linked judicial
power and its economic impact in a realist-influenced essay dispelling any lingering
naive thoughts that the Court might be above contemplating its real-world impact
on the distribution of wealth and power.[41] Thomas Reed Powell attempted to de-
mystify the Court's thought processes.[42] Former Justice (and future Chief Justice)
Charles Evans Hughes provided a laudatory yet realistic look at the Court's power,[43]
while the dean of the Columbia Law School (and another future Chief Justice),
Harlan Fiske Stone, endorsed some of the critical thought concerning the Court's
work.[44] In 1930 Felix Frankfurter and Nathan Greene brought out their critical survey of the ways that courts used the labor injunction to suppress organized labor.[45]

Liberal or Neo-Progressive Interpretations, 1940–1970

A unified approach to classical thought dominated historiography at mid-century. I
will call this interpretation "liberal," with the connotations of 1960s liberalism, or
"neo-Progressive," meaning that its proponents traced their ideological heritage
back to Progressive thought early in the century.

As Edward S. Corwin dominated the earlier period, so two analyses determined
the intellectual content of the neo-Progressive interpretation. These were Richard
Hofstadter's treatment of social Darwinism[46] and Morton G. White's discussion of
the "revolt against formalism."[47] Between them, Hofstadter and White impressed on
mid-century historical consciousness the image of a dominant pattern of thought
(competition, struggle, survival of the fittest) and the reaction to it (antiformalism).

Hofstadter was a remarkable historian. Though associated with the dominant approach to American history in the 1950s, labeled "consensus history," he transcended it by the durability of his insights, so that when consensus history was scuttled in the 1960s, Hofstadter's influence floated serenely above the wreckage. We still recur to his interpretations for insight and inspiration.

The gravamen of the neo-Progressive indictment focused on the classical jurists' ideological prepossessions, social vision, and juristic method, as well as the substantive elements of the classical outlook. The synopsis of liberal thought presented in the next few pages is slightly overdrawn, but it conveys the condemnation of classicism common to writers of the post–World War II era.

To the liberal eye, classical jurists were ideologically driven.[48] In a negative sense, they were tormented by the incubus of socialism. Chief Judge Holmes was the fountainhead of the interpretation that ascribed classical doctrine to this antisocialist mentality. "The comfortable classes of the community" were frightened by the bogey of socialism, and that fear "has influenced judicial actions both here and in England," he averred in his 1897 lecture, "The Path of the Law."[49]

[S]omething similar has led people who no longer hope to control the legislatures, to look to the courts as expounders of the Constitution, and . . . in some courts new principles have been discovered outside of the bodies of those instruments [constitutions] which may be generalized into acceptance of the economic doctrines which prevailed about fifty years ago.

On a positive note, the liberal interpretation insisted that classical judges were devout believers in the secular creed of laissez-faire, derived from their commitment to classical economics.[50] They were also social Darwinians, believing that progress was the result of a struggle for survival.[51] Regret for a child condemned to labor in mine or mill was as misplaced as pity for the herbivore condemned by natural selection to be the prey of the carnivore. The only function of the state was to protect property and enforce contracts; otherwise, classical creed taught, the state must get out of the way lest it disturb the beneficent workings of the natural order. If that natural order condemned the many to penury and rewarded the few with opulence, well, who was to question the workings of a benevolent (or at least impartial) regime of free contract? All of this, neo-Progressives charged, the classical jurists believed was ordained and protected by the federal and state constitutions.

Classicists' ideology shaped their vision of society. After the general strikes of 1877 and 1886 roused them from torpid complacency, classical jurists saw a society curiously resembling that of the socialists' vision: a Hobbesian world of class struggle, in which workers, immigrants, and the poor were contained only by iron Malthusian laws from below and the armed force of the state from above. The classical social vision in the 1890s was pessimistic and fearful, based on a dour view of human nature. The poor, left to themselves, were feckless and improvident, envious of the property of the more industrious and unrestrained by inner constraint from seeking to despoil it. Any form of organizing the working poor, whether in labor union, political party, or social group, threatened to lend the power of united force to collectivized avarice. Classicists were unfeeling about the sufferings of working people,[52] and they positively loathed unions. The immigrant hordes pouring in from eastern and southern Europe, Mexico, and Asia boded ill for the permanence of Anglo-Saxon institutions. Strangers to enlightened religion and democracy, the immigrants might cooperate with another group of eugenically condemned unassimilables, only recently freed from slavery, and other scourings of society to overturn the institutions that had bestowed prosperity on the deserving.

Classicists, in the liberal view, were antidemocratic, fearing popular political power and its consequences. The worst of these consequences would be redistribution of wealth. Vague notions of the French Revolution were refreshed for classical jurists by the more recent revolutionary upheavals in Paris in 1870–1871, by the wave of assassinations that plagued Europe in the late nineteenth century, and by the anarchist, syndicalist, and socialist sects that flourished on the Continent. To the skeptic who might note that the crowds were not exactly storming the Bastille in America, the classical jurist could point to the violence that seemed inevitably to mar efforts to unionize mines and railroads. Clearly Justice Brewer was hag-ridden by just such a vision when he wrote the *Debs* opinion in 1895.

But the meritorious could be despoiled of their property in ways that did not involve dynamiting or shoot-outs. They might have agreed with Woody Guthrie that some men rob you with a gun, some men rob you with a fountain pen — in this case, the pen that signed confiscatory legislation into law. Taxation was the most obvious route, but there was no limit to legislative ingenuity in the service of plunder. Thus classical jurists feared the regulatory state. It was a structural innovation, if nothing else, and it carried the potential to hobble industrialists in their pursuit of profits and markets.

Classicists' social vision was out of touch with reality. Perhaps one source of the "cultural lag" hypothesis was jurists' view of American society in their time, a vision not only dated and impoverished, but also disabled in severely dysfunctional ways from comprehending the reality about them (think of Stephen J. Field's apocalyptic and hallucinatory vision of impending class warfare in the *Income Tax Cases*).

Social vision produced the classicist image of law, a simplistic, reductionist enterprise that sought to identify some minimal number of fundamental principles, universally and at all times valid, to which all law must conform. To make such a vision work, the classicists relied on a highly formalistic, abstract mode of reasoning, and inculcated that "artificial reason of the law" (Coke's phrase) in the recently developed Langdellian law school curriculum. Under such a regime, the limited Marshallian conception of judicial review bloated into the doctrine of judicial supremacy that would lead Peckham to pontificate in *Lochner* that "we do not believe in the soundness of the views which uphold this law."

The classical jurists' attitude suggests a title of one of Goya's drawings: "The sleep of reason begets monsters." The classical mind was fecund with doctrinal monsters: substantive due process, liberty of contract, hostility to the police power. Artificial distinctions without differences sprang spontaneously to the classical jurists, the more dichotomous the better. Conservative casuistry was up to the task of inventing impediments to legislative power never dreamed of by the Framers.

The neo-Progressives did not, however, contend that the classical jurists were merely mouthpieces for their investor/capitalist masters. They avoided a simplistic vision that might have seen judges as being driven solely by class self-interest or subservience to ruling elites. However captivated some original Progressives may have been with the vision of "The People versus the Interests," later neo-Progressives did not fall into that oversimplification. Liberals tended rather to the idealist end of the intellectual continuum, attributing causal effect to ideas — which is precisely why they took the thought of the classical jurists so seriously.

Building on the image of American elites in the grip of classical economic pre-suppositions, constitutional historians of the liberal era generally portrayed judges and lawyers of the Progressive era as *devotés* of laissez-faire. This perception provided the theses for a quartet of interpretive studies that, taken together, explained, in the subtitle Benjamin Twiss chose for the first of them, "how laissez-faire came to the Supreme Court."[53] Treatise writers like Cooley, Dillon, and Tiedeman bore some of the responsibility, according to Clyde Jacobs.[54] Sidney Fine portrayed them as part of a wider intellectual tradition of laissez-faire that came into conflict with modern society in which it was obsolete, irrelevant, and obstructive of progress.[55] The colli-sion between laissez-faire and modernity occurred in the 1890s, producing what Arnold Paul termed a "conservative crisis" among most leading American judges, who reacted to it fiercely.[56] The magisterial authority of the previous era, Edward S. Corwin, endorsed this view.[57]

The influence of the liberal vision is incalculable. It represented interpretive or-thodoxy in its time. It enjoyed an extraordinary persistence, dominating without rival all interpretive texts that were used to teach constitutional history and related topics, including Robert G. McCloskey's *The American Supreme Court* (1960; 2nd and posthumous ed., 1994); the influential Mason and Beaney public law textbook in political science;[58] the Kelly and Harbison constitutional history textbook;[59] Carl B. Swisher, *American Constitutional Development* (2nd ed. 1954); and Benjamin F. Wright, *The Growth of American Constitutional Law* (1942). Because its premises underlay and permeated these widely used undergraduate texts, and because it con-tinues to be influential even today in college classrooms, liberal historiography has been the introduction to classical thought for two generations of undergraduates who have become today's lawyers, judges, historians, and law professors. The vision of laissez-faire ideology and social-Darwinian outlook dominating constitutional adjudication in the Progressive era continues to structure some constitutional law casebooks.[60]

In addition to informing classroom texts, the neo-Progressive view dominated interpretive studies of the period. McCloskey elaborated on it in his treatment of Justice Stephen J. Field in *American Conservatism in the Age of Enterprise*.[61] The two later volumes of the constitutional subset in the New American Nation series, written by Loren Beth and Paul Murphy, covering the period from 1877 to 1969, adopted the liberal perspective.[62] The preceding volume, which touched on the con-stitutional foundations of the Gilded Age, also assumed its validity.[63] Thus all the ex-tant volumes of that monument of mid-twentieth-century scholarship, the New American Nation series, were written within the liberal paradigm.[64] Other leading constitutional interpretations, including those of William Swindler,[65] Leo Pfeffer,[66] and Bernard Schwartz,[67] similarly affirm neo-Progressive assumptions.[68] The liberal interpretation even extended its influence into an unlikely venue, a history of the Su-preme Court written by a well-placed amateur historian, William H. Rehnquist.[69]

It perdures into the present. A recent example of its tenacious hold appears in *Make No Law*, Anthony Lewis's best-selling account of *New York Times v. Sullivan*:

> In the latter part of the nineteenth century and the early years of the twentieth the Supreme Court focused on protecting the economic interests of business. It found in the Fourteenth Amendment's rule against deprivation of liberty or property without due process of law a "liberty of contract," enforcing this by, for example, holding maximum-hour laws and restrictions on child labor unconstitutional.[70]

Linked in critics' eyes with the neo-Progressives were scholars of the Left in the 1960s. There is an irony in such an identification, for Left historians generally rejected the liberal vision more emphatically than they did the conservative. Apparently, however, since both liberal and Left were critical of classical thought, they must be related. Though obviously sympathetic to the socialist vision,[71] historians of the Left were not entirely dismissive of its antithesis, the intellectual environment of classical thought. James Weinstein[72] and Gabriel Kolko[73] developed the concept of "corporate liberalism," rejecting a "robber barons" image of corporate leaders as implacably opposed to regulation and the administrative state. Instead, both demonstrated the ways in which large corporations welcomed, when they did not clamor for, extensive administrative oversight to avoid destructive competition. In this, Left historians advanced beyond the somewhat two-dimensional liberal landscape.

Revisionist Interpretations, 1970–Present

Orthodoxy stimulates challenges to its dominance. Thomas Kuhn has sketched one influential description of the process.[74] A dominant paradigm (here, an orthodox explanation of a phenomenon like legal classicism) guides research and structures thought. In conducting investigations within this paradigm, researchers occasionally note the existence of anomalies: phenomena not anticipated or explained by the paradigm. They may advance new theories to explain the anomaly, which are then incorporated into the paradigm if possible. Kuhn terms this a paradigm change: the paradigm shifts or adjusts to take the new theory into account. In other cases, investigators may see the old paradigm as failing in some fundamental way to explain its basic phenomena, in which case a crisis of scientific explanation ensues. New theories appear as candidates to replace the regnant paradigm. The classic example was the Copernican theory of a heliocentric solar system challenging the Ptolemaic geocentric model.[75] When the old paradigm is overthrown and a new one substituted in its place, a scientific revolution has occurred.

The succession of revisionist to liberal explanations of legal classicism is following the former model of paradigm shift and adaptation, rather than the latter one of scientific revolution.[76] Since the 1960s, historians have been exploring some particular topic, often in biographical research, and find that the restricted categories of neo-Progressive thought fail to account satisfactorily for some apparent idea or behavior of their subject; in Kuhn's terms, they come across an anomaly. When the anomaly persists or reappears in other areas, obviously a new explanation or a revision of the old paradigm is called for.

Historical writing about classical thought since 1970 has been rich in interpretive innovation, but it has not yet yielded a unitary, coherent explanation that has displaced its orthodox rival.[77] Rather, like the Progressives, the revisionists are heterogeneous in their challenges to liberal orthodoxy. Thus it is misleading to regard revisionism as the antithesis to liberalism's thesis in a Hegelian sense.

The term "revisionist" comes freighted with distracting connotations, however, and is even less satisfactory as a descriptor than "liberal." Lynne Cheney on one hand, and Holocaust deniers on the other, have corrupted the term "revisionist" almost beyond rehabilitation. A brief digression on the concept of historical revisionism in general is necessary. *All* written history is revisionist. The only point to writing history at all is to revise previously held beliefs about the past, which are based on earlier written work or on tradition. Corruptions of the term, like Cheney's usage,[78] suggest that there is something subversive, suspect, or unnatural about revising history. Nonsense; we write to revise. Revision has no inherent ideological spin; it is the normal activity of rethinking the past. Thus attributing the term "revisionist" to an individual or a group is not pejorative (or flattering either). It merely indicates, in a neutral way, that normal historical activity is going on.

The revisionist historians of the last quarter-century have sought to redeem classical jurists from the imputation that their decisions were driven by class interest. Recent historians depict the classicists as dedicated to ideals of liberty, economic opportunity, or competitive capitalism, not as simply seeking to protect business from governmental regulation or to impose some abstract system of classical economics on the Constitution.[79] Instead, revisionists argue, classical jurists defended venerable traditions of the American constitutional order.

The classical jurists were confronted with bewildering, threatening economic and social change at a time when they lacked intellectual resources, such as well-developed methods of investigation in the social sciences, to understand these problems and deal with them. By default, classicist judges fell back on what they understood to be core values of the American experience, values that had been established in the Revolution and affirmed by the Civil War. Revisionists fault the liberal interpretation for judging those responses by the standards of a later era, and insist that the hopes, fears, and achievements of the classical jurists be considered in the light of their times, not ours. One acerbic criticism[80] suggests that liberal historiography was winners' history, a reinterpretation of the Progressive Era meant to vindicate the achievements of the New Deal by casting classical jurisprudence in as unfavorable a light as possible.

Respectful biographies of two judges who dominated the classical era first challenged neo-Progressivism's dominance. Willard King brought out a study of Fuller[81] that was precocious at the date of its publication, 1950, in rejecting the dismissive estimate of Fuller then prevalent. Joel Paschal produced less apologetic studies of George Sutherland, limning with delicacy and jurisprudential depth the thinking of a judge he epitomized as "A Man against the State".[82]

Other biographies of giants of the classical era, including Thomas M. Cooley[83] and Stephen J. Field, depicted a depth and dimensionality in their outlook that redeemed their subjects' reputation from neo-Progressive criticisms. Even David Brewer, one of the most hopeless of liberal *bêtes noires*, has enjoyed something of an on-going rehabilitation.[84] Charles McCurdy's work on Field disclosed a jurist who had outlived his times, a man attached to Jacksonian Democratic visions of the social order, clinging to a social vision rapidly obsolescing in the last two decades of the nineteenth century.[85] McCurdy reconsidered the emergence of the regulatory state and classicist decisions like *Knight* in a different light, as a manifestation of lingering state power orientation.[86] His compelling reconsiderations of Field's thought rescued that jurist's reputation from such unfortunate consequences of staying on too long as his *Income Tax Cases II* concurrence.

McCurdy's emphasis on lingering antebellum state power influences in judicial thought bore fruit in the work of his student Robert Stanley, whose remarkable study of the federal income tax and its rejection in the *Pollock* cases rethinks the nineteenth-century judicial order.[87] Stanley respects the Progressive historiographic tradition but rejects it as fundamentally beside the point in its treatment of taxation. His work, which eschews modern vogues of both Right and Left, calls into question the very possibility of reform.

The early forays into revision, focused or derived from biographical studies of individual jurists, led to broader interpretations that concentrated on topics, like substantive due process, or on periods of the Court's history, such as the Fuller era. McCurdy, for one, revisited the origins of liberty-of-contract doctrine.[88] Other scholars analyzed "styles of reasoning" or the "rhetoric" of the classical jurists.[89] They concluded that a single-minded emphasis on formalism as a defining characteristic of classical judging was insufficient to explain the results or spirit of that judicial era.

One of the revisionists' most valuable criticisms was that liberal historians had paid insufficient attention to those decisions of the classical era, principally from the United States Supreme Court, that had upheld regulatory legislation. It would not do (as this present book does) simply to note their existence and their inconsistency with their antiregulatory opposites. Melvin Urofsky retraced the work of Charles Warren two generations earlier and reconfirmed that both federal and state courts had sustained a broad sweep of regulatory legislation.[90]

Mary C. Porter did not attempt to defend the "progressiveness" of the Supreme Court as the Warren/Urofsky approach did. Rather, she suggested that in default of modern regulatory agencies and a tradition of administrative government, the Court attempted to serve as a sort of national regulatory pseudocommission, at least for supervising state rate regulation.[91] She might have buttressed her thesis by reviewing the role of federal courts in supervising railroad refinance at the end of the nineteenth century, where the federal court system did indeed serve as an informal national railroad administration.

Neo-Progressives displayed little interest in the inner dynamics of judicial decision-making on the Fuller, White, and Taft Courts. A closer attention to voting patterns, Stephen Siegel has demonstrated,[92] yields finer distinctions than a crude classicist-Progressive dichotomy. His analysis disclosed three blocs on the Fuller Court, corresponding to conservative-moderate-liberal shadings on an ideological continuum. Emphasizing the "constitutional conceptualism" (roughly, formalism) of those jurists he terms "laissez-faire constitutionalists," Siegel locates their thought as a continuation of antebellum trends and as a transition to modern constitutional thought, seeing in classicism both tradition and modernity. Siegel's work provides the finest available discussion of historicism in American law.[93]

A culmination of this reinterpretive trend came with the 1985 publication of Michael Les Benedict's review of the ideological foundations of laissez-faire constitutionalism.[94] Like all other revisionist scholars, Benedict rejected the imputation of class-based motivation to the classical jurists. Instead, he explored the moral and normative aspects of classical economics as expounded by men like Francis Wayland and Amasa Walker, who in their day were called "moral philosophers" or political economists, and who condemned economically discriminatory legislation not because it was inefficient but because it was "partial" or class legislation. Classical legal thought thus rested on an ethical libertarian foundation, rather than on the greed or fears of a governing elite.

Benedict traced the lineage of a venerable American philosophical tradition supporting that view, from Revolutionary-Era incorporation of the commonwealth principle in the first state constitutions, to the numerous antimonopoly, antiprivilege provisions in those same constitutions, to Jacksonian Democratic hostility to special privilege, through antislavery resistance to the privileges of the slavocracy and concurrent Republican commitment to the ideology of free labor. He concluded that on the eve of laissez-faire's explosive impact on the Supreme Court in the 1890s, jurists and treatise writers invoked hostility to "class legislation" or "special legislation" as a justification for condemning state legislation having a differential economic impact. Such legislation included taxation of urban property, regulation of the terms of labor contracts, enactments permitting strikes and boycotts, the regulation of railroad and warehouse rates, protective tariffs, monetary policy, subsidies, and taxation having a nonuniform incidence. It was this dedication to liberty defined in economic terms, rather than overt class bias, that accounted for classical constitutional thought, Benedict contends.

Daniel Ernst seconded Benedict's emphases in a study that explored the law of industrial relations. He contended that labor-related decisions were essentially "moralistic," stressing the moral value of work, the equivalence of rights of workers and employers (the first to work, the second to manage), and the irreducibly private nature of the employment contract.[95]

The article-length studies noted above broke new ground; they suggested shortcomings of the liberal interpretation; they offered important discrete theses about the classicist courts. But the typical length of an article, even the lengthy, massively footnoted pieces found in law reviews, is too short for an author to develop a comprehensive explanation of an important subject and defend it adequately. None of them individually or all of them collectively established a new canon, however much they might have disturbed the old. The appearance of monographic studies in the revisionist framework signaled the maturity of the new interpretation. Only the larger field offered by the monograph could be sufficient to enable scholars to establish a new direction of thought.

John Semonche produced the first monograph written under the new dispensation, *Charting the Future* (1978).[96] In it, he relied on an unusual but useful device, of analyzing the Fuller and White Courts in five-year segments, which provided a better sense of day-to-day continuity in the court's work and diluted the impact of analytical categories such as "labor legislation." The perspective thus provided enabled him to discredit the idea of a monolithic Court hostile to all economic reform.

As the revisionist work began to make its impact felt, two pivotal studies of the Holmes Devise series, *History of the Supreme Court of the United States*, appeared.[97] The earlier of the two, covering the White Court, was written by Alexander Bickel and Benno Schmidt, and appeared in 1984.[98] It represented the earlier tradition of lawyers' history in the Holmes Devise, then under the general editorial supervision of the eminent constitutional authority and law professor Paul Freund. Bickel's part of the volume reflected his lawyer's approach to the topic, giving scrupulous attention to cases of lesser importance an historian might have overlooked, but displaying little sense of a broad interpretive vision. For example, Bickel gave the vitally important case of *Coppage v. Kansas* (1915) only the briefest passing notice, even though he recognized it as "notorious." Schmidt's segment, dealing with civil rights cases, provided a contrast: it displayed awareness of historiographic controversy, something to which Bickel was utterly indifferent. Thus the White Court Holmes Devise volume simply passed by the controversy over classicism with scarcely an acknowledgment that it existed or mattered.

It was quite otherwise with Owen Fiss's volume on the Fuller Court, published in 1993 and reflecting the editorial influence of Freund's successor as general editor, historian Stanley N. Katz.[99] Though Fiss too is a lawyer rather than a historian, his volume addressed historiographic questions. He concedes that he "labor[s] uneasily against a scholarly tradition that treats all of the talk of liberty by the Fuller Court as mere camouflage or subterfuge and insists that Fuller and his colleagues were simply using their power to further class interests."[100] The Fiss volume is one of the major reinterpretive contributions of the revisionist effort. While recognizing the influence and importance of classicist modes of thought, Fiss contended that the Fuller Court was dedicated to its own conception of liberty, rooted in an older vision of American society. Classical judges were determined to protect that liberty against the threatening social disruptions of the late nineteenth century, especially those emanating from the labor movement.

Taking up the truly difficult cases — *Debs*, *Income Tax*, *Knight*, *Lochner* — Fiss provides an account of the period at odds with the neo-Progressive interpretation. He maintains that "liberty was the guiding ideal of the Fuller Court," but it was "conceived of as something that belonged personally to the individual, like a special kind of property or possession." It was defined by "the social contract tradition," which reduced "liberty to a demand for limited government. The state was seen as the natural enemy of freedom, prohibiting individuals from doing whatever they wished, setting limits on their conduct, or requisitioning their property." Under such a regime, "government power — that of the states as well as the federal government — was held to be limited to the accomplishment of discrete, previously defined ends."[101] Fiss is sensitive to the flow and ebb of historical interpretation, seeing the Rehnquist Court as reverting to this older contractarian tradition.

Howard Gillman has approached the problem of *Lochner*-era jurisprudence from the perspective of political theory.[102] He maintains that classical jurists were motivated not by class bias or adherence to some economic creed, but rather to the older constitutional ideal of hostility to "partial" legislation. This older tradition insisted that, to be valid, legislation must promote the general welfare and not the interests of one or another interest group or class. The Jacksonian ideals of political equality and government neutrality among classes and economic interests confirmed the Framers' effort to prohibit government from using state power to advance special interests. This outlook had become obsolete in the social conditions of industrial America, so *Lochner's* vice consisted of fidelity to an older jurisprudential outlook, not an innovative imposition of a new-fangled Spencerian economic/social philosophy on the constitutional structure. William E. Nelson's prize-winning reinterpretation of the Fourteenth Amendment[103] reinforces this position, stressing late-nineteenth-century precedents that condemned "class legislation" while sustaining laws that had been enacted to benefit the entire society. Richard Maidment emphasizes the constraining discipline of precedent, logic, and shared judicial culture as determinants of classicism.[104]

The appearance of synthetic studies, which combine recent interpretations into a synthesis designed to bring newer work to a wider audience, often undergraduate classrooms, is a sign that an interpretive trend has reached maturity. James W. Ely's survey of the Fuller Court performs that function,[105] as does Kermit Hall's classroom text, which approaches the subject in a more qualified, nuanced spirit than the liberal texts had.[106] Another sign that revisionist approaches have arrived and been widely accepted is the publication of monographs that explore some subset of the larger topic, within the new or reconfigured understanding provided by more comprehensive revisionist work. Such an effort is William LaPiana's reconsideration of one foundation of classicism, Langdellian legal education.[107] Appearing after a string of studies on the impact of the Harvard Law School published during the prior three decades, LaPiana's book brings a refreshingly positive attitude toward the contributions of Langdell's pedagogical legal science, partially rescuing it from the scorn in which it has languished since Holmes' crushing review in 1880.

Ensconced within the revisionist effort, yet distanced from it, are several works ideologically driven, avowedly retrograde in the sense that the authors proclaim their belief that classicism was not only understandable in its time — the position of all other revisionist studies — but also normatively, objectively, and enduringly *right*. The earliest such effort, and one whose ideological posture contributed in some unknown measure to the author's failure of confirmation to the United States Court of Appeals for the Ninth Circuit, was Bernard Siegan's *Economic Liberties and the Constitution*,[108] an effort to rehabilitate economic substantive due process. Siegan has complemented this pioneering effort (if that is the phrase) with other works extolling the Spencerian world of *Lochner* and recommending it to moderns as normatively preferable to the regulatory state. Only one of these, *The Supreme Court's Constitution*,[109] is historical in its approach.

Richard Epstein has gone back to the property law component of classical legal thought to propose far more extensive curbs on regulatory activity than are permissible in the postclassical world.[110] Promoted by the advocacy of conservative activist groups and legal foundations, Epstein's thoughts have found a sympathetic audience on the Supreme Court. Several modern decisions inhibiting state regulatory authority[111] suggest that public law may be moving toward an outlook congenial to the approach of *Pennsylvania Coal Co. v. Mahon*. David E. Bernstein provides a bizarre variant on this theme, contending that labor-protective legislation and decisions supporting it were hostile to the interests of black Americans, apparently in their capacity as strikebreakers and reserve labor pool. He goes so far as to blame New Deal labor legislation, like the Wagner Act, for creation of a "black underclass."[112]

Two studies use historical revisionism to influence legal change in the present.[113] Both advocate a return to classical jurisprudence in its purest form, and thus assume the burden of arguing that the past half-century of legal development has been wrong. Each regards the anticlassical legal traditions established by Holmes, Brandeis, and Cardozo, to say nothing of more modern jurists, as misguided. Stephen Presser's polemic endorses some major beliefs of classical legal thought,[114] while Hadley Arkes's apologia for Justice Sutherland is more historically and jurisprudentially oriented.[115]

Despite the powerful current of revisionist arguments, some scholars continue to work in the neo-Progressive tradition. Duncan Kennedy established the basis for this inquiry in a theoretical analysis of "The Rise and Fall of Classical Legal Thought, 1850–1940" (1975), probably the most influential unpublished manuscript in modern legal theory.[116] He published a brief, allusive *précis* of this manuscript in 1980, focusing on the *Lochner* case as an exemplification of classical legal thought.[117]

Kennedy's exploration of private and public law's foundations enabled other scholars to build up solid historical investigations on the theoretical armature he provided. Morton J. Horwitz first sketched the elements of the classical view in *The Transformation of American Law, 1780–1860* (1977),[118] and then followed up with a lengthier treatment in *The Transformation of American Law, 1870–1960: The Crisis of Legal Orthodoxy* (1992). The subtitle of his later book expresses one of the principal theses of my study.

Others elaborated on the theme of orthodoxy. Elizabeth Mensch briefly sketched classicism's rise and fall.[119] Robert Gordon treated lawyers' outlook in the classical period as a function of their experience in practice, which led them to emphasize juristic equality, the autonomy of individual will, and the formal qualities of the legal system that protected both.[120] Thomas Grey explored classical thought as an ideological system in the pedagogical theory of Christopher C. Langdell, the father of modern legal education.[121] Donald Gjerdingen developed an analytical framework that establishes linkages between legal and political thought, integrating the beliefs of judges both with the larger societal background and with the methods of their adjudication.[122] Gary Peller compared classical with realist thought using approaches derived from literary criticism. Unlike most others who have concluded that the two were incompatible, Peller sees an underlying similarity between them, derived from their shared assumptions of "transcendental subjectivity."[123]

Other scholars have not explicitly addressed the challenges of interpreting orthodoxy as Kennedy and others have, but their more specialized approaches reflect assumptions about classical thought resonant with the Kennedy/Horwitz/Grey approach.

Labor history has been especially fruitful and influential for modern rethinking of the classical era.[124] William Forbath[125] and Christopher Tomlins[126] in particular have reoriented the way that legal historians who are not labor specialists think about the relationship between organized labor and the legal order. Since that subject loomed so large in classical thought, any reinterpretation of classicism must shape itself around the work of Forbath and Tomlins. Tomlins and Andrew King have compiled a collection that showcases the work of younger scholars in the area of law and labor history, which demonstrates the vitality of work in that field.[127] Among these, the work of Karen Orren[128] and Victoria Hattam,[129] in particular, stands out. These scholars, in turn, have relied on a rich and compelling tradition of labor history, whose luminaries include David Montgomery[130] and Irving Bernstein.[131]

Another issue of major concern to the classical jurists was antitrust. Martin Sklar has surveyed the evolution of antitrust policy in a larger ideological context than the numerous specialized antitrust studies,[132] and his sense of the dynamics of ideology and politics has affected the ways that we think about the judicial response. James May also analyzed the evolution of antitrust policy from the starting-point of classical thought.[133]

Different scholars have returned to classical thought from a variety of perspectives. Neil Duxbury revisited its jurisprudential foundations, finding much less of a contrast between classicists and their prerealist and realist critics than most historians have supposed.[134] James C. Foster suggested that both conservative ("Hobbesian," in his terms) and liberal lawyers ("Lockeans") attempted to shore up the tottering legitimacy of liberal capitalism in an era of social crisis.[135] Robert W. Gordon traced elite lawyers' influence in a more theoretically-sophisticated integration of their formal thought with their achievements in practice, pursuing turn-of-the-century legal ideology back to its antebellum roots.[136]

Two studies that are focused specifically on the Supreme Court demonstrate how valuable the older critical attitude of the liberal era continues to be in illuminating the Justices' thought. Aviam Soifer has detected a strain of paternalism in their attitudes that extended beyond the usual objects, women and children, to include some male workers as well.[137] Paul Kens has revisited *Lochner* to produce the most convincing monographic interpretation of that case to have yet appeared.[138] In the same vein, Charles Lofgren's study of *Plessy*, though not directly relevant to classicism, documents the high-classical mind at work.[139]

And so the dance of historiography goes on, and will so long as we think about the ways that earlier judges tried to come to grips with the issues of their times.

Notes

1. For an excellent example of this technique creatively done, see William J. Novak, *The People's Welfare: Law and Regulation in Nineteenth Century America* (1996), 1–18.

2. Daniel T. Rodgers, "In Search of Progressivism," in Stanley I. Kutler and Stanley N. Katz, eds., *The Promise of American History: Progress and Prospects* (1982), 113–132.

3. Peter G. Filene, "An Obituary for 'The Progressive Movement,'" *American Quarterly* 22 (1970), 20.

4. Nell I. Painter, *Standing at Armageddon: United States, 1877–1919* (1987).

5. See generally Richard Hofstadter, *The Progressive Historians: Turner, Beard, Parrington* (1968).

6. Peter Novick, *That Noble Dream: The "Objectivity Question" and the American Historical Profession* (1988), 86–108.

7. Charles A. Beard, *An Economic Interpretation of the Constitution of the United States* (1913; rpt. 1986), 324.

8. Charles A. Beard, *The Supreme Court and the Constitution*, ed. Alan F. Westin (1912; rpt. 1962).

9. Holmes to Frederick Pollock, 12 July 1916, in Mark DeWolf Howe, ed., *Holmes-Pollock Letters: The Correspondence of Mr. Justice Holmes and Sir Frederick Pollock, 1874–1932* (1941), vol. 1, 237.

10. Carl L. Becker, *The History of Political Parties in the Province of New York, 1760–1776* (1909).

11. Carl L. Becker, *The Declaration of Independence: A Study in the History of Political Ideas* (1922).

12. J. Allen Smith, *The Spirit of American Government* (1907).

13. Vernon Louis Parrington, *Main Currents in American Thought: An Interpretation of American Literature from the Beginnings to 1920* (1927–1930).

14. Ernst Breisach, *American Progressive History: An Experiment in Modernization* (1993); Cushing Strout, *The Pragmatic Revolt in American History: Carl Becker and Charles Beard* (1958).

15. Herman Belz, "The Constitution in the Gilded Age: The Beginnings of Constitutional Realism in American Scholarship," 13 *Am. J. Legal Hist.* 110 (1969).

16. Beard, *An Economic Interpretation of the Constitution*, 324.

17. Herman Belz, "The Realist Critique of Constitutionalism in the Era of Reform," 15 *Am. J. Legal Hist.* 288 (1971).

18. Gustavus Myers, *History of the Supreme Court of the United States* (1912), 9.

19. Some of his most important article-length pieces are collected in Alpheus T. Mason and Gerald Garvey, eds., *American Constitutional History: Essays by Edward S. Corwin* (1964); a bibliography of his writings is at pp. 216–229.

20. Edwin S. Corwin, "The Supreme Court and the Fourteenth Amendment," 7 *Mich. L. Rev.* 643 (1909). His debut piece was "The Supreme Court and Unconstitutional Acts of Congress," 4 *Mich. L. Rev.* 616 (1906), in which he defended the power of judicial review as being derived form the common law and therefore antedating 1787.

21. Corwin, *The Twilight of the Supreme Court* (1934) (the Storrs Lectures 1933); *Commerce Power versus States Rights* (1936); *Court over Constitution* (1938); *Constitutional Revolution, Ltd.* (1941).

22. Charles E. Shattuck, "The True Meaning of the Term 'Liberty' in Those Clauses of the Federal and State Constitutions Which Protect 'Life, Liberty, and Property,'" 4 *Harv. L. Rev.* 365 (1891).

23. An extensive bibliography of the controversial literature is in Beard, *The Supreme Court and the Constitution*, 134–139. For the views of one especially significant (and representative) lawyer (soon to become a Justice of the United States Supreme Court), see Louis D. Brandeis, "The Living Law," 10 *Ill. L. Rev.* 461 (1916).

24. Walter Clark (North Carolina Supreme Court): "Is the Supreme Court Constitutional?" *The Independent* 63 (1907), 723; "Back to the Constitution," 50 *Am. L. Rev.* 1 (1916); "Government by Judges," 11 *Ohio L. Reporter* 485 (1914); William Trickett, "The Great Usurpation," 40 *Am. L. Rev.* 356 (1906); "Judicial Nullification of Acts of Congress," *North American Review*, 185 (1907), 848; Alfred Spring, "The National Government," 42 *Am. L. Rev.* 79, at 103 (1908).

25. Frank J. Goodnow, *Social Reform and the Constitution* (1911); Walter F. Dodd, "The Growth of Judicial Power," *Political Science Quarterly* 24 (1909), 193; Charles G. Haines, *The American Doctrine of Judicial Supremacy* (1914); Haines, "Judicial Review of Legislation in the United States and Doctrines of Vested Rights and of Implied Limitations on Legislatures," 2 *Texas L. Rev.* 257, 387; 3 *Texas L. Rev.* 1 (1924–1925).

26. Among others: Gilbert Roe, *Our Judicial Oligarchy* (1912); Horace Davis, *The Judicial Veto* (1914); George W. Wickersham, "The Police Power: A Product of the Rule of Reason," 27 *Harv. L. Rev.* 297 (1914).

27. Theodore Roosevelt, "Criticism of the Courts," *Outlook* 97 (1910), 526; "National-

ism and the Judiciary," *Outlook* 97 (1911), 383, 488, 532, 574; "Do You Believe in Rule of the People," *Outlook* 100 (1912), 526; "A Charter of Democracy: Address before the Ohio Constitutional Convention," *Outlook* 100 (1912), 390; "The Right of the People to Rule: An Address at Carnegie Hall . . .," *Outlook* 100 (1912), 618.

28. Louis B. Boudin, "Government by Judiciary," *Political Science Quarterly* 26 (1911), 238, later expanded into a scholarly two-volume study of the same title (1932).

29. Ernst Freund, *The Police Power, Public Policy and Constitutional Rights* (1904); Ernst Freund, "Limitations of Hours of Labor and the Federal Supreme Court," *Green Bag* 17 (1905), 411 (criticizing the majority position in *Lochner*).

30. Rodney L. Mott, *Due Process of Law: A Historical and Analytical Treatise of the Principles and Methods Followed by the Courts in the Application of the Concept of the "Law of the Land"* (1926).

31. Charles Warren, "The Progressiveness of the United States Supreme Court," 13 *Colum. L. Rev.* 290 (1913); Charles Warren, "A Bulwark to the State Police Power—The United States Supreme Court," 13 *Colum. L. Rev.* 667 (1913).

32. E.g., Charles Warren, *Congress as Santa Claus; Or, National Donations and the General Welfare Clause of the Constitution* (1932).

33. Charles Warren, "New Light on the History of the Federal Judiciary Act of 1789," 37 *Harv. L. Rev.* 49 (1923); Erie R.R. v. Tompkins, 304 U.S. 64, 72–73 (fn. 5) (1938).

34. Horace H. Lurton, "A Government of Law or a Government of Men," *North American Review* 193 (1911), 9.

35. William H. Taft, *Popular Government: Its Essence, Its Permanence and Its Perils* (1913).

36. Andrew C. McLaughlin, *The Courts, the Constitution, and Parties: Studies in Constitutional History and Politics* (1912), 3–107.

37. William M. Meigs, "Some Recent Attacks on the American Doctrine of Judicial Power," 40 *Am. L. Rev.* 640 (1916).

38. Joseph H. Choate, "The Supreme Court of the United States: Its Place in the Constitution," *North American Review* 176 (1903), 927.

39. E.g., John R. Commons, *Legal Foundations of Capitalism* (1924); Robert L. Hale, "Rate Making and the Revision of the Property Concept," 22 *Colum. L. Rev.* 209 (1922); Donald Richberg, "Value—By Judicial Fiat," 40 *Harv. L. Rev.* 567 (1927).

40. John Dewey, "The Historical Background of Corporate Legal Personality," 35 *Yale L.J.* 655 (1926); Dewey, "Logical Method and Law," 10 *Cornell L.Q.* 17 (1924); Morris Cohen, "The Ethical Basis of Legal Criticism," 41 *Yale L.J.* 201 (1931); Cohen, "Transcendental Nonsense and the Functional Approach," 35 *Colum. L. Rev.* 809 (1935).

41. Max Lerner, "The Supreme Court and American Capitalism," 42 *Yale L.J.* 668 (1933). A later study in the same vein demonstrates the lasting influence of Lerner's essay: Arthur S. Miller, *The Supreme Court and American Capitalism* (1968).

42. Thomas Reed Powell, "The Logic and Rhetoric of Constitutional Law," *Journal of Philosophy, Psychology, and Scientific Method* 15 (1918), 654.

43. Charles E. Hughes, *The Supreme Court of the United States: Its Foundation, Methods and Achievements: An Interpretation* (1928).

44. Harlan Fiske Stone, "Some Aspects of the Problem of Law Simplification," 23 *Colum. L. Rev.* 319 (1923); "Fifty Years' Work of the United States Supreme Court," 14 *A.B.A. J.* 428 (1928).

45. Felix Frankfurter and Nathan Greene, *The Labor Injunction* (193).

46. Richard Hofstadter, *Social Darwinism in American Thought* (1944); its influence was extended by a revised edition brought out in 1955.

47. Morton G. White, *Social Thought in America: The Revolt against Formalism* (1949).

48. The only exception to this generalization among writers of this period was John P.

Roche, who contended that classical jurists were simply opportunists, having no consistent ideological framework, not even a conservative one. Rather, he contended, they sought to advance the spirit of the age, "entrepreneurial liberty": "Entrepreneurial Liberty and the Commerce Power: Expansion, Contraction, and Casuistry in the Age of Enterprise," 30 *U. Chic. L. Rev.* 680 (1963); "Entrepreneurial Liberty and the Fourteenth Amendment," *Labor History* 4 (1963), 3.

49. Oliver Wendell Holmes, "The Path of the Law," in Sheldon M. Novick, ed., *The Collected Works of Justice Holmes: Complete Public Writings and Selected Judicial Opinions of Oliver Wendell Holmes* (1995), vol. 3, 398.

50. Wallace Mendelson, "Mr. Justice Field and Laissez-Faire," 36 *Va. L. Rev.* 45 (1950).

51. Max Lerner, "The Triumph of Laissez-Faire," in Arthur M. Schlesinger Jr. and Morton White, eds., *Paths of American Thought* (1963), 147.

52. See, e.g., a late neo-Progressive monograph: Judith A. Baer, *The Chains of Protection: The Judicial Response to Women's Labor Legislation* (1978).

53. Benjamin R. Twiss, *Lawyers and the Constitution: How Laissez Faire Came to the Supreme Court* (1942).

54. Clyde E. Jacobs, *Law Writers and the Courts: The Influence of Thomas M. Cooley, Christopher G. Tiedeman, and John F. Dillon upon American Constitutional Law* (1954).

55. Sidney Fine, *Laissez Faire and the General-Welfare State: A Study of Conflict in American Thought, 1865–1901* (1956).

56. Arnold M. Paul, *Conservative Crisis and the Rule of Law: Attitudes of Bar and Bench, 1887–1895* (1960).

57. Edward S. Corwin, *Liberty against Government: The Rise, Flowering, and Decline of a Famous Juridical Concept* (1948).

58. Alpheus Thomas Mason and William M. Beaney, eds., *American Constitutional Law: Introductory Essays and Selected Cases*, 3rd ed. (1964), 320–337.

59. Alfred H. Kelly and Winfred A. Harbison, *The American Constitution: Its Origins and Development* (1st ed. 1948 through 5th ed. 1976). Another text written in the same spirit is Melvin I. Urofsky, *A March of Liberty: A Constitutional History of the United States* (1988), 494–541, 616–632.

60. Paul Brest and Sanford Levinson, *Processes of Constitutional Decisionmaking: Cases and Materials*, 3rd ed. (1992), 296–299. As a graduate student, Sanford Levinson worked with Robert McCloskey.

61. Robert G. McCloskey, *American Conservatism in the Age of Enterprise* (1951), 72–126.

62. Loren P. Beth, *The Development of the American Constitution, 1877–1917* (1971); Paul L. Murphy, *The Constitution in Crisis Times, 1918–1969* (1972).

63. Harold M. Hyman and William M. Wiecek, *Equal Justice under Law: Constitutional Development, 1835–1875* (1982). The first volume of the constitutional subset, covering the period up to 1835, has not yet been written.

64. As were the general political interpretive volumes, which are classics of liberal scholarship in their own right: John A. Garraty, *The New Commonwealth, 1877–1890* (1968); Harold U. Faulkner, *Politics, Reform, and Expansion, 1890–1900* (1959) (see also the same author's *The Decline of Laissez Faire, 1897–1917* [1951]); George E. Mowry, *The Era of Theodore Roosevelt, 1900–1912* (1958); Arthur S. Link, *Woodrow Wilson and the Progressive Era, 1910–1917* (1954); John D. Hicks, *Republican Ascendancy, 1921–1933* (1960).

65. William F. Swindler, *Court and Constitution in the Twentieth Century: The Old Legality, 1889–1932* (1969); *Court and Constitution in the Twentieth Century: The New Legality, 1932–1968* (1970).

66. Leo Pfeffer, *This Honorable Court: A History of the United States Supreme Court* (1965).

67. To cite only the most recent contribution of Prof. Schwartz's massive output: Bernard Schwartz, A History of the Supreme Court (1993), 174–225.

68. William M. Wiecek, Liberty under Law: The Supreme Court in American Life (1988) was also written in this tradition, though it noted the revisionist critique.

69. William H. Rehnquist, The Supreme Court: How It Was, How It Is (1987).

70. Anthony Lewis, Make No Law: The Sullivan Case and the First Amendment (1991), 68.

71. James Weinstein, The Decline of Socialism in America, 1912–1925 (1967).

72. James Weinstein, The Corporate Ideal in the Liberal State, 1900–1918 (1968).

73. Gabriel Kolko, The Triumph of Conservatism: A Re-interpretation of American History, 1900–1916 (1963); Kolko, Railroads and Regulation, 1877–1916 (1965).

74. Thomas S. Kuhn, The Structure of Scientific Revolutions, 2nd ed. (1970).

75. Thomas S. Kuhn, The Copernican Revolution: Planetary Astronomy in the Development of Western Thought (1957).

76. Charles W. McCurdy, "The Roots of 'Liberty of Contract' Reconsidered: Major Premises in the Law of Employment, 1867–1937," 1984 Yearbook of Supreme Court Historical Society 20, disagrees, asserting that "the progressive synthesis in American constitutional history" had already collapsed when he wrote.

77. Mary C. Porter offers an historiographic survey of this subject in "Lochner and Company: Revisionism Revisited," in Ellen F. Paul and Howard Dickman, eds., Liberty, Property, and Government: Constitutional Interpretation before the New Deal (1989), 11–38. See also the brief survey by the author of one of the earliest and most influential revisionist pieces: Michael Les Benedict, "Law and the Constitution in the Gilded Age," in Charles W. Calhoun, ed., The Gilded Age: Essays on the Origins of Modern America (1996), 289.

78. Lynne V. Cheney, "The National History (Sub)Standards," Wall Street Journal, 23 Oct. 1995, A18.

79. David M. Gold, "Redfield, Railroads, and the Roots of Laissez-Faire Constitutionalism," 27 Am. J. Legal Hist. 254 (1983); Frank Strong, "The Economic Philosophy of Lochner: Emergence, Embrasure and Emasculation," 15 Ariz. L. Rev. 419 (1973).

80. Morton J. Horwitz, "Progressive Legal Historiography," 63 Or. L. Rev. 679 (1984).

81. Willard L. King, Melville Weston Fuller: Chief Justice of the United States, 1888–1910 (1950).

82. Joel F. Paschal, Mr. Justice Sutherland: A Man against the State (1951); Paschal, "Mr. Justice Sutherland," in Allison Dunham and Philip B. Kurland, eds., Mr. Justice (1956), 203–228.

83. Alan R. Jones, The Constitutional Conservatism of Thomas McIntyre Cooley: A Study in the History of Ideas (1987), the print version of his 1960 University of Michigan dissertation. Jones presented his interpretation as one of the earliest published pieces of revisionist scholarship in "Thomas M. Cooley and Laissez-Faire Constitutionalism: A Reconsideration," Journal of American History, 53 (1967), 751, a harbinger of the coming paradigm shift.

84. Robert E. Gamer, "Justice Brewer and Substantive Due Process: A Conservative Court Revisited," 18 Vand. L. Rev. 615 (1965); Owen M. Fiss, "David J. Brewer: The Judge as Missionary," in The Fields and the Law (1986), 53; Joseph G. Hylton, "David Josiah Brewer: A Conservative Judge Reconsidered," 1994 J. Sup. Ct. Hist. 45; Michael J. Brodhead, David J. Brewer: The Life of a Supreme Court Justice, 1837–1910 (1994).

85. Charles W. McCurdy, "Justice Field and the Jurisprudence of Government Business Relations: Some Parameters of Laissez-Faire Constitutionalism, 1863–1897" Journal of American History 61 (1975), 970; McCurdy, "Stephen J. Field and the American Judicial Tradition," in The Fields and the Law, 5. See also Robert Goedecke, "Justice Field and Inherent Rights," Journal of Politics 27 (1965), 198 (Field as devoté of philosophy of natural rights).

86. McCurdy, "The *Knight* Sugar Decision of 1895 and the Modernization of American Corporation Law, 1861–1903," *Business History Review* 53 (1979), 304.

87. Robert Stanley, *Dimensions of Law in the Service of Order: Origins of the Federal Income Tax, 1861–1913* (1993).

88. McCurdy, "The Roots of 'Liberty of Contract' Reconsidered."

89. William E. Nelson, "The Impact of the Antislavery Movement upon Styles of Judicial Reasoning in Nineteenth-Century America," 87 *Harv. L. Rev.* 513 (1974); cf., however, Harry N. Scheiber, "Instrumentalism and Property Rights: A Reconsideration of 'Styles of Judicial Reasoning' in the Nineteenth Century," 1975 *Wis. L. Rev.* 1; Walter F. Pratt, "Rhetorical Styles on the Fuller Court," 24 *Am. J. Legal Hist.* 189 (1980).

90. Melvin I. Urofsky, "Myth and Reality: The Supreme Court and Protective Legislation in the Progressive Era," *Yearbook 1983* of the Supreme Court Historical Society 53; Urofsky, "State Courts and Protective Legislation during the Progressive Era: A Reevaluation," *Journal of American History* 72 (1985), 63.

91. Mary C. Porter, "That Commerce Shall Be Free: A New Look at the Old Laissez-Faire Court," 1976 *Sup. Ct. Rev.* 135.

92. Stephen A. Siegel, "*Lochner* Era Jurisprudence and the American Constitutional Tradition," 70 *N.C. L. Rev.* 1 (1991).

93. Siegel, "*Lochner* Era Jurisprudence," 66–78; Siegel, "Historism [*sic*] in Late Nineteenth Century Constitutional Thought," 1990 *Wis. L. Rev.* 1431.

94. Michael Les Benedict, "Laissez-Faire and Liberty: A Re-evaluation of the Meaning and Origins of Laissez-Faire Constitutionalism," 3 *Law & Hist. Rev.* 293 (1985).

95. Daniel R. Ernst, "Free Labor, the Consumer Interest, and the Law of Industrial Disputes, 1885–1900," 36 *Am. J. Legal Hist.* 19 (1992).

96. John E. Semonche, *Charting the Future: The Supreme Court Responds to a Changing Society, 1890–1920* (1978).

97. For a critical review of the publication history of the Holmes Devise and its leading patron, see Eben Moglen, "A Bold Leap Backward?" 108 *Harv. L. Rev.* 2047 (1995) (review of Owen M. Fiss, *Troubled Beginnings of the Modern State, 1888–1910* (1993).

98. Alexander M. Bickel and Benno C. Schmidt Jr., *The Judiciary and Responsible Government, 1910–21* (1984), 415. This was the last book written by the senior author before his untimely death in 1974.

99. Fiss, *Troubled Beginnings of the Modern State*.

100. Fiss, *Troubled Beginnings of the Modern State*, 12. Fiss incorrectly attributes these views to Paul and Westin; both were too sophisticated and subtle to subscribe to the simple caricature Fiss imputes to them.

101. Fiss, *Troubled Beginnings of the Modern State*, 389.

102. Howard Gillman, *The Constitution Besieged: The Rise and Demise of Lochner Era Police Powers Jurisprudence* (1993).

103. William E. Nelson, *The Fourteenth Amendment: From Political Principle to Judicial Doctrine* (1988), 176–192.

104. Richard Maidment, *The Judicial Response to the New Deal: The United States Supreme Court and Economic Regulation, 1934–1936* (1991).

105. James W. Ely, *The Chief Justiceship of Melville W. Fuller, 1888–1910* (1995).

106. Kermit Hall, *The Magic Mirror: Law in American History* (1989), 226–246.

107. William P. LaPiana, *Logic and Experience: The Origin of Modern American Legal Education* (1994).

108. Bernard H. Siegan, *Economic Liberties and the Constitution* (1980).

109. Bernard H. Siegan, *The Supreme Court's Constitution* (1987).

110. Richard A. Epstein, *Takings: Private Property and the Power of Eminent Domain*

(1985). Michael J. Phillips has reviewed Epstein's and others' proposals for a revitalization of economic substantive due process and has concluded that the doctrine should be allowed to molder away in its grave, its costs outweighing any advantages: Phillips, "Another Look at Substantive Due Process," 1987 *Wis. L. Rev.* 265.

111. Nollan v. California Coastal Commission, 483 U.S. 825 (1987); Lucas v. South Carolina Coastal Commission, 112 S. Ct. 2886 (1992); Dolan v. Tigard, 114 S. Ct. 2309 (1994).

112. David E. Bernstein, "Roots of the 'Underclass': The Decline of Laissez-Faire Jurisprudence and the Rise of Racist Labor Legislation," 43 *Am. U. L. Rev.* 85 (1993) ("[L]abor legislation, not its invalidation, was the major tool of oppression of workers during the Lochner era," pp. 137–138); Bernstein, "The Supreme Court and 'Civil Rights', 1886–1908," 100 *Yale L.J.* 725 (1990).

113. In addition, Earl M. Maltz has endorsed conservative judicial activism in "The Prospects for a Revival of Conservative Activism in Constitutional Jurisprudence," 24 *Ga. L. Rev.* 629 (1990).

114. Stephen B. Presser, *Recapturing the Constitution: Race, Religion, and Abortion Reconsidered* (1994).

115. Hadley Arkes, *The Return of George Sutherland: Restoring a Jurisprudence of Natural Rights* (1994).

116. I thank Professor Kennedy for the courtesy of letting me read this manuscript. Ironists savor the factoid that Professor Kennedy occupies the chair at the Harvard Law School endowed by none other than James C. Carter, a leading figure among the classical lawyers.

117. Duncan Kennedy, "Toward an Historical Understanding of Legal Consciousness: The Case of Classical Legal Thought in America, 1850–1940," *Research in Law and Sociology* 3 (1980), 3.

118. Morton J. Horwitz, *The Transformation of American Law, 1780–1860* (1977), 253–268.

119. Elizabeth Mensch, "The History of Mainstream Legal Thought," in David Kairys, ed., *The Politics of Law: A Progressive Critique*, 2nd ed. (1990), 13–37.

120. Robert W. Gordon, "Legal Thought and Legal Practice in the Age of American Enterprise, 1870–1920," in Gerald L. Geison, ed., *Professions and Professional Ideologies in America* (1983), 70–110.

121. Thomas C. Grey, "Langdell's Orthodoxy," 454 *U. Pitt. L. Rev.* 1 (1983).

122. Donald J. Gjerdingen, "The Future of Our Past: The Legal Mind and the Legacy of Classical Legal Thought," 68 *Ind. L.J.* 743 (1993); see also Gjerdingen, "The Future of Legal Scholarship and the Search for a Modern Theory of Law," 35 *Buff. L. Rev.* 381 (1986).

123. Gary Peller, "The Metaphysics of American Law," 73 *Calif. L. Rev.* 1151 (1985).

124. See Wythe Holt, "The New American Labor Law History," *Labor History* 30 (1989), 275.

125. William E. Forbath, *Law and the Shaping of the American Labor Movement* (1991).

126. Christopher L. Tomlins, *Law, Labor, and Ideology in the Early American Republic* (1993); *The State and the Unions: Labor Relations, Law, and the Organized Labor Movement in America, 1880–1960* (1985).

127. Christopher L. Tomlins and Andrew J. King, eds., *Labor Law in America: Historical and Critical Essays* (1992).

128. Karen Orren, *Belated Feudalism: Labor, the Law, and Liberal Development in the United States* (1991).

129. Victoria C. Hattam, *Labor Visions and State Power: The Origins of Business Unionism in the United States* (1993).

130. David Montgomery, *The Fall of the House of Labor: The Workplace, the State, and American Labor Activism, 1865–1925* (1987).

131. Irving Bernstein, *The Lean Years: A History of the American Worker, 1920–1933* (1960); *The Turbulent Years: A History of the American Worker, 1933–1941* (1970).

132. Martin J. Sklar, *The Corporate Reconstruction of American Capitalism, 1890–1916: The Market, the Law, and Politics* (1988).

133. James May, "Antitrust in the Formalist Era: Political and Economic Theory in Constitutional Law and Antitrust Analysis," 50 *Ohio St. L.J.* 257 (1989).

134. Neil Duxbury, *Patterns of American Jurisprudence* (1995), 9–64.

135. James C. Foster, *The Ideology of Apolitical Politics: The Elite Lawyers' Response to the Legitimation Crisis in American Capitalism: 1870–1920* (1986).

136. Gordon, "Legal Thought and Legal Practice in the Age of American Enterprise," 70–110.

137. Aviam Soifer, "The Paradox of Paternalism and Laissez-Faire Constitutionalism: United States Supreme Court, 1888–1921," 5 *Law & Hist. Rev.* 249, 254 (1987).

138. Paul Kens, *Judicial Power and Reform Politics: The Anatomy of Lochner v. New York* (1990).

139. Charles A. Lofgren, *The Plessy Case: A Legal-Historical Interpretation* (1987).

Index